Ethnic Groups of Africa and the Middle East

Ethnic Groups of Africa and the Middle East

AN ENCYCLOPEDIA

John A. Shoup

Ethnic Groups of the World

ABC-CLIO

Santa Barbara, California • Denver, Colorado • Oxford, England

Library of Congress Cataloging-in-Publication Data

Shoup, John A.
  Ethnic groups of Africa and the Middle East : an encyclopedia / John A. Shoup.
    p. cm. — (Ethnic groups of the world)
  "This book is also available on the World Wide Web as an eBook."
  ISBN 978–1–59884–362–0 (hard copy : alk. paper) — ISBN 978–1–59884–363–7 (ebook)
1. Ethnology—Africa—Encyclopedias. 2. Ethnology—Middle East—Encyclopedias.
3. Ethnicity—Africa—Encyclopedias. 4. Ethnicity—Middle East—Encyclopedias. 5. Africa—Ethnic relations—Encyclopedias. 6. Middle East—Ethnic relations—Encyclopedias. I. Title. II. Series: Ethnic groups of the world.
GN645.S527   2011
305.80096′03—dc23   2011022343

ISBN: 978–1–59884–362–0
EISBN: 978–1–59884–363–7

15 14 13 12 11   1 2 3 4 5

This book is also available on the World Wide Web as an eBook.
Visit www.abc-clio.com for details.

ABC-CLIO, LLC
130 Cremona Drive, P.O. Box 1911
Santa Barbara, California 93116-1911

This book is printed on acid-free paper ∞

Manufactured in the United States of America

Contents

Preface

This encyclopedia is designed for both the beginner and the expert looking for information on particular ethnic groups living in the vast region of the African continent to the eastern limits of the Middle East. The groups selected are based on ethno-linguistic classifications, and not all individual ethnicities are included. When possible, those speaking closely related languages are grouped together, and only those with particular historical or political importance have been listed separately. For example, there is an entry for **Berbers** and a separate one for **Tuareg**, even though the Tuareg are also Berber-speakers.

This encyclopedia of the peoples of the Middle East and Africa was a difficult undertaking. The geographical region is vast, covering the entire continent of Africa as well as the Middle East. The Middle East is defined here as the Arab heartlands of the Levant, the Arabian Peninsula, and Iraq in addition to Turkey and Iran. The Caucasus and Central Asia are covered in other, separate volumes in this series. Afghanistan is always difficult to pinpoint where it fits culturally because it can be included with Central Asia, Iran, or South Asia, depending on how its cultures are being classified. It has not been included in this work.

When choosing how to classify the peoples of Africa and the Middle East, only closely related languages, and where there is a common feeling of something more shared between subgroups, have been combined. For example, **Berbers** of North Africa are one major entry with subdivisions within the entry for the different regional groups. In addition, there are entries for the **Copts** of Egypt and the **Assyrians** of Iraq, both of whom can be argued are religions and not ethnicities, since it is possible to convert to these religions. However, both are mainly composed of ancient populations with distinct languages, even if they are only used in church services today.

Arabs are difficult to define, and they are one of the ethnicities with the widest geographical spread in both the Middle East, across North Africa, down the East African coast, and out into the Indian Ocean. Today Arabs form the majority population in 19 countries, and in 3 other countries, Somalia, Djibouti, and the Comoros Islands, the majority of people have such a strong cultural connection to the Arabs that they are included in the Arab League. In addition, Arab minorities are found in other Middle Eastern and African countries. Arab identity is primarily linguistic, speaking a form of the Arabic language, and it has been historically easy to adopt an Arab identity through marriage, for example. Berbers in Morocco, Tunisia, and Libya have and continue today to shift identity between Berber and Arab with great ease.

Each entry in this encyclopedia provides all alternate names and spellings for the group, and identifies major population centers, estimated population figures, primary languages and religions, and similarities with other closely related groups. Each entry briefly examines the group's origins and early historical developments, describes cultural life and traditional customs, and discusses recent history, economic factors, politics, and major concerns or issues related to the group. Further readings are listed at the end of each entry, in order to provide readers with additional research opportunities. A Geographic Index provides a list of each country covered and the ethnic groups found in those countries that are discussed in this work.

Ethnicity is not a sociopolitical organization and is not based on an idea of lineages, but on a wider set of ideas that serve to unify people. Ethnicity can include regional identity, shared history and common experience, shared language, geographical isolation, shared kinship system, and/or religion. Jews, no matter the language they speak or their particular history, share a common religion that serves to unify them. Arabs have a somewhat shared history and language, even if there are numerous dialects. The Arabic language serves as means to unify them from Mauritania and Morocco on the west to Iraq and the Gulf States on the east.

Language is, more often than not, the main vehicle for a sense of unity between people. As a result, ethno-linguistic groupings were used to set the entries in this volume. It can be argued that in doing so, certain people have been left out or not covered properly, but to cover all people in the Middle East and Africa would be such a large undertaking that it would be nearly impossible to do. Countries such as Nigeria, Congo, and the Sudan each have well over 100 different language groups. Many, however, are related languages, and the people have similar religions, economics, and political systems. Rather than have separate entries on each, they are presented as a larger ethno-linguistic group to the reader. For any mistakes or objections by those who find this method of organization too simplistic, the author would like to ask your forgiveness and indulgence.

Acknowledgments

There are always a large number of people involved in a project like this without whose help it would never come to be. I would like to thank everyone at ABC-CLIO Press for their assistance at all stages of the work. I would like to particularly thank Kaitlin Ciarmiello, Nina Gomez, and Magendra Varman. I would also like to thank those people who have contributed to the text; Pade Badru, Tierno Bah, Jack Kalpakian, Scott Mattoon, Karen Milbroune, Connell Monette, K.P. Moseley, and Geri Shaw. I would also like to make special mention of Houssam Jedda, a student at Al Akhawayn University in Ifrane, Morocco who helped with the final stages of the project. This project belongs to all who assisted to bring it to light.

Introduction: Ethnicity in Africa and the Middle East

Ethnicity

The region covered in this volume is not only vast, but the populations are greatly varied and have suffered from being classified by colonial officials into frequently meaningless categories. In a good number of cases, contemporary labeling for different people were the direct result of colonial interference and attempts to classify people into categories, often for easier recognition and labeling rather than for any real reason to combine or divide peoples. These became hardened into the names used in the postcolonial period by independence governments. As noted above, labels are not always useful and, in a number of cases in Africa, have set peoples against each other over competition for resources or where one group was given privilege over others, such as the **Hutu** and **Tutsi**. Some groups, such as the Samburu (**Nilotic**), have been separated from larger entities, in their case the Maasai (Nilotic), and were not called the Samburu until into the 19th century. For the purposes here, ethno-linguistics has been used to denote the different ethnicities. Thus, Zulu and Xhosa are found in the entry **Nguni** rather than in separate, individual entries. It was felt by the main author of the volume that ethno-linguistic groups have a basis for distinction, while other labels are misleading or even wrong.

Ethnicity is defined by a shared historical experience, regional isolation, specific religion, kinship type, or language or dialect of a language that distinguishes a population from others. Ethnic groups can be fluid, such as **Arab** or **Berber**, and it is possible to be both an Arab and a Berber at the same time. Ethnicity can be defined as much by what a group is not as much as what it is; that is, it can be defined by those who are not members as much as those who are. It is possible to negotiate belonging to one group or another and, when language is the main means of defining a group, such as with the Arabs, it is possible to have multiple identities. Generally speaking, language or dialect is more of the marker of an ethnic group than, say, religion, though **Jews** are distinguished as much by their specific religious demands as by their historical experience no matter what language they speak. Ethnic tolerance or intolerance in much of the region under discussion (the Middle East and Africa) has become an issue more as a result of

European colonialism and the subsequent attempts to build nationalism with the modern, European-type state such as Kemalist Turkey or Iran. Such issues were rarely part of how older states behaved. Most of the pre-modern states in the Middle East and Africa had policies that are referred to as pluralist, meaning that the state included other religions or other peoples, but their interaction was generally economic and the state allowed for their own leaders to deal with internal problems as long as the communities paid their taxes. Nationalism is a 19th-century European invention, and it can be threatened by ethnicity. Few countries in the Middle East and Africa have multiculturalism as a policy. Instead, there are numerous problems around the concept of nationalism, a nationalist consensus, a national language, religion, food, costume, or how to teach a national history. Ethnic groups may be considered minorities and subject to discriminatory state policies. Nigeria is a state struggling with this issue, while South Africa is attempting to develop a multicultural policy.

When deciding on how to organize this volume, ethnicity, and in particular ethnolinguistics, makes more sense in deciding who to include and how to include them. Africans have often been subjected to arbitrary classifications that make little local sense. Ethnicity, or ethno-linguistic groupings, is an attempt to use ethnicity in its least offensive meaning.

Bands, Tribes, Chiefdoms, and States

The four main sociopolitical organizations, as classified by the American anthropologist Elman Service in his work *Primitive Social Organization: An Evolutionary Perspective* (1962), include bands, tribes, chiefdoms, and states. Africa and the Middle East include all four types of organization within the borders of modern states. In bands, tribes, and chiefdoms, membership is based on kinship; all members of the group believe they share a common ancestry/origin, even if it is fiction. Fictive kinship is as real as real kinship with the same obligations, responsibilities, and duties between members of the group, and often is created for economic or political gain. Lineages are named and, as a member, one can recount his ancestors back to the founder of the entire group; again, real or fictive. Such genealogies help establish "blood" relationships and set obligations between the members.

There are a few band peoples still in Africa, though they have been greatly marginalized by both the colonial powers and other Africans. Bands are hunter-gatherers that live without domesticated plants and animals, with the notable exception of the dog. They live a nomadic lifestyle, shifting campsites with the seasons and the availability of natural resources. Bands are small in size, and membership is based on real or fictive kinship. Bands have no formal leadership; leadership duties are assumed by different people at different times according to need and expertise, and decision making is done by the group as a whole. Settlement programs in South Africa and Botswana have greatly altered the hunter-gathering life of the San (**Khoisan**), better known as the Bushmen, of the

Kalahari, and few have been able to maintain their traditional lifestyle. The **Pygmies** of the Central African rain forest are also organized into bands, but, unlike the San, Pygmy populations take on the languages and even some of the cultural practices of their neighbors. Exploitation of the rain forest by commercial corporations and by national governments has greatly impacted their traditional hunter-gatherer economy.

"Tribe" is a term misused in most instances when referring to different peoples in the Middle East and Africa. A "tribe" is a sociopolitical organization, not an ethnicity. In this text, the term tribe is used only when the group under discussion is tribal in its sociopolitical organization. Tribes are permanent descent groups composed of different lineages, all of whom claim a common ancestor. Leadership is dispersed and weak, emerging when and where needed along kinship lines, and decisions are by consensus. The position of leader is not necessarily inherited, but goes to the person seen as most able or wise. Tribal leaders have developed different strategies in order to lead their people, such as talents in oratory, ability to apply social pressure, negotiation skill, and honorable behavior. Leaders are to be just but lack strong authority; they do not have the ability to order others to do anything, but should command respect for their wisdom and should be good orators to persuade. Tribal leaders can use social pressure to force someone to agree with the majority decision, or can lead by example. Tribal organization is often described as Segmentary Lineage Organization, based on the British anthropologist Edward Evan Evans-Pritchard's seminal work *The Nuer: A Description of the Modes of Livelihood and Political Institutions of a Nilotic People* (1940). Evans-Pritchard developed the theory of Segmentary Lineage Organization, which he applied in his study of the Sanusi Sufi Brotherhood in Libya, *The Sanusi of Cyrenaica* (1949). Subsequent studies of tribes in the Middle East, for example, have found that tribes frequently do not respond in the ways outlined by Evans-Pritchard, but his theory of segmentary lineage still serves as an important base for understanding how tribes are politically organized. Tribal peoples are often pastoralists, raising camels, sheep, goats, and cattle, and the more dispersed leadership and the strong sense of mutual dependence between lineages give security, especially when the population lives in greatly dispersed locales for at least part of the year. Most nomadic pastoral tribal peoples live in camping units of closely related families, sharing duties and responsibilities. For example, the "Arab" tribe called Tekna in Morocco and Mauritania is even today composed of two main lineages, one Berber-speaking and one Arabic-speaking. Each has important grazing lands, and the formation into a single "tribe" was of clear economic importance for them. They have mutual obligations to help each other as if they were real blood kin, and, through marriage, real blood relationships are established and maintained.

Today tribal leaders in the Arab world walk a political tightrope between obligations to states and to their tribesmen. Should a leader be seen as too close to the government, he will lose his position to someone else. Tribal structure gave pastoral nomads security in that there is shared responsibility for individual action. Tribal peoples have long had contact with nontribal people and have lived within the borders of states controlled by nontribal governments. Some scholars who study tribal people in the Middle East have proposed that "tribe" as a political structure not only developed after the development of states, but as a response to states. Tribally organized pastoral nomads in the Middle East and North Africa have long been integrated into local and regional economic systems, providing needed milk, meat, wool, and hair to major markets and buying the goods they do not produce themselves.

While there are still tribal groups in North Africa and the Middle East, they no longer have political independence. Some states in the Middle East and North Africa have been able to incorporate them into the state system through service in the military and/or border police, such as the cases of Egypt, Jordan, and Saudi Arabia. Others have focused on breaking the political organization of tribes, such as in Morocco and Algeria, but recognizing the social organization may persist in marriage patterns.

The refusal of later colonial powers to use the term "state" and instead use the term "tribe" has created confusion for many general readers today. Most Africans do not use the word "tribe" and see it as a colonial legacy as well as insulting. Some Africans prefer to use indigenous terms to describe local political organization, but in general, it is best to not use the term "tribe" or to think of people as "tribal" for most of the Middle East and Africa. News reports of civil conflicts in Rwanda, Congo, Angola, Nigeria, Sierra Leone, Liberia, and other countries are frequently and incorrectly described in mainstream press such as CNN and BBC as "tribal." Such labeling not only serves to trivialize the problems, but continues the mental picture of "primitive" peoples and "savage" actions. Conflicts have long, complicated histories, and it is much easier to simply call them "tribal" than to try to gain a real understanding of their origins.

African art is also frequently called "tribal" and/or "primitive," whether it is produced by a tribally organized people or not. African art was "discovered" by Western collectors in the late 19th century, when Europeans began to admire and buy African art. Pieces were originally brought to Europe or North America as curiosities or as war booty, with little care or interest about indigenous usage or meaning. As tastes developed, Africans began to make things specifically for sale to Europeans and later for tourists. African art is today appreciated like any world art, but it is still called "tribal" by most, even by art experts. There are a large number of Arab, **Kurd**, and Berber tribes, but, in sub-Saharan Africa, tribe was not a common form of sociopolitical organization.

In sub-Saharan Africa, tribe has not been a major form of sociopolitical organization, though some tribally organized pastoral nomads were and are still found there; for example, among pastoral Somalis and some of the famous pastoral people in East Africa such as the Maasai, Samburu, and Turkana. However, most people have been settled agriculturalists with stronger central political organization of a chiefdom or state. Chiefdoms are similar to states in that there is strong central leadership in the person of the chief. While chiefdom still makes use of principles of lineage, there are defined class differences based on the concept of senior and junior lineages, and chiefs have far more authority than a tribal leader. The social classes are based on closeness of kinship to the person of the living chief; those closest to the living chief are the most senior lineages, while as a person becomes further away in relationship, the more junior the lineages. New lineages can be absorbed into the system, but as the most junior of lineages. The position of chief is inherited and children may inherit it, in which case elder relatives such as uncles serve as regents until time of maturity. Chiefs need a number of officials to help manage large populations and natural resources. Like states, the population of chiefdoms can be large, and the economy is based on intensive agricultural production. Surplus production is controlled by the chief, who can dole it out as a means of payment, reward, or in times of need. With large settled populations living in permanent villages and towns, chiefdoms have borders and may need some form of military to protect themselves from others. Chiefs need a trained army, not a militia, for protection or for conquest of others, and as noted above, newly conquered peoples could be absorbed into the political system as the most junior of lineages. Paramount chiefs are very similar to kings and send out deputies or subchiefs to help govern and collect surplus agricultural production. Unlike states, chiefdom membership is still by kinship, and conquered people are absorbed into the junior lineages at the bottom of society.

A number of important states emerged in sub-Saharan Africa prior to the arrival of European traders and colonists. States are old in Egypt, Ethiopia, along the Nile in the Sudan, along the Mediterranean coast, in West Africa, along the East African coast, and inland in what is today Zimbabwe. While Egypt and the Mediterranean are well known, other early African states are not except among African specialists. States first arose in the Middle East and Egypt around 6000 BCE. Later, contact with Europeans usually brought quick transformation from chiefdom to state in much of sub-Saharan Africa. For example, the Zulu transformed not only into a state, but into an empire in the early 19th century under the leadership of Shaka, in response to the growth of competition for European trade in southern Africa. The Zulu push was to gain control over the flow of these goods, which had caused constant conflict between different chiefdoms in Natal. Shaka built on the work of Dingiswayo, paramount chief of Mtetwa Chiefdom, who had protected the young Shaka and his mother from the wrath of his father. Shaka revolutionized warfare and transformed his people into a highly efficient military machine, and his conquests had long-lasting effects throughout much of southern and central Africa.

In states, there are significant percentages of the population who are not engaged in primary food production, but working in government, trade, craft, police, military, and religious sectors. Membership in a state is not based on kinship, and there are defined social classes. In some instances, these classes allow no vertical mobility, and a person is bound for life to the class to which he or she was born. Specialization in crafts such as iron working, weaving, woodworking, leather working, poetry and music, law, religion, military training, fishing, and even farming provided the basis for different social classes.

Language Classifications in the Middle East and Africa

The region covered in this volume includes a number of macro language groups, also known as phyla. Each of the language phyla includes separate languages often employing different scripts. Arabic, Tifinagh, Hebrew, Syriac, Ethiopic or Ge'ez, Greek (Coptic is a modified version of Greek), and Latin scripts are used. Arabic is the language of Islam and the Qur'an, and thus has loaned a wide range of vocabulary not only of terms related to religious practice, but in law, sciences, medicine, and even agriculture to many of the other languages of the region. In more recent years, contact with European colonial powers has spread English, French, and Portuguese loanwords into many African and Middle Eastern languages. Several types of **Creole** have developed in Africa and it is argued that **Swahili** is an Arabic-based Creole. It must also be noted here that some of the linguistic groupings are still subject to a good deal of study, and the names of some macro language groups have changed over time as linguists refine their knowledge.

The American linguist Joseph Greenberg developed a typology of the languages of Africa that fall into four macro phyla, which he named Niger-Congo Kordofanian, Nilo-Saharan, Khoisan, and Afro-Asiatic. His major work *The Languages of Africa* was first published in 1963 and has subsequently been revised in 1966 and 1970. He used a comparative method and established the four macro groups by combining already established family groupings. His work has been criticized, with some linguists stating that certain of these macro groups need to be split into several smaller, distinct ones while still others think that some can be combined into even larger macro groups.

The Niger-Congo group is one of the largest identified by Greenberg, and it makes up the largest part of the broader Niger-Kordofanian phylum. Some linguists have argued that the Nilo-Saharan and Niger-Congo macro groups should be combined into one even larger phylum called Kongo-Saharan. The Niger-Congo group is divided into six major family groups: Kwa, **Mande**, Voltaic, Atlantic, Bantu, and Adamawa. It is the largest in Africa, both in number of speakers and in geographical distribution, having over 1,000 languages and 400 million speakers, while the Kordofanian languages number some 20 languages found in and around the **Nuba** Mountains of Sudan. Bantu is the widest spread of the families, and its movement from the proposed home area in West Africa into central, eastern, and southern Africa had important cultural significance. Bantu speakers brought with them technologies in metalworking and agriculture that supported large, settled populations. Hunter-gathering and herding peoples were forced out of productive agricultural areas and into more marginal zones such as arid steppes, desert, and mountains. The debate over the time of the Bantu arrival in South Africa, whether for an early date of the 4th century CE or the late date of the 18th century, was part of the ideology of the **Afrikaner**-dominated government of South Africa following the end of World War II. The Afrikaners took the position that the Bantu arrived in South Africa in the 18th century, meaning that the Afrikaners were in South Africa as long if not longer than the Bantu.

Nilo-Saharan was named by Greenberg to indicate the language phyla found along the Nile north from its origins in Lake Victoria to near where the Sudanese capital of Khartoum stands at the confluence of the White and Blue Niles as well as a number of related languages that fan out into the Sahara, reaching as far as the Niger Bend in Mali, thus the name Nilo-Saharan. The American linguist Merritt Rehlun estimated that the total number of Nilo-Saharan speakers was 11 million in 1987 (*A Guide to the World's Languages*, 2nd ed.). There are four main families: Eastern Sudanic, Central Sudanic, Saharan, and **Songhai**, with another possible eight proposed as large family groups. Songhai is not fully accepted by a number of linguists, who think it should be considered as its own, separate language group unrelated to any other.

Khoisan or Click languages are spoken by perhaps less than 100,000 people today. Once widespread over much of southern and eastern Africa, the Khoisan peoples live in marginal areas of Botswana, South Africa, Namibia, and Tanzania. Greenberg invented the name taking it from Khoikhoi, the more acceptable local name for the Hottentots, and San, the more acceptable local name for the Bushmen. There is a good deal of debate over the validity of including certain language groups as Khoisan, but in general they are divided into two main families, Khoikhoi and San. Click languages make use of around 30 click consonants, and some of their Bantu neighbors have borrowed clicks into their languages over centuries of contact.

Afro-Asiatic (formerly known as the Hamito-Semitic family) consists of 375 languages still spoken today by over 350 million people in North Africa, the Horn of Africa, the Sahel and West Africa, and southwest Asia. The largest single language group today is Arabic, with an estimated 280 million speakers worldwide. Linguists do not agree about the subgroupings or families of Afro-Asiatic but, generally speaking, there are five with a possible sixth: Semitic, Egyptian, Berber, Chadic, and Cushitic, as well as Omotic, which Greenberg classified as part of Cushitic. Each of these is further broken down into a number of separate languages and then into smaller regional dialects. For example, Semitic includes Arabic, Hebrew, Amharic, and Tigrinya. Arabic has some eight or nine major regional dialects (Maghribi, Hassani or that of Mauritania and the Western Sahara, Nile Valley, Levant, Iraq, Khaliji or Gulf, Najd or central Arabia, Hijaz or the west coast of the peninsula, and Yemen) and each of these is further divided into smaller regional dialects. Coptic is the only living Egyptian language today, and Arabic has replaced it as the medium of everyday communication.

The term Indo-European was first coined by the English scholar Thomas Young in 1813, but the systematic and scientific comparative study of Indo-European languages began with the German linguists Franz Bopp and his major work *Comparative Grammar*, published between 1833 and 1852. Today there are some 443 languages classified as Indo-European with an estimated 3 billion speakers worldwide. The main subgroup found in the Middle East is the Iranian of the Indo-Iranian family, which includes **Persian**, Kurdish, **Luri**, and **Bakhtiyari**. Afrikaans is a recent development of Dutch and is an important language of southern Africa where an estimated 6.45 million speak it as a first or second language. Other major Indo-European languages used in the Middle East and Africa include English, French, and Portuguese, and to a lesser extent Spanish and Italian.

The Ural-Altaic language phylum was first proposed by the Finnish ethnologist and philologist Matthias Castrén in the mid-19th century. He proposed that the two linguistic families of Altaic and Uralic were really one macro language phylum, but today many linguists see them as two, unrelated macro phyla though some still hold to Castrén's proposal. The Altaic language group is composed of five main subgroups; Turkic, Mongolian, Tungusic, Korean, and Japonic. There are six major subgroups of Turkic further divided into some 30 Turkic languages spoken by 180 million people, of which close to 40 percent of them live in Anatolia. Other Turkish languages in the Middle East include the Qashqa'i and Azeri (**Turks**) both spoken in Iran.

Geographical Regions and Cultural Areas

Geographical regions and/or cultural areas are convenient means of organizing and discussing the different cultures of a huge area such as the Middle East and Africa. Geography and environment play significant roles in economic activities, which can influence social and political organization. The link between specific geographical areas and specific cultural type is referred to as a cultural area.

The idea of cultural areas was first advanced by American anthropologists in the 19th century as a means to organize exhibits of mainly Native American cultures. The idea was further developed by American anthropologists Clark Wissler and Alfred Kroeber. However, it would be one of Kroeber's students, Julian Steward, who developed the idea into the theory of cultural ecology. Cultural ecology looks at the relationship between environment and a society and how the environment shapes that society. Steward proposed the idea that cultural change is caused when societies need to adapt to a particular environment in his work *Theory of Culture Change: The Methodology of Multilinear Evolution* (1955).

For the Middle East and Africa, a number of cultural areas have been devised by scholars. For the Arabic-speaking countries, the cultural areas are defined not only by the geography, but also by the dialects spoken. The main divisions are the Maghrib (Morocco, Algeria, Tunisia, and western Libya); the Nile Valley (Egypt, Sudan, and eastern Libya); the Levant or Greater Syria (Lebanon, Syria, Jordan, Palestine, and Sinai); Iraq; the Arab Gulf (Kuwait, eastern Saudi Arabia, Bahrain, Qatar, and the United Arab Emirates; the Najd (central Saudi Arabia); the Hijaz (Red Sea coast of Saudi Arabia); Yemen; Dhofar (includes parts of Yemen and Oman); and Oman. Morocco's Western Sahara, Mauritania, the Azwad of northwestern Mali, and the western part of Saharan Algeria is the homeland of the Awald Hassan Arabs who have a distinct dialect, Hassaniyah, as well as a culture that includes elements of their Bedouin Arab ancestral culture, that of the Sanhaja Berbers who lived in the region in historic times, and that of the great African kingdoms of Ghana and Mali. Hassani culture is a true bridge between Arab and Berber North Africa and West Africa.

Africa is oftentimes divided into large geographical areas; North Africa, West Africa, the Horn of Africa, East Africa, Central Africa, and southern Africa. Within each of these, there are further divisions based on social, political, and economic typologies. Unfortunately, such conveniences frequently obscure cultural differences and lump disparate peoples together in large categories.

The Sahara: Not the Great Divide

Africa is too often divided between North Africa and sub-Saharan Africa, with the idea that the Sahara Desert has been a natural barrier to the movement of ideas and peoples. Recent scholarship has begun to challenge this idea, and rather than being a barrier, it has been discovered that the desert has been crossed by peoples since the Neolithic period. The introduction of the camel from the Middle East in the fourth century BCE allowed movement of peoples across the desert as well as the development of local cultures dependent on the camel that live all year round in the heart of the Sahara such as the **Teda** and the **Tuareg**. Even before the arrival of the camel, people crossed the Sahara and trans-Saharan trade dates well into antiquity. Rock art depicting horses and chariots are found into the central Sahara and follow along well-established trade routes. Movement of people, goods, and ideas continues across the Sahara today.

This work attempts to present the great diversity of the Middle East and Africa. Both of these regions are complex with ancient histories and emerged from foreign domination following World War II. Borders drawn up by colonial powers with no or little regard for how it carved up ethnic groups have been maintained by agreements by major political bodies such as the Arab League and the African Union (formerly called the Organization of African Unity). Nationalism and citizenship today challenge older identities built on historical experience and linguistic unity. For example, the **Mande** are the heirs of a large empire that ruled most West Africa between the 13th and 15th centuries, and when it collapsed, many Mande peoples had settled throughout the region. The memory of the glory of the empire, especially that of its founder Sundiata Keita, are kept alive in epic poetry and music, which helps unify all Mande no matter where they live. Much the same can be said of Arabs, who have a feeling of unity of culture even if the states they live in are hostile to each other. It is hoped the brief entries presented here will help give an understanding of this complexity and encourage the reader to research more on the peoples of the Middle East and Africa.

Note on Spelling

Names of people and places in the Middle East and Africa are often hard to reconcile. The same names have numerous spellings given if it is spelled as it is pronounced or if there has been an attempt to follow an original spelling in another script. For example, in Arabic, Persian, Turkish, and other Middle Eastern languages with long histories of written texts, there are a number of "standard" ways of transliterating them from their original into a European script. These, nonetheless, give different ways of spelling the same word. For example the Arabic word *wadi*, for valley or river course, is rendered as *ouedi* in French, and using the clipped pronunciation of North African Arabs, it is often written as *oued* on maps and in texts. It is more difficult to deal with Arabic when those recording often did not speak the language and instead wrote down what they thought they heard, rather than the way a name is written. For example, in Mauritania, the town *Shinqit* is spelled *Chinguetti* in French and English texts, and the original *Shinqit* is rarely used except in Arabic. More confusion can be caused when a people use a name others call them, but do not use it when speaking to each other. For example, Arabs of Mauritania only called themselves *Moors* (English) or *Maure* (French) when speaking to non-Arabs; but when speaking to Arabs, particularly to each other, they refer to themselves as *Baydani*. In Morocco, the same peoples are called *Sahraoui* (*Sahrawi*) by other Moroccans, while most *Sahrawis* again call themselves *Baydani*. Mauritania was selected as the name of the county by a romantic French officer, Xavier Coppolani, in 1903, based on the Roman-era provinces of Mauretania Ceasariensis and Mauretania Tingitana inhabited by a Berber people the Romans called the *Mauri*. More famous in the Western world are the *Tuareg*, but this is the Arab name for them, and their own name is *Kel Tamasheq*.

In non-Arabic-speaking Africa, spellings of people and places were done by colonial officers sometimes with little real knowledge of local people, history, languages, or culture. Spanish, Portuguese, French (including Belgians), Dutch, German, and English languages have been used to help spell a variety of African languages. *Sesotho*, the language of the *Basotho* of *Lesotho* was developed by French evangelical missionaries in the 1830s. However, *Setswana*, the language of the *Bastwana* of *Botswana* and closely related to the *Basotho*, was developed by English missionaries around the same time and they used English orthography; thus, for them, the *Basotho* are the *Basutu*.

Generally, this work has followed well-accepted spellings and have, at the head of each entry, given a variety of spellings or alternative names for ethnic groups. For Middle Eastern and North African entries, the American Library of Congress system of transliteration has been used, minus the dots under letters that differentiates emphatics from those that are not. Arabic has emphatic and nonemphatic letters; thus there are two H's, two D's, two T's, two S's, and two Dh's. Arabs believe that the emphatic D or *dad* is unique to Arabic and thus one of the ways they have to refer to the language is *Lughat al-Dad* or "language of the letter *dad*." Arabic has three vowels: a, i, and u. In addition, Arabic has a glottal stop, the *hamza*, which is usually marked with ' and the letters *'ayn* transliterated as ', and *ghayn* transliterated as *gh*. Arabic has what it calls *Shamsi* (sun) and *Qamari* (moon) letters that, when at the start of the word, either elide into the definite article of *al* or not. They take the two names for how these letters deal with the definite article, *ash-Shams* and *al-Qamar*. However, these deal with pronunciation and not how the words are spelled. The Library of Congress system notes how words are spelled, not changes for pronunciation; thus, using the system, it is *al-Shams*, and this is what is used in this work.

Persian borrowed Arabic letters, but it is an Indo-European language and does not differentiate emphatic and nonemphatic letters, but keeps them in the words borrowed from Arabic that have them. Some letters are pronounced the same, though written differently; for example, *qaf* (or q in Arabic) and *ghayn* are both pronounced as *ghayn* in Persian. In addition, Persian has more vowels, including e and o, and added modified Arabic letters to represent *f, v, ch*, and *g*. Ottoman Turkish borrowed the Arabic alphabet and made many of the same modifications as Persian, but in 1928, the president of Turkey, Mustafa Kemal Atatürk, ordered the change from Arabic script to the Latin alphabet with its own way of dealing with how to write Turkish, an Altaic language. Turkish has sounds that were difficult to transcribe in Arabic, such as umlauted letters like ö and ü.

Similarly, some African peoples had literacy in Arabic and developed ways of using Arabic letters to represent the sounds of their languages. Often called *'Ajami* from the Arabic meaning "foreign" or "non-Arab," the use of Arabic both as a language of scholarship and as a means of writing local languages is wide spread in the Sahel region and along the Indian Ocean coast.

Ge'ez, or more properly Gi'iz, the written language of Ethiopia, is a development of the South Arabian script used by the D'mt civilization in the fifth century BCE. Gi'iz script or *abugida* was used during the Aksumite period (1st century CE to the mid-10th century CE) and spread to be used by a number of languages in the Horn of Africa including Amharic, Tigrinya, and Tigre. Like Arabic, Gi'iz has emphatics as well as a glottal stop.

The other main African script that is still used today by the Tuareg of Algeria, Mali, and Niger is called *Tifinagh* (spelled *Tifinar* in French, noting that the French letter *r* sounds like the Arabic letter *ghayn*). It is argued by some that *Tifinagh* is an African invention, predating the arrival of the Phoenicians on the North African coast. Others argue that it is a modification of the alphabet invented first in Ugarit on the Syrian coast and later spread with trade to other parts of the Mediterranean. The name *Tifinagh* means "of the Phoenicians" from *Finiq*, meaning "Phoenicians" in Semitic languages such as Arabic. Several versions have been developed and, with the rise of Berber nationalism in the second half of the 20th century, there has been a recent revival of the script in places like Morocco, where it was chosen as the script for Berber in 2003. Berber has also been transcribed into Arabic and Latin scripts, but nationalists want to use their own alphabet.

Despite the best attempts by governments following independence, spellings of African peoples and places have remained in a multitude of ways: *Tubu* or *Toubou*; *Timbuktu*, *Tinbuktu*, or *Toumbouctou*; or, among the most confusing, what to call the *Fulani*, *Fula*, *Ful Fula*, *Ful Fulda*, *Haapulaarin*, *Peul*, or *Pulaar* peoples who inhabit a wide range of countries and have fought Arabs, Berbers, the French, the Germans, and the British. In recognition of the fact that all of these such names are still used, all entries begin with a list of the names readers will most likely encounter, making the entries easier to use by the nonexpert reader. Within each entry, one main way of spelling is used based on what is the most common method found in most scholarly works.

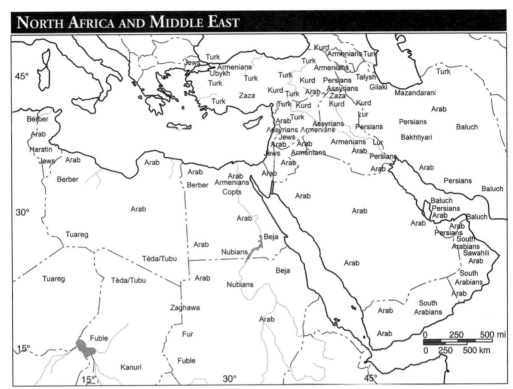

Ethnic groups in the North Africa and Middle East

Ethnic groups in West Africa

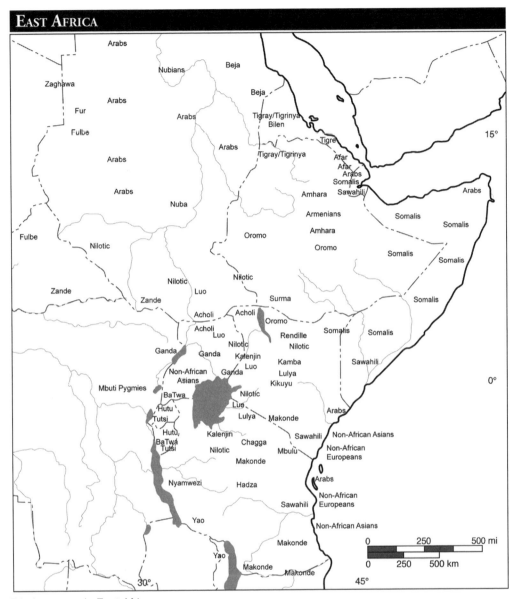

EAST AFRICA

Arabs

Nubians

Beja

Zaghawa

Arabs

Beja

Fur

Tigray/Tigrinya
Bilen

Fulbe

Arabs

Tigre

15°

Arabs

Tigray/Tigrinya

Afar
Afar
Arabs
Somalis
Sawahili

Arabs

Arabs

Nuba

Amhara

Arabs

Armenians

Somalis

Somalis

Amhara

Fulbe

Oromo

Oromo

Somalis

Somalis

Nilotic

Zande

Nilotic

Nilotic

Surma

Somalis

Zande

Luo

Acholi

Acholi

Oromo

Somalis

Somalis

Acholi

Rendille
Nilotic

Ganda

Acholi

Luo

Sawahili

Ganda

Nilotic

Kalenjin

Kamba

Non-African
Asians

Luo

Lulya

Ganda

Kikuyu

0°

Mbuti Pygmies

BaTwa

Nilotic

Hutu

Luo

Arabs

Tutsi

Lulya

Makonde

Hutu
BaTwa
Tutsi

Kalenjin

Chagga

Sawahili

Non-African Asians

Nilotic

Mbulu

Non-African
Europeans

Makonde

Nyamwezi

Hadza

Arabs

Non-African
Europeans

Sawahili

Yao

Non-African Asians

Makonde

Yao

Makonde

Makonde

30°

45°

| 0 | 250 | 500 mi |
| 0 | 250 | 500 km |

Ethnic groups in East Africa

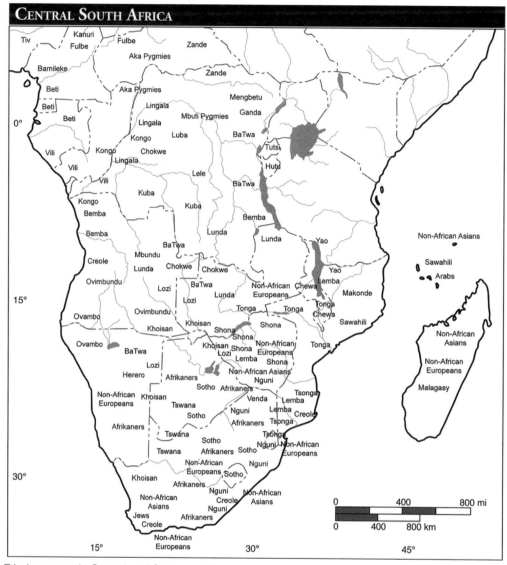

Ethnic groups in Central and Southern Africa

A

Acholi

The Acholi or Acoli are a western **Nilotic** people who live in southern Sudan, Uganda, and northern Kenya. They are most closely related to the **Luo** of Kenya and the Shilluk of Sudan. They number around 2 million, with the largest number, over 746,000, living in Uganda. Their name *Acholi* comes from the term 19th-century **Arab** traders gave them, *Shûli*, meaning speaking a mix of Arabic with another language.

The Acholi believe they moved into their current homeland some 300 years ago from the north. They began to coalesce into the Acholi as an identifiable group in the 17th century, and today there are six main subdivisions of the Acholi as well as three main ethnic groups: the Patiko (related to the Luo), the Ateker-speakers (who seem to have migrated earlier), and the Sudanic-speakers (who came from the west). Arab and **Swahili** slave traders from Zanzibar arrived in the 19th century, and the Acholi suffered greatly at their hands. Acholi villages were raided and burned, high numbers were enslaved, and local economies subsequently suffered because people fled to escape further raids.

Like most other Nilotes, Acholi life and culture revolve around their cattle. Until the 19th century, they possessed large herds, but diseases introduced by Europeans and raids by neighbors have greatly reduced the numbers of their cattle. Subsequent droughts in the 1980s and 1990s have put a great deal of stress on their ability to remain pastoralists.

The Acholi have made an effort to use their rather remote location to resist change. They are the least economically developed and least acculturated of Uganda's people. Nonetheless, the Acholi have had large numbers of men serving in the Ugandan army. The Acholi were severely punished during the rule of Idi Amin (1971–1979) for their service in the colonial army and for their support for President Milton Obote (1964–1971). Idi Amin became suspicious of Acholi soldiers, officers, and civilian leaders following an attempt in 1972 to restore ousted president Obote. Acholi soldiers were massacred in their barracks, and by the end of his purge, some 5,000 Acholi had been killed.

The Acholi have become important far beyond their mere numbers because of the Lord's Resistance Army, founded by Alice Auma in 1986. Auma became a spirit medium after she was possessed by the spirit Lakwena and took the name Alice Lakwena. Her movement began as a religious movement called the Holy Spirit Movement. The movement is directly connected with the defeat of the Acholi general Tito Okelo, who briefly was president of Uganda as the result of a coup. However, Okelo was driven from office and his Acholi soldiers fled back to their homeland, and subsequently the Acholi homeland was occupied by southern Ugandans. After a series of local victories, Alice Lakwena began a march to Kampala that was joined by other ethnic groups with grievances against the Museveni government, but the Ugandan army firmly defeated them in a battle outside of Kampala. Alice claimed that Lakwena then left her, and she fled to a refugee camp in northern Kenya where she died in 2007.

The movement lives on in Uganda led by Joseph Kony. He has similar claims to Auma of being possessed by spirits that direct his actions. Using symbols from traditional belief, Christianity, and on occasion Acholi nationalism, Kony has been able to resist the central state and spread fear beyond the borders of Uganda. He has an army of child soldiers, most of whom he has kidnapped from their home villages. The total of his strength is not known and guesses range from only 500 to up to 3,000 soldiers.

John A. Shoup

Further Reading

Behrend, Heike, Mitch Cohen, and John Middleton. *Alice Lakwena and the Holy Spirits: War in Northern Uganda, 1985–1997.* Athens: Ohio University Press, 2000.

Otiso, Kefa. *Culture and Customs of Uganda.* Westport, CT: Greenwood Press, 2006.

Twesigye, Emmanuel. *Religion, Politics, and Cults in East Africa: God, Warriors and Saints*, vol. 11. Bern, Switzerland: Peter Lang Publishing, 2010.

Afar

The Afar, also referred to as Danakil, are pastoral nomads living in the harsh deserts of Dankalia in southern Eritrea, Djibouti, and adjoining lowlands of northeastern Ethiopia. The only fertile land is near the Awash River. The Afar number approximately 2 million, with most living in Ethiopia. The people are Muslim and speak Afar, a Cushitic language.

Afar are a Hamidic people, closely related to the **Somali** and Saho. In the 10th century, **Arab** immigrants introduced Islam to the indigenous people, with whom they intermarried. There are two classes of Afar, the Asaimara (nobles) and Adiomara (commoners), each consisting of numerous patrilineal clans. Clans formed into petty *Sultanates*, most important of which was the *Sultanate* of Aussa on the Awash River, established in the 16th century. Life revolved around subsistence pastoralism with salt, gathered from desert lakes, providing the main trade commodity.

Historically, Afar men were fierce fighters. They formed a major part of Arab armies in wars against Christian Ethiopia and for centuries served as guides for Arab slavers. They plundered caravans along trade routes and raided neighbors, killing and castrating enemies as a sign of prowess. Afar men still wear their traditional curved knife or *jile*.

The majority of Afar today remains nomadic, moving between water sources with herds of camel, sheep, and goats. The Awash district provides grazing in dry seasons. Women are responsible for the camp, constructing huts, gathering wood and water, weaving mats used for their dwellings, and tending herds. Meat, milk, hides, and salt are traded for necessities. Fishing is an important industry along the Red Sea.

Afar religious beliefs mingle Islam with an earlier Sky-God religion. A cult of the dead tradition has continued in the annual festival of *Rebina*, which includes animal sacrifice. Common cultural practices include both male and female circumcision and preference for first-cousin marriages.

Recent history has been marred by conflict with national governments. Ethiopian expansionism in the late 19th century brought the *Sultanate* of Aussa under Ethiopian control. In the 20th century, Modernism established commercial farming in the Awash valley, eliminating vital grazing areas. In 1975, the socialist Derg government nationalized rural lands and ended the traditional *sultanate*, sparking ethnic rebellion. Galvanized by the newly formed Afar Liberation Front (ALF), the insurrection continued in the region until after the collapse of the Derg in 1991. The creation of an autonomous Afar Region in 1994 brought peace; however, drought, famine, fighting, and corruption have all taken a toll on the Afar.

Geri Shaw

Further Reading

Central Statistical Agency of Ethiopia (CSA). "Census 2007." http://www.csa.gov.et.

Collins, Robert O. *Africa: A Short History*. Princeton, NJ: Markus Wiener Publishers, 2008.

Insoll, Timothy. *The Archaeology of Islam in Sub-Saharan Africa*. Cambridge: Cambridge University Press, 2003.

Lewis, I. M. *Peoples of the Horn of Africa: somali, Afar and Saho*. London: International African Institute, 1969.

Lewis, I. M. *Saints and Somalis: Popular Islam in a Clan-Based Society*. Lawrenceville, NJ: Red Sea Press, 1998.

Meredith, Martin. *The Fate of Africa: A History of Fifty Years of Independence*. New York: Public Affairs, 2005.

Pankurst, Richard. *The Ethiopians: A History*. Oxford: Blackwell Publishing, 2001.

Said, Ali. "Afar Ethnicity in Ethiopian Politics." In *Ethnicity and the State in Eastern Africa*, edited by M. A. Mohamed Salih and John Markiles. Uppsala: Nordiska Africainstitutet, 1998.

Afrikaner

Afrikaners are descendants of Dutch, German, and French settlers who speak *Afrikaans*, a form of Dutch. There are between 2.2 million and 3 million Afrikaners living in South Africa, Namibia, Botswana, and Zimbabwe, though the majority live in South Africa. Afrikaners are also called Boers from the Dutch word meaning "farmers." In South Africa they comprise around 60 percent of the white population, but only 10 percent of the total population of the country. Afrikaner identity is closely tied to their language, Afrikaans, to the Dutch Reformed Church, and their history of conflict with both the British and the native peoples of South Africa. Afrikaners have a strong feeling of being Africans and not Europeans.

Afrikaner settlement in South Africa began in 1652 when Jan van Riebeeck of the Dutch East India Company established a colony at Table Bay. The Cape Colony was to serve as a station for ships going to and coming from the Dutch East Indies (Indonesia), a place where ships could replenish with fresh fruits, vegetables, meat, and water. The employees working the land were kept under strict control by the administration, but within a decade, some of the employees were allowed to settle lands outside of the original colony. The free burghers proved to be more cost efficient for the directors in Holland, and so others were released from their contracts to establish more freehold farms. To work the land, slaves from the Dutch East Indies, India, Ceylon, and Portuguese Mozambique were imported. The indigenous Khoikhoi (Hottentots; **Khoisan**) were defeated and forced into servitude. In 1688, the colony received new blood from French Huguenots (Protestants), who had been forced to flee France in 1685.

The Afrikaans language developed during the first 200 years of European settlement in Africa. Dutch was the base, but in order to speak to slaves from Indonesia and Africa, vocabulary from those languages were borrowed and Dutch grammar was simplified. The arrival of French Huguenots brought French vocabulary into the language as well. English became an important influence as Afrikaans developed in the first decades of the 19th century. Afrikaans was not a written language (formal Dutch was used until after 1900), but has a rich oral history in songs and poetry. Following World War I, the language quickly developed a literary corpus, and in 2003, Afrikaner John Maxwell Coetzee won the Nobel Prize for Literature.

During the Napoleonic Wars, the Cape Colony came under British rule in 1795. The British were forced to leave in 1803, but were back permanently starting in 1806. British control was confirmed by the peace agreements between European powers in 1814. British relations with the

Leander Jameson's forces attempt to fend off the Boers during the Jameson Raid in South Africa in December 1895. It was this attempt by the British to annex the Transvaal that sparked the Boer War. (Library of Congress)

Boers were poor, and in 1815, the Boers rose in the Slagtersnek Rebellion. In 1820, the first British colonists arrived in the Cape, which to the Afrikaners seemed a threat to their religion, language, and culture. The British government became increasingly abolitionist, and in 1834, the Cape administration emancipated all slaves. The result was the Great Trek, where some 5,000 Boers left the territory of the Cape Colony to find a new life free of British control. The Great Trek is an important part of shaping Afrikaner identity; framed in Old Testament symbols, it developed into the idea of a covenant between the Righteous and God and the founding of a new Zion. The defeats of powerful kingdoms, such as the Zulu (**Nguni**) at the Battle of Blood River in 1838, were later embodied in Afrikaner political ideology. Around 500 Boers stood off and defeated an army of 10,000 Zulus. Zulu losses were put at 3,000 dead, with no losses on the Boer side—this seemed to be a clear sign of God's approval of the Boers. December 16, the date of the battle, became a holiday called Day of the Vow.

The Boers established three independent states: Transvaal, the Orange Free State, and Natalia. The British annexed them, but later gave Transvaal and the Orange Free State their independence. British-Boer relations were strained, and after 1867, when the first diamonds were found near Bloemfontein, British prospectors, miners, and speculators moved into the two Boer republics. British imperialist interests in southern and central Africa were blocked by the republics, and in 1896, the Jameson Raid, an attempt to annex the Transvaal by a pro-British conspiracy, provoked war. The Boer War (1899–1902) created great bitterness among the Boers toward the British. To crush Boer resistance, the British devised concentration camps for Boer women and children where 28,000 died of starvation and disease before the end of hostilities.

Boers were militarily defeated, but Boer resistance was not. It took on a different mode in the form of political parties and secret brotherhoods. In 1914, the National Party was founded to protect Afrikaner economic interests and to take South Africa out of the British Empire. Afrikaners were able to get a number of laws passed in the South African parliament, which favored them between 1910 and 1948. The year 1938 marked the centennial celebration of the Battle of Blood River, and the event was celebrated with the erection of a monument at the battle site as important expression of Afrikaner culture. In 1948, the National Party was able to win the election and gain control of the government. The National Party imposed policies based on *apartheid*, a racist doctrine of separate development for different peoples. Opposition was often branded as communist, and those in opposition were exiled, imprisoned, or banned. In 1991, the reform element in the National Party controlled parliament and ended all apartheid laws, and in 1994, South Africa had its first nonracial elections. Afrikaners remain among the more affluent South Africans, owning large commercial farms. Unlike many of British origin, Afrikaners have not

---

Fighting Apartheid

Apartheid was the official policy of forcing South Africa's peoples into separate, distinct living spaces. The word "apartheid" is Afrikaans and simply means "separation" or "apartness." The idea of needing a policy of separateness began as early as the 1870s–1880s; the Afrikaner S. J. du Toit advocated separation of the Afrikaner people in order to keep their race "pure" from mixing with the English.

Resistance to Apartheid began as early as 1912, when the African National Congress (ANC) was founded. Africans, Coloreds, and Indians, though all directly affected by the growing restrictions on their communities, did not unite in action against the racist laws. Each fought for greater rights for their own communities, but until 1948, they did not see a common interest. This changed in the 1948 elections, and the ANC was more and more inclusive of South Africa's people. Incidents such as the Freedom Charter of 1955, Sharpsville Massacre in 1960, the Treason Trial of Nelson Mandela and others in 1964, and Steve Biko's South African Students Organization founded in 1968 all helped bring a greater unity to the opposition. A general countrywide strike in 1973 and the Soweto student uprising in 1976 help galvanize the opposition. Outside pressure was applied as well with the United Nations embargo on weapons sales to South Africa imposed in 1977 and disinvestment movements, forcing companies to withdraw from their investments in South Africa.

In 1990, the South African government lifted the ban on the ANC, and Nelson Mandela was released from prison; he had been a prisoner for 22 years. In 1994, Mandela was elected the first postapartheid president of the Republic of South Africa, the first black president, and first to be elected where all South Africans were allowed to participate in the process.

---

generally joined the white flight from postapartheid South Africa.

John A. Shoup

Further Reading

Afolayan, Funso. *Culture and Customs of South Africa*. Westport, CT: Greenwood Press, 2004.

Meredith, Martin. *The Fate of Africa: A History of Fifty Years of Independence*. New York: Public Affairs, 2005.

Morris, Donald. *The Washing of the Spears: The Rise and Fall of the Zulu Nation*. Cambridge, MA: Da Capo Press, 1998.

Stokes, Jamie, ed. "Afrikaner." In *Encyclopedia of the Peoples of Africa and the Middle East*. New York: Facts on File, 2009.

Thompson, Leonard. *A History of South Africa*. New Haven, CT: Yale University Press, 1995.

Worden, Nigel. *The Making of Modern South Africa: Conquest, Apartheid, and Democracy*. Oxford: Wiley-Blackwell, 2007.

Akans

The Akans are one of the most culturally dominant ethnic groups in West Africa. Located in modern-day Ghana, formerly the British Gold Coast, the Akans are organized into matrilineal groups in which social and political power is wielded by the female head of household, and lineage reckoning is through the female side. The Akans are made up of several sub-ethnic groupings, of which the Ashantis (Asantes) are the most prominent. In modern-day Ghana, the Akans have a population of 8,562,748, representing more than 46 percent of the total national population of 18,412,247. The other members of the Akan family are Ahanta, Akuapen, Akwanu, Akyem (Ahuakwa, Bosome, Kotoku), Buaho, Fante, Kwaku, Sefwi, and Wasa. Of these, the Asantes constitute 30.1 percent of the Akan population, making them the largest of the group. Geographically, the Akans are spread over a large area of modern Ghana, covering areas as far as the Asante region, Bonon Aha-fo, central and eastern regions, and some remote parts of the Volta region. The most commonly spoken language among the Akans is "Twi" with many dialects, depending on the location of the sub-group. These include Fante, Akuapem, Asante, and Akyem. Other dialects within the Twi language can also be

The Asante king Otumfuo Opoku Ware II sits next to the Golden Stool (on right), symbol of the Asante nation. The Asante king is not the son of the previous king; instead, he is the son of the king's sister, mother, or aunt. (AP/Wide World Photos)

found in the southwest area of Dankyira, Twifo, Wasa, and Ahanta.

According to historians, the Ashanti kingdom (also known as Asante kingdom) was one of the last kingdoms to have emerged after the decline of the kingdom of Akuapem. The kingdom of Akuapem was itself founded by refugees fleeing the Bono kingdom by moving southward toward modern-day Kumasi, where it was believed that the first Asante kingdom, known as Asante Manso, was established by the Queen mother, Nkansa. The first paramount king of this kingdom was Obiri Yeboa, who was the first son of King Ansa Sasraku I of Asamankese-Akwamu. Shortly after the installation of the new king, other refugees from Ayoko, led by Akyeampong Tenten, soon settled in the new kingdom. With the new arrival, the title of the king was changed from *Asamankese* to *Asantehene*, and Ossei Tutu I, the grandson of Akyeampon's sister, Nana Abena Gyapa, became the first *Asantehene*. As Asante society is matrilineal, the *Asantehene*, the king, can be chosen only from among the male children of the king's sister, the Queen mother, or from his aunt's male children. The Queen mother is not the mother of the king; she could be the sister or the aunt, and she has tremendous power over the royal household.

The Akan people are ruled under an elaborate system of governance at the top of which is the king, the *Asantehene*. As the principal chief, the king acts under the authority of the ancestors and he is seen, by his subjects, to be the embodiment of their power and will. However, with the conquest of the kingdom by the British around the end of the 19th century, the authority and the influence of the king have greatly diminished. The king now wields symbolic power, which is restricted to traditional and customary matters, while issues of jurisprudence are now taken over by the constituted authority of the modern state. In the day-to-day governance of his kingdom, the king is assisted by several lesser chiefs. Chieftaincy position is hereditary, and each of the selected chiefs has a symbolic right to a blackened tool, which is a sharp stick that has been hardened in fire. The Queen mother also plays an important role in the administration of the royal court and of the kingdom. She maintains order within the royal court in addition to mobilizing popular support for the king's authority and influence. Besides the Queen mother, the Council of Elders also plays a prominent role in running the kingdom and in advancing the authority of king over his subjects.

Under the direction of the king, the Council of Elders is set up as an advisory body to the royal court. The council consists primarily of elders, selected from different clans, who are considered to be knowledgcable of the clan's history and rules guiding descent. Within the Council of Elders, there are three prominent figures. The *Krontihene* is in charge of overall administration of the kingdom. The *Okyeame* is the noted linguist within the royal court, and through him, the king speaks to his subjects. The third position is the *Gyasehene*, who is solely responsible for the day-to-day administration of the royal palace. He is also responsible for maintaining an elaborate system of royal servitude, which in many cases may consist of several hundreds of royal servants and court attendants selected from lower ranks of the Asante society.

Among the Akans, the extended family is the norm, which may be comprised of the spouse, uncles, aunts, grandparents, and other related siblings. The clan is the basis of social organization among the Akans, and members of the clan have claim to common ancestry and, in some instances, are united by one language. The oldest female member of the household, often the maternal grandmother, oversees the running of the household, and through the recognition of her authority, order and respect for elders are maintained within the unit. Matrilineal descent is the norm, and family properties are passed down through the female line. Rules of consanguinity, often determined by the female elders of the household, are used to decide on which member of the clan one can take as a bride. In most cases, the Akans practice exogamous marriage, which prohibits one from marrying one's cousin. Marriage is seen as uniting two families or clans as opposed to uniting the bride and the groom; the maternal grandmother of the bride or the aunts have more say as to whom the bride takes for a husband.

Like most ethnic groups in West Africa, the Akans of Ghana believe in a very complex system of ancestor worship, and their worldview is still guided by superstition and oracular beliefs. The Akans believe in the existence of a universal God, the creator of all living things. They also believe in the existence of other lesser gods or spirits through which they relate to their primary God, *Odonmankoma* or the Supreme God. The most important of these lesser gods are *Bonebone*, the creator; *Omaomee*, the granter of satisfaction; *Omaowia*, the giver of sunlight; *Toturobonsu*, the giver of rain; *Onyan-Koropon*; and *Twereampton*, the supporter. These lesser gods or spirits are represented by different objects, the most common of which are blackened stools, and a tree (*Nyaamedua*), under which foods or eggs are left as sacrifice to the ancestors. Overall, the Akans believe in their ancestors (*Nsamanfo*) as medium spirits between them and the Supreme God. They also believe that life continues after death and there is no clear separation, in their belief system, between heaven and earth; both are seen as a continuum.

In the Akan society, polygyny, a practice whereby a man can marry more than one woman, is the norm. Polyandry (a practice where a woman can have more than one husband) is very rare. A man can only marry a woman outside his clan (exogamous marriage). Mate selection is usually done by the parents of the groom, often the mother or aunt of the groom. Once a match is made and both families have agreed on the suitability of the couple for marriage, the groom's family offers a "bride price" to the family of the bride. The bride price can be in the form of articles of clothing, labor service in the bride's father's farm, and, more recently, money. The groom also presents to the father of the bride local drinks (*Odo Nsa*) to seal the relation. This process represents the marriage contract; however, the bride price should be seen not as a purchase price of the bride, but as a symbolic offering that recognizes the emerging bond between the two families. Other types of marriage exist among the Akans, and one of these is the marriage of an unborn baby to a prospective suitor. This is known as *Asiwa* (or betrothal), in which a man requests the hands of the unborn baby in marriage, assuming the unborn child is going to be a girl, which often can be predicted by the oracles. Once the request is accepted, the man then becomes the sole provider for the unborn baby's mother, and after the baby is born, he continues to support the baby and the mother until she reaches the age of puberty. Female twins are automatically reserved as wives to the king.

One of Akan's great historical figures was a female warrior, Nana Yaa Asentewaa, who mobilized her people on March 28, 1900, against British occupation of the Asante kingdom. Born of noble origin in 1840, Yaa Asentewaa was appointed Queen mother of Ejisu kingdom, one of several loose confederacies of the greater Asante kingdom. In 1896, Yaa Asantewaa's brother, King Ejisu, was exiled to Seychelles along with the Asante king, Prempeh I, and other prominent members of his royal court. The king had opposed the British occupation of his kingdom. With the absence of Prempeh I, the kingdom was in disarray, and agitation for his immediate release became the rallying point of revolt against the British occupying force. As a leader of the Asante confederacy, Yaa Asentewaa appointed her grandson to replace her brother as the new *Ejisuhene*. Together they became the rallying point of protest and opposition to the British governor-general of the Gold Coast, who earlier had humiliated King Prempeh I by seizing his Golden Stool before exiling him to Seychelles. Now as a regent of the Ejisu-Juanben, Yaa Asantewaa organized and led a powerful force of 14,000 armed men and women in Kumasi in revolt against British occupation. This marked the beginning of the Asante's rebellion against British rule throughout the Gold Coast. Several attacks were mounted against British soldiers by Yaa Asantewaa and her followers before she was finally captured in 1901 and sent to exile in Seychelles, where she died on October 17, 1921. Yaa Asantewaa's courage, and her dedication to freeing the Asante's nation from British occupation, in the face of one of the most brutal British military campaigns in colonial West Africa, made her a legend in the Akan society today.

Today the Akans are part of the modern state of Ghana. While still maintaining their culture and tradition, which are often seen in their mode of dress, especially the *Kente*, the authority of the *Asantehene*, Ossei Tutu II, has been relegated solely to customary matters. After gaining independence in 1957, the country of Ghana adopted a British-type parliamentary democracy; but today, it has opted for an American-style presidential system after the country went through several violent military coups.

Pade Badru

Further Reading

Adu Boahen. *Topics in West African History.* London: Longmans, 1966.

Akyeampong, Emmanuel. "Christianity, Modernity and the Weight of Tradition in the Life of Asantehene Agyeman Prempeh I." *Africa* 69, no. 2 (1999): 279. Academic Search Premier. EBSCO. Web. October 13, 2009.

Al-Bakri, Kitab al-masalik wa 'l mamalik. An Arabic Account of the Culture, Politics, and Geography of the Empire of Ghana. (Book of Routes and Realms, 1068).

Badru, P. "Family and Social Trends in Ancient West Africa." In *World Eras, Volume 10: West African Kingdoms, 500–1590,* by Pierre-Damien Mvuyekure. New York: A Manly, Inc. Book & Thompson-Gale Publisher, 2004.

Boahen, Adu, et al. *Topics in West Africa History.* Harlow, UK: Longman Press, 1986.

Buah, F. K. *A History of Ghana.* London: MacMillan Education Ltd., 1980.

Busia, K. A. *The Position of the Chief in the Modern Political System of Ashanti: A Study of the Influence of Contemporary Social Changes on Ashanti Political Institutions.* London, New York, and Toronto: Oxford Press, 1951.

Clark, Gracia. "Negotiating Asante Family Survival in Kumasi, Ghana." *Africa* 69, no. 1 (1999).

Danquah, J. B. *The Akan Doctrine of God: A Fragment of Gold Coast Ethics and Religion.* London: Cass, 1968.

Danquah, J. B. *The Gold Coast Akan.* London: United Society for Christian Literature, 1945.

Ehret, Christopher. *The Civilizations of Africa: A History to 1800.* Charlottesville: University Press of Virginia, 2002.

Fortes, M. "The Structure of Unilineal Descent Groups." *American Anthropologists* 55 (January–March), 1953. GhanaNation.com (Official Web site of the Ashanti Region).

Goody, Jack. "Bridewealth and Dowry in Africa and Euro-Asia." In *Bridewealth and Dowry,* by Jack Goody and S. J. Tambiah. Cambridge: Cambridge University Press, 1973.

Isichei, Elizabeth. *History of African Societies to 1870.* Cambridge: Cambridge University Press, 1997.

Kyeremateng, Nkansa, K. *The Akans of Ghana: Their Customs, History and Institutions.* Accra, Ghana: Sebewie Publishers, 2004.

Lystad, Robert A. "Marriage and Kingship among the Ashantis and Agai; A Study of Differential Acculturation." In *Continuity and Change in African Cultures,* edited by William R. Boscon and Melville Herskovits. Chicago: University of Chicago Press, 1959.

Magesa, L. *African Religion.* New York: Orbis Book, 1997.

Mbiti, John. *Introduction to African Religion.* London: Heinemann Press, 1975.

McKissack, Patricia, and Fredrick McKissack. *The Royal Kingdoms of Ghana, Mali, and Songhay. Life in Medieval Africa.* New York: Henry Holt and Company, 1994.

Ofosu-Appiah, L. H., and Keith Irvine. *Encyclopaedia Africana: Dictionary of African Biography Volume 1: Ethiopia–Ghana.* Algonac, MI: Reference Publications, Incorporated, June 1997.

Owirendu, P. A "The Akan System of Inheritance Today and Tomorrow." *African Affairs* 58, no. 9 (1959): 161–65.

Ross, Doran H. *Wrapped in Pride: Ghanaian Kente and African American Identity.* Los Angeles: UCLA Fowler Museum of Cultural History, 1998.

Thompson, Farris, R. *Flash of Spirit: African and Afro-American Art and Philosophy.* New York: Random House, 1983.

Yankah, Kwesi. "Proverb Speaking as a Creative Process: The Akan of Ghana." DeProverbio.com 6, no. 2 (2000). http://www.deproverbio.com/display.php?a=3&r=119 (accessed January 26, 2010).

Aka Pygmies

The Aka pygmies (also called BaAka, Gba-Aka, Bi-Aka, Bekà, Yakwe, Yakpa, and Yakpawe) live in the Central African Republic and Congo (Brazzaville) and number around 5,000. Like the **Mbuti** and Efe of the Ituri forest, the Aka are true pygmies and adults are no taller 150 centimeters (4 feet, 11 inches). According to geneticists they, along with the Mbuti/Efe and **Khoisan**, have the Y chromosome haplogroup B and mt (mitochondrial) DNA haplogroup L1, making them perhaps the oldest living group of modern man. The Aka speak their own language, Diaka, as well as the Bantu languages of the populations close to them.

The Aka are among the oldest of living groups of modern man and are most likely the descendants of the Tschitolian industry that dates back to around 25,000 years ago on the fringes of the rain forest. An ancient Egyptian (6th dynasty, 2300 BCE) account of an expedition that may have reached into central Africa records bringing back a pygmy dancer, and other ancient Egyptian references call pygmies "Aka."

The Aka traditionally are hunter-gatherers and developed relationships with some 11 Bantu peoples who moved into the region. Aka provide skins, ivory, and wild rubber to their Bantu neighbors in exchange for foodstuffs that are not found in the wild. The Aka live in particlan groupings, or camps of three to four adult males who belong to the same male line of descent.

The Aka have become well known for their distinctive contrapuntal polyphony vocals accompanied by drums and hand clapping. They perform the music to mark the making of a new camp, funerals, and other special occasions. In 2003, the United Nations named their music one of the world's Intangible Cultural Heritage of Humanity.

The Aka were brought into the world economy in the late 19th century to help supply the European market with ivory. Elephant hunting brought about a change in their society as elephant hunters gained prestige from their earnings. Later, with the introduction of coffee, many Aka now spend significant parts of the year working on village farms during the best time of year to trap and net game. Like the Mbuti and Efe, the Aka have been targets for killing squads called *Les Efaceurs* (erasers), who also are accused of cannibalism. It is reported to the UN representatives in several central African states that some of the rebel groups in the region hunt and kill pygmies, eating parts of their victims to gain the skills of those eaten, believing they can take on some of the abilities of those they eat.

John A. Shoup

Further Reading

Hewlett, Barry. Biographical sketch. http://www.vancouver.wsu.edu/fac/hewlett/introaka.html (accessed December 30, 2009).

Kent, Susan. *Cultural Diversity among Twentieth Century Foragers: An African Perspective.* Cambridge: Cambridge University Press, 2006.

Kisliuk, Michell Robin. *Seize the Dance! BaAka Musical Life and the Ethnography of Performance.* New York: Oxford University Press, 2000.

Newman, James. *The Peopling of Africa: A Geographic Interpretation.* New Haven, CT: Yale University Press, 1995.

"Safeguarding Intangible Cultural Heritage." http://www.unesco.org/culture/ich/index.php?lg=EN&topic=mp&cp=CF (accessed December 30, 2009).

Vansina, Jan. *Paths in the Rainforests: Toward a History of Political Tradition in Equatorial Africa.* Madison: University of Wisconsin Press, 1990.

Woodfork, Jacqueline. *Culture and Customs of the Central African Republic.* Westport, CT: Greenwood Press, 2006.

Amhara

As a group, the Amhara are a mixture of people who speak a common language, Amharic. They occupy the central highlands of Ethiopia, west to the Sudanese boarder. Their state includes the regions of Wollo, Gojjam, Gonder, and north Shoa. Typically, people think of themselves in terms of their regions, rather than as a distinct ethnic group. While the majority of people are sedentary farmers, the Amhara have been the ruling class of Ethiopia over most of its long history, and have provided almost all of the imperial rulers. They have been seen as synonymous with the Ethiopian State. The people are Orthodox Christian and speak Amharic, a Semitic language related to Tigrinya and **Tigre**, though strongly influenced by Cushitic and Sidama languages. They are a large group, numbering about 18 million, approximately 30 percent of Ethiopia's population. They are closely related to the Tigray people, their main political rivals.

Amhara ancestors are believed to have come from southern Arabia and intermarried with the local Cushite inhabitants in the south Wollo area. From here, the Amharic language and culture spread, absorbing non-Amhara ethnic groups, and creating a mixed culture and language. Amhara imperial tradition claims that the first Ethiopian kingdom was established by Menelik I, son of the Judean king Solomon and the queen of Sheba. The line of kings and emperors that followed remained unbroken for 2,000 years. Menelik is also said to have brought the Ark of the Covenant from Jerusalem to Ethiopia. The Ark of the Covenant still figures prominently in Amharic religious beliefs.

The first important kingdom was the Kingdom of Axum from the first to the ninth century. Centered to the north in Tigray, Axum controlled a large area with important trade connections with southern Arabia. *Ge'ez*, the language of Axum, is the foundation of the Amharic language and writing system. Orthodox Christianity was adopted by the Axumites in the fourth century and spread throughout the kingdom. The church remains at the core of Amhara culture, and *Ge'ez* is still the language of the church. As Axum declined in the ninth century, the center of power gradually shifted southward to the Amhara.

During the decline of Axum, **Arab** influence pushed inland along trade routes, bringing Islam into the regions surrounding the highlands, isolating the Christian Church. The only outside contact was with the Orthodox or **Coptic** Church of Alexandria in Egypt. In the 16th century, the Christian kingdom was attacked in an Arab holy war against Christians led by Ahmad Gran. The Arab army massacred people, burned churches, and sent the imperial ruler into hiding. Only the highest mountainous regions were unconquered. The invasion was brought to an end with the intervention of the Portuguese, preserving Amhara rule and the Christian faith.

For the Amhara, the Orthodox Christian Church is the center of community and cultural life. Over the long centuries of isolation, the Orthodox Church developed its own distinctive form, noted for its Judaic elements. The many churches are a typical part of the landscape and appear in every village. A distinctive form of artwork has developed around the religion, and numerous religious feast days are observed throughout the year. On holy days, the *Tabot*, replicas of the Ark of the Covenant, are carried in colorful processions led by priests who wear elaborately designed robes. The processions are accompanied by music and dancing, evoking images from the Old Testament. It is the possession of *Tabot* that gives sanctity to churches. Sites of pilgrimage include the many churches carved out of solid rock into hills and cliff faces. The most important are the medieval churches of Lalibela, purportedly built with the help of angels.

Almost 90 percent of Amhara are rural people, whose lives have changed little over time. They are sedentary farmers living in villages surrounded by cultivated fields. Amhara were among the earliest peoples in Africa to develop plows and harnessing for oxen to pull them. Grains such as millet, corn, and *tef*, a small local grain, are the dietary staples. During the harvest, animals are used to thresh the grain. Most cultivation is subsistence. Amhara also raise cattle, goats, and sheep, with donkeys serving as draft animals. Coffee, indigenous to the highlands, is the cash crop. Men tend the fields and herd larger animals while children tend smaller animals and women take care of household tasks. Drought, famine, and political unrest have created hard times for the rural Amhara.

The 19th century brought expansion of Amhara political dominance as regions were brought under imperial control. From the north, foreign invasions from the Ottomans of Egypt and Mahdists of Sudan were fought off. French, British, and Italian colonial powers made inroads along the coastal regions. The Italians, having taken control of Eritrea, invaded Tigray, but were stopped by the Ethiopian armies of Menelik II at the Battle of Adowa in 1896, effectively ending the Italian colonial enterprise. The Amharic empire remained free of European colonization.

Under Haile Salassi, the last emperor in the early 20th century, a process of modernization and assimilation began. Amhara culture was promoted and Amharic became the official language at the expense of non-Amharic cultures and languages. Regional ethnic groups in the country resented the push toward Amharization and sporadic unrest ensued. Salassi was overthrown in 1975 by the socialist, military Derg regime, ending 2,000 years of monarchy. The Derg used harsh tactics to subdue unrest. Famine in the 1980s compounded the problems, and the economy deteriorated. Ethnic groups rose up in defiance of the government, in pursuit of self-determination and as a reaction to centuries of Amhara dominance. Leading the struggle was the Tigray People Liberation Front (TPLF) in the Tigray region. After bitter fighting, the Derg government fell in 1991. The federal republic that followed created several ethnic states, one of them the Amhara State. Politically, the federal republic is dominated by the Tigray, who control the current ruling political party. Having lost political control, the Amhara are now beginning to form political parties to promote their political interests.

Geri Shaw

Further Reading

Adhana, Adhana H., "Tigray—the Birth of a Nation within the Ethiopian Polity." In *Ethnicity and the State in Eastern Africa*, edited by M. A. Mohamed Salih and John Markakis. Uppsala: Nordiska Africainstitutet, 1998.

Central Statistical Agency of Ethiopia (CSA). "Census 2007." http://www.csa.gov.et

Henze, Paul B. *Layers of Time*. New York: Palgrave, 2000.

Pankhurst, Richard. *The Ethiopians: A History*. Oxford: Blackwell Publishing, 2001.

Stokes, Jamie. "Amhara." In *Encyclopedia of the Peoples of Africa and the Middle East*. New York: Facts on File, 2009.

Teka, Tigegne. "Amhara Ethnicity in the Making." In *Ethnicity and the State in Eastern Africa*, edited by M. A. Mohamed Salih and John Markiles. Uppsala: Nordiska Africainstitutet, 1998.

Ullendorff, Edward. *The Ethiopians*. London: Oxford University Press, 1965.

Annang

The Annang or Anang live mainly in the Cross River area of southern Nigeria. Their language belongs to the Kwa group, which is the same Benue-Congo branch of the Niger-Congo phylum of languages, as do all of the Efik-Ibibio-speaking peoples. The Anang belong to the Western branch of the Ibibio people, and today the Anang number around 800,000 people.

The Anang, like others of the Ibibio group, have a long history in the Cross River region of Nigeria. They developed generally democratic independent villages, rather than strong, central states, and following the arrival of Europeans eager for slaves, the **Igbo** pushed the Ibibio peoples, including the Anang, further to the south and east. The Anang grew rain-forest crops of yams, taro, and cassava, and in the 19th century, following the collapse of the Atlantic slave trade, palm oil become the staple of the economy.

The Anang, like other Ibibio peoples, have a number of secret societies called *ekpo* linked to the traditional religion of the ancestral spirits. Most of the *ekpo* societies use a number of masks, and during important festivals, the masks are paraded in what are called "theatrical staging of the masks." Masks represent the spirits of the ancestors as well as of the *idiok* spirits, which are considered to be dangerous and can only be seen by members of the *ekpo* societies.

The Anang are patriarchal, and people trace their ancestry from their original compound or *ufok*. Several *ufok* make up an *ekpuk* or extended families, and several *ekpuk* make up an *idung* or village. Political power rests with lineage elders and elected village leaders. Women have both economic and political importance and have been able to rise to high political positions. Bride fattening is part of the political and economic power that women once had, and some scholars note that prior to the arrival of Christian missionaries, the Anang may have been at least partially matriarchal. The fattening room was where the potential bride was taught how to be a good wife, how to cook, clean, and perform other duties. In addition, she was encouraged to add to her weight because fat was an essential part of beauty. Anang argue that being fat was not just a sign of wealth, and since Anang did not suffer hunger, fat people did not separate wealthy from the poor. Instead, it was simply an aspect of local concepts of beauty.

Political organization of the Anang has remained village headmen who are elected by the leaders of the main lineages. Equally important are the leaders of the three *ekpo* societies who help plan the main annual rituals. The council of elders assists the elected chief.

In 1929, during the colonial period, women in the southern region of Nigeria protested attempts by the British to control trade, much of which was done by women. Nigeria became independent in 1960 and, due to the military rule that began in 1966, the southeastern region of the country, led by the Igbo, declared independence as the Biafra, sparking a long civil war. The civil war ended in 1970 with the surrender of Biafra, but only after between 500,000 and 2 million people died. The Anang, like all peoples of the region, suffered from the war.

Following the civil war, the region has been reintegrated into the Nigerian republic, and some of the issues that sparked the rebellion to begin with have been addressed by the Nigerian state.

John A. Shoup

Further Reading

Falola, Toyin. *Culture and Customs of Nigeria.* Westport, CT: Greenwood Press, 2001.
Stokes, Jamie. "Ibibio." In *Encyclopedia of the Peoples of Africa and the Middle East.* New York: Facts on File, 2009.
"Tribal African Art: Anang (Annang)." http://www.zyama.com/anang/index.htm (accessed May 2, 2010).

Arabs

Arabs are the largest single ethnic group in the Middle East and North Africa, numbering around 325 million people living in 22 countries that make up the League of Arab States, including Somalia, Djibouti, and the Comoros Islands. In addition, there are important Arab minorities in Turkey, Iran, and Israel as well as in a number of Saharan and Sahel states in Africa including Mali, Niger, and Chad. Arabs have had a long historical presence in East Africa where they founded several trade cities, and as a result, there are Arab minorities in Kenya and Tanzania, especially on the island of Zanzibar.

Arabic is the largest and most widespread Semitic language today. Most Arabs are Muslims, and Arabic is closely tied to the religion as it is the language of the Qur'an and Islamic practice. Arabs comprise around 20 percent of Muslims worldwide. There are between 20 million and 30 million Christian and **Jewish** Arabs and, in Lebanon, Christians make up around 44 percent of the total population. Since the foundation of Israel in 1948, many Jewish Arabs have immigrated, leaving behind small communities numbering only in the few hundreds or few thousands. Arab ethnicity is difficult to define, and it is generally accepted that it is primarily

Sunni or Shi'ite

The main division between Muslims is between the Sunnis and the Shi'ites, which goes back to the succession of the temporal and spiritual leadership of the Muslims following the death of the Prophet Muhammad in 632. The first four who succeeded him, Abu Bakr (632–634), 'Umar ibn al-Khattab (634–644), 'Uthman ibn 'Affan (644–656), and 'Ali ibn Abi Talib (656–661) were all from the close companions of the Prophet and elected by a council called the *shura* or consultative council made up of the companions as a whole. 'Uthman ibn 'Affan was assassinated and 'Ali, the Prophet's cousin and husband of the Prophet's daughter Fatimah Zahrah, was elected, but the governor of Syria and a relative of 'Uthman, Mu'awiyah, refused to recognize 'Ali and said that he suspected 'Ali, or his supporters, had a hand in 'Uthman's death. The two met in battle at Siffin in 657, but agreed to arbitration. The attempts to arbitrate between the two did not bring an end to the problem, and until 'Ali's death in 661 both men ruled as the "successors" to the Prophet, Mu'awiyah from his base of support in Syria and 'Ali from his base in Iraq. Sunnis believe the succession of Mu'awiyah in 661, following the death of 'Ali, is politically acceptable, while Shi'ites believe that 'Ali and his sons should be the legitimate rulers of the Islamic world. Most Sunnis today do not feel that the contest over power in the seventh century is that important and, in general, have followed the "rule of law" and thus the appellation of "Sunni." Shi'ites, on the other hand, see the legitimate succession as extremely important and have taken their support for 'Ali and his descendants as central to their belief and are thus "Shi'itu 'Ali" or "partisans of 'Ali."

based on speaking the Arabic language. The language serves as a means of separation into regional dialects, but is also the unifying force in the form of classical/literary Arabic (*Fusha*). A modified form of *Fusha* called Modern Standard Arabic is used in print and broadcast media.

In the Qur'an (and the Bible), Arabs are the descendants of the patriarch *Ibrahim* (Abraham) and his Egyptian bondwoman *Hajar* (Hagar) through their son *Isma'il* (Ishmael) and are thus close cousins to the Hebrews. In Arabic sources, *Isma'il* founded the various North Arabian tribes including that of the Prophet Muhammad, which are collectively called the *'Arab al-Musta'arabah* or the Arabized Arabs. *Qahtan* (the Biblical Joktan) was the founder of the *'Arab al-'Arabah* or Arabian Arabs who are the South Arabian tribes. The rivalry between northern (*Qaysi/'Adnani*) and southern (*Yamani*) tribes played a major role in Arab history.

Arabs originated in the Arabian Peninsula, and the first recorded use of the term "Arab" is found in an Assyrian inscription dated 853 BCE; Shalmaneser III notes that among those he defeated was Jindibu, king of the Arabs, at the Battle of Qarqar. Settled populations in South Arabia formed states early and were in contact with Egypt, while in the Arab (Persian) Gulf, **South Arabian** peoples traded with India, Iran, and Mesopotamia. Copper from Oman and frankincense and myrrh from Dhufar were the major items traded. South Arabians established the Kingdom of Axum in Ethiopia around 400 BCE. There were a number of South Arabian states, but among the best known were Sabaean and Himyarite that ruled Yemen and the Hadramawt from the fourth century BCE to the rise of Islam. North Arabian kingdoms such the Nabateans emerged in the fourth century BCE, controlling trade between Yemen and the Mediterranean. The oasis city of Tadmur (Palmyra) controlled the trade from Iraq and assisted the Romans in their wars against Persia. The Palmyrene queen Zenobia (ruled 267–274), briefly challenged Roman rule over the eastern parts of the Empire including Egypt. The Roman emperor Marcus Julius Philipus (ruled 244–249) was born in what is today southern Syria and was known as Philip the Arab.

In the fifth century CE, several Arab buffer states arose on the borders between the Roman and Persian empires. The Bani Ghassan served the Romans/Byzantines and the Lakhamids served the Persians. The Kingdom of Kinda in what is today Saudi Arabia remained outside of imperial control and briefly united much of Arabia, but it was eventually destroyed by the Lakhamids. The last prince of Kinda, the poet Imru' al-Qays, sought the help of Emperor Justinian I (ruled 527–565) to reclaim his throne.

Pre-Islamic history is usually called the *Jahiliyah* Period in Arabic, meaning the Age of Ignorance, indicating ignorance of Islam. It is also called *Ayyam al-'Arab* or Time of the Bedouin because Bedouin tribes and their conflicts dominated the events. The Prophet Muhammad was born around the year 571 in Makkah to the ruling Quraysh tribe. He was orphaned early in his life and was raised first by his grandfather 'Abd al-Mutalib and then by his paternal uncle Abu Talib. Muhammad was uncomfortable with the religion of his fathers and took to deep meditation. In 610, he had the first revelation of the Qur'an during the month of *Ramadan* and declared that he was chosen to be the Prophet of God.

In 622, Muhammad was invited to come to the oasis of Yathrib (Madinah) and help settle the dispute between its main tribes. In Yathrib, Muhammad effectively became both the head of the new religious community and of a new state that challenged Makkah's position in Arabia. Muhammad was able to defeat coalitions formed by the Quraysh and entered Makkah in triumph in 630. The Prophet died in 632, and Abu Bakr, a longtime friend and one of the first converts to Islam, was elected to be the Prophet's Successor or *Khalifah*.

After a short period of consolidation, the Arabs set out to challenge the power of the Byzantines and the Persians, and by 636, Syria and, in 642, Egypt were taken from the Byzantines; by 652, most of Persia was in Arab hands. The Arabs continued to expand after the establishment of the Arab Muslim first imperial dynasty the Umayyads (660–661 to 750).

The Umayyads moved the capital from Madinah to Damascus in Syria. The Umayyad period brought the Arabs into contact with Hellenistic and Persian cultures, helping to forge a larger Islamic identity. Under the Umayyads, the Arabs successfully expanded into North Africa and by 711 had conquered the Visigoth Kingdom of Spain. Initially, the new empire relied on the people and institutions of the old empires they conquered, but during the reign of 'Abd al-Malik (ruled 685–705) the government was Arabized; Arabic replaced Greek and Persian in official government records.

The Umayyads were unable to deal effectively with the continual rivalries between *Qays* and *Yaman* and the growing dissatisfaction among recent converts to Islam who did not have equal rights with Arabs. The descendants of 'Ali ibn Abi Talib rose in a rebellion that weakened Umayyad rule. Eventually, the Umayyads fell to their distant relatives, the 'Abbasids, in 750. The Umayyads continued in a separate state in Spain, which lasted from 755 to 1031. The Umayyads of Spain produced one of the most remarkable societies of their time, with Muslims, Christians, and Jews living together in tolerance. The cultural dialogue of Umayyad Spain or the *convenvincia* remains unique and one of Islam's greatest periods.

The 'Abbasids moved the capital of the empire to Baghdad in Iraq and styled their government on the Persian model. The position of *Wazir* or chief minister was adopted by al-Mansur (ruled 754–775) and was first held by the Persian Barmakid family. During the 'Abbasid period, the position of *Khalifah* became more of a figurehead as powerful military commanders called *Sultans* took control of the government. The empire broke into numerous small states ruled by local dynasties, though most continued to give official recognition of the 'Abbasids as their overlords. The last 'Abbasid *Khalifah* al Mu'atasim (ruled 1242–1258) was killed by the Mongol Hülagü Khan at the fall of Baghdad in 1258. A branch of the 'Abbasid family was saved by the Mamluks of Egypt where they would be figureheads until 1517, when the Ottomans conquered Egypt and forced the last of the 'Abbasids to sign over the title of *Khalifah* to the Ottoman *Sultan*.

Arabs have a long history of cultural contributions in literature, architecture, fine arts, and music. Arabic became the language not only of literature and religion, but also of medicine, optics, biology, history, geography, astronomy, and linguistics for the vast Muslim society. Many non-Arabs contributed to the corpus of Arabic literature. Even today, most religious scholarship on Islam is written and studied in Arabic, no matter the origin of the person.

Poetry is an Arab art, and few people enjoy both making and listening to verse as much as Arabs. During the pre-Islamic period, poetry had already emerged as the primary Arab art form in the *Suspended Odes* or *al-Mu'allaqat*. The Classical period of Arab-Islamic literature produced a long list of poets who developed such forms as satire, elegy, panegyric, and the ode. Princes such as Firas al-Hamadani of Aleppo became famous, and collections or *Diwan*s of poetry were edited and published in large numbers. Another format at which the Arabs excelled was rhymed prose or *belle lettre*. 'Ali ibn Hazm's (d. 1064) works on courtly love greatly influenced that of medieval Europe.

The Qur'an and its commentaries (*Tafsir*) were important not only in understanding and developing law, but also for a better understanding of the language. Grammars were written to help instruct non-Arabs in proper style and pronunciation, and the language of the Qur'an remains a standard few have been able to match. The Syrian poet al-Mutannabi (d. 965) earned his name (meaning "prophet-like") for being able to compose poetry said to equal the high standards of the Qur'an. Arabs also developed literature

Najib Mahfuz

Najib Mahfuz (1911–2006) was the first Arab author to win a Nobel Prize for Literature in 1988 to the delight of the whole Arab world. Mahfuz was born to a poor family in Gamaliyah in old Cairo. His father was a low-level civil servant; nonetheless, he made sure all of his children had a solid religious education in a traditional Islamic school. The family moved from Gamaliyah to 'Abbasiyah, at that time one of the newer parts of the city. One of the major incidents that had a profound effect on the young Najib Mahfuz was the 1919 Egyptian uprising against the British. Though only seven years old at the time, he long remembered seeing events from the window of his family's house.

Mahfuz graduated from King Fouad I University (now Cairo University) with a degree in philosophy in 1934. He worked as a journalist and began his career as a writer. His first novels were set in ancient Egypt, and though their sales were not bad, it was not until 1947 and the publication of *Midaq Alley* (*Zuqaq Midaq*) that he came into his full stride. He followed *Midaq Alley* with *The Mirage* (*al-Sirab*) in 1948 and then another of his classics, *The Beginning and the End* (*al-Bidayah wa al-Nihayah*), in 1950.

Between 1956 and 1957, he wrote the Cairo Trilogy that trace the family of al-Sayyid 'Abd al-Gawad from World War I through the Free Officers Revolution in 1952. His next novel, *Children of Gabalawi* (*Awlad Harratna*) was banned for being blasphemous since the novel's characters were Cain, Abel, Moses, Jesus, and Muhammad, and the patriarch Gabalawi (God). Only Lebanon allowed the book to be printed, and Egypt finally allowed it to be published in 2006.

Mahfuz wrote 50 novels, numerous short stories, and screenplays for a number of films, including those based on his own novels. He was an outspoken critic of censorship and, in 1989, spoke in favor of Salman Rushdie when Ayatollah Khomeini condemned *Satanic Verses*. Mahfuz suffered death threats from religious fundamentalists in his own country and survived an attack by a knife in 1994. He died in 2006 as a result of a fall.

on the *Hadith* (sayings of the Prophet Muhammad) as well as on mystical Islam (*Sufism*). The works of al-Ghazali (d. 1111) were an attempt to reconcile mysticism with orthodox belief and the folly of philosophy. In the Arab West, ibn Tufayl (d. 1185) responded to al-Ghazali to defend human reason with his book *Hayy ibn Yaqzan* (*Alive Son of Awake*) which later served as a model for Daniel Defoe's *Robinson Crusoe*.

Arabs adopted and adapted the writings of the Greek philosophers such as Aristotle and Plato through translations into Arabic. Al-Kindi (d. 873) and al-Farabi (d. 951) gave the works of Plato an Islamic bent and developed his *Republic* into the Islamic ideal state *al-Madinah al-Mufadilah*. In Muslim Spain, ibn Rushd (d. 1119) wrote on philosophy and reason, and his works greatly influenced Thomas Aquinas and the rise of European thought.

Arabs produced a large corpus of histories, geographies, and travel narratives. The North African Ibn Khaldun (d. 1406) produced the first social theory of history in the *Muqaddimah* (*Prologue*) to his monumental history of the **Berber** dynasties. Ibn Battutah (d. 1368–1369) wrote an extensive and detailed description of his numerous travels. His accounts of the Kingdom of Mali still serve as valuable information on it and its culture.

Arabic literature suffered a decline with the rise of **Turkish** and Persian dynasties and the subsequent elevation of both Turkish and Persian to the level of court languages. The Arabic literary revival began in the 19th century, with Egypt and the Levant being the main centers. Arabs not only revived ancient forms such as poetry, but

quickly adopted new literary forms from the West such as the novel, short story, plays, and free-verse poetry. Cairo became the center for literary publications because its upper class had the finances and the desire to patronize journals, newspapers, and book publishing houses. Arabs from Lebanon, Syria, and Palestine moved to Cairo to pursue their careers.

Egyptians took the lead and major authors such as Taha Hussein (d. 1973), Tawfiq al-Hakim (d. 1987), and Nagib Mahfuz (d. 2006) became well read both in and out of the Arab world, and Nagib Mahfuz won the Nobel Prize for Literature in 1988. The Syrian poet Adonis (b. 1930) has taken modern Arabic poetry to unknown limits, breaking standard conventions, and has been nominated for the Nobel Prize for Literature four times since 2005.

Arabic music is one of the major musics of the world, and there are a wide variety of forms today. Arabic music developed in the early Islamic period to include not only indigenous Arab styles of the Arabian Peninsula, but also instruments and scales adopted from the Byzantines and Persians and based on a system of modes/scales or *maqamat*. The composer/teacher Ziryab arrived in Muslim Spain in 822 after falling out with the 'Abbasids. He introduced a number of innovations to Arabic music, including adding a string to the *'ud* and developing the *muwashshahat* form of *zajal*. *Muwashshahat* became a major source for the medieval European troubadour music, and the Andalusian ibn Quzman (d. 1160) is considered the first troubadour.

Arabic music was also revived in the 19th and early 20th centuries. In the

Postmodern architecture marks most of the contemporary Arab world. Buildings, such as these in downtown al-Shariqah (al-Sharjah) are the new urban feature of Arab cities. (John A. Shoup)

1920s, the Egyptian Umm Kulthum (d. 1975) established a reputation unchallenged in her ability to produce *tarab* (a state of ecstasy) in her listeners. The Egyptian composer/singer Muhammad 'Abd al-Wahhab (d. 1991) was the opposite of Umm Kulthum, including a wide range of Western innovations in his music. The Syrian Farid al-Atrash (d. 1974) was an accomplished *'ud* composer and player and wrote a large number of songs both light and popular as well those with strong classical influences. The Syrian singer Sabah al-Fakhri (b. 1933) carries on the classical style of music, noted for his ability to induce *tarab* among his listeners. Today, Arab music includes a range of popular styles: *Khaliji* from the Gulf and

Saudi Arabia, *Rai* from Algeria, and *Jil* from Egypt as well as Arabic rap.

Calligraphy is a well-developed Arab art, and it is not only used in books, but in decoration on buildings. Six "classic hands" or calligraphic styles were developed, and that of ibn Bawwab (d. 1031) became the standard for others to imitate. The Arab West developed its own styles called *maghribi* and *andalusi* from which the Arabic script in West Africa, *sudani* or *'ajami*, developed. In addition to the beauty of the calligraphy, many books include illumination and miniatures were a specialty of books produced in the Islamic world. Miniature illustrations arose in the 13th century in Iraq at a time when large numbers of manuscripts were produced. Miniatures were quickly adopted by the Persians and Turks, who developed the art form in the 15th and 16th centuries.

Arab architecture has developed over a wide geographical area responding to climate and available building materials. There is no single Arab type, and Arab architecture is influenced by the classic traditions of Rome (stone) and Persia (brick). The typical Arab house is built around a central courtyard where much of the housework is done. The courtyard can be simple as in a rural farmhouse, or elaborate with side *iwans* (alcoves) such as in houses in Damascus. Courtyards in urban homes were paved in stone such as marble and included a fountain and oftentimes fruit trees such as lemon. In the Arab Gulf, houses had a wind tower that helped catch the slightest breeze and funnel it into the house. In Yemen and the Hadramawt, houses were built in mud brick as much as five stories tall. Most Arab palaces consist of a series of pavilions in large gardens of flowering trees and bushes and flowing water from fountains in an attempt to imitate heaven; the Arabic word for garden, *junaynah*, is a diminutive of the word for paradise, *jannah*.

Mosques, *madrasahs* (Islamic schools), hospitals, fountains, and other such public buildings developed over the centuries, incorporating local influences as well as those of Rome, Iran, and Central Asia. Public buildings served as a means for the upper class to demonstrate both their wealth and their generosity. Regional styles developed such as "Andalusian" Muslim Spain and North Africa and "Mamluk" in Egypt and Syria. The Ottoman Turks had a profound influence on public buildings in the Arab world between the 16th century and the early 20th century, when they ruled most of the Middle East and North Africa.

Modern history of the Arabs begins in the 19th century with the rise of Arab nationalism and European colonization. Muhammad 'Ali's (d. 1848) period of rule in Egypt marks the beginning of the modern era. He arrived in Egypt in 1801 with the Ottoman army sent to expel the French. Muhammad 'Ali destroyed the last of the Mamluks and set about reforming the army along European lines. He came to the aid of the Ottomans and defeated the Wahhabis in the Arabian Peninsula 1814 and added the Sudan to Egypt in 1820. He expanded into Syria in 1831 and was quickly able to advance into Anatolia, where he defeated the Ottoman army. The European powers forced him to return to Egypt, giving up control of

Syria to the Ottomans. However, the brief period of Egyptian occupation forced the Ottomans to begin their own reforms. Between 1839 and 1876, the *Tanzimat* (Reform Movement) tried to modernize the Ottoman government and army. A number of new acts were promulgated, including equality between all citizens of the empire and a national assembly. However, the movement was killed when the new *Sultan* 'Abd al-Hamid II (ruled 1876–1909) came to the throne in 1876. Suspicious and reactionary, he dissolved the parliament and ruled by decree until he was overthrown by the Young Turks in 1908.

The Arab provinces of the empire had been stripped from the *Sultan* one by one by the European powers; Algeria in 1830, Tunisia in 1881, Egypt in 1881, and Libya in 1911. The Arab Gulf rulers had been placed under British protection by a series of treaties in the 19th century, and Britain occupied Aden in 1839 in order to help protect British shipping to India. Europeans were interested in the Levant, the French in Lebanon and the British in Palestine, though they were not able to detach them from the empire.

Arab nationalism grew in the 19th century, and many young Arab men were educated in foreign mission schools or went to Europe to complete their education. While in Europe, they formed a number of secret societies and began publishing nationalist materials to distribute back home. When the Young Turks came to power, their Turkish nationalism clashed with Arab nationalism and, when World War I started, many Arab citizens reluctantly fought for the Turks. In 1916, the *Sharif*

The Voice of Egypt: Umm Kulthum

Umm Kulthum has been called the Voice of Egypt, but she was also the Voice of the Arab World. She was born sometime between 1899 and 1902 in the village of Tammay al-Zahayra and her father, *al-Shaykh* Ibrahim al-Sayyid al-Baltaji, was the *Imam* of the local mosque. Her father made very little money as the village *Imam* and substituted his salary by singing at wedding parties along with his son and nephew. When Umm Kulthum was between five and eight years old, she was allowed to also come along and sing, but dressed as a boy wearing the long robes and head dress of a Bedouin.

By 1934, her voice was so well known that she was asked to be opening singer for the new Radio Cairo. Umm Kulthum had the distinction of being asked to perform for the Egyptian king, King Faruq, and for Gamal 'Abd al-Nasir. Umm Kulthum joined forces with the major poet Ahmad Shawqi and composer Riyadh al-Sumbati in 1946 and took the chance to sing lyrics fully in classical Arabic. The result was an immediate success. Kulthum had a powerful contralto voice. Her voice was so strong that she had to stand about three feet (one meter) from a microphone. She had a tremendous range, being able to sing all five Arabic scales, a feat she shares with only four other women in Arab history (Asmahan, Fairuz, Sabah, and Therka). She performed nearly until her death in 1973, and her vocal range was barely affected. Her funeral was a mass outpouring of grief and was perhaps the largest funeral ever, with an estimated 1 million people lining the streets of Cairo. In 2008, the Institute du Monde Arabe in Paris put on an exhibition about her life and music.

of Makkah declared the Arab Revolt and joined the Allies.

Following the war, the Arabs thought they would be able to have their independence, with Damascus as the capital. However, neither France nor Great Britain would allow an independent Arab state, and instead Arab provinces became mandates with the British in charge of Palestine, Transjordan, and Iraq, and France in charge of Lebanon and Syria. The British declared Egypt an "independent" *Sultanate* at the start of hostilities in 1914. In 1919, Egyptians rose in revolt when their delegation to the Peace Conference was refused a seat, and by 1921, the British had negotiated Egyptian independence, but Great Britain still controlled most of the country's affairs. Great Britain granted Iraq independence in 1932, and Jordan was granted its independence in 1946. The Syrians rose in rebellion in 1925 and, though crushed by 1927, the rebellion forced France to allow elections for a national parliament, which the opposition won. Syria became independent in 1944, though French troops stayed until 1946 and Lebanon became independent in 1943. Only Saudi Arabia and

Northern Yemen were independent and not occupied by foreigners.

Morocco was the last of the North African states to fall under European control and, in 1912, split between France and Spain while the city of Tangiers was internationalized. Morocco was a protectorate with a French resident general who was to work with the Moroccan *Sultan*, though in reality the resident general administered the country. In 1927, Muhammad V became the *Sultan*, and he formed an alliance with those Moroccans who wanted to see the end of foreign rule. He was exiled in 1953 and the French tried to replace him, but were forced to return him in 1955 and, in 1956, Morocco became independent as did Tunisia. Algerians fought a long war of independence with France, which they won in 1962. Mauritania gained its independence in 1960, and the last of the Arab world to receive full independence were the Gulf States in 1970.

Much of recent Arab history has been driven by the Palestinian conflict with Israel. With roots in promises made during World War I, the conflict has not been resolved. Of the nearly 1 million Palestinians in 1948, two-thirds were made refugee in the first war. The Arabs have fought three major wars with Israel, in 1948, 1967, and 1973, as well as a number other conflicts such as 1956, when Israel joined the British and French attack on Egypt as a result of Egyptian president Gamal 'Abd al-Nasr's nationalization of the Suez Canal and the 1978, 1982, and 2006 Israeli invasions of Lebanon and the 2008–2009 Israeli invasion of Gaza. Some Arab states had diplomatic ties with Israel following the 1990–1991 Gulf War; but relations remain stagnant, and as long as the conflict in Palestine continues, diplomatic representation is difficult. Mauritania cut its diplomatic ties with Israel following the 2008–2009 invasion of Gaza.

Arab states include a range of different political systems, from monarchies to republics. Meaningful political participation is limited, and most Arab counties are accused of human rights abuses. Censorship of the media still occurs, although general wide access to satellite television makes censorship less important. Since the 1980s, governments have been challenged by the rise of militant Islamism. Egyptian president Anwar Sadat was assassinated during a military parade in 1981 by Islamic militants, and Algeria fought a civil war from 1991 to 2002 with several different Islamist groups. All of the Arab states have had to deal with bombings or other acts of violence perpetrated by organizations such as Al Qaeda.

John A. Shoup

Further Reading

Amiry, Suad, and Vera Tamari. *The Palestinian Village Home*. London: British Museum, 1989.

Andrews, Peter, with excerpts from Odette du Puigaudeau. "The Hassaniya-Speaking Nomads: Tekna, Trearza, and Brakna." In *African Nomadic Architecture: Space, Gender, and Power*, edited by Labelle Prussin. Washington, DC: Smithsonian Institution Press and National Museum of African Art, 1995.

Coulson, Noel C. *A History of Islamic Law*. Edinburgh: Edinburgh at the University Press, 1999.

Danielson, Virginia. *The Voice of Egypt: Umm Kulthum, Aribic Song, and Egyptian Society in the Twentieth Century*. Chicago: University of Chicago Press, 1997.

Du Puigaudeau, Odette. *Arts et coutoumes des Maures*. Paris: Ibis Press, 2002.

Hitti, Philip. *History of the Arabs*. Revised 10th ed. New York: Palgrave MacMillan, 2002.

Hourani, Albert. *A History of the Arab Peoples*. New York: Warner Books, 1991.

Hunwick, John O. *West Africa, Islam, and the Arab World*. Princeton, NJ: Markus Wiener Publishers, 2006.

Hunwick, John O., and Alida Jay Boye. *The Hiddent Treasures of Timbuktu: Rediscovering Africa's Literary Culture*. London: Thames and Hudson, 2008.

Jabar, Faleh A. *The Shi'ite Movement in Iraq*. London: Saqi Press, 2003.

Keenan, Bridgid. *Damascus: Hidden Treasures of the Old City*. London: Thames and Hudson, 2000.

Khalili, Nasser. *Islamic Art and Culture: Timeline and History*. Cairo: American University of Cairo Press, 2008.

Lane, Edward William. *An Account of the Manners and Customs of the Modern Egyptians*. London: East-West Publications, 1989 (reprint of the 1836 ed.).

Lapidus, Ira. *A History of Islamic Societies*. Cambridge: Cambridge University Press, 1997.

Le Quellec, Jean-Loïc. *Maisons du Sahara: Habiter le désert*. Paris: Editions Hazan, 2006.

Lunde, Paul. *Islam: Faith, Culture, and History*. New York: DK Publishing Inc, 2002.

Mahfuz, Naguib. *The Cairo Trilogy: Palace Walk, Palace of Desire, and Sugar Street*. New York: Everyman's Library, 2001.

Mahfuz, Naguib. *Midaq Alley*. New York: Anchor, 1991.

Provence, Michael. *The Great Syrian Revolt and the Rise of Arab Nationalism*. Austin: University of Texas Press, 2005.

Racy, A. J. *Making Music in the Arab World: The Culture and Artistry of* Tarab. Cambridge: Cambridge University Press, 2003.

Shoup, John A. *Culture and Customs of Jordan*. Westport, CT: Greenwood Press, 2006.

Shoup, John A. *Culture and Customs of Syria*. Westport, CT: Greenwood Press, 2008.

Smith, Dan. *The State of the Middle East: An Atlas of Conflict and Resolution*. Berkeley: University of California Press, 2006.

Vérité, Monique. *Odette du Puigaudeau et Marion Sénones: Mémoire du Pays Maure, 1934–1960*. Paris: Ibis Press, 2000.

Weir, Shelagh. *The Bedouin*. London: British Museum, 1990.

Weir, Shelagh, and Serene Shahid. *Palestinian Embroidery*. London: British Museum, 1988.

Young, William C. *The Rashaayda Bedouin: Arab Pastoralists of Eastern Sudan*. Belmont, CA: Wadsworth/Thomson Learning, 2002.

Armenians

The Armenians are a globally distributed ethnic group originating in Eastern Anatolia and the Trans-Caucasus region—where an independent state, Armenia, has emerged after the collapse of the Soviet Union. While they use Russian, Spanish, English, French, **Turkish**, and **Arabic**, their indigenous language is Armenian—a unique member of the Indo-European family of languages. About half of the world's Armenians use Armenian, and the rest rely on the languages of the broader societies in which they live. The worldwide population is estimated to be about 8–10 million people, with about 3 million dwelling in Armenia proper and the rest living in Russia (1.4 million), the United States (1.1 million), France (0.5 million), Georgia (0.5 million), Argentina (0.3 million), the self-declared

Republic of Nagorno-Karapakh (0.2 million), and the Middle East (0.5 million). Important Armenian communities currently exist in the Crimea, Greece, Cyprus, Poland, Bulgaria, Belgium, Ethiopia, Canada, Brazil, the Central Asian Republics, Australia, and Egypt. Historic centers of population included Mughal India, the early modern Netherlands, and Dutch Indonesia as well as the Ottoman Empire—which included most of the traditional Armenian lands. The Armenian community in Turkey today numbers about 70,000 individuals, largely concentrated in a few districts in the Asiatic side of Istanbul. Aside from Istanbul, the only remaining Armenian communities in Turkey are in Malatya, Diyarbakir, and Arapgir—where fewer than 5,000 Armenians live today.

The dispersion of the world's Armenians tends to reflect the country's difficult history as a crossroad on one of the main East-West invasion routes in Eurasia as well as a borderland region between the powers that dominate Anatolia and the Iranian plateau. The earliest references to Armenians include descriptions of the Armenian units in the Persian army invading Greece by Herodotus. The Behistun stele in Iran, set up during the reign of Darius, also refers to the Armenians as one of the peoples constituting the Persian Empire who had risen in revolt. While independent at many and long stages of their history, Armenians have often known imperial rule, with is benefits and costs.

Unlike most of their immediate neighbors, with the notable exception of the Georgians, Armenians tend to be at least confessional Christians. The dominant Armenian Church is the indigenous Gregorian Apostolic Church (often called the Armenian Orthodox Church), a Jacobite miaphysite denomination in communion with the national churches of Egypt and Ethiopia. There is also a Uniate Armenian Church within the Roman Catholic Communion as well as Protestant Armenians often organized as autonomous branches of the Congregational and other mainline Protestant denominations in the United States. There is also a small community of **Jewish** Armenians in Yerevan.

Historically, there have been some Muslim Armenians such as the medieval Shah-Armen princely dynasty as well as the recent Hashmen Armenian community in contemporary northeastern Turkey, Ajaria, Georgia proper, Abkhazia, and southern Russia. Armenian Muslims have been either largely assimilated into the Turkish mainstream or simply no longer regard themselves as Armenian, preferring a Hamshen identity instead. With the incorporation of Armenia into the Soviet Union in 1920, the state worked against religion, and as a result, there are some atheists among the Armenian post-Soviet nomenklatura. While present, atheism has generally failed to gain adherents, because it faced the cliff-face of Armenian Christian heritage; Armenia converted to Christianity under the rule of King Tiridates III in 304 CE, who was brought into the faith by his cousin, Gregory the Illuminator, in part because of his sense of guilt over his execution of Christian missionary nuns Saints Hripsime and Gayane.

Reflecting on the Christian faith informed Armenian art and literature to this day. Second only to the Bible for

Armenian widows and children, about 1915. The Armenian genocide of 1915–1916 resulted in the deaths of an estimated 600,000 to 1.5 million Armenians and the deportation of most of the remainder of Armenians from Anatolia. (Library of Congress)

many Armenians, the *Lamentations* of Saint Gregory of Nareg (951–1003) could be found in any Armenian home. Armenian music was systematized by Komitas (1865–1935) in Istanbul, who wrote sheet music for the *Divine Liturgy* as well as religious anthems. In the domain of poetry, Sayat Nova (1712–1795) wrote poems and performed music in Armenian, **Persian**, Turkish, Azeri, and Georgian, before hanging up his lyre to become a priest. Nova's life was chronicled by Sergei Parajanov (1924–1990) in his opus magnum film, *The Color of Pomegranates*. Other Armenians to make a significant cultural contributions include Mkhitar Gosh (1130–1213), whose legal texts informed the pre-

partition Polish legal code, and William Saroyan (1908–1981), whose novels in English replicated traditional Armenian storytelling in an American context.

Before 1915, Armenians practiced farming, animal husbandry, carpet weaving, iron working, coppersmithy, and meat preservation. These lifestyles have disappeared in nearly all Armenian communities outside Armenia, Georgia, and Nagorno-Karapakh. While there are some Armenian farmers in the Central Valley region of California, their operations can be described as corporate. Today most Armenians are urban dwellers working in factories, the professions, and retail trade as well as in services such as photography, bronzing, and shoe repair. Other current professions include restaurants and specialty stores selling automotive parts as well as vehicle repair and customization.

The relationship with the Ottomans was generally positive throughout the existence of the empire, but as the Porte went into decline, internal tensions increased. The arrival of nationalism in the Balkans and the rise of independent Christian nation-states led to the development of Armenian nationalism, which was politically articulated by the Armenagan (National Democratic), Ramgavar (Liberal Nationalist), Hunchak (Social-Democratic and Nationalist) and Tashnak (Socialist and Nationalist) parties. While the Armenian movements participated in and were included in the revolutionary Ottoman government of 1908, the First World War brought unprecedented stress to the Ottoman system, whose collapse saw attempts to ensure the population's loyalty through demographic engineering by massacres between 1915 and 1923. While contemporary Armenian and Turkish narratives differ on the meaning of these events, most historians as well as the International Center for Transitional Justice call these massacres genocide. The events of 1915 led to the establishment of the diaspora communities in the Middle East, Europe, Australia, and the Americas.

The smaller Russian portion of historic Armenia saw the rapid integration of Armenians into the Russian imperial system. The Russian portion of Armenia also served as the core of the Democratic Republic of Armenia (1918–1920) and the Armenian Soviet Socialist Republic (1936–1991). With the collapse of the Soviet Union, Armenia emerged into a world where a significant portion of its original territory and population was placed under Azeri rule by the Soviet Union. Azerbaijan refused to return the territory to Armenia, and a war resulted in its forceful eviction from the territory and the decision of Turkey to provide its ethnic Azeri kin with political support through the imposition of a blockade on a landlocked Armenia.

Turkey's decision directly led to the rebirth of Armenian diaspora political pressure to isolate it from the Western community through the use of genocide as a political weapon, causing heightened friction and threatening to pit Turkey and its friends in the Organization of the Islamic Conference against France, Russia, and 20 additional states that recognized the Armenian genocide of 1915. Diaspora political activity directly resulted in U.S. pressure on both Turkey and Armenia to sign a normalization accord in 2009, but whether the documents are implemented remains to be seen.

Jack Vahram Kalpakian

Further Reading

Abrahamian, Levon, Nancy Sweezy, and Sam Sweezy, *Armenian Folk Arts, Culture and Identity*. Bloomington: Indiana University Press, 2001.

Arkun, Aram. "The Hemshin: A Community of Armenians Who Became Muslims." *Armenian Reporter*, November 13, 2008. http://www .reporter.am/index.cfm?furl=/go/article/ 2008-11-13-the-hemshin-a-community-of -armenians-who-became-muslims&page wanted=all (accessed December 2, 2009).

Armeniadiaspora.com. *Population.* http://www.armeniadiaspora.com/population.html (accessed December 1, 2009). Used by the Armenian Ministry of Foreign Affairs for Diaspora Relations.

Cowe, Peter. "Medieval Armenia: Literary and Cultural Trends." In *The Armenian People from Ancient to Modern Times, Vol. I—The Dynastic Periods from Antiquity to the Fourteenth Century,* edited by Richard Hovannisian. New York: Palgrave Macmillan, 2004.

Hamalian, Leo. "Preface." In *William Saroyan: The Man and Writer Remembered,* edited by Leo Hamalian, 11–22. London: Associated University Presses, 1987.

Lang, David Marshall. *Armenia: Cradle of Civilization.* 3rd ed. Boston: Unwin Hyman, 1980.

Melkumyan, Lusine, ed. "Biography of Komitas." *Virtual Museum of Komitas.* http://www.komitas.am/eng/brief.htm (accessed March 29, 2010).

The Mother See of Holy Etchmiadzin. *The Armenian Church Past and Present.* Armenian Church Web site, 2003. http://66.208.37.78/index.jsp?sid=1&id=10&pid=2 (accessed April 2, 2010). See particularly the subpages "Official Adaption" and "Present Day."

National Conference on Soviet Jewry. *Armenia Country Page.* http://www.ncsj.org/Armenia.shtml (accessed April 1, 2010).

Oeler, Karla. "A Collective Interior Monologue: Sergei Parajanov and Eisenstein's Joyce-Inspired Vision of Cinema," *Modern Language Review* 101, no. 2 (April 2006): 472–87.

Payaslian, Simon. *The History of Armenia.* New York: Palgrave Macmillan, 2007.

Samuelian, Thomas J. "Introduction." In *Speaking to God from the Depth of One's Heart–Narek.* 2001. http://www.stgregoryofnarek.am/intro.php (accessed December 2, 2010).

Stone, Nira, and Michael Stone. *The Armenians, Art, Culture and Religion.* London: D. Giles Ltd., 2007.

Tolman, Herbert Cushing. *The Behistun Inscription of King Darius.* Nashville, TN: Vanderbilt University, 1908. http://mcadams.posc.mu.edu/txt/ah/Persia/Behistun_txt.html (accessed April 2, 2010).

Assyrians

The Assyrian people are closely related to other speakers of Semitic languages, including **Arabs** and **Jews**. Assyrians use several forms of Neo-Aramaic as well as Arabic, **Persian**, **Turkish, Armenian**, Swedish, French, English, and Russian. They are also known as Chaldeans, Syriacs, and Arameans. Depending on the criteria used in determining membership in their community, there may be as many as 3 million Assyrians worldwide. While the 20th- and early 21st-century conflicts have led to the migration of many Iraqi Christians, including Assyrians, there may be as many as 1 million Assyrians in Iraq. Syria and Lebanon may host an additional 0.4 million, the United States 0.1 million. Other significant populations can be found in Iran, Turkey, Jordan, Sweden, Russia, Armenia, the Netherlands, and Canada. There are two districts in the Nineveh province of Iraq with slight Assyrian majorities. According to the Ethnologue, about 400,000–500,000 can speak either the Chaldean or Assyrian versions of Neo-Aramaic. There are large and visible Assyrian communities in Turlock, California; Detroit, Michigan; and Chicago, Illinois. As a native Mesopotamian population, Assyrians are traditionally farmers and townspeople engaged in crafts.

The community differs concerning its name, with some preferring the term

Iraqi Chaldean Catholic worshippers attend Sunday mass at a Chaldean church in Amman, Jordan, on February 18, 2007. The Catholic Church in Iraq prefers the designation "Chaldean" over "Assyrian." (AP/Wide World Photos)

"Aramean" while others preferring the term "Assyrian," and there are closely related communities that use Aramaic in their liturgy but not in their daily lives, such as the Maronites of Lebanon and Syria. Some Maronites now reject Arab identity and prefer to be designated as either Phoenician or Aramean instead. While there is a clear basis for this claim in terms of liturgical language as well as self-identification, common use of the terms Assyrian, Chaldean, Syriac, and Aramean has not historically included the Lebanese and Syrian Maronite communities. To complicate matters, the appearance of an independent Arab state bearing the name "Syria" increased the level of confusion concerning who is an Assyrian. Some of the confusion has been

fed by the existence of several national churches among Assyrians. These include the Chaldean Catholic Church, the Syriac Orthodox Church (Miaphysite), the Assyrian Church of the East, the Ancient Church of the East, and the Syriac Catholic Church. Depending on how the community is defined, the list may also include the Antiochian Orthodox Church and the Maronite Catholic Church. The existence of separate churches for a community that spoke dialects of the same language prevented the rise of a unified Assyrian identity until the modern period. While there are also Muslims who use the Aramaic language, they generally do not maintain an Assyrian or Chaldean identity, and much the same applies to Jewish users of the same language. The Catholic

Church in Iraq generally resists the designation "Assyrian," preferring "Chaldean" instead.

As with other Middle Eastern Christians, Assyrians and Chaldeans celebrate a number of Christian holidays including Easter, Christmas, and All Saints Day. These holidays are celebrated on different days by each denomination, but the celebrations are usually similar to those among other Christians. All Saints Day is celebrated as an aid to fasting; young men dress in frightening costumes and visit Assyrian homes to motivate children into abstaining from animal products. Uniquely Assyrio-Chaldean celebrations include the Nineveh fast (a three-day period of fasting associated with Job) and the feast of the Bride of the Ascension, which commemorates Assyrian resistance to Tamerlane. The Assyrian New Year (*Kha B-Nisan*) begins on April 1, and the day is marked with parties and parades. While marriage, birth, and burial traditions vary by community and location, there are some commonalities. Marriage includes ritually cleaning the groom and placing cross pins on his coat or cloak during the wedding ceremony, the passing of a symbolic blanket to the bride a few days before the wedding, and the payment of a symbolic bride price. These rituals combine pre-Christian traditions with church procedures. Turkey banned the Assyrian New Year celebrations, and the country is not alone in proscribing Assyrian cultural practices—Syria has banned commemorations of the attempts by Iraq to destroy Assyrian culture in the 1930s.

Like other Ottoman Christians, the Assyrians faced massacres and attempts at liquidation in 1915. While the Assyrians and most historians describe these events as genocide, Turkey does not, insisting that the deaths were a result of World War I; the estimated numbers of dead range between 200,000 and 500,000. The Assyrians had been encouraged to rebel by the British, and their leader, Agha Petros, was able to help the British drive the Ottoman military out of northern Iraq; having served his purpose, the British exiled Petros to France after they joined Mosul to Faisal's Iraq. The Assyrians' relationship with Great Britain, despite its fruitlessness, made them suspect to their Arab neighbors, and Iraq responded by inducing Kurdish tribes to target and massacre Assyrians in over 60 villages in northern Iraq in 1933. The Simele massacre was the beginning of a series of attacks that arguably continues to this day, carried out by Kurdish and Arab nationalists, Islamists, and Baathists alike, despite the close association of the now-condemned Tariq Aziz with the previous Baathist government. The removal of Saddam Hussein revived calls for autonomy in Assyrian areas, and there are signs that the current Iraqi government seeks to reverse earlier policies. The Assyrian Democratic Movement is represented in the Iraqi parliament with one seat. While the instability and the targeting of Christians in Iraq by violent Islamists has led to the migration of thousands of Assyrians, the funeral of Emmanuel "Ammo Baba" Dawud, an Assyrian soccer coach and former star, was conducted in an atmosphere of national mourning and empathy towards his family.

Jack Vahram Kalpakian

Further Reading

"Assyrian Population." Zinda Magazine, Assyrian Iraqi Documents Project, April 2003. http://www.zindamagazine.com/iraqi_docu ments/assyrianpopulation.html (accessed December 2, 2009).

"Funeral Held for Iraqi Football Legend Dawud." British Broadcasting Corporation, May 29, 2009. http://news.bbc.co.uk/2/hi/ middle_east/8074225.stm (accessed December 2, 2009).

Giwargis, Ashur. "The Assyrian Liberation Movement and the French Intervention (1919–1922)." Assyrian International News Agency, 2011. http://www.aina.org/articles/ almatfi.htm (accessed April 1, 2010).

Hanoosh, Yasmeen. "The Politics of Minority: Chaldeans between Iraq and America." PhD thesis, University of Michigan, 2008. http://deepblue.lib.umich.edu/bitstream/ 2027.42/61663/1/yhanoosh_1.pdf (accessed December 3, 2009).

Iraq: Continuous and Silent Ethnic Cleansing— Displaced Persons in Iraqi Kurdistan and Iraqi Refugees in Iran. International Federation for Human Rights and Alliance International pour La Justice, January 2003, 17. http://www.fidh.org/IMG/pdf/iq350a.pdf (accessed April 1, 2010).

Lewis, M. Paul, ed. *Ethnologue: Languages of the World.* 16th ed. Dallas, TX: SIL International, 2009. http://www.ethnologue .com (accessed December 5, 2009).

Travis, Hannibal. "Native Christians Massacred: The Ottoman Genocide of the Assyrians in World War I." *Genocide Studies and Prevention* 1, no. 3 (December 2006): 327.

B

Bafur

Bafur, Imrawgen or Imraguen, and Nemadi represent what are most likely some of the most ancient populations in the Sahara, and their language may belong to the Niger-Congo group. What little of their language is left seems to be similar to Azer, a form of Soninke (**Mande**). Today they all speak Hassaniyah Arabic, the Arabic of the dominant **Arabs** of Mauritania, the Azwad region of Mali, and the Western Sahara, but the Imrawgen and Nemadi still maintain a few words related to fishing, hunting, and houses as well as other grammatical features of their original language when speaking Hassaniyah. Depending on the sources, some 1,000 Imrawgen still speak their form of Azer.

In total, all three groups number only in the few thousands; the Imrawgen number around 5,000 found along the Atlantic coast of the Western Sahara and Mauritania. Most live in and around the Banc d'Arguin National Park in Mauritania. The Nemadi number perhaps no more than 200 in the Tagant and Hawdh of Mauritania either as nomadic hunters or settled in towns such as Tishit and Walata, where they make up 20 percent of the population. The Bafur exist in small numbers in the Adrar, Trarza, and Senegal River valley and are dominated by the Hassani Awlad Banyug. The Mauritanian scholar Wuld Hamidun notes that the Hajjah people, a minority group in Senegal, is Bafur.

Very little is known of the origins of the three groups, though it can be speculated that they are descendants of the Neolithic populations of Mauritania. During the Neolithic period, the Sahara was a lush savanna and the population in Mauritania produced rock art illustrating hunting, fishing, and the beginnings of domestication of cattle, sheep, and goats. The Bafur are mentioned in early Islamic geographies and histories as occupying the Adrar region of central Mauritania south to the Senegal River. They were fierce adversaries of the pastoral nomadic **Berber** Sanhajah and at first resisted Islam. The Murabatin eventually defeated the Bafur, took their capital *Madiat al-Kilab* (City of Dogs, named for their use of trained dogs in combat), and forced them to retreat south of the Adrar.

All three groups have been subjugated first by Berber-speaking Sanhajah and later by Arabic-speaking Awlad Hassan. *Imrawgen* is a Berber term meaning fishermen, and *nemadi* is a Berber word meaning master of dogs. The Imrawgen were dominated by the Awlad Ahmad bin Daman and the Awlad Dulaym, to whom they paid a form of tribute into the 20th century. The Nemadi lived from hunting and once roamed the vast region from Wadan in the north to Kiffa in the south and N'imah in the east. They still raise and use dogs to hunt today, thus their Berber name meaning "master of dogs." Studies by Jean Gabus, such as "Contribution à l'étude des Némadis," remain the most complete studies to date.

The Imrawgen's traditional fishing grounds became a national park in 1976, and in 1989, it became a UNESCO World Heritage Site. The park has split the community between those who wish to maintain their traditional fishing methods and those who have "modernized." Competition from international fishing fleets has created a major problem for them. In conjunction with the World Wildlife Federation, the Mauritanian government integrated the Imrawgen into the park by officially making them guards. Other international organizations have come to assist, and in 2007, traditional Imrawgen-preserved fish was introduced to the market.

John A. Shoup

Further Reading

"Banc d'Arguin: The Imraguen Guards of Culture and Nature." http://www.afrol.com/features/10598 (accessed November 18, 2009).

Gabus, Jean. "Contribution à l'étude des Némadis." *Bulletin Societie Suisse d'Anthropologie-Neuchâtel*, 1951.

Lopez Bargados, Alberto. *Walata, La Ciutat de les Caravanes/Walatah Madinat al-Qawafil*. Barcelona: Mon-3, 2005.

Norris, H. T. "Muritaniya." In *Encyclopaedia of Islam*, 2nd ed., CD-ROM.

Ould Cheikh, Abdel Weddoud. *Eléments d'histoire de la Mauritanie*. Nouakchott: Centre Culturel Français, 1991.

Vérité, Monique. *Odette du Puigadeau et Marion Sénones: Mémoire du pays Maure 1934–1960*. Paris: Ibis Press, 2000.

Wuld Hamidun, al-Mukhtar. *Hayat Muritaniya: al-Jughrafiya*. Rabat: Manshurat Ma'had al-Dirasat al-Ifriqiyah, 1994.

Bakhtiyari

The Bakhtiyari is one of the major tribal sections of the **Lur** and live mainly in the Zagros Mountains in Southwest Iran. They number around 800,000 and speak the Lur-i Buzurg (Greater Lur) dialect of Luri, which has features of **Kurdish**. Luri (and Kurdish) are closely related to *Farisi* or **Persian**, an Indo-Iranian language of the Indo-European phylum.

Like others who comprise the Lur tribal confederacy, the Bakhtiyari is most likely of Kurdish origin coming from Syria between the 9th and 12th centuries. Other ethnic groups, such as **Arabs**, have been absorbed into the Bakhtiyari as well. They were under the Khushidi *Atabek*s and became 12er Shi'ites along with the other Lurs supporting the Safavid *Shah* Isma'il I (1501–1524).

The Bakhtiyari have played important roles in Iranian history. During the period following the collapse of the Safavids in 1722, Bakhtiyari tribal leaders were involved in the political intrigues and led Bakhtiyari troops both for the state and against it. The Qajar dynasty (1779–1925) had generally poor relations with the Bakhtiyari and, despite numerous military expeditions sent against them, the Qajars were never able to bring them fully under state control.

The Bakhtiyari are divided into two major groups, the Haft-Lang and the Chahar-Lang, which are further divided into subgroups; the Haft-Lang is composed of 55 sub-tribes and the Chahar-Lang is composed of 24 subtribes. Tribal leaders are called *khans*, who are judges called upon to settle disputes inside the group and are representatives for their people to the outside, including to governments. Wives of the *khans* are able to stand in for their husbands to settle disputes between tribespeople when the *khans* are absent, and the wives' decisions are binding.

The yearly migration from the lowlands at the foot of the Zagros Mountains to highland summer grazing areas is legendary. The trek was the subject of a Hollywood documentary in 1925 called *Grass: A Nation's Battle for Life*. The film crew was the first group of Westerns to make the journey across the Zagros with the nomads. In 1976, a similar documentary was made of the yearly migration called *People of the Wind*, which was nominated for the Oscar (1976) and for the Golden Globe (1977) for best documentary.

There is a good deal of Bakhtiyari oral literature; stories, proverbs, poems, and the like. Some of this has been collected and translated into English by a number of scholars. In addition, Bakhtiyari women are noted weavers. Bakhtiyari weaving is easily recognizable by their designs; the main field of the rug is divided by squares, diamonds, and other such shapes that are filled with floral patterns. Settled sections of the Bakhtiyari have adopted elements from urban Persian designs, but keep their distinctive Bakhtiyari use of floral-filled geometrics. Like most "tribal" carpets, Bakhtiyari are mainly red with designs in green, brown, yellow, and blue.

Like other pastoral nomads in Iran, attempts were made in the 1920s and 1930s to force the Bakhtiyari to settle. Most of these settlements failed, and they returned to pastoral nomadism once Reza Shah (1924–1941) was removed from power. Sections of the Bakhtiyari have remained resolutely pastoralist, and their great migration has been aided by the building of roads and bridges along their route.

Many Bakhtiyari have held important positions in the Iranian government. Perhaps the most famous was Soraya Esfandiary-Bakhtiayri, who was queen of Iran. In 1951, Muhammad Reza Shah married her as his second wife. Soraya Esfandiary-Bakhtiyari was the daughter of Khalil Esfandiary, a Bakhtiyari *khan* and Iran's ambassador to Western Germany, and the niece of Sardar Assad, a major figure in Iranian politics and constitutional movement. They divorced in 1958 due to her infertility.

John A. Shoup

Further Reading

Abecassis, Michael. "War Iranian Cinema: Between Reality and Fiction." http://www.st-andrews.ac.uk/anthropologyiran/abstracts.html (accessed January 4, 2010).

Bamborough, Phillip. *Antique Oriental Rugs and Carpets*. London: Blandford Press, 1979.

Melkonian, V. "Bakhtiyari." In *Encyclopaedia of Islam*, 2nd ed., CD-ROM.

Minorsky, V. "Lur." In *Encyclopaedia of Islam*, 2nd ed., CD-ROM.

"Soraya Esfandiari Bakhtiari." http://www.bakhtiarifamily.com/soraya.php (accessed January 4, 2010).

Baluch

The Baluch (Balush) are an Indo-European people whose language, Baluchi, belongs to the Indo-Iranian family and is closely related to **Kurdish**. The Baluch occupy a large region in southeastern Iran and across the border into Afghanistan and Pakistan; historic Baluchistan meaning "land or home of the Baluchi." There are a number of Baluchi dialects, but they can be placed into three main geographical divisions: Western, Southern, and Eastern. In addition, there are minorities of Baluchi in the Gulf States such as the United Arab Emirates, Bahrain, and Oman. In Oman, they make up around 25 percent of the population today. Oman's overseas empire included a number of coastal Baluchi towns and people, and it was only in 1958 that the last Omani possession, Gwadar, was incorporated into Pakistan. There are between 6 million and 7 million Baluchi speakers, but some 2 million "Baluchis" speak Brahui or Brahvi, the only Dravidian language spoken outside of the Indian Subcontinent. Iranian Baluchistan is one of the provinces of the Islamic Republic, and its population is estimated to be close to 2.3 million, the majority of which are ethnic Baluchis. Baluchis make up 2 percent of Iran's population.

It is thought that the Iranian element in the Baluchis arrived after the **Arab**-Islamic conquest between the seventh and eighth centuries. Arab-Islamic expansion came mainly from the direction of Kirman in Iran and was mainly administered from Kirman. Most of today's Baluchistan was conquered by 750. Baluch tribes moved into the region and raided Khurasan and Sistan, which brought punishment from first the Buwayhid ruler 'Adud al-Dawlah (978–982) and then later by the Ghaznavid ruler Mahmud (998–1030).

Raids by Baluchis caused the Brahui in the Kalat highlands to form a confederacy that included other Baluchi and Afghani tribes. Most of the information on the time between the Saljuq (1040–1194) and Safavid (1501–1722) periods is mainly in the form of oral histories, poems, and stories detailing the raids and expansion of various Baluch tribes into India. There are occasional mentions of them in official histories, such as the assistance some Baluch tribes gave to the Mughul rulers Babur (1526–1530) and to Humayun (1530–1540, 1555–1556) in his reconquest of Dehli in 1555.

Most Baluchis are Sunni Muslims. The Baluchis were not brought under Safavid rule when the Iranian state imposed 12er Shi'ism. Iran was not able to establish firm authority over its part of Baluchistan until 1872 in a treaty between Iran and the British in India. Shi'ism has subsequently spread, and some of the Iranian Baluchis have become Shi'ites. Today only 4 percent of Iranians are Sunni, mostly among the Baluchis, Kurds, and Turkmen.

Baluchis are organized into tribes and tribal confederacies with *khans* to measure out justice and deal with states. Over the course of the 17th century, the Kambarani *khans* were able to develop into something close to a state where the *khans* were able to assert a good deal of authority over their people and deal with the Persian and British states.

Along the Persian Gulf coast, Oman gained control of a number of ports and towns that provided troops for the *Sultan*'s army. Baluchi tribesmen had a reputation for both loyalty and as fierce fighters, which made them sought after as soldiers in the personal guards of the Omani rulers. Oman lost most of its overseas empire to the British in the course of the 19th century, including most of its holdings in Baluchistan. Nonetheless, individual Baluchis still serve in the Omani military. In addition, the Bani Hadiyah section of the Shihuh tribe in the Musandam Peninsula is of Baluchi origin, and they still speak a dialect of Baluchi in addition to Arabic.

Like many pastoral peoples, the Baluchi women are master weavers using a horizontal loom. Baluchi carpets are distinctive with the use of dark blue and red wool or natural beige camel-hair backgrounds and use designs from a number of sources including Central Asia, Afghanistan, and the Caucasus. Baluchi carpets are sold through regional centers such as Mashhad in Iran and Sharjah in the United Arab Emirates.

Contemporary history begins with the Brahui Kambarani *Khanate* that emerged as the local power in the 17th century. The height of their power was under Nasr Khan (d. 1795) who was able to even challenge the Moghul emperor, Ahmad Shah (1748–1754); however, he was defeated and agreed to supply the emperor with troops. In the 19th century, the British expanded their control over India and began to minimize Arab control over the Gulf. In 1872, the British and Iranians signed a treaty, revised in 1895–1896, which established the boundaries of Iran, British India, and Afghanistan, splitting Baluchistan between the three. In general, the Baluchi tribesmen ignored the borders until well into the 20th century.

Baluchi nationalism began in the 1920s with an attempt to separate Kalat under the *khan* of Kalat in what is today Pakistan when the British left, but it was ignored by Muhammad 'Ali Jinnah. Various Baluchi political organizations have grown in Iran, and perhaps the best known is the *Jund Allah*, meaning Soldiers of God, formed in 2003 under the leadership of 'Abd al-Malik Rigi. The group claims to be fighting for the rights of Iran's Sunni minority and has been responsible for a number of terror acts in Iran. Iran claims the group has connections to both the Taliban in Pakistan and Afghanistan and to officials in the U.S. CIA.

John A. Shoup

Further Reading

Daniel, Elton L., and Ali Akbar Mahdi. *Culture and Customs of Iran*. Westport, CT: Greenwood Press, 2006.

Frye, R. N., and J. Elfenbein. "Balucistan." In *Encyclopaedia of Islam*, 2nd ed., CD-ROM.

Heard-Bey, Frauke. *From Trucial States to Untied Arab Emirates*. Dubai: Motivate Publishing, 2004.

"Jundallah." http://www.sourcewatch.org/index.php?title=Jundullah (accessed January 5, 2010).

Khalili, Nasser. *Islamic Art and Culture: Timeline and History*. Cairo: Cairo University Press, 2008.

Lapidus, Ira. *A History of Islamic Societies*. Cambridge: Cambridge University Press, 1997.

Malik, Iftikhar H. *Culture and Customs of Pakistan*. Westport, CT: Greenwood Press, 2008.

Shoup, John A. "Ethnic Groups." In *Saudi Arabia and the Gulf States Today: An Encyclopedia of Life in the Arab States*, edited by Sebastian Maisel and John A. Shoup. Westport, CT: Greenwood Press, 2009.

Smith, Dan. *The State of the Middle East: An Atlas of Conflict and Resolution*. Berkeley: University of California Press, 2006.

Bamileke

The Bamileke are one of the largest groups in Cameroon, numbering between 3.5 million and 8 million people. The Bamileke speak a number of Bantu languages of the Niger-Congo phylum. The main language groups include the Ghomala', Fe'fe', Nda'nda', Yemba, Medumba, Mengaka, Ngiemboon, Ngomba, Ngombale, Kwa, and Ngwe. Though the languages are closely related, there are at least 17 dialects that follow a continuum of change that makes it possible for people to understand each other. The Bamileke live in several provinces in the highlands area or the grasslands region covering the western part of the country.

Bamileke trace their origins to ancient Egypt and claim to have left Egypt in the ninth century CE. After nearly two centuries of moving across the continent, they arrived in their present location in the 11th century. The history of their journey from the Nile to the plateau of western Cameroon includes tales of magic and even levitation of the entire population over wide rivers and deep chasms. They arrived in western Cameroon in the 11th century, and in the middle of the 14th century, they began to split into different local kingdoms called *fon* or *fong*, and the first to be established was Bafoussam by Prince Yendé. He was followed later by a royal sister who also founded an independent *fon*. The pattern was repeated by others, and Bafoussam was the original home of many of the subsequent kingdoms. A number of waves of new people arrived; according to their legends, five separate waves arrived and were absorbed into the Bamileke identity, as were those who already lived in the area. Today, little difference can be noted even in language, but those who live along the western and southern limits of Bamileke territory are most likely descendants of those people who already lived in the area and were incorporated into the Bamileke. They share some cultural traits with the forest Bantu who live nearby.

The Bamileke are patrilineal, and a man's children belong to the *fon* of their father. Property is inherited by one single heir, a son. Men can marry large numbers of women and, in the past, wealthy men could have literally hundreds of wives. Strict inheritance meant that wealth would not be spilt upon the death of a head of household and group cohesion gave other, less lucky sons, the ability to share in their father's wealth, though not inherit it outright. Families live in grouped housing surrounded by their fields. Each village is governed by a chief, also called a *fon*, who has nine advisers. The position of *fon* is also inherited and, in the past, the decision of who would be the heir was kept a secret until after the *fon*'s death.

As noted above, Bamileke men are able to marry a large number of wives. In general, the man pays a bride price to the bride's family, and all of her children belong to the *fon* of the man. Men work to clear agricultural fields, but the actual farming is left to the women. Like many agricultural societies, women and children are important sources of farm labor. Even today, Bamileke villages produce quantities of taro, peanuts, maize, and yams. Men are also engaged in trade and entrepreneurship. Starting in the 17th century,

Bamileke men have moved out of their home area as traders and entrepreneurs spreading throughout Cameroon. Following the introduction of colonial authority in the second half of the 19th century, Bamileke traders and craftsmen have expanded into other parts of Africa and, with colonial empires, to other parts of the world.

The Bamileke are skilled craftsmen, though it is said that since colonial times many of their skills have been lost. They have reputations as carvers of wood, horn, and ivory. Many of their sacred masks are made from cloth heavily beaded, using imported glass beads. Several types of masks associated with different societies are still made—and many sought on the international African art market. Among the most spectacular are the elephant masks, which represent the power of the *fon*. It is believed the *fon* has the ability to change his shape into that of a leopard, a buffalo, or an elephant. All three of these animals are the embodiment of what a *fon* is; powerful, fierce, and willing to defend his people. The elephant mask is made of dark (often in deep indigo) cloth and covered in beads and cowrie shells, symbols of wealth that outline and fill in the main features, including large ears. The mask falls down the front of the wearer in imitation of the trunk. The person wearing the mask also wears a long, decorated tunic, again of dark indigo cloth, and has a large feathered crown on the top of his head. Masks are worn during special ceremonies and at funerals of important men.

The *Kuosi* Society is the most important of the men's societies and in the past was made up of warriors. Today, it is composed of important and wealthy businessmen, and even the *fon* himself may decide to wear a mask and join the masquerade. *Kuosi* Society members wear elephant and leopard masks, both animals associated with the political power of the *fon*. The *Kwifo* Society is another specific mask group and each local *Kwifo* Society has their own mask. The masks are worn during trials or when the *fon* is receiving local petitioners. The *Kwifo* masks are worn in groups of up to 50 individuals and are accompanied by an orchestra of xylophones, drums, and rattles. Unlike the *Kuosi* masks, the *Kwifo* masks are a large, helmet type made of carved wood and decorated with brass and copper. The masks are of men and frequently include elaborate hairstyles that in the past were associated with high-ranking dignitaries.

Christianity was introduced to the Bamileke during the colonial period and subsequently, there have been some conversions. Islam has also penetrated from the north where Fulani and Hausa have come into contact with the Bamileke. Most, however, adhere to the religion of their ancestors that focuses on the honoring of ancestors. The skulls of ancestors are kept so as to provide a place for the spirits of the departed to live. If it is not possible to keep the skulls, a ceremony is held periodically to ask for the help of the ancestors even if there is no place for them to live. The Bamileke have a supreme god called *Si*, though he had little to do with the affairs of man. Ancestors are appealed to and can send messages through illness or dreams. Women are seen to be the embodiment of fertility of the land, and it is advanced by the Bamileke—this is the reason women are the planters and cultivators of the soil.

Germany extended its control over the Bamileke in 1884 and were the first to use the term Bamileke for the entire population as an easy means of identifying and classifying African peoples in the colony; the Bamileke used names of local *fon* to identify themselves. Following World War I, the German colony of Kamerun was divided between the British and the French, and most of the Bamileke fell under French control. Resistance to European domination grew in French Cameroon, and in 1955, the Union des Populations du Cameroon (UPC) was founded demanding independence. The French quickly outlawed the organization and attacked those supporting the UPC, and the Bamileke were among those to suffer. The attacks against the Bamileke were so severe that in some texts they are called the "Bamileke genocide." The exact count of dead is not fully known, but Bamileke see the killings as the first, but unreported, genocide in contemporary African history. They compare the French operations against them to be similar to the German attacks on the **Herero** in Namibia and later **Hutu** and **Tutsi** attacks against each other in Rwanda and Burundi. The war with the UPC continued until its leader, Ruben Um Nyobé, and his subsequent replacement, Félix-Roland Mounié, were both killed by the French in 1958 and 1960, respectively.

Cameroon became independent in 1961, with British Cameroon deciding to join French Cameroon rather than Nigeria. Following independence, the Bamileke have prospered, using their entrepreneurial skills to become among the best-known businesspeople in the country. Bamileke music,

called *Mangambe*, was fused with other Cameroonian sounds by Manu Dibango in the 1970s to create the dance style called *Makossa*. According to Manu Dibango, "what makes the *makossa* popular is that every Cameroonian can find himself in the *makossa*" (Ewens, 109). Since the original music began, it has been taken up and developed by groups such as Les Tetes Brulées.

John A. Shoup

Further Reading

Bacquart, Jean-Baptiste. *The Tribal Arts of Africa: Surveying Africa's Artistic Geography.* London: Thames and Hudson, 2000.

"Campagne militaire Francaise en Pays Bamileke." http://www.scribd.com/doc/125988/Bamileke-genocide (accessed February 14, 2011).

Crabtree, Caroline, and Pam Stallerbrass. *Beadwork: A World Guide.* London: Thames and Hudson, 2002.

Ewens, Graeme. *Africa O-Ye! A Celebration of African Music.* London: Guinness Publishing, 1991.

Toukam, Dieudonné. *Histoire et anthropologie du peuple bamileke.* Paris: l'Harmattan, 2010.

Van Custem, Anne. "Les coiffures d'Afrique subsharienne." In *Costumes et Textiles d'Afrique: Des Berbères aux Zulu.* Milan: 5 Continents Press, 2008.

Bassa

The Bassa are one of the main 28 ethnic groups in Liberia, living mainly in the Marshall and River Cess Territory. The Bassa speak a Western Kru language, which belongs to the Atlantic branch of the Niger-Congo phylum. The last noted census of them in 1991 states that there were more than 350,000, most of whom were rural farmers.

The Kru peoples moved into the rain forests of West Africa, most likely between 1000 BCE and 300 CE. Ironworking seemed to have spread into the region in the first millennium CE, and the economics shifted from yam production to sorghum and rice. Others moved into the rain forest, following the paths of the more ancient Kru speakers. Bassa language and identity emerged as they moved further to the west and eventually into the area where they are found today. A separate identity based on language shifts gave rise to Bassa identity.

The Bassa remain notably small farmers producing mainly cassava, yams, and plantains. While some have converted to Christianity or Islam, many have remained followers of their traditional religion like most of the other ethnic populations of the country. Only the Americo-Liberians are majority Christians. The Bassa have their own script to write their language called Vah. It was devised in 1910 by Syracuse University graduate Dr. Thomas Narvin Flo Lewis, who began teaching it once he returned to Liberia. Dr. Lewis had a printing press made in Germany and began printing materials in using the Vah alphabet in 1920.

Traditional Bassa political organization consisted of several chiefdoms of closely related lineages. Each chiefdom was further divided into numerous smaller clans. There were three main chiefdoms that coincide today with the political divisions of Grand Bassa, Marshall Territory, and River Cess Territory.

The founding of modern Liberia and the return of American slaves to Africa starting in 1822 had important consequences for the non-slave population of the country. At first the newly created town of Monrovia was the main base for the new community, and disease claimed many of the new inhabitants. By 1840, the population numbered only 17,000, but they were able to declare their independence by 1847. The result was that the Bassa began to build a number of strong villages along the Atlantic coast. The Bassa and other Kru speakers had to confront the growing Americo-Liberians as they began to expand areas of control.

Following the fall of President William Tubman in 1980, the Americo-Liberians lost their long-term control over Liberian politics. His successor Samuel Doe was from the Krahn, while his main rival, Charles Taylor, was backed mainly by the Gio and Mano, who are closely related to the Bassa. As a result of the long, bloody civil war, thousands of civilians were killed and hundreds of thousands were forced to flee their homes During the civil war, ethnic affiliation became important as a person's political orientation was seen as support for one side or another. In 1996, opposition leader Charles Taylor won the presidential elections, and over 150,000 Liberians had lost their lives. Taylor was forced to leave the capital in 2003, and subsequently multiparty elections have been held. The country seems to be on the road to recovery with foreign economic aid and investments.

John A. Shoup

Further Reading

"Bassa Alphabet." http://www.omniglot.com/writing/bassa.htm (accessed May 2, 2010).

Charles Taylor, leader of a rebel army during the fighting in Liberia, celebrates a military victory with his troops on July 21, 1990. The Liberian civil war, fueled by the corrupt exploitation of natural resources, ended when Taylor was elected president on July 24, 1997. (Pascal Guyot/AFP/Getty Images)

Ehret, Christopher. *The Civilizations of Africa: A History to 1800*. Charlottesville: University Press of Virginia, 2002.

Olukoju, Ayodeji Oladimeji. *Culture and Customs of Liberia*. Westport, CT: Greenwood Press, 2006.

Stokes, Jamie. "Bassa." In *Encyclopedia of the Peoples of Africa and the Middle East*. New York: Facts on File, 2009.

BaTwa

The Twa or BaTwa are pygmy peoples who live in the forests and savannah plains stretching from Uganda in the north down along the Lakes Region of Central Africa to Rwanda, Burundi, and the Democratic Republic of Congo (formerly Zaire). In addition, there are BaTwa populations scattered in Botswana, Angola, Zambia, and Namibia, where they have adopted to living conditions in deserts and swamps as well as their more familiar forests. In 2000, BaTwa numbered around 80,000 in total, and in some of these countries, they represent significant minorities.

Like other pygmies, the BaTwa have been dominated by their Bantu and Cushitic neighbors and speak their languages. Most BaTwa speak Kirundi and Kinyarwanda, the languages of the **Hutu** and **Tutsi**. In Rwanda and Burundi, the BaTwa make up 1 percent of the population in each country and, due to the heavy demands for farming and grazing lands, much of the natural

BaTwa pygmies perform a traditional dance in the Kabale District in southwestern Uganda. Much of the BaTwa way of life was destroyed by colonization; however, they have managed to preserve some aspects of their culture, such as traditional dances. (Torsius/Dreamstime.com)

forest habitat has been lost over the last several centuries. Like other pygmies, little of their own culture still exists.

The BaTwa are thought to be among the oldest living groups connected to the Tschitolian culture dating back some 25,000 years ago. They seem to have lived in a widespread area before the Bantu expansions starting in the second millennium BCE and lasting, with different waves and patterns, into the first centuries CE. The BaTwa, as hunters and gatherers, helped provide meat and honey to the Bantu in trade for iron goods and agricultural products. In some situations, the two were able to develop a symbiotic relationship, and the **Kuba** of Angola and southern Democratic Republic of Congo have brought BaTwa into their mask societies. That is, among the masks made and worn at special occasions are those that represent BaTwa with a noticeably large head, large, bulging forehead, and wide nose. Called a *bwoon* mask, they are worn at funerals of important men who belonged to the initiation societies.

In the colonial period, BaTwa society began to unravel in a number of places. Their hunting and gathering skills were less and less needed, and their natural habitat was quickly cut down. BaTwa began to gather on the outskirts of Bantu towns and villages and became a source of menial labor, in often very abusive terms. They were generally ignored in the postcolonial developments, and their communities still suffer today from the lack of schools, electricity, water, and medical treatment. Missions did not seek them out, and today it is estimated that only some 7 percent of BaTwa are Christians. The largest number of them adheres to syncretic Apostolic forms that combine Christian belief with indigenous systems of belief or still follow indigenous (mainly Bantu) forms of belief. BaTwa have been able to preserve some of their specific cultural practices such as dances and songs during social gatherings. Hunting was banned in the 1970s, and though BaTwa men still know how to make bows and arrows, they have been persecuted and jailed for continued hunting.

In the fighting between the Hutu and Tutsi in Rwanda in 1994, the BaTwa suffered greatly, and some 30 percent of the BaTwa in Rwanda died at the hands of the Hutu *Interahamwe*. According to the UN Office of Unrepresented Nations and Peoples, some 10,000 BaTwa were killed in the Rwandan Genocide and another 8,000 to 10,000 fled to nearby countries ("Batwa").

BaTwa communities suffer from problems of alcoholism and are treated with contempt by their countrymen. In 2007, it was reported that with no source of income, over 40 percent of the BaTwa in Rwanda earned a living through begging. The majority are illiterate, and many BaTwa children drop out of school due to harassment by other students in the classes, and the UN Office of Unrepresented Nations and Peoples states that 91 percent of BaTwa have no formal education ("Batwa"). BaTwa women are subject to harassment, including sexual harassment from Bantu men. A source of income and of cultural identity is pottery making; however, the swamp lands where the BaTwa have enjoyed joint land rights for centuries with Hutu farmers came into danger starting in 2005 when plans to develop rice plantations emerged. In both Rwanda and Burundi, the BaTwa are not legally recognized, have no representation in government, and have no land rights. In 2009, Burundi began the process of bringing the BaTwa into the government in an attempt to finally deal with the situation. In addition, a number of different organizations have taken up the cause of not only the BaTwa, but other pygmy peoples in Africa such as Act and Empower, based in Washington, D.C., and Uganda; Communauté des Autochtones Rwandais, (CAURWA) in Kigali, Rwanda; and Pygmy Survival Alliance, Seattle, Washington.

John A. Shoup

Further Reading

Adekunle, Julius O. *Culture and Customs of Rwanda.* Westport, CT: Greenwood Press, 2007.

Afolayan, Funso. "Bantu Expansion and Its Consequences." In *Africa: Volume 1 African History before 1885*, edited by Toyin Falola. Durham, NC: Carolina Academic Press, 2000.

"Batwa." http://www.unpo.org/article/7861 (accessed February 14, 2011).

Oyebade, Adebayo. *Culture and Customs of Angola.* Westport, CT: Greenwood Press, 2006.

"Rwanda: Indigenous Batwa Opening Channels of Cooperation with Conservation." http://www.wrm.org.uy/bulletin/70/Rwanda.html (accessed February 14, 2011).

Baule

The Baule (Bawle, Baoulé, Ton, Kotoko, Baba, and Po) belong to the Twi group of the **Akan** language, part of the Kwa branch of the Niger-Congo language phylum. They number between 1.5 million and 2 million people living mainly in central Côte d'Ivoire, making them one of the largest ethnic groups in the country. There are also a large number living in Ghana. They are closely related to the Anyi, also of Côte d'Ivoire and Ghana, and broke away from the Asante (**Akans**) in the mid-18th century. Most of the Baule today are Christians or adhere to their traditional religion, though around 2 percent of them have converted to Sunni Islam of both the Maliki and the Shafaʻi schools of jurisprudence.

The Baule originated when the Asante Kingdom in today's Ghana needed to expand farming lands in the 18th century. The Baule, like other Akan peoples, are matrilineal; thus it was not difficult for a woman to be a political leader. According to the Baule founding legend, a woman named Awura Poku (a variant of the name is Alba Poku) brought her people to the eastern side of the Bandama River and established settlements. These were the origins of both the Baule and the Anyi. Later, another woman named Akwa Boni took her followers across the river and into central Côte d'Ivoire, but in order to cross the river, she had to make a sacrifice to the river god. She sacrificed her son and in doing so gave name to her people, *bauli*, meaning "the son is dead" (other sources credit Awura Poku with both the establishment of settlements along the eastern

shore of the Bandama as well as for taking her people on into central Côte d'Ivoire and say that she sacrificed her son). The queen and her followers were able to take control of the important gold-producing areas along the west of the Bandama region.

The Baule remain not only matrilineal but matriarchal, with women occupying political office. The Baule maintained the office of a queen who ruled them until the end of the colonial era. Nonetheless, the queen had limited authority to act, and each village was more or less independent of others with their own local council of elders. Villages were divided into wards, and each ward further divided into family compounds. Decisions were made with the entire group being involved, and the Baule were remarkable for allowing not only women but also slaves into the discussions. The Baule were truly egalitarian. The Baule did not develop any societies or associations with hierarchy as many other West African peoples did. They did not organize age sets, or initiation ceremonies, nor did they circumcise boys. They did foster a great deal of tolerance and individualism, which, it is argued, helped them become among the most influential people in Côte d'Ivoire today.

Traditional religion was and still is centered around the ancestors. While the father's line is not completely forgotten, the mother's line is the more important, and important traits and spiritual connections are inherited through her. Each family has an ancestral stool that embodies the ancestral spirits or *amuen*. They do have a creator god (male) figure called *Nyamien*, who is unseen and inaccessible and no longer concerned with human affairs. This is left to the earth god *Asie*, who controls humans and animals alike. Offerings are made to the ancestral spirits such as the first yam of the harvest.

The Baule are a farming people, and they occupy both forest and savanna areas. They are still mainly farmers and produce crops of yams and maize and grow cash crops of cocoa, kola nut, and coffee. Traditionally, crops have been supplemented with hunting and fishing, though they do raise some small stock.

Baule art is another major source of income today. Unlike other West Africans with traditions that bind people to specific professions, among the Baule, to become a wood carver is a matter of personal choice. The Baule make a number of wooden statues and masks that are sought by art dealers. Among the most interesting of statues are the spirit spouses that each married person has. In addition to the living spouse, each man has a *blolo bian* and each woman has a *blolo bla*. It is believed that every person has a spirit spouse, and the statue helps focus contact through offerings of food. The statues are made under supervision of the village diviner and are kept in a person's room. The spirit spouses contact people through erotic dreams and can cause a person problems in their life if not properly attended to. Since the late 19th century, Baule carvers have made statues for the tourist market, and among the first were figures of Baule people dressed as colonials.

There are a number of different types of Baule masks, but generally they were only to be worn by men. The *Bon Amwin* mask, originally worn by men ready to go to war, is of a buffalo head with crescent horns.

Pablo Picasso was greatly impressed with them and incorporated them into one of his costume designs. Today, the masks are used to protect the village. Masks for the *Goli* festival to celebrate harvests developed after 1900. They are also used to welcome official visitors and during periods of mourning.

The Baule were the last people to submit to European rule. European interest began with the arrival of the Portuguese in 1482, and the French established a mission post at Assinie in 1637. French presence in Côte d'Ivoire remained precarious until 1843–1844, when French admiral Bouët-Williuamez signed treaties with the kingdoms of Grand Bassam and Assinie, which made them French protectorates. This allowed French explorers, traders, and missionaries the ability to access the interior. As a result of the Franco-Prussian War of 1871, France withdrew much of its military from West Africa, but in the 1880s, France again expanded into its colonies, and in 1889, Great Britain recognized French rights to Côte d'Ivoire. French direct military expansion began and met with resistance. The Baule continued to resist the French until they were finally defeated in 1915.

While only a few Ivoirians were able to get French citizenship during the colonial period, most remained subjects of France and, lacking political rights, were able to be drafted for the military or for work. As a result of African loyalty to France during World War II, Charles de Gaulle gave all Africans French citizenship; however, continued discriminatory practices pushed educated Ivoirians toward independence in 1960 under the leadership of a Baule chief's son, Félix Houphouet-Boigny. He first came to politics in 1944 when he formed an African trade union to protect the rights of African cocoa farmers like himself. When in 1945, France abolished the forced labor law, Houphouet-Boigny became a good friend of France and thought Côte d'Ivoire would benefit from long-term connections with France.

When the country became independent in 1960, its economy boomed, becoming the third-largest producer of coffee in the world. With French engineering help, it became Africa's largest producer of pineapple and palm oil. In 1983, he decided to move the capital from Abidjan to his hometown of Yamoussoukro and spent millions to improve the city, but the world economic crisis hit when world prices for sugar and timber fell, and so did the Ivoirian economy. Houphouet-Boigny died in 1993 and was followed as president by Henri Konan Bédié.

Many Baule are highly educated, and many hold positions in the government and in the professions. They are hard-working farmers, and many still produce the basic commodities that are Côte d'Ivoire's main sources of income.

John A. Shoup

Further Reading

Bacquart, Jean Baptiste; *The Tribal Arts of Africa: Surveying Africa's Artistic Geography.* London: Thames and Hudson, 2002.

"Baule." http://www.archaeolink.com/africa_indigenous_people_baule.htm (accessed December 20, 2010).

"The Baule People." http://www.nmafa.si.edu/exhibits/baule/map.htm (accessed December 20, 2010).

Boyer, Alain-Michel. *Visions of Africa: The Baule.* Milan: 5 Continents Press, 2007.

Ivory Coast president Félix Houphouët-Boigny waves to an audience in 1971. His political career began in the 1940s when he formed a trade union to protect African cocoa farmers. (AP/Wide World Photos)

"Tribal African Art: Baule (Baoule, Bawule)." http://www.zyama.com/baule/index.htm (accessed December 20, 2010).

Vogel, Susan Mullin. *Baule: African Art, Western Eyes.* New Haven, CT: Yale University Press, 1997.

Weiskel, Timothy C. *French Colonial Rule and the Baule Peoples: Resistance and Collaboration, 1889–1911.* New York: Oxford University Press, 1981.

Beja

The Beja are comprised of a number of tribal peoples inhabiting the region between the Nile on the west and the Red Sea on the east, from the borders of Eritrea along the south to the region near Luxor in Upper Egypt. Most of them speak Tu-Bedawiye, an Afro-Asian language belonging to the Hamitic/Kushitic family, as well as Arabic. The northernmost group, the 'Ababda, speak Arabic, while the southern Bani 'Amir include a **Tigre**-speaking section. They number over 2 million, with the largest numbers in Sudan.

Many of the Beja peoples now claim **Arab** genealogies connecting themselves with Arab tribes such as the Bani Hilal, the Awlad Kahil, the Juhaynah, and the Rabi'a, while the 'Ababdah claim to descend from Zubayr ibn al-'Awwam, a companion of the Prophet Muhammad.

The Beja have been living along the Red Sea coast for millennia, though attempts to connect them with the Blemmyes noted in texts of the late Roman period have been questioned. At least some of the Beja were missionized from **Coptic** Egypt or by the Christian kingdom of **Nubia**. In the 10th century, the Arab Rabi'a tribe came to dominate much of the Beja territory through intermarriage with the leadership of the Hadarib section of the Beja, taking advantage of the matrilineal system of succession of many Sudanese peoples. By the 14th century, most Beja had converted, and Islamization brought the change from matrilineal to patrilineal system of descent.

With the arrival of Arab tribes and through intermarriage, Arabic language and social customs mixed with Sudanic ones. Many of the Beja were pastoral nomads and, for example, the Bisharin subgroup, who live south of Aswan in Egypt, became famous for the high quality of their riding camels. Others settled and grew millet, sorghum, and other subsistence crops.

The Beja kept certain Sudanic practices such as matrilocality and taboos about milk, as well as living in tents made from mats rather than the woven goat-hair tents of the Arabs. In addition, the Beja still use large charms of made of stiffened straw shapes covered in bright cloth, and decorated with glass beads and ostrich feathers to protect newlyweds from harmful spirits. Until the early 20th century, many Beja men wore their hair in what was called the *dirwa*, what the British soldiers called "fuzzy-wuzzy" and from which African Americans in the 1960s took as the model for the "Afro" style.

The Sufi saint al-Shadhali is buried in 'Ababdah territory, and many celebrate the Islamic festival *'Id al-Adha* at his tomb, where they leave as offerings the sacrificed animals' ear to al-Shadhali. The 'Ababdah also have yearly visitation to the tomb of 'Abad, their ancestor near Edfu in Upper Egypt, where they also sacrifice animals.

The Beja were defeated and brought under Ottoman-Egyptian rule by Ibrahim Pasha, son of the Ottoman governor Muhammad 'Ali, in 1820. Egyptian misrule in the Sudan provoked a general rebellion in 1881 led by an Arab Sufi *shaykh* from Dongola named Muhammad Ahmad, who was proclaimed the *Mahdi*, meaning a special guide to reform society. The Beja, particularly the Hadanduwa, joined the ranks of the Mahdi's army. They were led by one of their leaders, 'Uthman ibn Abi Bakr Diqna, who was successful in containing the Egyptians and later the British to the Red Sea port at Suakin. In 1884, Diqna's men defeated an expedition at Trinkitat in an attempt to relieve Anglo-Egyptian forces besieged at Tokar. Later, strong British expeditions were able to inflict two defeats on Diqna's forces, but in the end, they were not able to help relieve the ill-fated General Gordon, the governor-general of the Sudan, who was besieged by the Mahdi's forces in Khartoum. The British defeats of Diqna's forces did little to their morale or the ferocity of their attacks, and Beja support for the Mahdi, and for his successor 'Abdallah al-Ta'ishi, continued after British forces took Tukar in 1891. Diqna remained loyal to the Mahdist cause, lost an arm in battle with the British in 1888, fought in the last Mahdist campaign in 1899, and was not captured and forced to surrender until 1900. In the period between 1899 and 1956, Sudan was ruled as a condominium between Egypt and Great Britain, and during that time, the Beja were "pacified," schools were built, and contacts with the outside increased due to the construction of a rail link to Port Sudan from Kasala and between Kasala and the Nile Valley.

Following Sudanese independence in 1956, relations with the central government have been strained on occasion. Beja formed the Beja Congress in 1957, and it has served as a focal point for Beja opposition to the government. It even became an armed resistance group several times. It joined the National Democratic Alliance in 1989 to oppose the government of 'Umar al-Bashir, and in 2006, the Beja, under the name of the Eastern Front, signed a separate peace agreement with the government in Khartoum.

John A. Shoup

Further Reading

Barthrop, Michael. *War on the Nile: Britain, Egypt, and the Sudan, 1882–1898.* London: Blandford Press, 1984.

Collins, Robert O. *A Modern History of Sudan.* Cambridge: Cambridge University Press, 2008.

Hillelson, S. " 'Ababda." In *Encyclopaedia of Islam*, 2nd ed., CD-ROM

Holt, P. M. "Bedja." In *Encyclopaedia of Islam.* 2nd ed., CD-ROM.

Insoll, Timothy. *The Archeology of Islam in Sub-Saharan Africa.* Cambridge: Cambridge University Press, 2003.

Lapidus, Ira. *A History of Islamic Societies.* Cambridge: Cambridge University Press, 1997.

Young. William C. *The Rashaayda Bedouin: Arab Pastoralists of Eastern Sudan.* Belmont, CA: Wadsworth/Thomson Learning, 2002.

Bemba

The Bemba, also called the Awemba, Wemba, and Babemba, are one of the largest ethnic groups in Zambia and are also found in Tanzania and in the Democratic Republic of Congo (formerly Zaire). Two other groups, the Hemba and the Katanga, are considered to be part of the Bemba. The Bemba number close to 1 million in total and make up between 20 percent and 37 percent of the total population of Zambia. The Bemba language Chibemba, also known as Cibemba, Ichibemba, Icibemba, or Chiwemba, belongs to the Bantu language group and is spoken by others since it has become the language used in the copper industry. Chibemba is one of the most widely spoken of indigenous languages in Zambia.

The Bemba originated in the Katanga region in today's Democratic Republic of Congo, and they claim to have close connections to the **Luba** and **Lunda**. These three peoples appear to have originated in the Shaba area in the Congo and, some 300 years ago, began their migrations south into Zambia and Angola. It has been noted that the Bemba belong to the group known as the Sabi, who have a matrilineal system of inheritance. In the 1650s, they founded the Bemba kingdom, and in the 19th century, they expanded into the Luapala and the Luangwa River valleys. Between 1750 and 1800, the Bemba expansions caused a number of splits, with smaller units becoming new kingdoms such as the Chishinga, Unga, and Bisa. The Bemba became involved in the slave trade with **Arab** and **Swahili** traders from the coastal regions of the Indian Ocean during the 19th century. In 1889, the British South African Company was granted control over what was called Northern Rhodesia, and by 1900, all of the African peoples in this area had submitted to European rule. Bemba lands were particularly important due to the copper deposits located there. The Bemba were among those recruited to work the mines, which revolutionized life for them.

The Bemba are an agricultural people, but because of the poor soils of the area where they lived, villages had to be relocated every four or five years. With the introduction of fertilizers and crop rotation methods, they no longer need to move. They raise crops of millet, sorghum, maize, and cassava, and some keep livestock such as sheep and goats; but because of the tsetse fly, few have cattle. Since the introduction of wage labor in the copper mines and other employment opportunities opened up due to mission education, many Bemba have moved to the major cities to live and work.

The majority of Bemba are Christians, but their traditional religion, which focused on ancestral spirits and women, has been incorporated into Zambian Christianity. One custom of traditional religion was that there was a shrine in every household, which was maintained and managed by married women. Married women kept in touch with the ancestral spirits or *ngulu* through spirit possession. In the 1700s, with the growth of the political power of the Bemba king, power of the household spirits was undermined by that of the kings; and in the late 19th century, Christianity also undermined the traditional religion and the place of women. Christianity spread rapidly among the Bemba following its introduction in the 1890s. The Bemba converted mainly to Roman Catholicism, and today the Roman Church is the largest single Christian domination in the country. However, Christianity in Zambia was greatly influenced by the ancestral spirits, and spirit possession of both men and women is part of Christian worship.

Traditional Bemba society is matrilineal, and a man inherits even his political position through his mother. The Bemba are composed of 30 clans, each claiming to descend from a distant ancestor named for an animal, plant, or mineral. For example, the Bena Yanda clan, the clan that became politically dominant, takes their name from the crocodile. Each of the clans is governed by a hierarchy of leadership from the local village level up to the top authority, called the *Chitimukulu* from the name of the great leader Chiti of the 18th century. His place of burial, called *Mwalule*, is still where leaders of the Bemba are buried.

The British South African Company turned over control of the three territories, Northern and Southern Rhodesia and Nyasaland, to the British colonial office in 1923 as the Central African Federation. The three territories had numerous differences, but the principal one was the amount of land granted or bought by whites. Problems over rights of indigenous peoples, especially in Southern Rhodesia, eventually caused the union to break, and Southern Rhodesia declared its independence with a minority-white government in 1963. Northern Rhodesia became the new state of Zambia in 1964 under its first president, Kenneth Kaunda. Kaunda's father was himself a Christian missionary and Kenneth was the product of a mission school. The Bemba, being generally well educated with an urban as well as a rural base, were among the most active opposition populations during Kaunda's rule, and many Bemba were arrested and accused of plotting against the government in 1981. In 1991, Kaunda lost the presidential elections to the Bemba political leader Frederick Chiluba.

John A. Shoup

Further Reading

Mbajekwe, Patrick U. "East and Central Africa in the Nineteenth Century." In *Africa Volume 1: African History before 1885*, edited by Toyin Falola. Durham, NC: Carolina Academic Press, 2000.

Stokes, Jamie. "Bemba." In *Encyclopedia of the Peoples of Africa and the Middle East*. New York: Facts on File, 2009.

Taylor, Scott D. *Culture and Customs of Zambia*. Westport, CT: Greenwood Press, 2006.

Wills, A. J. *An Introduction to the History of Central Africa: Zambia, Malawi, and Zimbabwe*. 4th ed. Oxford: Oxford University Press, 2002.

Berbers

Berbers are the indigenous inhabitants of North Africa who generally call themselves *Imazighen* (singular *amazigh*) meaning the "free people." Berbers inhabit a wide area from Siwa Oasis in Egypt's Western Desert to the Atlantic coast of Morocco and from the Mediterranean south to the Sahel in Niger and Burkina Faso. The total number of Berbers is difficult to determine, mainly because of the different ways people can be counted as Berber or not. In Morocco, between 30 percent and 60 percent of the population can be counted as Berber, depending on whether or not speaking Berber as the language of the home is part of the identity. If speaking Berber as the first language is considered, then around 30 percent to 40 percent of Morocco's people are Berbers; but if other aspects are taken into consideration, such as family name, place of origin, and cultural affinity, then as many as to 60 percent of Moroccans are Berbers. Berbers number at least 10 million, with the largest populations in Algeria and Morocco.

The term Berber derives from the Greek word *barabaroi*, which they used to mean those who could not speak Greek. It was borrowed into Latin as *barbar*, from which the English language takes the word *barbarian*. The Latin term was also borrowed into Arabic as *barbar* (plural *barabar*) and generally was applied to much of North Africa or *Barbary* by Europeans. Arabic speakers usually referred to Berbers as *Shluh*, which derives from the Arabic for someone who speaks a broken form of Arabic, though recently, the more proper *amazigh/imazighin* has been adopted by most North African countries. The Berber language, generally called *Tamazight*, belongs to the Afroasiatic group and seems to have divided from Semitic sometime around 11,000 BCE.

The origin of the Berbers has been a source of controversy, especially after the emergence of the highly romantic *Berberisme* or Berber Myth movement supported by Europeans and Americans in the early 20th century. The Berber Myth originated with the work of the French officer Robert Montagne, who was commissioned by the French Governor-General of Morocco, Hubert Lyauty, to study the Berbers. He sought to find Berber origins in Europe, perhaps related to the Basques. The Berber Myth of lost Europeans pushed an agenda to "free" the Berbers from their occupation and suppression by the **Arabs** and Islam. Medieval Arab historians and geographers followed Berber genealogies that gave themselves Yemeni origins claiming to descend from the Himyarites. Berbers sought to place themselves on an equal footing with Arabs by claiming prestigious Arab genealogies. Recent studies by physical and medical anthropologists note the Y chromosome and DNA place Berbers as sharing common links to African and Middle Eastern peoples.

Archeologists believe that what they call proto-Berbers inhabited most of the Mediterranean coastal regions of North Africa in the late Paleolithic period (formerly called the Mesolithic) and produced the Capsian culture. By the Neolithic period, around 7000 BCE, Berbers produced some of the rock art found in the Sahara. Evidence is backed up not only by genetic research, but also by representations of nomadic life, tent structures, and clothing that are very similar to those found in ancient Egyptian representations of the Libu and other Berber peoples from historic times.

The ancient Egyptians provided a good amount of detail about the Libu/Rebu, Tehenu, and Temehu peoples who lived in the Western Desert and in eastern Libya. The Algerian archeologist Malika Hachid argues that the **Tuareg** are the modern-day descendants of the ancient Garamantes mentioned by Greek and Roman geographers. Some of the Berbers, mainly those in contact with Egypt and Punic Carthage, organized themselves into states. Numidia arose in the fourth century BCE in the region close to Carthage and divided into two main lineages/kingdoms of Massyles and Masaeyles. A third kingdom, Mauritania (no connection with the modern country of Mauritania) under the Bogud lineage, emerged in the first century BCE. The Berber kings were greatly influenced by Punic culture and took on a number of elements, including worship of the two principal Punic gods Tingit and Ba'al-Hammon. The Numidian rulers became embroiled in the conflict between Rome and Carthage. The last independent Numidian ruler, King Jugurtha (118–105 BCE), fell out with Rome, with whom he fought a seven- year war. Jugurtha was eventually betrayed by his cousin, the king of Mauritania, and was taken to Rome for execution. Numidia was allowed to continue to exist, but was broken up into small, contesting city-states until the civil war between Julius Caesar and Pompey when King Juba I (68–46 BCE) tried to use the civil war for his own benefit. However, Pompey's forces were beaten by Caesar and Numidia was annexed as the Roman province of Africa.

The Kingdom of Mauritania remained a "Friend and Ally of Rome." Its last major ruler, Juba II (25 BCE–23 CE), was taken to Rome, where Julius Caesar had him educated in Latin and Greek. During this time, he became a close friend of Octavian and they remained close the rest of their lives. His kingdom was annexed by Rome in the year 40 CE after the emperor Caligula had King Ptolemy (23–40 CE) poisoned. The city of Volubilis rose in resistance under the command of the Aedemon, King Ptolemy's servant, but, in 42, the rebels were defeated. Rome controlled all of North Africa including the provinces of Africa (Tunisia), Numidia (eastern Algeria), Mauritania Ceasaria (western Algeria), and Mauritania Tingitania (Morocco). Berber resistance led by Tacfarinas (17–24 CE) in what is today Algeria was also crushed. As the empire weakened, Rome withdrew from Mauritania in 285, though it kept the ports of Tangier and Sebta/Ceuta.

During the later Roman period, Berbers in Tunisia and eastern Algeria were attracted to the Donatist and Arian forms of Christianity and rose in rebellion against the Catholic Church and the wealthy landowners. However, Saint Augustine of Hippo (340–430), who was of Berber origin, wrote to defend the Church of Rome, and he argued against the theological points of Donatists, Arians, and Palegians as well as against the ideas of the last of the pagan philosophers. His major work, *The City of God* (*De Civitate Dei*) argued for the supremacy of the Catholic Church of Rome, which formed the basis for the secular as well as religious power that the Church was able to maintain throughout the European medieval period as the true inheritor of imperial Rome.

By the fifth century CE, the edges of the Roman possessions in Africa were under pressure from camel pastoral nomadic Berber tribes and, with the arrival of the Arabs in 647, Rome/Byzantium lost Libya and Tunisia to the Muslims. Berber resistance to the Arabs was led by two remarkable figures. The first was Kusaylah ibn Lamzan, who was able to push the Arabs out of Tunisia briefly, and the second was the queen of the Gerawa Berbers, *al-Kahinah* or the Priestess, who was not defeated until 701. Following the collapse of the last resistance, Berber conversion to Islam happened quickly, and by 711 when the Muslims conquered Spain, nearly everyone in the army, including their commander, Tariq bin Ziyad, were Berbers.

Berbers were attracted to both early Shi'ism and *Kharaji* forms of Islam. Both forms of Islam were brought to North Africa by populations from the Middle East trying to escape persecution by the Umayyads and 'Abbasids. Along Morocco's Atlantic plain, the Barghwata Berbers developed their own version of Islam following their prophet Salih ibn Tarif, who compiled his own Berber version of a "revealed book" to rival the Qur'an. In central Morocco, the proto-

Shi'ite Idrisi dynasty was established by Idris I (788–791/792), a descendant of the Prophet, in 788. Berbers also were the main supporters of the Isma'ili Shi'ite Fatamids who arose in Tunisia in 909.

Sunni Orthodoxy of the Maliki *madhhab* (School of Law) was firmly established in North Africa with the rise of the al-Murabatin (Almoravids), who developed in the Sahara among the pastoral nomadic Sanhaja tribes. By 1056, they had begun their conquest of Morocco, and by 1070, they had consolidated their control over all of Morocco and expanded into Algeria as far as the city of Algiers. The al-Murabatin were asked by the Muslim rulers of Spain to assist them against the pressures from the king of Castile. In 1086, they responded, and by 1110, all of the Muslim states of Spain were under Murabati rule, creating a unified state from the Ebro River in Spain to the Senegal River.

The al-Murabatin were replaced by another Berber dynasty, the al-Muwahhidin (Almohades), by 1147 when the Murabati capital Marrakech fell. The al-Muwahhidin had their main support among the settled farming Masmuda Berbers of the High Atlas. The al-Muwahhidin claimed the al-Murabitin were not truly pious, but in 1212, the al-Muwahhidin were defeated by the Christian king of Castile at the Battle of Hisn al-'Uqab or Las Navas de Tolosa, and the subsequent abandonment of the Muslims of Spain caused them to lose moral authority. Al-Muwahhidin control weakened, and the Bani Ghaniya in southern Tunisia broke from them in the early 13th century as did the Hafsids of Tunis. The Bani Marin of the Berber Zanata tribal confederacy began their slow conquest of Morocco between 1244 and 1274. The Marinids were unable to halt the advance of both Spanish and Portuguese expansion along the coasts of Morocco, and in 1415, the Portuguese seized the port of Sebta/Ceuta. Between 1486 and 1550, nearly every Atlantic port of Morocco was taken by the Portuguese, and the Marinids lost popular support. The Marinids marked the last of the major Berber dynasties, and they were followed by the Arab Sa'adians who claimed legitimacy through direct descent from the Prophet Muhammad.

Today, most Berbers are Sunni Muslim, belonging to the Maliki school or *madhhab*. The Berber al-Murabitin imposed Sunni Islam and the Maliki school and ended both Shi'ite and *Kharaji* forms of Islam, though small communities of *Kharaji* Muslims have been able to survive in the Mzab of Algeria, on the Island of Jerba in Tunisia, and the Jabal Nafusa in Libya. In addition, many of Morocco's **Jews** were Berber-speaking and belonged to one of the oldest Jewish communities outside of the Middle East. Their own history states that they were sent with Phoenician traders by King Solomon. Christianity was embraced by some Berbers in the past, but most Berber Christians today were converted during the French colonial period, with the majority found among the Kabyli Berbers of Algeria.

Berber society was mainly tribally organized. People belonged to particular lineages and, like the Arabs, they had demonstrated descent, meaning that it would be possible to name a person's ancestors back to the founder of the lineage. Berbers were pastoral nomads, with mixed economies of husbandry and farming, while those who lived in oases practiced intensive agriculture. Each lineage among the nomads was under the leadership of an *amghar*, similar to the Arab *shaykh*, while the settled population had elected assemblies (of leading lineages) generally called *jama'a*.

Until recently, Berber culture was sidelined to folklore by most North African governments. Berber contributions to Andalusian architecture and music have not been well studied, but the three main Berber dynasties that ruled most of North Africa and Muslim Spain between 1050 and 1510 patronized the arts. The al-Muwahhidin marked their empire with major mosques with massive minarets in Marrakech, Rabat, Seville, and Tunis. The Marinid period marks the high point in Andalusian architecture, and they encouraged the best and brightest from Spain to work for them. The al-Murabatin court promoted poetry and philosophy, in the universal language of education in the Muslim world, Arabic, and made Arabic the official language of the state.

Berbers nonetheless have a rich heritage in domestic architecture, building in stone, mud brick, and *pisé* or pounded earth. This architecture shows a sophisticated knowledge of thermal and structural aspects of the building materials. Among the most notable structures are the fortified granaries or *agadir* that often stand in the middle of villages.

Berber literature is mainly oral, and most of the texts written in *Tifinagh* or Libyan script are monumental inscriptions. Berbers wrote in Latin or, with the arrival of Islam, in Arabic. Some Berber

Berber village of Shali in the Egyptian oasis of Siwa, the furthest east of any Berber-speaking population. Most of the traditional village has been abandoned following a heavy rain in the 1970s, and today most live in a new village with full amenities. The weekly market is held at the foot of the old village as it always has been. (John A. Shoup)

language texts in southern Morocco are written using Arabic letters. In general, most Berber literature is in the form of poems that are preserved by the *imdiyazin* or bards. These poems are frequently sung, and two major types of dance are associated with them, the *ahidus* of the Middle Atlas, and the *ahwash* of the High Atlas and Sus.

Other Berber arts include silver jewelry, often very large and heavy. Silver jewelry has a wide variety stretching from Siwa to the Atlantic, though use of geometric designs such as triangles is common. Berber weaving is famous, and Berber kilims are excellent, though knotted carpets have large "clunky" knots and are not as refined as those from Iran or Turkey. Use of embroidered patters of sunbursts, sun wheels, and triangles in bright orange, red, and yellow silk floss link communities as distant as Siwa in Egypt and the Tafilalt in Morocco. Berber silver jewelry, embroidery, and carpets have become collectors' items.

Berbers in Algeria and Morocco have recently engaged in a revival of their identity and culture. In Algeria, where Berbers have been able to develop a sense of nationalism, a political movement began in the late 1970s. In 1980, the Berber Spring occurred with a widespread strike by Kabayli Berbers in response to the government banning a conference where the Kabayli intellectual Mouloud Mammeri was scheduled to speak. Subsequently, several Berber associations were founded, and eventually the Algerian government made some concessions, including declaring Berber to be a national language in 2001, though Arabic remains the official language.

In Morocco, King Muhammad VI instituted the Royal Institute for Berber Culture (IRCAM) with the main purpose of studying and publishing on Berber language, history, and culture. Nonetheless, the Amazigh Moroccan Democratic Party (AMDP), formed in 2005, was declared illegal by Moroccan courts in 2008. Moroccan Berbers have been able to get Berber introduced as a language of instruction in regions where Berber is the main language of the home, but have not been able have it declared on par with Arabic. Some still say that they

have difficulty having local officials register their children with Berber names.

John A. Shoup

Further Reading

Abun-Nasr, Jamil. *A History of the Maghrib in the Islamic Period.* Cambridge: Cambridge University Press, 1987.

Amal, Pascal, et al. *Splendeurs du Maroc.* Paris: Editions Plume, 1998.

Basset, R., et al. "Berbers." In *Encyclopaedia of Islam*, 2nd ed., CD-ROM.

Becker, Cynthia. *Amazigh Arts in Morocco: Women Shaping Berber Identity.* Austin: University of Texas Press, 2006.

Brett, Michael, and Elizabeth Fentress. *The Berbers.* Oxford: Blackwell Publishing, 1997.

Fakhry, Ahmed. *Siwa Oasis.* Cairo: American University in Cairo Press, 1990.

Hachid, Malika. *Les Premiers Berbères: Entre Méditirranée, Tassili, et Nil.* Paris: Ina-Yas Edisud, 2001.

Hoffman, Katherine, and Susan Gilson Miller, eds. *Berbers and Others: Beyond Tribe and Nation in the Maghrib.* Bloomington: Indiana University Press, 2010.

Lapidus, Ira. *A History of Islamic Societies.* New York: Cambridge University Press, 1997.

Lunde, Paul. *Islam: Faith, Culture, and History.* New York: DK Publishing, Inc., 2002.

Panetier, Jean-Luc. *Volubilis: Une cité du Maroc antique.* Paris: Maisonneuve and Larosse, 2002.

Parker, Richard. *A Practical Guide to Islamic Monuments in Morocco.* Charlottesville, VA: Baraka Press, 1981.

Pean, Richard. *Tunisia's Berber Heritage: From Prehistoric Times up to the Present.* Tunis: Agence Nationale du Patrimoine, 1995.

Shoup, John A. "Are There Still Tribes in Morocco?" in *Nomadic Societies in the Middle East and North Africa: Entering the 21st Century*, edited by Dawn Chatty. Leiden: Brill, 2006.

Sorber, Frieda. "Afrique du Nord: Des fibres au fil à travers le Maghreb." In *Costumes et Textiles d'Afrique: Des Berbères aux Zulu*, by Anne-Marie Bouttiaux et al. Milan: 5 Continents Press, 2008.

Tahi, Mohand Salih. "North African Berbers and Kabylia's Berber Citizens' Movement." http://www.tamazgha.fr/article.php 3?id_article=225 (accessed December 30, 2009).

Beti/Beti-Pahuin

The Beti are composed of 20 Bantu speaking peoples living mainly in Cameroon, Gabon, Equatorial Guinea, and Sao Tomé and Principe. There are two main divisions, the Beti and the Fang, which are the northern and southern division of the same people. Population figures for individual ethnic groups are difficult to deduce following independence, where such distinctions can be seen as counterproductive to nation building, but it is estimated that the Fang in Gabon and Cameroon number 800,000. Other sources give numbers for the Fang at over 2 million and for the Fang and Beti at over 3 million spread over three main countries. Whether Fang or Beti, all speak different dialects of the same Bantu language called Beti. Beti includes a third group, the Bulu, which makes up about one-third of the Beti-Fang in Cameroon. Bulu speak a dialect that is spoken by some 800,000 people in southern Cameroon, and is further divided by more local dialects of Bene, Yelinda, Yembana, Yengono, and Zaman. All of the regional dialects are considered to be dialects of one main language, Beti, and all of them are mutually intelligible.

Originally, the Beti and Fang migrated from east of the Sanaga River and moved primarily as well-armed farming families into western Cameroon and Gabon. Their migration began perhaps in the 17th or 18th century. It has been noted that the term *Fang* or *Pahouin* come from language shifts of "p" and "f" in the Myene language, since Myene-speakers served as translators for 19th-century French, British, and German explorers. The Beti and Fang call themselves after their lineage; thus there are a number of different groups who claim a common identity. The Beti and Fang were pressured by raids by the **Fulbe** in the early 19th century and moved into areas with lower population densities.

Among the first Europeans to contact the Beti and Fang was Franco-American Paul du Chaillu, whose book *Voyages et aventures dans l'Afrique équatoriale* was published in 1863. His journey took place in 1856, and he seems to be the first European to visit them. Du Chaillu had been told by peoples along the coast that the Fang were cannibals and their warnings seemed to be true when he noticed heaps of human bones, though in truth these were bones of Fang ancestors kept in sacred areas where *so* and *ngil* initiations took place. Rumors of cannibalism were sustained by other 19th-century travelers and explorers such as by Mary Kingsley's 1893–1895 expedition. Her book about her travels, when translated from French, was entitled *A Victorian Woman Explorer among the Man-eaters*. The first true ethnographic account was produced in 1912 by Father Trilles, who learned to speak the Beti language.

European powers did not establish themselves in Beti and Fang areas until near the end of the 19th century. In 1884, the Germans created the colony of Kamerun. German rule was harsh, but following World War I, in 1920, the German colony was divided between the French and the British. Most of the region inhabited by the Beti and Fang went to the French, who found it hard to defeat them. During the French colonial period, large numbers of men were taken away to work in large-scale commercial timber and plantation production, which left too few at home to produce enough food, resulting in famine. Starvation was followed by outbreaks of contagious diseases such as smallpox and influenza, which initiated strong Fang nationalism.

Beti-Pahuin/ Fang society is formed at the level of the village. Each village is a fortified outpost in its organization, reflecting the manner of their penetration into the rain forest. Social organization is based on patrilineal lineages or *ayon/ mvog*, but each village is independent of others. Each village is ruled by a headman of the most important lineage with a council made up of the heads of the other lineages living there.

Important in the traditional belief system are the bones of important ancestors that used to be periodically paraded in the community and kept in reliquary boxes called *byeri*. *Byeri* were stored near the bed of the head of household along with personal fetishes. Fang wood carvings of *byeri* proved to be some of the most beautiful and collectable African art with naturalistic human features and "a distinctive oily patina (that) was instantly appealing to collectors and artists alike" (Bacquart, 124). In addition to the reliquaries containing ancestors' bones, masks were used in initiation ceremonies called *so* and *ngil*, representing the spirit of the forest in the form of animals such as the snake, red antelope, and so forth. *So* and *ngil* are both the names of the masks as well as names of initiation ceremonies; *so* masks tend to be of horned animals, while *ngil* masks usually have a human face. Like the *byeri* figures, collectors and museums were interested in *ngil* masks and "since the thirties, every major international collection of 'Negro arts' and then 'tribal arts' has had to have a *ngil* mask from the Fang" (Perrois, 44). Initiation into the wearing of such masks was organized more like societies because those who had been initiated also helped in policing during other ceremonies, especially those ceremonies that brought out the bones of the ancestors to be viewed or paraded. Such displays of human bones led to rumors of Beti-Pahuin/Fang cannibalism. So common was the belief about their cannibalism and warlike demeanor that the writer Edgar Rice Burroughs decided to set his novel *Tarzan* in the Beti-Pahuin/Fang area. Between 1910 and 1920, French colonial authorities suppressed *so* and *ngil* societies and a new form emerged called *ngontang*, meaning young white girl. *Ngongtang* masks are helmet masks colored white and many are "janus" faced (two faces) and are used during funeral ceremonies. Since the colonial era, many Beti-Pahuin/Fang are Christians or belong to local Christian

Tarzan and the Beti

Edgar Rice Burroughs brought the character of Tarzan to the world audience in 1912 with the publication of the first illustrated "pulp" fiction story, *Tarzan of the Apes*. In the story, John Clayton, Lord Greystoke and his wife Lady Alice are left on the "wild" shore of central Africa—the coast of Cameroon—by mutineers. The stranded Lord, Lady, and infant son John begin life where British civilization is pitted against savage nature and cannibal natives. The infant John is found by the female ape Kala, who names him Tarzan, meaning "White-skin" in the language of the Great Apes.

Tarzan is raised by Kala, who protects him from the other apes as well as teaches him to fear the cannibal Africans led by their king Mbonga. The first European explorers who witnessed Beti rituals around the bones of their dead ancestors thought the bones were those of victims eaten by the Beti. The Beti lands were located only a short distance from the Atlantic shore and thus were easy for Burroughs to bring them into his story of stranded Europeans. The rumors of Beti cannibalism and aggression (fierce demeanor) perpetuated by other Africans and Europeans made them an excellent foil to the "pure" uncorrupted soul of Tarzan.

Tarzan of the Apes and the subsequent titles became among the best-selling titles of the 20th century. In 1921, the first Broadway play based on the novels was staged, and in 1929, it was published as a syndicated cartoon strip in newspapers. Burroughs himself published 26 Tarzan books, and other authors, under license, published another 18 novels. Hollywood made 89 Tarzan movies and since the 1930s, both radio and television produced Tarzan series. Tarzan, despite criticism of racism, stereotype, and colonialism, is one of the best-known characters of the 20th century worldwide.

churches that blend traditional belief with Christianity.

Each Beti-Pahuin/Fang community was built like a fortress with a single street lined with houses and defended by watchtowers. The villages were also protected by traps making it difficult to surprise any such village. Houses were built to be small with one single room and a single, small entrance. The Beti-Pahuin/Fang practiced double exogamy—marriage out from the lineages of both mothers and fathers—but group genealogy was passed on in *melan* initiation. They also practiced a type of *potlatch* called *mebala*, in which the rich redistribute excess wealth to less prosperous members of the community.

The modern community has been split between three main countries with very different histories. Gabon became independent in 1960, Cameroon in 1961, and Equatorial Guinea in 1968. Equatorial

Guinea has been controlled since independence by Fang from the Esangui lineage. The government is accused of human rights violations, and the president is accused of authorizing the arrest and torture of political opposition leaders.

John A. Shoup

Further Reading

Bacquart, Jean-Baptiste. *The Tribal Arts of Africa: Surveying Africa's Artistic Geography*. London: Thames and Hudson, 2002.

Burroughs, Edgar Rice. *Jungle Tales of Tarzan*. http://www.literature.org/authors/burroughs-edgar-rice/jungle-tales-of-tarzan (accessed May 3, 2010).

"Fang." http://www.encyclopedia.farlex.com/Fang (accessed May 3, 2010).

"Fang Information." http://www.uiowa.edu/~africart/toc/people/Fang (accessed May 3, 2010).

Mbaku, John Mukum. *Culture and Customs of Cameroon*. Westport, CT: Greenwood Press, 2005.

Perrois, Louis. *Visions of Africa: Fang*. Milan: 5 Continents Press, 2006.

Vansina, Jan. *Paths in the Rainforests: Toward a History of Political Tradition in Equatorial Africa*. Madison: University of Wisconsin Press, 1990.

Bilen

The Bilen or Bilin (alternate names include Balen, Belen, Beleni, and Bogo, among others) live in the Keren region of Eritrea and **Tigray** Province in Ethiopia. As of 2006, they numbered around 91,000 in Eritrea, Ethiopia, and Djibouti. Around 60 percent of Christians speak Tigrinya, and 70 percent of Muslims speak Tigré and use either the Ethiopic or Latin scripts. Tigrinya and Tigré languages belong to the Cushitic branch of the Afro-Asiatic phylum of languages, and they are a division of the Agaw people. Agaw is the general name given to all speakers of Central Cushitic. Bilen identity arose during the early Christian era, and currently a Bilen nationalist Web site states that they are the oldest human population in the world.

Between 3500 and 1000 BCE, the Agaw established themselves in the Ethiopian Highlands. Small immigrant populations of Semitic settlers from Yemen brought with them a number of cultural innovations, including wheat and barley cultivation, to add to the cultivation of *teff* and millet, as well as oxen and the plow. Agaw communities grew in population, and more of the mountains were cleared for cultivation. Population exchange between the Ethiopian Highlands and Yemen continued introducing religious elements, including Judaism, into Ethiopia. Urban cultures grew with the improved agricultural practices that could support much larger numbers. The great pre-Christian kingdom of Aksum in the first century CE and among the servants of the king of Aksum was a governor of the Agaw. Later, Christianity also found fertile ground in the same region and it spread among the Agaw. The Agaw Kingdom of D'mt under the Zagwé dynasty revolted against Aksum control in the 970s, which eventually brought the downfall of Aksum.

Following the collapse of the Zagwé kingdom around 1270, the Agwa withdrew into isolation and emerged again with the Islamic conquests of the 16th century. The Agaw joined the *jihad* armies as they moved inland, which by the 1530s had most of Ethiopia in Islamic control, and a Bilen identity seems to have emerged. However, thanks to Portuguese intervention on behalf of Christian Ethiopia, by the 1550s, most of the country was recovered and the notably rebellious, Islamic principality of Damot was forced to submit.

The Agaw people are both Christian and Muslim and the Bilen are around two- thirds Muslim today. The Christian one-third is mainly Roman Catholic—the religion of the Italian occupiers—rather than the **Coptic** Christianity of the Ethiopians. There are small minorities of Copts and Protestants as well.

The Agaw emerged again in the 19th century with the completion of the Suez Canal in 1869, once again making the Red Sea an important commercial thoroughfare. The British, French, and Italians all became interested in the once-remote area, and in the 1930s, the Italians employed Bilen troops in its invasion of Ethiopia. The British and Ethiopians forced the Italians out of Ethiopia in 1941, and in 1952, under United Nations order, Eritrea was added to Ethiopia. In 1962, Ethiopia annexed Eritrea and a number of separatist movements arose. Long, protracted war began, and in 1993, Eritrea gained its independence from Ethiopia. The war had displaced as many as one-half of all Bilen who are scattered throughout Eritrea. Today, many are concentrated around the cities of Keren and Asmara in the State of Eritrea.

John A. Shoup

Further Reading

"Bilen Dynasty." http://www.bilendynasty.ning.com (accessed May 22, 2011).

"Languages of Eritrea." http://www.ethnologue.com/show_country.asp?name=ER (accessed June 20, 2011).

Pankhurst, Richard. *The Ethiopians: A History.* Malden, MA: Blackwell Publishing, 2001.

Bini/Edo

The Bini/Edo belong to the Kwa group of the Benue-Kwa family of the Niger-Congo phylum of languages. The language is usually called Bini, and they numbered 3.8 million at the turn of the 21st century. They are found mainly in the Edo State in southern Nigeria and claim direct descent from the Edo, who founded the state of Benin in the 14th century.

The Bini/Edo emerged sometime around 1000 in the rain forest of Nigeria. The Bini/Edo moved from the savanna into the forest, building large sites and excavating around them to reduce the problems of disease. They built large and densely populated settlements; often larger ones grew into and incorporated smaller ones. They developed a highly centralized business elite with far-reaching trade links to the **Hausa**, **Songhay**, and **Yoruba** states, and expanded southward into regions of less centralized Ijoid peoples.

In the 14th and 15th centuries, the Benin kingdom, as it was called, became one of the most powerful in the region. The height of the Benin Kingdom lasted from the 14th to the 17th century, and their wealth was due to trade in ivory, pepper, palm oil, and slaves, though the state resisted the idea of sale of slaves. Benin City had wide, straight streets and was surrounded by earthwork walls. Matrilineal descent patterns helped shape the management of the smaller villages in the kingdom, and women had a say in the politics of the kingdom through the 17th century. Europeans bought African cloth, which brought not only economic growth, but greatly enhanced the position of women, who were the main producers of cloth. Benin began to decline in the 18th century as many of their main exports were taken over by other producers outside of Africa.

The period of political height was also the height of its artistic production, especially in bronzes and carved ivory. Contact with the Portuguese along the coast starting at the end of the 15th century introduced other metalworking techniques such as brass gilding. When Benin City fell to the British in 1897, some 3,000 brass, ivory, and wooden objects were taken away to Europe and later sold to pay for the expedition's costs. Around 1,000 brass plaques from the palace of the king, or *oba*, dating from between the 16th and 17th centuries were among the booty taken, and their beauty and sophistication astonished Western art scholars. The vast amount of materials were due partially to the fact that each *oba* had a state monopoly on ivory, coral, brass, and wooden objects, which were an important part of public displays and ceremonies that were paraded, or were objects for ancestral altars.

The Edo people are well known for both music and dance, much of it part of official holidays. The *Igue* festival is still held every December, and the *oba* welcomes the New Year and gives thanks for the bounty of the outgoing year. There are 27 other masquerades held every year, with different masks representing different natural powers. There are a large number of well-known Edo musicians who play a variety of music, from traditional styles to Nigeria's internationally known Highlife.

The head of the Benin state was the *oba*, who had a sacred status. The *oba* was selected on the principle of primogeniture or to the eldest son, and he held political, economic, and religious power. He had monopolies on items such as ivory, and anyone who killed an ivory-bearing animal, such as an elephant, had to give one-half of the ivory to the *oba*, who also had first right of purchase to the rest. Matrilineal principles of inheritance were part of village leadership, and villages were usually divided into age sets or age grades that were responsible for different aspects of running the day-to-day affairs of the village.

The modern history of Benin begins with economic collapse in the 18th century. The *oba*s surrounded themselves with the aura of divine kingship, and human sacrifice was introduced. The British used the excuse of what they called large-scale human sacrifice to justify their invasion and burning of Benin City in 1897. The power structures were more or less left in place, but Benin was incorporated into British Nigeria and eventually became part of independent Nigeria in 1960.

Today, the Bini/Edo live in a region called Edoland, which comprises Edo and the Delta States in modern Nigeria. The Edo and the **Yoruba**-dominated states did not join with other southerners when in 1967 the **Igbo** seceded from the Nigerian federation. When Nigeria reorganized the federal states in 1996, the State of Edo was formed, with the ancient capital of Benin named the new state's capital.

John A. Shoup

Further Reading

Bacquart, Jean-Baptiste. *The Tribal Arts of Africa: Surveying Africa's Artistic Geography.* London: Thames and Hudson, 2002.

Collins, Robert O. *Africa: A Short History.* Princeton, NJ: Markus Wiener Publishers, 2008.

Falola, Toyin. *Culture and Customs of Nigeria.* Westport, CT: Greenwood Press, 2001.

Falola, Toyin, and Matthew Heaton. *A History of Nigeria.* Cambridge: Cambridge University Press, 2009.

Vansina, Jan. *Paths in the Rainforests: Toward a History of Political Tradition in Equatorial Africa.* Madison: University of Wisconsin Press, 1990.

C

Chagga

The Chagga, Chaga, Wachagga, Jagga, Dschagga, or Waschagga are a Bantu-speaking people who traditionally live on the slopes of Mount Kilimanjaro and Mount Meru. The Chagga are the third-largest ethnic group in Tanzania, numbering some 2 million people. Their language is called Kichagga and, though mainly Bantu, the language includes some elements of other peoples the Chagga encountered when they migrated from west of qake Victoria starting in the 11th century CE. There is no one single Kichagga language, but it is made up of a number of closely related dialects, including Kivunjo, Kimarangu, Kiromba, Kimachame, and Kikibosho. Some linguists note that the **Kamba** of Kenya speak a language with many similarities to Kichagga. The Chagga are related to the Pare, Tateva, and Teita, who remained in the Pare Mountains south of Kilimanjaro when the Chagga migrated to their current homeland.

The Chagga were part of the Bantu expansion into Kenya and Tanzania that began around the start of the 11th century and lasted until the mid-15th century. The Bantu brought with them knowledge of highland cultivation that could support large populations, and the Chagga found the highlands of Mounts Kilimanjaro and Meru ideal for the cultivation of bananas. They developed a large number of banana types and developed agricultural methods including terracing, irrigation systems, and use of animal waste for fertilizer. The Chagga did not have large areas to graze livestock, but kept them in stalls or pens and collected the manure to fertilize their fields. It is debated if the Chagga invented some of these methods, or if they were partially already in place, brought by Southern Cushitic peoples from Ethiopia, where similar techniques were in use for centuries. Southern Cushitic peoples had been in the region since the first millennium BCE.

The Chagga absorbed the remnants of those who already lived on the mountain slopes and developed a close trading relationship with the **Nilotic** peoples, who dominated the plains by the end of the 11th century. The Nilotic Ongamo in particular had a major role in shaping Chagga culture. The Chagga borrowed a number of Nilotic practices including female circumcision, the drinking of cattle blood (originally a Cushitic practice), and age sets. Drumming, associated in Bantu culture with the chieftaincy, was lost among the Chagga, who no longer practice it. In the second half of the 19th century, the Ongamo were increasingly acculturated into the Chagga. Chagga-Ongamo interaction blended their religions; Bantu concepts of the Creator God and Cushitic-Nilotic concepts of the life-giving sun whom the Chagga combined into *Ruwa*. *Ruwa* is also the Chagga word

Bicycles for delivering bananas stand outside a storehouse in Tanzania. The Chagga develo-ped methods for cultivating bananas on Mount Kilimanjaro and Mount Meru. (iStockPhoto)

for "sun," and as a god, he is a provider; kind, and tolerant. The Bantu importance of ancestor spirits remains to this day among the Chagga, but in general, their traditional religion has been replaced by Christianity and Islam.

The Chagga are patrilineal, and the center of their society is the *kihamba* or family plot of land. The *kihamba* is passed from one generation to the next and was the source of family wealth. Chagga farmers in the past grew bananas, finger millet, beans, and cassava and raised small numbers of livestock, cattle, goats, and sheep. With colonization, new crops were added including coffee, maize, and tobacco, which helped them remain wealthy in the face of colonial commercial farming.

Politically, the Chagga developed a number of competing chiefdoms that were more territorial based than lineage based. The need to expand viable agricultural lands met the challenge of space on the mountain slopes and the *kihamba* system is seen today as one of the best examples of multi-cropping and with less environmental damage than other agricultural systems. Environmentalists have urged others to study how the Chagga are able to maintain high production on small quantities of land and not damage the natural environment. Today the *kihamba* produce crops of coffee, bananas, millet, maize, beans, cassava, sweet potatoes, yams, sugar cane, tobacco, pumpkins, and squash. In addition, they grow fodder crops for their livestock, and keep fish in the irrigation canals to help keep them clean. Chagga chiefs are called *mangi*, which means more of "an arranger" or "planner" than "head of a clan." Rivalries between Chagga chiefs led to a continual need for iron ore to make needed weapons. Iron ore deposits are located in the Pare Mountains, and Chagga chiefs maintained good trade relations with the Bantu Pare, Tateva, and Teita who inhabit the Pare Mountains. Conflicts between Chagga chiefs allowed the interference of colonial powers, who took one side against another.

Toward the end of the 19th century, two major *mangi* were in rivalry, *Mangi* Rindi and *Mangi* Sina, both with large, well-armed armies. The Germans established their colony in the 1880s and entered into the conflict assisting *Mangi* Rindi against *Mangi* Sina, and in 1891, a German column assisted in the defeat of Sina. *Mangi* Rindi had already signed a treaty with the Germans in 1885 and his town of Moshi became the German colonial capital. The Germans, and later the British, used the rivalries between the Chagga leadership to manipulate them; however, in 1952, the Chagga decided they needed better means to deal with colonial administrators and elected the *Mangi Mkuu* or "Paramount Chief." The *Mangi Mkuu* became their representative with colonial authorities until he came into conflict with Western-educated Chagga and growing power of the Tanganyika African National Union (TANU) under the leadership of Julius Nyerere.

Chagga split their support between the *Mangi Mkuu*, who formed a rival party called the Chagga Democratic Party that pushed for democratization of the chieftaincy, and those who supported Julius Nyerere. By 1959, the position of *Mangi Mkuu* was abolished and with

independence, the role of traditional chiefs was reduced.

The Chagga are one of the most highly educated people in Tanzania, with over 80 percent literacy in the 1980s. During the colonial period, Chagga welcomed missionaries and the majority of them are Christian, perhaps as much to do with the combination of Christianity and schools. There are also a smaller number who are Muslim. As the most educated population of Tanzania, they exercise a great deal of influence in economics and politics and have the highest number of people in government, education, and the arts.

John A. Shoup

Further Reading

Ehret, Christopher. *The Civilizations of Africa: A History to 1800*. Charlottesville: University Press of Virginia, 2002.

Mbajekwe, Patrick U. "East and Central Africa in the Nineteenth Century." In *Africa Volume 1: African History before 1885*, edited by Toyin Falola. Durham, NC: Carolina Academic Press, 2000.

"People of Kilimanjaro: The Chagga." http://www.climbmountkilimanjaro.com/the-people-of-kilimanjaro-the-chagga/index.html (accessed December 20, 2010).

Chewa

The Chewa or Chichewa (Chuas, Achewa, Ancheya, Masheba, or Cewas) are the largest ethnic group in Malawi and the third-largest ethnic group in Zambia. The Chichewa number around 57 percent of the total population of Malawi and total over 1.5 million in Malawi and Zambia. They are a Bantu-speaking people, and their language is called Chicewa, Chinyanja, or Banti.

The Chewa arrived in the region of Lake Malawi in the 15th century and was part of the Maravi or Mravi chieftaincies that eventually merged into a state; Lake Malawi is a corruption of Lake Maravi and was named so by the Portuguese. In the 18th century, the Portuguese believed the Chewa controlled a vast empire, though this seems to have been born more of rumor than solid facts.

The Chewa created at least one kingdom, Undi, and the leadership benefited from the trade routes from the interior that passed on to Zanzibar. North of Undi, the territory was divided into hundreds of chiefdoms that fell victim to the **Yao**, another Bantu people who lived to the east of Lake Malawi. Internal warfare among the Chewa, including the larger, more organized kingdom of Undi, supplied the Yao with war captives sold as slaves. Trade was not only in slaves, but in locally grown and woven cotton cloth.

The Chewa were peaceful and thus suffered from slave-taking raids by the **Arab**s, the Portuguese, and the Yao. In the 19th century, the **Nguni**, fleeing north from Shaka Zulu, also fell on the Chewa, taking some as slaves. From 1600 to 1870, the Chewa were subjected to warfare from the expanding **Luba**, **Bemba**, and Luyi from the north and the southern Nguni Bantu pushing north from Natal in South Africa. After 1856, the Bemba were supplied with guns by Arab traders from Zanzibar and, together with the Nguni, they devastated the Chewa.

Although contacted by the Portuguese in Mozambique in the 17th century, Portuguese ideas of the Chewa were rather negative. They were described as being "heathens very barbarous, and great thieves ... Their mode of speaking is in a loud harsh voice" (Wills, 51). Subjected to slave raids, it was not until British missionary David Livingston's travels through what was then called Nyasaland that the Chewa were absorbed into British ambitions in Africa. Between 1884 and 1900, the British in the "scramble for Africa" secured their control over Nyasaland in 1891. Originally called the British Central Africa Protectorate, the name was changed to the Nyasaland Protectorate in 1907.

The Chewa are settled agriculturalists and grow crops of sorghum, maize, beans, and rice. Droughts in the 1980s greatly affected the rural population, and many have left to find jobs in the cities. British and Portuguese Christian missions have converted many, but at least one-fifth of all Chewa are Muslims today. Despite the influence of Christianity and Islam, a good number of Chewa still hold to their ancestral belief system. Traditional belief centered on a single creator god called *Chiuta* or *Chaunta*, who made all living things on Mount Kapirintiwa that exists on the border of Malawi with Mozambique.

Most Chewa lived in densely compact villages managed by a hereditary village chief and a council of elders. Historically, the Chewa did not form into a single central state, but remained, for the most part, divided into hundreds of independent chiefdoms even after being attacked by more centrally organized peoples.

British and German troops were engaged during World War I on Lake Malawi and along the land frontier between their colonies. Though the British quickly put the one German boat operating on Lake Malawi out of commission, the Germans held a strong position on the land frontier until, in 1915, the British victory over a much larger German force in Nyasaland did much to boost the British image in the region. The last major German-British encounter along the northern shores of Lake Malawi took place after the armistice in Europe was signed and the German commander agreed to surrender a few days later.

Moves toward independence began in the 1950s, and more and more local people became involved in the administration of Nyasaland. Many were educated in British schools or in the United States, and in 1944, the Nyasaland African Congress Party was founded, which later changed its name to the Malawi Congress Party. In 1953, Great Britain consolidated all three territories of the two Rhodesia and Nyasaland, which gave more support to the independence movement. In 1961, the Malawi Congress Party won a majority in the elections and Hastings Banda was appointed prime minister. Nyasaland won full independence in 1964, and in 1966, Hastings Banda became the first president of Malawi. Banda ruled Malawi until 1994, when he was removed from office.

John A. Shoup

Further Reading

Gough, Amy. "The Chewa." http;//www.peoplesoftheworld.org/hosted/chewa/index.jsp (accessed May 3, 2010).

Stokes, Jamie. "Chewa." In *Encyclopedia of the Peoples of Africa and the Middle East*. New York: Facts on File, 2009.

Taylor, Scott D. *Culture and Customs of Zambia*. Westport, CT: Greenwood Press, 2006.

"Tribes and People Groups: Chewa." The Africa Guide. http://www.africaguide.com/culture/tribes/chewa.htm (accessed May 3, 2010).

Wills, A. J. *An Introduction to the History of Central Africa: Zambia, Malawi, and Zimbabwe*. 4th ed. Oxford: Oxford University Press, 2002.

Chokwe

The Chokwe are one of the main ethnic groups in Angola and live in the diverse ethnic region of eastern Angola and the southern Democratic Republic of Congo stretching into Zambia. They are associated with the former kingdom of **Lunda** and the related **Luba**. They have a number of variants for their name, including Kioko, Cokwe, Tschokwe, and Quioco, which stem from different languages and the linguistic slip between "ch" and "c." The Chokwe number over 1.16 million people and speak a Bantu language called Wuchokwe, which is only a little different from their two ancestral languages of Lunda and Luba.

Chokwe origin dates to sometime between the 15th and 17th centuries, when a Lunda woman of high lineage named Lweij married a Luba hunter named Chibinda Ilunga, also of high lineage. However, most of the Lunda nobility did not approve of the marriage, and the couple began their migration south into what would become Angola. The Chokwe grew from their descendants and subsequent attached peoples. In this period of origins, the Chokwe legendary hero figure Chibinda Ilunga (also spelled Kibinda

A pwo mask. (Swisshippo/Dreamstime.com)

Ilunga) emerged; by legend he is the son of the Lunda and Luba couple or the Luba "prince" himself. Chibinda Ilunga introduced a number of specific hunting practices that helped in developing a Chokwe identity. It has been noted that the Chokwe expanded by dispersing the population through setting up small hunting camps in the territory of a king. As the Chokwe grew in size and began to cultivate land, they would then reject the laws of the king in whose lands they have settled and eventually either defeat or simply absorb him into the growing "Chokwe" peoples, making everyone Chokwe. The Chokwe were unable to supply the needs for manpower,

and marriage with non-Chokwe women, even slaves, was common, and the children belonged to their father's lineage. It has been noted that the Chokwe men used ivory obtained through hunting to purchase women and then gained access to the rubber regions of the Congo basin, which was highly profitable.

The Chokwe were very successful in spreading their identity. By the 19th century, a number of Chokwe chiefdoms had emerged, and they began trading with the **Ovimbundu**. Fortified Chokwe villages dotted the landscape, and though they did not have a centralized head, they were able to raise enough highly trained men that by

1885 they were able to overwhelm the Lunda, taking their capital city. At the start of the 20th century, the Chokwe chiefdoms were split between the British (Northern Rhodesia in today's Zambia), the Belgians (Democratic Republic of Congo), and the Portuguese (Angola) as the colonial authorities divided them into colonial-administered provinces and districts.

The Chokwe produced some of the most sought-after art in Africa. Despite the decline in art following the collapse of Chokwe political power at the end of the 19th century, Chokwe pieces are still produced, particularly the *pwo* masks. *Pwo* masks consist of not only the face mask, but entire body costumes of twisted plant fiber called *makishi*. There are other *makishi* masks; some are of men and are used in a number of different celebrations including the *mukanga* initiation/circumcision ceremonies. The masks associated with circumcision in the past were burnt as soon as the ceremony had finished. It has been noted that today, artists tend to keep the masks from year to year rather than destroy them, and the parts that were once made from plant fiber have been replaced with nylon from flour and grain sacks.

The Chokwe believe in a creator called *Kalunga* and a number of spirits or *mahamba* who can be consulted by a *nganga* or diviner. Belief in spirits or *hamba* links the current generation with their ancestors and are shared with the Lunda and other peoples in the region. The Chokwe hero figure Chibinda Ilunga introduced specific orientation of *hamba* rituals to hunting in addition to the more shared idea of *hamba*

in connection to divination and fertility. Some of the ancestor statues made for *hamba* rituals began to fade in the 1860s and new, simpler styles became more common. As trade developed in the 19th century, another type of *hamba* spirit became important, that related to trade called the spirit of the wind, or *hamba e peho*. These were "scourges of unknown origin that behaved in unpredictable ways" (Wastiau, 18). The *hamba vimbali* (also spelled *imbali* or *imbari*, which is the Wuchokwe word for the Ovimbundu) represent the Ovimbundu and their Portuguese partners on the Atlantic coast. These *hamba* pieces show figures in European dress, smoking cigarettes, with facial hair, and sunburnt faces.

The Chokwe developed a dispersed form of government, and though they were able to defeat the Lunda, they did not have a recognized central authority. Each chief was called *mwana nganga*, who consults with a council of elders to make decisions. The leadership position is inherited, though usually it goes to the son of the chief's sister following a matrilineal system of governance. Generally sons go to live with their maternal uncles at around age six. Chokwe society is broken into two major groups: those who descend from the Lunda princess Lweij, and those who descend from people later absorbed into the Chokwe.

The Chokwe live in areas of Angola and Democratic Republic of Congo that are rich with minerals, including diamonds. During the Angolan civil war, which began in 1975, the Chokwe were again divided between pro-government and pro-UNITA (*Uniao Nacional para a*

Chokwe Art

The Chokwe are well known in the world of African Art for the beauty of their carvings and masks. "Of all the sculpture in Central Africa, ancient, traditional Chokwe pieces are now among the most admired: statues of mythological ancestor Chibinda Ilunga, cult statuettes, ritual masks, and prestige objects," all of which are avidly collected by art dealers, museums, and private collectors (Wastiau, 7). Chokwe art appeals to the Western aesthetic due to the natural, almost realistic representations of humans and animals.

One of the main collectable types of art is the statues representing the founder of the Chokwe people, Chibinda Ilunga. The figure always wears the chiefly headdress called a *mutwe wa kayanda*, which is an elaborate coiffure of hair, raffia, and glass beads, which in rolls, folds back over the head and on both sides, and separate rolls form horn-like sides. The figures always are bearded and in some instances, the beard hair is made of real hair. The statues always show a circumcised penis, and it is said that Chibinda Ilunga imposed circumcision on the people.

Walking sticks, scepters, and ceremonial clubs are also elaborately carved, often with human heads. The detail and natural representations of people as well as the high finished polish of each piece gives them the strong appeal to Western buyers. Other items, such as elaborately carved chairs and stools, are also made by Chokwe craftsmen. Masks are called *mukishi* from the Chokwe *kishi*, meaning to represent or express a living force. The masks are carved of wood and again, Chokwe masks are noted for their naturalism. Masks are divided into *pwo* (female) and *chihongo* (male). *Pwo* masks are worn now at parties of different kinds, including celebrating local events and at tourist attractions. Today, Chokwe artists make a living from selling masks and other art items for the international African Art market.

Independencia Total de Angola—the rebel movement under the command of Jonas Savimbi and supported by South Africa and the United States) villages. The rebels were attracted to the Chokwe area due to the mineral wealth of the region, and again in 1992, just before the brokered elections, UNITA forces occupied the diamond fields. UNITA rebels were financed by selling diamonds through Zaire (now Democratic Republic of Congo) at between US$300 million and $500 million a year, and by 1997 Jonas Savimbi, head of UNITA, was making an estimated US $2 billion a year from the sales of diamonds. Savimbi's last stand against government advances was in the Chokwe region of Moxico, where in 2002, Savimbi was surrounded and killed.

John A. Shoup

Further Reading

Bacquart, Jean-Baptiste. *The Tribal Arts of Africa: Surveying Africa's Artistic Geography.* London: Thames and Hudson, 2002.

"Chokwe Information." http://www.uiowa.edu/ ~africart/toc/people/Chokwe (accessed May 1, 2010).

Meredith, Martin. *The Fate of Africa: A History of Fifty Years of Independence.* New York: Public Affairs, 2005.

Mukenge, Tshilemale. *Culture and Customs of Congo.* Westport, CT: Greenwood Press, 2001.

Oyebade, Adebayo. *Culture and Customs of Angola.* Westport, CT: Greenwood Press, 2006.

Wastiau, Boris. *Visions of Africa: Chokwe.* Milan: 5 Continents Editions, 2006.

Copts

Copts are a Christian group native to Egypt and today make up around 10 percent of the total population of the country. The Coptic language belongs to the Afro-Asiatic group, but was generally replaced with Arabic by the 14th century and is reserved for religious services, though even some parts of the service are now in Arabic. Copts speak various dialects of Egyptian Arabic in daily life. The Coptic language is written in a modified version of Greek script, but the language is the last development of the language of ancient Egypt. The Coptic faith spread beyond the borders of Egypt into **Nubia** and Ethiopia early in the fourth century.

The word Copt, or *Qubt* in Arabic, comes from the name of the town Coptos (modern Quft) in Upper Egypt, though others argue that it comes from the Greek Aegyptos or Egypt. That term derives originally from the name of the ancient city of Memphis, *Ha-Ka-Ptah* or the House of Ptah, which the Greeks corrupted into Aegyptos.

Copts believe that Christianity was brought to Egypt by Saint Mark in the first century CE and the Coptic calendar, or Calendar of the Martyrs, dates from 284 CE when the Roman emperor Diocletian's persecutions of Christians included the martyrdom of the Coptic patriarch. The Coptic calendar is solar based and is linked to the agricultural year. It uses the ancient Egyptian names of the months divided into three seasons of four months each. Christianity spread quickly among Egypt's Greek-speaking urban population, but much more slowly among rural Egyptians. Because it is believed that Saint Mark first landed in Alexandria, it is the seat of the patriarch of the Church.

Copts diverged from the official Christianity of the Roman/Byzantine state in 451, leading to conflict between the *Malikite* or Christianity of the King (*malik*) and the monophysitism of the Copts. Byzantine persecution of Copts prior to the **Arab** conquest in 641–643 caused many Copts to welcome the Arabs. The Prophet's wife Maryam was a Copt, and she was the mother of his short-lived son Ibrahim. Copts served in the first Arab administrations of the province, and the Coptic language was used by the state until replaced by Arabic under the Umayyad *Khalifah* 'Abd al-Malik (685–705). Copts remained in government service, and a number rose to important positions under Islamic rulers.

Copts are mainly rural peasants with the largest numbers in Upper Egypt, exceeding 2 million. In Coptic marriage patterns, divorce is not allowed except in the case of adultery, and marriage can only be among their fellow Copts, indicating that they see themselves as the true descendants of the ancient Egyptians. Copts, like Muslims in Egypt or Sudan, practice circumcision for boys and girls, who have the clitoris removed. Excision of the clitoris is a practice shared with many other peoples in Africa. Most Copts tattoo a cross on their wrists, and according to folklore among the peasants, their fellow Coptic Ethiopians will one day conquer Egypt and spare only those who have the tattoo. In the past, Copts also had the date of their pilgrimage to Jerusalem tattooed on their arm. Cross confessional popular practices are common among the peasants, with Muslims and Christians visiting each other's shrines and asking for both blessings and protection against evil.

There are mixed Muslim-Christian villages, but others in Upper Egypt are predominately one or the other. Coptic villages or neighborhoods are dominated by the local church bell tower, and church services in the countryside are separated by gender; men and women are separated by a screen, and children are with the women.

Christian holidays of Christmas and Easter follow the Eastern Christian calculations using the Julian calendar. Holidays are preceded by fasts, and Copts are required to endure long periods of fasts. The holiday *Sham al-Nasim* ("sniffing the breeze" in Arabic) is an ancient Egyptian festival to welcome spring and usually falls on the Monday of Coptic Easter. *Sham al-Nasim* is today a national holiday celebrated by all Egyptians, Christians, and Muslims.

Official persecution of Copts increased especially during the Mamluk period (1250–1517). Copts rose in a number of rebellions but, in 1354, the rebellion resulted in large conversions to Islam. Under the Ottomans, and later under the dynasty founded by Muhammad 'Ali (1805–1849), the position of Copts improved. Copts were allowed to serve in the military, and Copts were part of the Wafd Party that emerged to counter British colonial interests in Egypt shortly after World War I.

Copts are full citizens in Egypt and are subject to a few constitutional restrictions, such as the president of the republic must be a Muslim—and therefore, any position that can fill in for the president cannot be held by a non-Muslim. Butrus Butrus Ghali, a prominent Copt, served as Egypt's foreign minister under Anwar al-Sadat and was the general secretary of the United Nations. Until 2005, there were restrictions on the construction and repair to churches and monasteries that require the approval—and signature—of the president. The Egyptian government also recognized January 7, Coptic Christmas, to be a national holiday in 2002. Despite these government decisions, many Copts feel the growing tide of Islamic fundamentalism and believe they are subject to attack.

In January 2010, a Coptic service in Alexandria was the target of a bomb that killed 21 people, and letters were sent to Coptic churches in Europe telling them they were also targets for more bombs by radical Islamists. The Egyptian government, as well as security services in France and

Germany, went on high alert for the Coptic Christmas mass, and there was a large outpouring of official and unofficial support for the Copts. The Christmas mass was attended by a number of leading public figures and was fully televised on a number of Egyptian channels. In subsequent weeks, Egyptian television has carried a number of interviews with Coptic officials including Baba Shenudah, head of the church. The unity of Muslims and Copts, a long historic theme that was emphasized during the 1919 Egyptian uprising against the British, was evoked by the Egyptian government.

John A. Shoup

Further Reading

Abdel Sayed, Gawdat Gabra. *Coptic Monasteries.* Cairo: American University in Cairo Press, 2002.

Atiya, A. S. "Kibt." In *Encyclopaedia of Islam,* 2nd ed., CD-ROM.

Ayrout, Henry Habib. *The Egyptian Peasant.* Translated by John Williams. Cairo: American University in Cairo Press, 2005 reprint of 1963 edition.

Blackman, Winifred. *The Fellahin of Upper Egypt.* Cairo: American University in Cairo Press, 2000 reprint of 1927 edition.

Capuani, Massimo, Otto Meinardus, and Marie-Helene Rutschowscaya. *Christian Egypt: Coptic Art and Monuments through Two Millennia.* Collegeville, MN: Liturgical Press, 2002.

Carter, Barbara Lynn. *The Copts in Egyptian Politics.* London: Routledge Kegan Paul, 1986.

Hasan, S. S. *Christians versus Muslims in Modern Egypt: The Century-Long Struggle for Coptic Equality.* Oxford: Oxford University Press, 2003.

Insoll, Timothy. *The Archaeology of Islam in Sub-Saharan Africa.* Cambridge: Cambridge University Press, 2003.

Lane, Edward William. *Manners and Customs of the Modern Egyptians.* London: East-West Publications, 1989 reprint of 1836 edition.

Lapidus, Ira. *A History of Islamic Societies.* Cambridge: Cambridge University Press, 1997.

Meinardus, Otto F. A. *Two Thousand Years of Coptic Christianity.* Cairo: American University in Cairo Press, 2010.

Wakin, Edward. *A Lonely Minority: The Modern Story of Egypt's Copts.* Backinprint.com, 2000.

Creole

Creole, Krio, Métis, Mestico, and Colored are terms that refer to the peoples of mixed-race ancestry in various parts of Africa depending on the language of the colonial power, French, English, or Portuguese. In the case of Sierra Leone, Krio (English mixed with local languages) is also the language for 98 percent of its people, though only 300,000 or 5 percent are actually descendants of freed slaves brought by the British to establish Freetown in 1787. Numbers of Creole communities vary greatly. There are about 500,000 (2009 estimate) people on the Cape Verde Islands, of which 71 percent are of mixed ancestry. The Mesticos in Angola and Mozambique number over 600,000. The Cape Coloreds number 4 million, or 10 percent of South Africa's population.

Creole peoples originated with the first European encounters in Africa at the trade stations established along the Atlantic coast. The Portuguese were the first and arrived on the coast of Senegal in 1444, and in 1462, they established themselves on the uninhabited Cape Verde Islands, bringing slaves from Africa as laborers. The Portuguese established trading centers on the Senegalese coast, such as Rufisque and Portudal, which remained under the control of African kings. The Luso-African or *Lançados* (mixed African and Portuguese ancestry) population began as well as the spread of Catholicism. Later, under the French, a Franco-African community developed called Métis, important in the commercial life of St. Louis and later Gorée. French trade interests in Senegal were in the hands of the *signares* or grand women. In 1652, the Dutch established the Cape Colony at the Cape of Good Hope in South Africa, and in 1658, the first ships with slaves from Dahomey and Angola arrived. Slaves from Mozambique, Madagascar, Indonesia, India, and Sri Lanka, including a substantial minority of Muslims, came to the Cape. With the expansion of the Cape Colony into the interior, local Khoikhoi (**Khoisan**) were forced into indentured servitude. Dutch was the common language between these various peoples, and intermarriage between the whites and their slaves and freedmen evolved into a special community by the middle of the 18th century. As the historian Leonard Thompson notes, "As a result of these relationships, the 'black' population of the colony became considerably lightened, and the 'white' population became somewhat darkened" (Thompson, 45).

Both Sierra Leone and its southern neighbor Liberia were created by the British and the Americans as a place where freed slaves could return to Africa. Sierra Leone was founded in 1787 and Liberia in 1822; Sierra Leone remained under British control, but Liberia became independent in 1847, modeling itself after the United States. Settlement of slaves freed from illegal slave ships and of freed American slaves continued until 1865 and the Americo-Liberian identity emerged, which today includes 2.5 percent of the total population.

The cultural life of the different communities varies a good deal. Most are Christians belonging to the various denominations of the colonizers. Métis in Senegal, Cape Verdeans, and the Mesticos are Roman Catholic for the most part. In Senegal, there is an important Catholic shrine at Popenguine with an annual pilgrimage. Creole in Sierra Leone and Liberia tend to be Protestants and the Cape Coloreds are both Protestant Dutch Reformed Church and Muslim. The Muslim Cape community prefers to be called Cape Malay and do not want to be "lumped" together with the Cape Coloreds.

Creoles have often been better educated than indigenous peoples and have been able to hold positions not only in commerce, but also in politics. Métis from St. Louis and Gorée were represented in the national assembly in Paris following the French Revolution. Métis began to hold the position of mayor of St. Louis in 1778. In some instances, Creoles, such as the Americo-Liberians, were able to maintain power over indigenous peoples. Liberia's president Tubman granted women and indigenous people who owned property the right to vote in 1951. Samuel

Doe led a military coup in 1980 that ended Americo-Liberian political dominance.

In South Africa, Coloreds had been given the same rights as whites in the Cape Province, but with the rise to power of the Afrikaner National Party in 1948, Coloreds were subjected to the same apartheid laws as blacks. In 1956, Coloreds lost their right to vote, and in 1962, Coloreds and blacks lost even white representation for them in Parliament. In 1984, attempts by the South African government allowed Coloreds to vote again but for their own house, separate from the whites. Indians were also allowed their own parliament in an attempt to separate Colored and Indian South Africans from the antiapartheid struggle. Since the end of apartheid, Coloreds still feel marginalized by the ANC-dominated government, though now they have complete political freedom.

John A. Shoup

William V. S. Tubman (in center, with glasses), president of Liberia (1944–1971), in 1967. During his presidency, Tubman instituted universal adult suffrage. (Gift of William R. Davis, Jr., Monrovia, Liberia/Library of Congress)

Further Reading

Afolayan, Funso. *Culture and Customs of South Africa*. Westport, CT: Greenwood Press, 2004.

Ndege, George. *Culture and Customs of Mozambique*. Westport, CT: Greenwood Press, 2006.

Olukoju, Ayodeji Oladimeji. *Culture and Customs of Liberia*. Westport, CT: Greenwood Press, 2006.

Oyebade, Adebayo. *Culture and Customs of Angola*. Westport, CT: Greenwood Press, 2006.

Robinson, David. *Paths of Accommodation: Muslim Societies and French Colonial Authorities in Senegal and Mauritania, 1880–1920*. Athens: Ohio University Press, 2000.

Ross, Eric. *Culture and Customs of Senegal*. Westport, CT: Greenwood Press, 2008.

Thompson, Leonard. *A History of South Africa*. New Haven, CT: Yale University Press, 1995.

D

Dan

The Dan, also called the Yacuba, Mebe, Samia, and Gyo (or Gio), live in the border area between Liberia and Côte d'Ivoire and number around 350,000 in total. Most Dan live in Côte d'Ivoire with much smaller numbers over the border in Liberia. The Dan Maou and the Dan Kran are subdivisions of the Dan in Côte d'Ivoire and speak the same language also called Dan, which belongs to the southern branch of the **Mande** of the Niger-Congo phylum. The Dan are a farming people cultivating crops of cocoa, rice, kola nuts, peanuts, cotton, millet, and manioc as well as small livestock. The region they inhabit includes forest and savanna, giving them a wide variety of corps they can raise.

Historically, the Dan lacked any form of political cohesion until the 19th century when a common language and the preference to marry from within the Dan and not choose marriage partners from neighboring groups helped foster a sense of unity. Before the 19th century, individual villages were independent, and it was possible to rise to the chieftaincy through success in farming, hunting, and through lavish gift-giving, which was subsequently institutionalized into the *tin* ceremony. Social hierarchy was achieved through community recognition of hard work— and a person seeking such recognition needed to hold feasts and give gifts. Relationships between Dan villages also

involved lavish feasting and exchanges of gifts, which gave both leaders further social prestige as well as lessened tensions between communities. In general, the Dan have few oral traditions and no written record of their earlier history. They are, nonetheless, known for resisting Islamization efforts from the Kingdom of Mali in the 15th and 16th centuries. Even though they generally resisted the first efforts to convert them to Islam, the majority are Muslims today.

Even though the majority of Dan today are Muslims, they still have a strong attachment to their traditional animist beliefs. For the Dan, all people have a spirit called a *du*. When a person dies, part of the *du* will be reborn in a new person, but part of it will also remain in the forest joining the myriad of forest spirits. The spirits are not only in humans, but in animals too, and were created by their god *Xra*. Any activity needs the cooperation of the forest spirits, and it is necessary to give them a physical form. When a living person is contacted by a *du*, usually during the initiation period, he must give the spirit a form, usually as a mask the person then wears when in touch with the spirit. In addition to a mask carved by the person, he may also need to learn a special dance when using the mask.

Traditional Dan religion is complicated, and they have developed societies to deal with spirits. Since the 19th century, the most important and most wide spread of the societies is the Leopard, or *Go*, Society. The Leopard Society controls boys' initiation and serves to regulate Dan life, since it also is charged with maintaining peace. It is a secret society, meaning that only initiates may know what happens at a meeting, the format they take, and any other information about them. Boys, when initiated, are taken into the forest for three to four months and are taught the secrets of the society. The influence of the Leopard Society is growing among the Dan, but villages still today try to maintain a degree of local independence.

The Dan make a number of cultural items that have a ready international market. African art has a wide appeal, and the Dan make both masks and wooden statues, though statues are less common. Originally, the objects on the art market had ceremonial uses and the masks represented *du* spirits, but some were worn for simply village entertainment. There are a wide variety of masks, but they fall into two main groups. The northern masks are known for having fine features, high, smooth foreheads, eyes set in the middle of the face, and a smooth, brown finish due to being soaked in mud. Southern masks are less refined with protruding features, and the brown finish is rough, being brushed on vegetal pigments. Dan put on mask shows for tourists and are known for a number of masked figures that dance on stilts. In addition, Dan make objects such as ornamental spoons that are exchanged as *tin* gifts.

The Dan are now among the labor force in Côte d'Ivoire's cities, where they have a deserved reputation for hard work. Dan men work as lumberjacks, dockworkers, and domestic labor, where young people put the Dan belief in hard work to practice. They use their earnings to finance feasts and gift giving when they return home to gain social status.

John A. Shoup

Further Reading

Bacquart, Jean-Baptiste. *The Tribal Arts of Africa: Surveying Africa's Artistic Geography*. London: Thames and Hudson, 2002.

"Dan Mask Art History." http://www.rebirth.co.za/Dan_tribal_art_history_and_culture.htm (accessed December 20, 2010).

"Dan Tribe: People of Africa." http://www.gateway-africa.com/tribe/dan_tribe.html (accessed December 20, 2010).

Diola

The Diola, also known as the Jola, Yola, Dyola, or Diula, is among the largest ethnicity in southern Senegal, mainly concentrated in the Casamance region. Recent data shows there are 1.2 million in Gambia (10 percent of the total), 1.2 million in Senegal (4 percent of the total), and another 800,000 in Guinea Bissau, with other smaller populations in Burkina Faso and Mali. Their language belongs to the Bak group of the West Atlantic family of languages of the larger Niger-Congo phylum. Following the break up of the Kingdom of Mali, Malinke/**Mande** nobility gained power over many other communities less politically organized, including the Diola. Mande influence grew both along the Gambia and Casamance Rivers, where a number of states emerged with Mande and later **Fulbe** leadership over a Diola base.

The Diola appear to have been living in the region between the Casamance and Gambia rivers in early historic times and were conquered by the Malian general Tiramakhan Traoré in the 1260s, though the lower river basin remained outside of Malian control. Mali's system was generally to not replace local political authority, but to make it subject to the Malian king or *mansa*. There does not appear to have been any political authority above the level of individual villages in the Diola region, leaving more organized state building to the Mande, who emerged as local nobility. Numbers of Mande moved into both the Gambia and Casamance and settled in separate villages from the local Diola. The Mande language became that of the state, and Islam was associated with the Mande and later with the Fulbe.

In 1360, the Malian empire suffered from problems over succession and much of the western part broke away, forming the **Wolof**-speaking kingdom of Jolof, but the Mande ruled the region called Kabu (Gabu) and remained tied to Mali until the 15th century. In the 15th century, contact with European traders developed along the Atlantic coast, and the Portuguese established trading posts. It is noted that the term *casamance* is the Portuguese rendering of the Mande *Kasa Mansa* or King of Kasa, the name of one of the Mande kingdoms in the region. Between the 16th and 17th centuries, English, French, and Dutch also arrived and set up trading posts to purchase mainly slaves.

By the end of the 17th century, nearly 1 million Africans, many from the Senegambia region, had already been taken to the Americas. However, by 1801, the numbers taken from the Gambia/Casamance region were less than 1 percent of the enslaved African total. The Diola were among the people greatly affected by the slave trade, and a number of their words passed into American English via West African slaves, such as the term *nguba* for the American plant peanut, which passed into usage as *goober pea*, and the term *bangoe* for the neck of the three- or four-stringed, long-necked lute, which passed into usage as *banjo*.

The Diola, in general, differ from the other groups in the Senegambia area because they did not develop distinct classes. They have remained generally organized into independent village communities; however, in the Oussouye region, the Floup Diola developed a monarchy with a king who presides over religious festivals, and still does today.

The Portuguese in the 15th century brought Christian missionaries, but few Diola were converted to Christianity until the French colonial period. Today, a good number of Diola are Catholics, though those who were under the control of *jihad* leaders in the 19th century to the early 20th century converted to Islam.

Most of the Diola remained followers of their traditional religion or had converted to Christianity before the *jihads* of the 19th century. In 1843, the Mande allied themselves with the Muslim Fulbe of Futa Jalon in the Guinea highlands and launched out to defeat the Diola and bring them into Islam. In the 1850s, Muslim forces gained the upper hand in the fighting, which spread north to the Gambia under British rule. The main *jihad* leader Ma Ba Diakhu was not defeated until the 1860s, when he

People shop at a local market in the region of Casamance, Senegal. It was in this region that a primarily Diolan civil war was fought from the 1980s to 2004. (Torsius/Dreamstime.com)

was defeated by the non-Muslim **Serer** kings of Sin and Salum and their French allies. Leadership of the *jihad* south of the Gambia fell to Fodé Kaba, who was eventually defeated by the French in 1901. Although the *jihad* was primarily among the non-Diola peoples of the region, the Diola suffered the effects of the wars the most. A number of them living in the areas under *jihad* leaders converted to Islam, and today around 50 percent Diola are Muslims.

Following Senegalese independence, the Casamance region felt that it was not receiving attention from the national government, and a mainly Diola resistance movement grew. From the 1980s into the 2000s, a low-level civil war was fought between a local separatist group and the Senegalese government. The Diola opposition to the Senegalese state formed into the Movement of Democratic Forces of Casamance (MFDC) led by a Catholic priest, Father Augustin Diamacoune. The conflict was brought to an end in 2004 in an agreement between the government of President Abdoulaye Wade and the MFDC.

John A. Shoup

Further Reading

Baum, Robert M. *Shrines of the Slave Trade: Diola Religion and Society in Pre-Colonial Senegambia*. Oxford: Oxford University Press, 1999.

Collins, Robert O. *Africa: A Short History*. Princeton, NJ: Markus Wiener Publishers, 2008.

Ross, Eric. *Culture and Customs of Senegal*. Westport, CT: Greenwood Press, 2008.

Schaffer, Matt and Christine Cooper. *Mandinko: The Ethnology of a West African Holy Land*. Prospect Heights, IL: Waveland Press, 1987.

Senegalaisement. http://www.senegalaisement
.com/senegal/ethnies.html.diola (accessed
May 1, 2010).

Dogamba

The Dogamba, also called Dagomba or
Dagbamba, speak Dagbani or Dagbane,
which belongs to the More-Dagbanli group
of Gur languages of the larger Niger-
Congo language phylum. They are one of
the main ethnic groups in Ghana and number over 650,000, according to the official
Ghana Web site; but according to the Joshua
Project (Christian site), the Dogamba number over 836,000 in Ghana and in Togo.
The majority of Dogamba are Muslims,
over 90 percent, with a very small minority
of only 3 percent Christians.

The Dogamba state arose in the 15th
and 16th centuries following the collapse
of the **Songhai** after the Moroccan invasion in 1591–1592. The numerous dependent states such as the Gonja, **Mossi**,
Wolof, **Serer**, and Dogamba were able to
survive and took advantage to develop further trade with the Europeans on the
Atlantic coast. The Dogamba capital was
first located at Tamale, but in the 1600s,
the Gonja forced them to abandon the
western part of their kingdom. They built
a new capital called Yendi closer to the
border of Togo. In the early 1700s, the
Dogamba rallied, pushing the Gonja back
and remaining the strongest state in the
north of Ghana until the British defeated
them in the early 20th century. The
Dogamba were in turn forced to pay tribute to the growing power of the Asante
(**Akans**) and were tributary to them until
the British defeated the Asante in 1874.

In 1884, the Germans conquered Togo
and forced most of the Dogamba out of
what became their colony of Togo in
1914, and most sought protection in
British Ghana. Following the German
defeat in World War I, some Dogamba
have returned to Togo, where they form a
minority living mainly in the northern
regions.

The Dogamba are small farmers and
raise millet, sorghum, beans, and yams.
The traditional monarch, whose position
still exists today, is called the *Ya-Na*, and
he holds court in Yendi. Under the *Ya-Na*,
other ethnic groups have lived for centuries with the Dogamba and have, historically, shared the same rights with them.
The throne of the *Ya-Na* is a pile of animal
skins and is often referred to as the Yendi
Skin. Most of Dogamba culture and literature is oral; despite conversion to Islam,
they did not produce a large corpus of
written material in **Arabic** or in local language using Arabic script. Drummers
played the role of oral historians, and
drumming today is both an integral part
of the oral culture and of recounting the
political history of the Dogamba in the
legend of Tohazie or the Red Hunter.

The Dogamba follow a patrilineal
descent pattern, which goes well with the
legal rights in Islam. Older forms of matrilineal descent still exist in that a person's
social status also includes the status of
the mother. Kinship groups are important
as political positions, such as that of the
king, are inherited. In addition to the two
main feasts of Islam, the Dogamba also
celebrate several of their own feasts, of
which the most important are *Damba* and
Bugum.

The Dogamba king, the *Ya-Na*, still exists, though the northern region of Ghana is divided into seven administrative districts. Rights of traditional monarchs and recognition of traditional law were allowed, though with the central government being supreme and overriding local, traditional systems of rule. Despite internal conflict in Ghana and the extension of government rule in the country, traditional monarchies are recognized as are their rights to apply common or traditional law.

John A. Shoup

Further Reading

Collins, Robert O. *Africa: A Short History.* Princeton, NJ: Markus Wiener Publishers, 2008.

"Dagbon and Its People." http://www.ghana web.com/GhanaHomePage/tribes/dagomba .php (accessed May 10, 2010).

Olson, James. *The Peoples of Africa: An Ethnohistorical Dictionary.* Westport, CT: Greenwood Press, 1996.

"People-in-Country Profile: Dagomba of Ghana." http://www.joshuaproject.net/ peopctry.php?rog3=GH&rop3=102372 (accessed May 10, 2010).

Salm, Steven J., and Toyin Falola. *Culture and Customs of Ghana.* Westport, CT: Greenwood Press, 2002.

Dogon

The Dogon, also called Habé and Cadau, number between 400,000 and 800,000 and live mainly in Mali and Burkina Faso, with the majority found in the Bandiagara Escarpment in Mali. The Dogon speak 12 distinct dialects with around 50 recognized subdialects, which have been classified as belonging to the Niger-Congo phylum, though this is far from definitive. It may be that Dogon is its own language unrelated to any other.

The Dogon resisted conversion to Islam, and various oral histories of the Dogon state that they came to the Bandiagara Escarpment some 1,000 years ago from either north or west from areas under **Mande** control. They say that they were led to their current homeland by the snake *Lébé*, and when they arrived at the escarpment, they found an older population living there, the Tellum and the Niongom, whom they conquered. Some dispute this and believe that the Tellum were the original Dogon. Other groups arrived as late as the 15th century to escape Islamization and created the diverse and complex language situation of today's Dogon.

The Dogon have a rich cultural life that remained well protected in their isolation from the strong forces of Islam in the Mande-speaking areas. Dogon cosmology was first studied by the French ethnographer Marcel Griaule for over 20 years, starting in the 1930s. Making sure to get information from Dogon who had not converted to either Christianity or Islam, or who had been in long-term contact with whites, Griaule's research revealed that the Dogon had astronomical knowledge of the Dog Star, Sirus, as well as of other heavenly bodies that are not visible to the human eye. Griaule made no attempt to explain how the Dogon have such knowledge; but popular Western imagination has subsequently run rampant, including contact with extraterrestrials.

Traditional Dogon religion is animist, and there are totem spirits or *Binou* that protect

Dogon masked dancers participate in the Lébé celebration in Mali. This celebration is held once each year for three days and is popular with tourists. (iStockPhoto)

villages. Totem animals are not killed and their parts, including hides, cannot be used. *Amma* is the creator, and he is the focus of all other religious celebrations as well as having a yearly celebration of his own. The *Sigui* celebration is done in cycles of every 60 years. It is connected to the cycle of the Dog Star and can last for several years. It celebrates the death of the first man, Lébé Serou, and the time until man acquired speech. It is marked by dances and long lines of masked dancers that have become famous among tourists. Other celebrations include that of *Lébé Serou*, who was transformed into a snake. The Lébé celebration is done once a year and lasts for three days.

Traditional religion has a body of holy men or *hogon* who preside over ceremonies and make sure all is done properly. They are elected to hold the position and learn wisdom during a six-month period of near isolation, during which they are not to shave or wash. A *hogon* wears white, and his food needs are taken care of by a young virgin girl who has not yet had a period. At night, the snake *Lébé* comes to him and gives him the knowledge he will need.

The Dogon have a history of art, and theirs was among the first to be sought after by Western art dealers and collectors. Dogon masks are used in a number of ceremonies, including funeral masquerades. Dogon granaries are gender divided, and their doors are decorated with carved images that have become not only collectors' items, but an important source of money from the tourist trade. Dogon statuary includes ancestor figures often with raised arms connected to rainmaking ceremonies, and equestrian figures and carved house posts have found their way onto the world art market as well. Dogon-like art is now made not only by Dogon, but by other wood carvers and metal workers in Mali.

The Dogon are patrilineal, and the eldest-living male is the head of the extended family or *guinna*. Men are allowed to marry more than one wife, though today few have more than one. Women join the *guinna* of their husbands only after the birth of their first son. Divorce is considered to be a very serious step, and though it is possible, it is discouraged. Among traditional Dogon, divorce is decided upon after the participation of the entire village.

In 1860, the Dogon came under the control of al-Haj 'Umar Tall's Islamic *jihad* and then by the French in 1893, though the French did not defeat the Dogon until 1920. Since then Dogon have converted to either Islam (approximately 35 percent of Dogon are Muslim) or Christianity (10 percent) and the rest practice their ancestral religion. In recent years, Western interest in Dogon ceremonies and arts has brought tourism and needed tourist dollars. Tourist companies in Bamako set up group visits, and Dogon perform masked dances for them. Tourists are allowed to stay in Dogon villages, but most of these are eco-friendly and blend in with the local architecture of the traditional Dogon architectural style. Tourist development has become a much-needed source of income, but recent disturbance in Mali, starting in 2009 involving Al Qaeda militants, has greatly reduced the numbers today.

John A. Shoup

Further Reading

Bacquart, Jean-Baptiste. *The Tribal Arts of Africa: Surveying Africa's Artistic Geography*. New York: Thames and Hudson, 2002.

Bouttiaux, Anne-Marie. "Afrique Occidental: Comment tisser les couleurs et le sens." In *Costumes et Textiles d'Afrique: Des Berbères aux Zulu*, by Anne-Marie Bouttiaux et al. Milan: 5 Continents Press, 2008.

Calame-Griaule, Genevieve and Agnes Pataux. *Dogon: People of the Cliffs*. Milan: 5 Continents Press, 2006.

Doyle, Margaret, et al., eds. *Peoples of West Africa*. New York: Diagram Group, Facts on File, 1997.

Huet, Jean-Christophe. *Villages perches des Dogon du Mali: Habitat, espace et societe*. Paris: L'Harmattan, 1994.

Olson, James. *The Peoples of Africa: An Ethnohistorical Dictionary*. Westport, CT: Greenwood Press, 1996.

Scranton, Laird. *The Science of the Dogon: Decoding the African Mystery Tradition*. Rochester, VT: Inner Traditions, 2006.

Sidibé, Samuel, et al. *Le Musée National du Mali*. Bamako: Musée National du Mali, 2006.

E

Ewe

The Ewe live in the region stretching from the southern side of the Volta River in Ghana to the Togo Mountains in Togo and are divided into four main groups: the Ewe "proper," the Anlo Ewe, the Wtyi, and the Mina, which includes the **Ga**. The Ewe number over 2 million and are one of the main groups in Ghana. The Ewe speak several dialects of the Ewe language, and Anlo has become the literary language. Ewe belongs to the Gbe language cluster that also includes **Fon**; Gbe belongs to the Kwa family of the Niger-Congo phylum.

The Ewe originated in the border region between Benin and Nigeria and migrated to their current location in Ghana and Togo in the mid-1600s. Some Ewe remained in what is today known as Benin, where they form a very small minority. In 1784, the Ewe warred against the Danes, who established forts along the coastal region; but generally Ewe relations with European traders were fairly good, and the Ewe sold war captives to the Europeans as slaves. Great Britain abolished the slave trade in 1807, and the Ewe turned to other economic activities such as producing and selling copra and palm oil. The Ewe were divided by British and German colonial enterprises; the British established the Gold Coast in 1874, and the Germans established Togoland colony in 1884. During World War I, the Ewe were caught in the fighting between the European powers, and after the war, former German Togoland became a joint protectorate shared by Great Britain and France.

The Ewe are organized around lineages headed by the senior male. Land was seen as a "gift" of the ancestors not to sell, though in recent years with the penetration of cash-crop economies, land sales do occur. Leaders of a village's founding lineage traditionally hold political power, but a council of all lineage elders serves to help guide decision making. Colonial authorities ruled through pliant village leaders, and those who resisted colonial power were replaced. This upset the preexisting political structure, which allowed for the removal by their own people of leaders who were abusive of their power.

Ewe women play a major role in markets as do many West African women. They are wholesalers as well as retailers, and they hold a near monopoly over trade in many coastal ports. They deal in a wide variety of items, many of which are produced by men such as a woven cloth called *keta*. *Keta* is similar to the better-known *kente* cloth woven by the Asante (**Akans**). *Keta* is woven by men in narrow strips that are then sewn together. At first the cloth was white and blue, with blue being the only dye that they had access to; but, like *kente* cloth, other colors were available after trade with Europeans offered other sources, such as unraveling silk belts from Morocco imported and sold by Portuguese traders.

Aja

The Aja or Adja are part of the Ewe of southern Benin and Togo. Their language Aja-Gbe forms the foundation of the all of the languages between the Volta River and the Oueme River. Today the Aja number over 500,000 people.

The Aja split from the Yoruba in Oyo in the 13th century and established themselves in the Adja-Tojo region. The Aja, along with the Ewe and Fon, populated the Bight of Benin region, existing on a mixed economy of crops, mainly millet, fishing, and livestock. Because of the lack of good harbors, the Portuguese and other European traders did not bother with the area until the 1620s, when they needed sources of slaves. In the 18th century they spilt into two groups; one went south and became the Ewe, while the other established the Allada kingdom in what is today Benin. Allada fell to the Fon, and the Aja became a major source for slaves sold to European dealers of the trans-Atlantic trade. Newman notes that the Aja lost 3 percent of their population annually for a period of 40 years. The Aja intermarried with the Fon, who were eventually defeated by the French in 1893.

The Aja are mainly farmers producing crops of maize, millet, manioc, and plantains. The region they inhabit, stretching between the borders of Togo and Benin, is heavily populated and, as a result, many Aja have migrated to Nigeria, Ghana, and as far away as Guinea Bissau.

Voodoo is the traditional Ewe religion. The word "voodoo" is borrowed from the Fon word meaning "spirit." Voodoo gives life to all objects (animism), and powerful spirits of nature are able to inhabit the body of a believer during rituals and give the person incredible physical abilities. The Ewe are able to know which spirit is possessing a person from the direction the eyes roll (back or to the sides), leaving only the whites visible. Today around 50 percent of Ewe are Christians or combine Christianity with traditional belief.

The Ewe are also well known for their drumming. Ewe drumming accompanies dance, drama, poetry, and singing. Drums accompany religious celebrations such as those that contact spirits associated with voodoo ceremonies. A special aspect of Ewe drumming is a type called *halo*, which is a humorous exchange of insults between villages.

The Ewe were able to maintain a sense of group identity despite being separated between two colonial states. In 1954, they founded the Togoland Congress to push to unify the Ewe people and land. Some Ewe in Togoland voted to join Ghana, which became independent in 1957. However, the Ewe remain separated in two states that became independent in 1960, Ghana and Togo, and they represent about 40 percent of the population in Togo. In Togo, the political elite were mainly Ewe, and following independence, Ewe culture was used in an attempt to build a national culture. Ewe domination ended in 1967 when Gnassingbe Eyadema, a Kabre from the north, became president in a coup. The Ewe represent about 12 percent of Ghanaians and, although ethnic tensions have existed, such problems have not plagued Ghana as they have other African countries following independence.

John A. Shoup

Further Reading

Beckwith, Carol, and Angela Fisher. *African Ceremonies*. New York: Harry N. Abrams, Inc, 2002.

Bouttiaux, Anne-Marie. "Afrique Occidental: Comment tisser les couleurs et le sens." In *Costumes et Textiles d'Afrique: Des Berbères aux Zulu*. Milan: 5 Continents Press, 2008.

Giles, Bridget, ed. *Peoples of West Africa*. New York: Diagram Group, Facts on File, 1997.

Salm, Steven J., and Toyin Falola. *Culture and Customs of Ghana*. Westport, CT: Greenwood Press, 2002.

Stokes, Jamie. "Ewe." In *Encyclopedia of the Peoples of Africa and the Middle East*. New York: Facts on File, 2009.

F

Fon

The Fon are one of the largest ethnic groups in Benin and represent around 40 percent of the total population of the country. Fon are also found in Nigeria, and together they number 3.5 million people, with over 1 million living in Benin. The Fon language is closely related to that of the **Ewe** and belongs to the Gbe subfamily of Kwa of the Niger-Congo language phylum.

The Fon developed a powerful, centralized state perhaps as a response to European trade, which began in the second half of the 15th century. Fon society had been organized along clan lines, and each community fiercely guarded its independence. Some Fon communities had fallen under **Yoruba** control, but others were able to expand their own control over neighboring Fon villages. The result was the rise of a strong state with a capable military by the middle of the 17th century. The Fon state based in Allada was able to conquer much of the interior. Over the grave of a defeated local ruler in Abomey, the first king of the newly formed Kingdom of Dahomey, King Agaja, built his new capital city.

Dahomey quickly expanded and with the military's use of guns, its army was able to take the trading center of Whydah/Ouidah in the 1720s. Following a brief period of chaos caused by the shift in power from older states in the area, Dahomey emerged as the most powerful of precolonial states in West Africa. The early kings gained a reputation for large human sacrifices of captured soldiers of defeated armies who were executed at annual ceremonies. However, Dahomey became engaged in the slave trade, and defeated peoples were sold to European traders rather than sacrificed. The Fon devastated many nearby peoples; for example, the Aja lost some 3 percent of their total population in a 40-year period. The Fon involvement in the trans-Atlantic slave trade was so great that their area was named the "Slave Coast." The Fon absorbed a number of defeated peoples, which helped to strengthen their regional domination. The Fon of Dahomey were able to remain outside of European control until the French conquest between 1892 and 1894.

The Fon word *vodun* was borrowed into European languages as *voodoo*, and belief in this traditional religion based on powerful spirits remains strong. Around 50 million people in West Africa and among the African diaspora in the Americas practice some form of voodoo, often mixed with Christianity. Approximately 40 percent of Beninese are Christians, but 20 percent follow *vodun*.

The Fon are primarily settled farmers with a mixed economy of agriculture, raising livestock, fishing, and trading, which supports a dense population. The region is where the tropical rain forest belt is broken, being both north and south of the Bight of Benin, by light forest and grasslands, which allowed early exploitation by settled

A Guardian of the Night dancer in Fouditi, Benin. The Fon word Vodun became Voodoo in European languages and is defined as the faith that is widely practiced in Benin. This straw costume is believed to be home to the Guardian of the Night spirit and dances on its own during a voodoo ceremony. (Corel)

agriculturalists. The coast of the Bight of Benin was not conducive to early European settlements due to the fact there were few good natural harbors.

The Fon produce a distinctive cloth appliquéd art often called Dahomey cloth. The form began as religious banners, standards and flags for chiefs, and on chiefs' headgear and clothes. Today, the art is primarily done for the tourist trade, and there is a ready market for Fon appliqué outside of the country. Fair-trade shops in Europe and North America carry Fon appliqué of village scenes, folktales, and other representations. In addition, the Fon produce wide variety of small carvings and cast figures called *boccio* or *bochio* that are offered for sale at local markets and only take on meaning after being animated by a *vodun* priest or acquire weathering from exposure to the elements.

The Fon were conquered by the French starting in 1883 when they were able to take the port of Porto-Novo. King Glele fought to keep the coast from falling into French hands, but by 1889, the French had taken all of the coastal areas and, in despair, King Glele committed suicide. The struggle was taken up by his son and successor King Behanzin who, in a war between 1892 and 1894, was eventually defeated. Many of the troops used by the French to fight the Fon were Yoruba and other West Africans that caused intercommunal distrust until recent years.

The French used local chiefs to administer the territory starting in 1892, and the system lasted into the 20th century. In 1904, Dahomey was incorporated into the federation of French West Africa, but the federation was dissolved in 1958. Dahomey became independent in 1960, but the newly independent country was subject to interethnic problems, some of which stemmed from the French conquest of the kingdom in the 19th century. In 1972, a Marxist government came to power and changed the name of the country from Dahomey to Republic of Benin, named for the Bight of Benin, which was considered to be more politically neutral. Subsequently, the country has emerged as one of the most stable and democratic countries in Africa.

John A. Shoup

Further Reading

Beckwith, Carol, and Angela Fisher. *African Ceremonies*. New York: Harry N. Abrams, Inc, 2002.

Collins, Robert O. *Africa: A Short History*. Princeton, NJ: Markus Wiener Publishers, 2008.

Egerton, Robert. *Warrior Women· The Amazons of Dahomey and the Nature of War*. New York: Basic Books, 2000.

"Fon." http://www.africadirect.com/other/peoples/peoples.php?people=Fon (accessed February 14, 2010).

Giles, Bridget, ed. *Peoples of West Africa*. New York: Diagram Group, Facts on File, 1997.

Keim, Curtis A. "Africa and Europe before 1900." In *Africa*. edited by Phyllis M. Martin and Patrick O'Meara, 3rd ed. Bloomington: Indiana University Press, 1995

Murrell, Nathaniel Samuel. *Afro-Caribbean Religions: An Introduction to Their Historical, Cultural and Sacred Traditions*. Philadelphia: Temple University Press, 2009.

Fulbe

Fulbe (plural) and Pullo (singular) is the proper name of this pastoral people who specialize in cattle herding of West and Central Africa. Roaming the Sahel and the Savanna expanses, these nomadic cattle herders are named differently by their hosts or neighbors: Peul, Fula, Ful Fula, Fule, Fulani, Fellatah, and Silmiga, among others. Today, the majority of Fulbe are sedentary and live in more than 17 African countries, from Senegal to Darfur, and from Mauritania to Cameroon. However, the Wodaabe of Niger to northern Nigeria and Cameroon remain nomads.

Main Fulbe regions include Futa Toro and Futa Bhundu (Senegal), Futa Jalon (Guinea), Maasina (Mali), Sokoto (Nigeria), and Adamawa (Cameroon). The major Fulbe urban centers are Podor (Senegal), Labe (Guinea), Dori (Niger), Sokoto (Nigeria), and Maroua (Cameroon). The overall population of Fulbe and related communities is estimated at 35 million people.

Fulbe speak a noun-class language split into two dialectal areas; Pular (also Pulaar) is spoken west of the Niger River Bend, whereas Fulfulde extends east of that line; hence the Pular-Fulfulde compound name. UNESCO ranks it among Africa's top 10 languages for numbers of speakers.

A wealth of linguistic resources enables the continued renewal of genres in both the oral (myths, legends, tales, epics, proverbs) and written *ajami* (meaning written in their language using Arabic script) literature. They shape and proceed from the quest for beauty, knowledge, and understanding: a hallmark of Fulbe culture. Folklore masters, court poets (griots) and scholars tap them to carry on a vibrant cultural heritage.

Theories on Fulbe origins abound, ranging from outlandish and superficial to plausible and heuristic. They have been varyingly called "distinguished Semites," "negricized" Caucasians, mysterious Hamites, a lost tribe of Israel, 12th-century dynasty Egypt, or Dravidian descendants.

Fulbe civilization rests on four major groupings identified by their family names, Baa, Bari, Jallo, and Soo, which correspond to the four natural elements (earth, water, fire, wind) and to the cardinal points (north, south, east, west). In contrast, 'Haal-Pular are nonethnic Fulbe communities who speak Pulaar/Fulfulde. In Futa Toro, they have a dozen family names. Conversely, while retaining the four-tiered naming system, some Fulbe communities (Khasonke, Wasulu) speak **Mande**, not Pular/Fulfulde. Similarly, **Hausa** has assimilated the Fulbe (Fulani) elite in northern Nigeria.

The Fulbe population displays physical traits (skin tone, hair, facial features) characteristic of a phenotype. Pular/Fulfulde reflects awareness of the phenomenon, hence Fulbe consider themselves non-blacks and call their neighbors Bhaleebhe (blacks). Yet, despite some phenotype peculiarities, it is more likely that Fulbe are indigenous to Africa. Accordingly, the timeline of their civilization breaks down into four periods: Prehistory, Antiquity, Middle Ages, and Modern Times.

Fulbe prehistory is likely embedded in the domestication of cattle. The recent description of the genome of the cow shows that the bovine achieved a genetic switch 15,000 years ago. The mutation meant the processing of low-quality food intake into high-grade output (milk, meat). The taming of the bovine constituted "one of humanity's first leaps forward" (Anselin 1981). Subsequently, humans marched with the cow into civilization. Between 12,000 and 5,000 years ago, "Proto-Fulbe" participated probably into adopting this ruminant as a lasting companion. In effect, the Pullo and the cow bonded strongly and became interdependent. A dictum reminds that "the strength of the Pullo is in the bovine; if he loses it he will face distress."

Fulbe devotion to their cattle started in the Sahara, when that region was a watered land of green pastures. Fulbe were among the area's likely inhabitants. Ever since, the Pullo has stuck to the cow like a stick. As the desert advanced, they emigrated southwest, leaving behind engravings of their pastoral lifestyle and hints of their cosmogony. Archeologist Lhote (1959) was the first to associate contemporary Fulbe with his findings in Tassili n'Ajjer (Algeria). Amadou Hampâté Bâ and G. Dieterlen (2009, 1961) agreed and pointed to similarities between today's Fulbe pastoral rites and some rock drawings. However, since rock art predates writing considerably, its analysis entails guesswork and, hence, warrants caution. Thus, scholars have expressed reservation about Fulbe Saharan legacy. However, no refutation of the Bâ-Dieterlen-Lhote hypothesis has yet appeared.

The Bovidian period (4500–2500 BCE) sealed the connection between Fulbe pastoral society and cattle herds. Practicing cow worship, Fulbe believed that *Geno*, the Supreme Being, created the universe from a drop of milk. A pantheon of adjunct deities (*laareeji*) oversaw animal husbandry and partook with herders in the animals' well-being. Strikingly, millennia later, Muslim Fulbe writers Mombeya and Bâ and mystic Sufis would merge *Geno* with that of Allah, thereby acknowledging God's oneness beyond language barriers.

Moving in on the banks of the Senegal River, Fulbe eventually achieved a dual specialization, nomadic pastoralists and sedentary agriculturalists. Between the 5th and the 13th centuries, Fulbe rulers led the centralized state of Takrur (a.k.a. Tukulor) running a standing army, engaged in domestic slavery, and alternating between vassal and rival of the Ghana Empire. Takrur probably was the result of nomadic leaders (*silatigi*)

Imam or religious leader of the region of Boghe in the Futa Toro with one of his students reading the Qur'an in the courtyard of the Imam's compound. The Imam controls a number of mosques in the immediate area around the town of Boghe. (John A. Shoup)

and trailheads (*arbe*, sing. *ardo*) turning their power into a pastoral monarchy dominated by the herder-in-chief, the *Aga*, symbol of wealth, might, and wisdom. King Yero Jaaje was one such ruler in the ninth century.

In that period, Takrur rulers converted to Islam, which became religion of the court but remained unknown to rest of the people. Historical records indicate the presence of a Takrur Fulbe regiment in the **Arab** conquest of Southern Spain. At the peak of its hegemony, Takrur designated generically all sub-Saharan Africans in Arabic writings.

In the 13th century, Sundiata Keita, emperor of Mali, vanquished both Ghana and Takrur. Fulbe scattered throughout the region during an interregnum that took place with the rise of the Koli Tenhella Baa dynasty in the West. They also marched eastward, and by 1200 CE, they had arrived in Hausa country. Until circa 1600, these non-Muslim rulers controlled noncontiguous territories, from northern Senegal to western Guinea.

Beginning in the 17th century, Muslim Fulbe scholars launched an Islamic hegemony that placed them to the forefront of history in the western Sudan. The *Jihad*-driven movement began in 1625 in Futa Bhundu, Senegal. Then it spread out south, north, and east to Futa Jalon (1725–1896), Futa Toro (1775–1885), Maasina (1804–1865), Sokoto (1814–1908), Adamawa (1815–1909), and lesser dominions. The main leaders of these Sunni theocracies were: Karamoko Alfa, 'Abd al-Qadir Kaan, Sheyku Amadu, Shehu Usman dan Fodio, and last but not the least, Al-Hajj 'Umar Taal. Imitating the model of the Prophet

Muhammad, these priest-warriors mastered the intellectual (esoteric and exoteric) and the aesthetic dimensions of Islam. They proselytized and built empires. Theirs were stratified societies of aristocrats, civil community, castes, and captives. Critics have emphasized the practice of slavery under Fulbe hegemony. However, this should not negate the achievements of those leaders, who learned, taught, wrote, and upheld the spiritual and temporal duality of their rule.

At the peak of the Fulbe states, two great minds, Tierno Muhammadu Samba Mombeya and Usman dan Fodio, separately took Pular-Fulfulde *ajami* literature to new heights. Yet, Muslim Fulbe supremacy also significantly altered tradition by replacing indigenous nomenclature (people, places) with Arabic designations. Furthermore, narratives of Muslim rulers sought to give Fulbe an Arab ancestry. However, this view should be construed as a secular dogma of the ruling clergy.

"West Africa's master cattle herders," the Fulbe's material art and intangible culture stand out as original and universal. *Pulaaku*, the Fulbe/Haal-Pular cultural heritage, is acknowledged throughout the world. It builds on three successive—and overlapping—stages: nomadic, Islamic, and modern; and it emphasizes both material culture and intangible art.

Fulbe creation myths and millennia-old way of life point to a perpetual quest for enlightenment and wisdom, as expressed in verbal art, speech mastery, and abundant poetry. Hence, in the epic poem *Kaydara*, the journey of the hero, Hammadi, evokes the quest—pre-Christian and Arthurian—for the "Holy Grail," or to seek the unattainable.

Fulbe material culture yields a precious inventory: the "home-in-the-bush" and antique pastoral altar (*kaggu*), decorated calabashes, iron and leatherwork, pottery, carving, basketry, jewelry, indigo tie-dyed fabric, woven textiles, embroidery, photos, paintings, signature pieces by modern sculptors.

The intangible culture features deeply substantive—pastoral initiation texts, the "haunting beauty" of legendary tales and epics, European language authors and masterworks, the inspiring life of mystic (Sufi) masters, an esthetic Islamic liturgy and an articulate teaching system, world-famous musicians, *haute couture* celebrities, photographers, filmmakers, painters, etc.

Traditional Fulbe images are known worldwide. Fulbe popular art and caste products, namely cotton weavers, goldsmiths, and indigo tie-dyers, are the topics of field studies. Delange (1974) has compared Futa Jalon women's Phrygian hairstyle (*jubaade*) to a mobile (hanging art piece) by the American sculptor Alexander Calder.

The defeat of Maasina by the army of al-Hajj 'Umar Taal in 1865 preceded the European Scramble for Africa in the late 19th century. As elsewhere in Africa, Fulbe indigenous states successively fell under foreign rule. They splintered between British West Africa/Sudan and France's Afrique Occidentale Française. "Proconsuls" and "Rulers of Empire" organized the exploitation of the economy and the administration of the people to the metropolis' advantage.

The *Institut Français d'Afrique Noire* (IFAN) and the School of Oriental and

African Studies (SOAS) specialized in research, libraries, archives, and museums. Colonial ethnographers collected and published extensive records on Fulbe history and culture, which are stored in documents conserved by those institutions. Secondary, professional (*Ecole normale* called William Ponty) and military schools trained teachers, researchers medical staff, and junior officers. Colonial administrator Gilbert Vieillard championed Fulbe studies. After extensive fieldwork he published detailed ethnographic works. Upon his death on the front during World War II, Fulbe Ponty graduates from Futa Jalon formed an association to carry on Vieillard's legacy. Eventually, the group switched to partisan politics in Guinea, reflecting similar trends elsewhere. Its members were among the forerunners of the emancipation struggle that led to independence.

Pointing to the aberrant and violent nature of slavery and colonialism, authors argue that the independence series of the 1960s reversed Europe's Scramble for Africa in the 1880s. However, given the dismal postcolonial record, others object that independence has been as much a blessing as a bane. Nonetheless, Hampâté Bâ undertook the promotion of Fulbe—and African—oral tradition. Drawing on serendipitous fieldwork and privileged access to core pastoral initiation, he wrote *Kumen* (1961) with G. Dieterlen. Then, he composed the beautiful *Kaydara* (1969) and *Koodal* (1974) epics. Bâ coined the phrase "In Africa, when an elder dies, a library burns down." His tireless efforts earned him the moniker of "pope of African oral tradition." Cheikh

Hamidou Kane (1954) and scores of modern Fulbe writers followed suit. And artists (Sori Bobo, Hamidou Baldé, Ali Farka Touré, Baaba Maal, Oumou Sy, Cole Ardo Sow, Ousmane Sow) contributed significantly to Fulbe cultural revival.

Finally, Fulbe politicians participated in the inception and the expansion of post–World War II African nationalism. In 1963, Guinea's Telli Diallo headed the Organization of African Unity. Today, Mali and Nigeria have Fulbe presidents. Yet, like elsewhere on the continent, the economic prospects are bleak. Wrong policies and climate deterioration threaten the Fulbe way of life (*Pulaaku*). Consequently, various grassroots associations try to rise to the challenge, and on the Internet, dozens of Web sites publish Fulbe content. Last but not least, the Wodaabe face painting and male beauty contests (*jeerewol*) are a topic of educational literature and a mainstay of world tourism. It is a fitting tribute to the originality, vitality, and universality of Fulbe-Haal-Pulaar civilization.

Tierno S. Bah

Further Reading

Adepegba, C. O. *Decorative Arts of the Fulani Nomads*. Ibadan: Ibadan University Press, 1986.

Aherne, T. D. *Gude Ngara: Exploring the Dynamics of the Creation, Use and Trade in Guinea's Indigo Cloths*. Bloomington: Indiana University, 2002.

Al-Naqar, 'Umar. "Takrur the History of a Name." *Journal of African History* 10, no. 3 (1969): 365–74.

Arnott, D., ed. "Literature in Fula." In *Literatures in African Languages*. Cambridge: Cambridge University Press, 1985.

Bâ, Amadou Hampate, and G. Dieterlen. *Cahiers de l'Homme*. Dakar: IFAN, 2009; originally published 1961.

Boser-Sarivaxenivanis, R. *Woven Blanket: Fulani, Yuvaru, Niger Bend, Mali, Wood, White Dots, Cotton Patterns in Brocade Tapestry*. Basel. Birkhäuser Verlag, 1979.

Bourdier, J.-P., and T. M.-H. Trinh. "A Drop of Milk (Fulbe)." In *African Dwellings*, by J.-P. Bourdier. Bloomington: Indiana University Press, 1996.

Bovin, M. *Nomad Who Cultivate Beauty: Wodaabe Dances and Visual Arts in Niger*. Uppsala. Sweden: Nordiska Afrikainstitute, 2001.

Brain, R. "The Art of Fishermen and Cattle Herders." In *Art and Society in Africa*. London: Longman, 1980.

Brenner, Louis. *West African Sufi. The Religious Heritage and Spiritual Search of Cerno Bokar Saalif Taal*. Berkeley and Los Angeles: University of California Press, 1984.

Brown, David. "Scientists Unravel Genome of the Cow. Signs of Human Intervention Seen." *Washington Post*, April 24, 2009.

Brown, K. H. *Fulani Textiles: An Annotated Bibliography*. Bloomington: Indiana University Press, 1983.

Cohen, William. *Rulers of Empire: The French Colonial Service in Africa*. Stanford, CA: Hoover Institution Press, 1971.

Delange, J. "Fulbe Art." In *The Arts of the Peoples of Africa*. New York: E. P. Dutton & Co, 1974

Elsik, Christine G., Ross L. Tellam, and Kim C. Worley. "The Genome Sequence of Taurine Cattle: A Window to Ruminant Biology and Evolution. The Bovine Genome Sequencing and Analysis Consortium." In *Science* 324, no. 522 (2009).

Fisher, A. *Africa Adorned*. New York: Harry N. Abrams, Inc, 1984.

Gann, L. H. and Peter Duignan, eds. *African Proconsuls. European Governors in Africa*. New York: Free Press/Collier Macmillan Publishers and Hoover Institution, 1978.

Imperato, P. J. "Wool Blankets Known as Khasa, Woven by Male Fulbe Weavers." *African Arts* 6, no. 3 (1973): 40–47.

Johnston, H. A. S. *The Fulani Empire of Sokoto*. London: Oxford University Press, 1967.

Kane, Cheikh Hamidou. *Ambiguous Adventure*. Paris: Plon, 1961.

Kirk-Greene, A. H. M., and Caroline Sassoon. *The Cattle People of Nigeria*. London: Oxford University Press, 1959.

Kueper, K. *Fulani Gold Earrings: Kwattenai Kanye, a Selected Bibliography*. Washington, DC: Smithsonian Institution, National Museum of African Art, 1985.

Last, Murray. *The Sokoto Caliphate*. Ibadan: Ibadan History Series. Humanities Press, 1967.

Lhote, H. *The Search for the Tassili Frescoes: The Story of the Prehistoric Rock-Paintings of the Sahara*. New York: E. P. Dutton & Co., 1959.

Loftsdóttir, Kristín. *The Bush Is Sweet: Identity, Power and Development among WoDaaBe Fulani in Niger*. Uppsala: Nordiska Afrikainstitutet, 2008.

Loftus, T. Ronan, David E. Machugh, et al. "Evidence for two independent domestications of cattle ..." *Evolution* 91 (1994): 2757–61.

Fur

The Fur people gave their name to the region they inhabit in western Sudan, Dar Fur, meaning the home of the Fur. Their language, also called Fur, belongs to the Nilo-Saharan phylum and they number close to 800,000 people today. The Fur are divided into three main groups, the Kunjara, the Tunjara, and the Daju.

It seems the Fur have inhabited the central region of Dar Fur for millennia, centered on the Jabal Marrah highlands. They were subjected to the slow invasion of **Arab** tribes, especially of the Juhaynah Bedouin in the 14th century, and more recently by the Baggarah Bedouin. The area held by the Fur became more important with the further spread of Islam. The Fur held a strategic pass over the Jabal Marrah, which was used by both Muslim pilgrims from West and Central Africa on their way to Makkah and for the *Darb al-Arba'in* or Forty Day Road, the major trade route that linked Sudan with Egypt.

It is not known when Islam became established among the Fur, but archeological excavations of sites date it to the early 13th century. By the time of the founding of the Kayra dynasty in the 17th century by Sulayman Solong, Islam was officially encouraged by the rulers. The capital was moved to the town of al-Fashir, the southern terminus of the Forty Day Road, in 1791. The *Sultanate* of Dar Fur continued until it was annexed in 1874 to Egyptian Sudan after the death of *Sultan* Ibrahim bin Muhammad Husayn in a battle with the semi-independent ruler of the Bahr al-Ghazal al-Zubayr Rahmah Mansur.

By the 19th century, the majority of Fur were Muslims belonging to the Maliki *madhhab* or school of Sunni Islam. Islam and Islamic piety are important to the Fur and one gains social status with greater knowledge of the religion. Islam seems to have been spread partially by *fuqaha'* (singular *faqih*) or scholars of religious jurisprudence or *fuqara'* (singular *faqir*) associated to Sufi brotherhoods. Kayra rulers encouraged Islamic mystics as well

as those trained in al-Azhar University in Cairo to settle in Dar Fur and gave them land grants as an incentive. As the 18th and 19th centuries progressed, the capital city of al-Fashir was surrounded by such privately owned religious properties. However, most observers noted that the Fur have not totally given up earlier, pre-Islamic practices that have been preserved in belief in local spirits. Hilltop shrines are maintained by older women, and visitors leave offerings of flour and water. Other Sudanic practices still exist including taboos about blacksmiths and rainmaking ceremonies. In general, the Fur living to the east of Jabal Marrah had greater exposure to both Islam and the Arabic language. The Fur court became Arabic speaking in the 18th century and the border of Islamization and Arabization was marked by the mountains. The Fur to the west of them, the Birgid, Mima, and the Berri, have not yet replaced their own language with Arabic and practice a much more syncretic form of Islam and traditional African religion.

The Fur are settled peoples who lived in stone-built structures called *Tora*. *Tora* houses are a unique feature of Fur architecture, "usually built of dry-stone facings and rubble core and composed of multiples of round huts with flat roofs and surrounded by a ring-wall pierced by two opposite entrances" (Insoll, 129). A fortified town is a *fashir* and there are a number of *fashir*, but the Kayra dynasty established *al-Fashir or* the Fort as their capital city.

Fur were ruled by kings with a central state for some 2,000 years. There is some evidence both from written accounts in

Arabic and from archeological evidence of the concept of divine ruler before the general conversion to Islam. The Dar Fur state was based in the Jabal Marrah, a rough mountainous region that gave them a place to retreat to in times of political weakness and a base to strike out from in times of political strength. Dar Fur was ruled by the Kayra dynasty and in the 18th century, the Kayra *Sultans* were able to force a number of non-Fur to submit to their rule, among them the non-Arab **Zaghawa**, Masalit, Mararit, Birgid, and Tunjur, and the Bedouin Arab Baggarah, particularly the Rizayqat. In the middle to the late 18th century, *Sultan* Muhammad Tayrab ibn Ahmad Bakr was able to build a large (the size of France) multiethnic state and extended his authority over Kordofan to the east. To the west, he was able to impose a peace with the Wadai Kingdom in today's Chad. The conquest of Sudan by Egyptian ruler Muhammad 'Ali's son Ibrahim followed the course of the Nile. Subsequently, the Egyptian state's expansion followed the development of private enterprises, which expanded control over the inland areas. In 1874, the Fur *Sultanate* was defeated and the *Sultan* killed by an invading force of such Arabs under the command of al-Zubayr Rahma Mansur, governor of the Bahr al-Ghazal Province. Dar Fur was annexed by Egypt and al-Zubayr was appointed the new governor. When Muhammad Ahmad al-Mahdi rose in rebellion against Egyptian rule in 1881, many in Dar Fur were pro-Mahdi. In 1883, Dar Fur formerly fell under the Mahdi, though ruled by shadow *Sultans* of the Kayra dynasty. Following the defeat of the Mahdist state by Britain in 1898,

there was a brief attempt to revive the state under the last *Sultan* 'Ali Dinar. 'Ali Dinar was recognized by the British as an independent ruler, and at first his ability to keep the French in Chad was appreciated. In 1901, the *Sultan* tried to force the Arab Rizayqat to pay him tribute, as his Kayra ancestors had been able to do, but the *Shaykh* of the Rizayqat refused and in 1913 the Fur army invaded leaving mass destruction, but at Tumburko the Rizayqat defeated the Fur. In 1914, 'Ali Dinar joined with the Ottoman *Sultan* when World War I broke out, which made him a target for the British and their allies the French. He was eventually defeated and killed by the British in 1916 and Dar Fur was annexed to Anglo-Egyptian Sudan, though some of the western parts were given to France.

British rule in Dar Fur can best be described as one of neglect. Education was limited to the sons of local elites, and no real health clinics were available to deal with repeated epidemics of various diseases. Sudan became independent in 1956, and nearly from the start the state has faced ethnic, linguistic, and religious problems. The Fur were split between those who had tried to assimilate into the River Arabs, had education, spoke Arabic, and those who had been too isolated. Into the mix were added the Baggarah *Ansar* who supported the lineage of the *Mahdi* in the person of al-Sadiq al-Mahdi, Lybian ruler Mu'ammar Qadhafi, and the rivalry in Chad between the Zaghawa and the **Tubu**.

Fighting erupted in Dar Fur several times and in the 1980s, large-scale fighting killed hundreds, forcing more to escape

Sudanese refugees rest at the Gaga refugee camp in eastern Chad on February 13, 2007. Many Fur women and children have been displaced or killed as a result of the conflict. (AP/Wide World Photos)

into Chad as refugees. The Arab Bedouin Bani Husayn moved into Masalit areas looking for better grazing and in the end the Masalit resistance was crushed. An attempt was made to consolidate resistance among the Masalit, Fur, and Zaghawa, but old grudges brought the attempt to ruin. At the turn of the century, two major rebel groups emerged in Dar Fur by 2003: the Sudan Liberation Movement (SLM) and the Justice and Equality Movement (JEM), and both are seeking equal social, political, and economic conditions for non-Arabs. In the subsequent conflict, between 200,000 and 400,000 have been killed and over 2 million displaced. The conflict is also a result of years of drought and the movement of pastoral nomads, mainly ethnic Arabs, into

settled farming ethnic Fur areas. Armed militias of Arab nomads called *janjaweed* (a term among the Masalit originally meaning bandits) have been accused of atrocities backed by the Sudanese state and, since 2004, of cross-border raids into Chad. Sudan has over 2 million pastoral nomads who use much of the more arid parts of the country. Pastoral nomads are difficult for governments to control as traditional grazing patterns conflict with state borders.

John A. Shoup

Further Reading

Collins, Robert O. *A History of Modern Sudan.* Cambridge: Cambridge University Press, 2008.

Holt, P. M. "Dar Fur." In *Encyclopaedia of Islam,* 2nd ed., CD-ROM.

Insoll, Timothy. *The Archaeology of Islam in Sub-Saharan Africa*. Cambridge: Cambridge University Press, 2003.

Lapidus, Ira. *A History of Islamic Societies*. Cambridge: Cambridge University Press, 1997.

Lunde, Paul. *Islam: Faith, Culture, History*. New York: DK Publishing, 2002.

McMicheal, H. A. *A History of the Arabs in Sudan: And Some Account of the People Who Preceded Them and of the Tribes Inhabiting Darfur*. 2 vols. Cambridge: Cambridge University Press, 2010 reprint of the 1933 edition.

G

Ga

The Ga or Gamashie belong to the Mina group of the much larger **Ewe** people of Ghana, Benin, and Togo, who are closely related to the **Fon**. The Ga live along the Atlantic coast of Ghana and Togo and are mainly fishermen. The Ga number some 50,000 and speak Ga mixed with the Ouatchi dialect of Ewe, which belongs to the Kwa family of the Niger-Congo phylum.

The Ga are part of the Ewe people who, according to their oral histories, migrated to Ghana from Benin and Nigeria in the 17th century. The Ewe settled in different parts of Togo and Ghana and engaged in the slave trade with Europeans until trade was brought to an end in the 19th century. The Ga settled along the Atlantic coast near what became the border between Togo and Ghana, with most of them in Ghana.

The Ga became settled farmers, fishermen, and traders, with women taking the lead in marketing. Following the end of the slave trade, many farmers began producing copra for the market. Copra is the by-product of making coconut oil, and is mainly composed of the dried coconut meat. Small, home-based industries such as cloth weaving also became important aspects of the economy.

Similar to other Ewe peoples, Ga society is based on lineages, with each lineage governed by the eldest male. The Ga have been influenced by Christianity, and their funerals mix elements of the traditional belief system of the soul returning to God and the "personality soul" returning to the ancestral lineage. Recently, the Ga have become famous for their fantasy coffins. Expert wood carver Kane Kwei first created a fantasy coffin for his uncle in the shape of a boat so that when his personality soul arrived back with the ancestors, he could continue his work as a fisherman. When Kane's mother died, he made her coffin in the shape of an airplane because she was fascinated with them. Since then most Ga, and many non-Ga neighbors, have requested master carvers to make fantasy coffins in the shapes that are meaningful to the individual, representing work, interests, or stations in life. Kane Kwei died in 1992, but his son and nephew carry on the tradition.

In 1954, the Togoland Congress was formed to try to unify the Ewe land and people, but Ghana gained its independence in 1957 and Togo in 1960. The Ewe remain scattered between three states, and since the independence of Ghana, many Ga have left their homes to work in Accra and other major urban centers.

John A. Shoup

Further Reading

Beckwith, Carol, and Angela Fisher. *African Ceremonies*. New York: Harry N. Abrams, Inc., 2002.

Giles, Bridget, ed. *Peoples of West Africa*. New York: Diagram Group, Facts on File, 1997.

Henderson-Quartey, David. *The Ga of Ghana: The History and Culture of a West African People*. London: Author, 2002.

Olson, James. "Ga" in *Peoples of Africa: An Ethnohistorical Dictionary*. Westport, CT: Greenwood Press, 1996.

Parker, John. *Making the Town: Ga State and Society in Early Accra*. London: Heinemann, 2000.

Salm, Steven J., and Toyin Falola. *Culture and Customs of Ghana*. Westport, CT: Greenwood Press, 2002.

Ganda

The Ganda (in singular Muganda and in plural Baganda or Waganda) are a Bantu people, and are the single largest ethnic group in Uganda, numbering over 3.7 million people. Their language, called Ganda or Luganda, belongs to the interlacustrine family of the Bantu group. They represent 17 percent of Uganda's population, and small numbers of them are found in Kenya, Rwanda, and the Democratic Republic of Congo.

The Ganda migrated to the region around Lake Victoria in 1000 CE from Central Africa, pushing out earlier groups of **Nilotic** and Cushitic peoples. The Baganda prospered and were able to effectively compete with other lake kingdoms, particularly Bunyoro. The Buganda kingdom seems to have first been a tributary to Bunyoro, but in the 16th century, Buganda expanded linking into the trade in dried fish, bark cloth, sorghum, salt, iron, and bananas.

Baganda people developed both a food and economic base in bananas, and their population increased as a result, giving them an advantage over Bunyoro, and by 1640 or 1650, they were able to exercise independence from Bunyoro. Buganda kings or *Kabaka* struck out and expanded through the conquest of other peoples, which continued into the 19th century. Baganda belief is that the first *Kabaka* named Kintu unified all of the clans of the Baganda, and the honorific title of *Sasabataka* or Head of the Clan Heads was first given to him.

By the time European travelers first encountered them, Buganda was a strong, highly organized kingdom ruling the region that included Lake Victoria, Lake Edward, Lake Albert, and Lake Kygoa. When Henry Stanley first visited the court of *Kabaka* Mutesa I in 1875, Stanley noted the king could raise an army of 150,000 men and a war fleet of 325 canoes of close to 21.95 meters (72 feet) in length. Each vessel was manned by a crew of 30 men of rowers and a steersman.

Mutesa I needed to balance growing foreign interest in Buganda, and in 1871, the British governor of the Sudan for Egypt, Sir Samuel Baker, annexed "Equatoria" to Egypt. Baker was succeeded in office by a fellow British officer, Charles Gordon, who placed the Austrian convert to Islam, Amin Basha as governor of Egyptian-Sudanese Equatoria. Amin was also Gordon's emissary to Mutesa I. As Buganda became of more interest to a number of outside powers, Mutesa converted to Islam, but refused to be circumcised. He brought **Arab** and **Swahili** merchants and Muslim scholars to his court, but also allowed Catholic and

Protestant missionaries to operate. Mutesa died in 1884, and his burial place, Kasubi, has become a shrine to the Buganda kings as all following *Kabaka* are buried there. Upon Mutesa's death, his son and heir, Mwanga, was unable to prevent the civil war that began in 1886 between the Catholics, Protestants, and Muslims in the kingdom. By 1889, the Muslims were able to force all of the Christian missionaries out, but in 1890, the British were successful in forcing Mwanga to agree to a treaty that gave primacy to the Protestants. In 1894, Buganda, along with Bunyoro, Kitara, and Ankole, was unified into the British protectorate of Uganda.

The British were willing to work with the local system, and in 1900, the Buganda Agreement was signed, making the kingdom officially a province in the Protectorate of Uganda and reorganizing its territories into counties, each headed by a chief. In 1955, the second Buganda Agreement was signed between Britain and the Buganda *Kabaka*, which made him a constitutional monarch and his council or *Lukiko* became an elected body.

Since the time of Mutesa I, Baganda have converted to Islam, Catholicism, and Protestantism. Muslims represent 20 percent of the population, while Christians represent around 60 percent. The remaining 20 percent follow the traditional Ganda religion, which is one of the most elaborate in Africa. There are numerous spirits that are associated with places, such as trees, and each god and spirit has its own traditions and priesthoods.

The Baganda are settled farmers and raise a variety of traditional crops as well as commercial crops of coffee, tea, sugar cane, and cotton introduced by the British. Coffee is an African crop, and the tree did grow wild in parts of Uganda; the domesticated type was introduced in the 20th century as part of British agricultural policies. Most commercial crops are grown in the milder climatic zone, which is frequently compared to the English countryside with rolling green hills.

The Baganda are famous for the huge buildings they can construct out of wood covered with thatching. The *Kabaka*'s traditional residence rises to 4.5 meters (15 feet) in height. They are also expert basket weavers, and their baskets are now

A family of coffee farmers in Uganda begin to husk their coffee beans. Selling free-trade coffee is a way for Ugandan families to earn a living. (Brian Longmore/Dreamstime.com)

sold online along with free-trade coffee from Uganda.

The *Kabaka* ruled with divine authority and, though the Baganda are patrilineal, the kingship is matrilineal. The system allows all Baganda clans to have the chance at providing the next monarch in that the succession goes to a male from among the relatives of the principal wife. The *Kabaka*'s court was served by those who could prove their abilities as military commanders or administrative services, meaning that any one could rise to positions of power and wealth. The Baganda were attracted to education, and a fairly large middle class emerged as a result. The Baganda are highly educated and have come to dominate various professions, government offices, and the commercial farms.

When Uganda became independent in 1962, the *Kabaka* Mutesa II was made the first president of the country. This lasted until 1966, when the serving prime minister, Milton Obote, arrested and dismissed him. The subsequent riots by many Baganda did not result in his return, but instead, in 1967, all of the traditional kingdoms were abolished by law. In 1971, Obote was overthrown by a military coup by Idi Amin Dada, who began a reign of terror that claimed perhaps as many as 300,000 people. Idi Amin was driven from office by an invading army from Tanzania in 1979 after the economic and intellectual life of the country had been destroyed. Obote returned and was reelected president in 1980, but eventually he too was forced from office by Tito Okello, who was from the small Nilotic group, the **Acholi**.

Okello was also forced to leave office by a coup in 1986, and Yoweri Museveni became the new president. In an attempt to improve relations with the main ethnic groups in Uganda, in 1993, Museveni restored the four kingdoms in Uganda including Buganda. The *Kabaka*, Ronald Mutebi II, was in exile in Great Britain, and he came back to be crowned the new *Kabaka* in front of some 20,000 loyalists. The new king was crowned on Buddo Hill, near the capital Kampala, and is the site of the ancestral throne of Buganda. His official duties are to ensure the continuation of Baganda culture and ceremonies, development of agriculture and local development projects, and to maintain ancestral shrines.

John A. Shoup

Further Reading

Beckwith, Carol, and Angela Fisher. *African Ceremonies*. New York: Harry N. Abrams, Inc., 2002.

Ehret, Christopher. *The Civilizations of Africa: A History to 1800*. Charlottesville: University Press of Virginia, 2002.

Lewis, David Levering. *The Race to Fashoda: European Colonialism and African Resistance in the Scramble for Africa*. London: Bloomsbury, 1988.

Newman, James. *The Peopling of Africa: A Geographic Interpretation*. New Haven, CT: Yale University Press, 1995.

Otiso, Kefa M. *Culture and Customs of Uganda*. Westport, CT: Greenwood Press, 2006.

Gilaki and Mazandarani

The Gilaki and Mazandarani peoples live along the southern coast of the Caspian Sea in Iran and make up about 8 percent of the Iranian population. Their two languages, Gilaki and Mazandarani, although Indo-European and related to **Persian**, belong to a separate language family and are more closely related to **Kurdish** and **Baluchi** than to Persian. The language family is called Mazneki or Tabari, while the two localized languages are Mazandarani (in the Mazandaran region) and Gilaki (in the Gilan region). Gilaki is not only closely related to Mazandarani, but shares some other linguistic features with **Talysh**. Gilaki and Mazandarani speakers number close to 6 million in total when looking at the 2006 census of the two provinces of Gilan and Mazandaran.

Both Gilan and Mazandaran regions have long histories dating to before the establishment of the Persian Empire under Cyrus the Great (576–530 BCE). Both fell to Alexander the Great, and though local dynasties ruled in both regions, they were incorporated into the subsequent Parthian and Sassanid dynasties. The area fell to the **Arabs** in 644, who brought with them Islam. The Arabs called the area Tabaristan, and the division into Gilan and Mazandaran reemerged with the arrival of the Saljuq **Turks** in the 11th century. The people of Tabaristan had early leanings towards the 'Alids (the descendants of 'Ali ibn Abi Talib) and as early as 864 sent for a member of the 'Alid family to come to rule over the area. Various 'Alid dynasties ruled over parts of Mazandaran into the 16th century, and they were able to withstand the attacks by the Safavid ruler *Shah* Isma'il (r. 1501–1524), but fell to *Shah* 'Abbas (r. 1587–1629) in 1597.

Gilan was brought more directly under central government rule by the Ilkanid Öljaytü (r. 1304–1316) in 1307, but local dynasties were able to survive. The Hanbali and Shafa'i Sunni *madhhabs* dominated in Gilan, but Zaydi Shi'ism remained strong in eastern Gilan and in Mazandaran. It was not until the time of Safavid *Shah* 'Abbas did 12er Shi'ism come to dominate Gilan and Mazandaran regions.

Both Sunni and Zaydi Shi'ite Islam found favor among the people of the region, as had Nestorian Christianity in the centuries before the Arab conquest. The great historian Abu Ja'afar Muhammad al-Tabari was born in the city of Amul in 839 in Tabaristan and died in Baghdad in 923. He was one of the greatest scholars of his day. Several other Islamic scholars have the name "al-Tabari" and were either born in Tabaristan or are descendants of those who emigrated from there. The founder of the first organized Sufi brotherhood, 'Abd al-Qadir al-Jilani (1077–1166) was from Gilan. In Arabic sources, those who originated from Gilan are often called al-Jilani or al-Kilani (Arabic has no letter "g," and the closest are either "j" or "k." Persian, however, does have the letter "g".).

In the 19th century, Mazandaran was at the heart of the *Babi* movement, and in 1848–1849, it was the center of a Babi uprising. The Babi movement is an offshoot of mainstream 12er Shi'ism, associated with the notion that it would be possible to have a living person be the *bab* or gate to God, with special, spiritual knowledge. In 1844, Mirza Muhammad 'Ali declared that he was the living *bab* and later said that he was the *mahdi*, or spiritual guide, expected to come either to bring a renewal (in the role of the *mujaddid*) or to pave the way for the return of the Hidden *Imam*. His followers caused revolts in Iran and he was caught and executed in 1850. The father of Mirza Hussein 'Ali, the founder of the *Baha'i* movement, was also born in Mazandaran. The Baha'i movement developed from the Babi and has been able to survive despite persecution by the Qajars, the Ottomans, and subsequent governments in Iran. The current Iranian government has placed restrictions on the actions of the Baha'i, such as preaching to non-Baha'i Muslims. Those who can, have left Iran, and many have come to the United States, where there is a good number of Baha'i today, both of Iranian and non-Iranian origin.

Gilan and Mazandaran were both involved with the Bolshevik rising in Iran from 1920 to 1921 under Küchuk Khan. Gilan had an active Bolshevik movement as early as 1917, which briefly formed the Soviet Republic of Gilan. The Bolshevik risings gave the Cossack Brigade under the command of the Mazandarani Reda/Reza Khan the opportunity to overthrow the Qajar dynasty (1779–1925) and become the new *shah* of Iran as Reda/Reza *Shah* Pahlavi in 1925. The Pahlavi dynasty was overthrown by the Islamic Revolution in 1979.

John A. Shoup

Further Reading

Bosworth, C. E. "al-Tabari, Abu Djafar." In *Encyclopaedia of Islam*, 2nd ed., CD-ROM.

Glassé, Cyril. "Bab." In *The Concise Encyclopedia of Islam*. San Francisco: Harper, 1991.

Glassé, Cyril. "Babis." In *The Concise Encyclopedia of Islam*. San Francisco: Harper, 1991.

Glassé, Cyril. "Baha'is." In *The Concise Encyclopedia of Islam*. San Francisco: Harper, 1991.

Minorsky, V. "Mazandaran." In *Encyclopaedia of Islam*, 2nd ed., CD-ROM.

Spuler, B. "Gilan." In *Encyclopaedia of Islam*, 2nd ed., CD-ROM.

Gwari

The Gwari have a number of different names: Gbari, Gbarri, Agbari, Gwali, Gbagyi, and Gwarri Baris, though they tend to use Gbagyi or Bagyi more. The word Gwari seems to come from the **Hausa** word meaning "slave," possibly because the Gbagyi have a long history of persecution by both the Hausa and the Fulani (**Fulbe**). The Gbagyi live primarily in the Niger Plateau in the Niger State in Nigeria near the new capital Abuja. They are also found in Kaduna and other northern states in Nigeria. The Gbagyi language is part of the Benue division of the Niger-Congo phylum, though it is broken into a large number of dialects. They number around 700,000 people today.

The Gbagyi trace their origins to the region of Bornu, though not to the Bornu people who inhabited the region. They are divided into three main religious groups: Muslims, who make up around one-third of the total; Christians of different sects; and traditional animists. Most are still small farmers and did not form into a unified, central political state despite years of being raided by the Hausa and Fulani for slaves; however, slave raiding did produce a group Gbagyi identity.

With Nigerian independence, the Gbagyi have felt they were singled out for persecution when the new capital city of Abuja was built in 1991. Gbagyi were forcibly removed and settled elsewhere, which they see as part of the larger Hausa-Fulani conspiracy against them. Nonetheless, one Nigerian president has been Gbagyi, General Ibrahim Babangida, who governed from 1985 to 1993.

John A. Shoup

Further Reading

Falola, Toyin. *Culture and Customs of Nigeria.* Westport, CT: Greenwood Press, 2001.

"Gbagyi." http://www.ethnologue.com/show _language.asp?code=gbr (accessed May 10, 2010).

Olson, James. *The Peoples of Africa: An Ethnohistorical Dictionary.* Westport, CT: Greenwood Press, 1996.

H

Hadza

The Hadza or Hatsa or Hadzabe'e (also called Hadzapi, Kingiga, and Tindiga) and the Sandawe are the last members of the original **Khoisan** inhabitants of East and southern Africa. They are both small in population; the Hadza number less than 1,000 and the Sandawe number no more than 40,000. Both populations live near Lake Eyasi in northern Tanzania, where tsetse fly infestation prevented others from wanting to take their land until recently. The Hadza language does include a number of distinctive click sounds associated with the Khoisan group, but it seems to not share any other features. Sandawe language does seem to be a Khoisan language, and though the two groups have lived close to each other for a very long time, the two are not related.

The Hadza and Sandawe belong to the earliest populations that once inhabited the whole of East and southern Africa which, according to archeological record, emerged around 19,000 BCE. Generally identified as the Khoisan peoples, they were hunter-gatherers. Around 1000 BCE, Cushitic peoples pushed into East Africa from north of Lake Turkana and absorbed most of the original inhabitants. Only a few of the Khoisan peoples were able to remain as distinct ethnicities after the arrival of the Cushites, including the Hadza and Sandawe. Around 500 BCE, **Nilotic** groups also moved in and pushed

as far as central Tanzania. They were followed by the expansion of the Bantu, who arrived from Central Africa after 500 BCE.

Both the Hadza and the Sandawe have resisted changing their way of life and have remained hunter-gatherers. Frank Marlowe of Harvard University has studied the Hadza for a number of years and notes that between 200 and 300 remain foragers, gathering honey, hunting game, digging for tubers, and gathering baobab fruit, while the rest have developed a mixed economy that includes working on farms, for the game department as well as in tourism.

Hadza religion involves a set to general rules that when broken cause illness. The belief is that spirits cause a person to become ill (physically or mentally) and not following the rules can anger the spirits. The result is the spirit, in anger, sends illnesses to the person. The *Epeme* dance is their most important ritual, which is held on moonless nights in the dark. Men tell a number of "why" and "how" stories, which entail the Hadza cosmology. There are puberty rites for girls, which are held during the season when berries ripen.

The Hadza and Sandawe are under pressure from the Tanzanian government to settle and give up their way of life. As early as 1964, the Tanzanian government tried to force settlement, but by 1966, most of those who tried to settle had left after a number had died of different

Hadza tribesman hunts game in Tanzania, March 8, 2008. Many Hadza people remain hunters and gatherers to this day. (Rosaria Meneghello/Dreamstime.com)

diseases. Other settlement projects were instituted in 1979 and in 1988, where Christian missionaries have come to work. There have been few conversions, and the Hadza remain uninterested in the settlements.

John A. Shoup

Further Reading

Collins, Robert O. *Africa: A Short History*. Princeton, NJ: Markus Wiener Publishers, 2008.

"Hadza." http://www.ethnologue.com/show_language.asp?code=hts (accessed December 31, 2009).

Jenson-Elliot, Cynthia. *Indigenous Peoples of Africa: East Africa*. San Diego, CA: Lucent Books, Inc., Gale Group, 2002.

Marlowe, Frank. *The Hadza: Hunter-Gatherers of Tanzania*. Berkeley: University of California Press, 2010.

Marlowe, Frank. "Why the Hadza Are Still Hunter-Gatherers." In *Ethnicity, Hunter-Gatherers, and the "Other": Association or Assimilation in Africa*, edited by Sue Kent. Washington, DC: Smithsonian Institution Press, 2002.

Newman, James. *The Peopling of Africa: A Geographic Interpretation*. New Haven, CT: Yale University Press, 1995.

Haratin

The Haratin are a social class, often seen as a caste (though this is subject to a good deal of debate), found in most of the oases in the Sahara. The Haratin have no language or special cultural practices different from that of the peoples who dominate them; thus, they speak Arabic or **Berber**, depending on which is the main culture around them. It is difficult to have an accurate count of their numbers as well because they can be either considered to be either **Arabs** or Berbers.

The origin and meaning of the name *Haratin* (singular *Hartani*) is controversial, as some say that it comes from the Berber term *Ahardan*, meaning dark or black. Others claim it comes from the Arabic phrase *al-Hurr al-Thani* or second class (second group of free people), though neither of these claims have much proof. Still others note that, in some Arabic dialects, the term is used to mean a horse of mixed breed or "wild" uncultivated land Both reflect the fact that Haratin are dark and that though they are technically free, their traditional social status was more like that of a serf in medieval Europe. Haratin share the culture and social practices of those who own their labor. In some of the oases in Jabal Bani or Anti Atlas Mountains in southern Morocco, Haratin in the same oasis can be either "Arab" or "Berber" depending on whose land they work.

Haratin origins may be traced to the Neolithic period when the Sahara was inhabited by a number of black-skinned peoples engaged in farming and animal husbandry. When the Sahara began to dry up, people were forced to find water, and the Haratin most likely were those who developed the oases resources and could be the same stock as the **Bafur** of Mauritania or perhaps the

Fulani/**Fulbe** of Senegal and Mali. They were first dominated by the Saharan Berbers. Then the Arabization and Islamization of North Africa brought about a similar change in their ethnolinguistic identity. In either case, whether dominated by Berbers or Arabs, the Haratin remained a servile people without rights to buy or inherit land or water until the end of the colonial period.

Haratin in some places include the descendants of freed slaves as well as those who descend from the original peoples of the oases. Many people think that Haratin means freed slaves, but this is not fully accurate. In the oases, both Haratin and *'Abid* (slaves) belong to the social classes defined as "not free to own land," and those slaves who were freed joined the ranks of the Haratin. Unlike the Haratin in Morocco, Algeria, and Tunisia, the Haratin in Mauritania have a stronger separate sense of identity. Though culturally part of the dominant Hassani culture speaking Hassani Arabic, they have their own songs, dances, and distinctive names.

During the colonial period, Haratin took advantage of educational opportunities, and following independence of North African countries, many migrated for work out of the oases to major cities or to Europe. Many have become financially successful, but they have not been accepted as social equals by their former employers no matter how wealthy they may have become. Despite national laws that allow them to buy, own, and inherit lands, they are still locked out of these rights in most of the oases, where all land is privately owned. Haratin in Mauritania have become politically active and, in the presidential elections in 2009, two of the candidates were Haratin.

John A. Shoup

Further Reading

Colin, G. S. "Haratin." In *Encyclopaedia of Islam*, 2nd ed., CD-ROM.

Du Puigaudeau, Odette. *Arts et coutumes de Maures.* Paris: Ibis Press, 2002.

Norris, H. T. "Muritaniya." In *Encyclopaedia of Islam*, 2nd ed., CD-ROM.

Vérité, Monique. *Odette du Puigaudeau et Marion Sénones: Memoire du Pays Maure 1934–1960.* Paris: Ibis Press, 2000.

Hausa

Spread across West Africa, the Hausa-speaking people had one of the most ancient civilizations in sub-Saharan Africa. The largest population of the Hausa can be found in the northern part of modern-day Nigeria, where with their historical rival, the Fulanis, they constitute more than 50 percent of the population of 140 million people. The population of native Hausa itself is put at around 15–20 million people. The Hausa are also found in significant numbers in northern Ghana, Niger, and Benin republic. Classified as being in Afro-Asiatic language group, the name Hausa refers to seven subethnic groups that are united by one language. These seven Hausa ethnic groups are located in the ancient states of Kano, Gobir, Zaria (Zazzau), Biram, Daura, Katsina, and Rano. Under 'Uthman dan Fodio (also known as Shehu Usman Dan Fodio), the **Fulbe** radical Muslim cleric, the traditional rulers of the Hausa states (Habe dynasties) were replaced by rulers of Fulbe origin, most of whom had migrated northeast from the Futa Jalon valley. With the destruction of the ancient Hausa states, the Sokoto Caliphate was established by Fulbe warriors, and 'Uthman dan Fodio soon became ruler, incorporating into his area of influence the remaining 15 Hausa principalities (emirates) including Zaria and Katsina.

Myths of early origin, like the **Yorubas**, centered on a single ancestor, Bayajidda, who like Oduduwa, the proclaimed ancestor of the Yorubas of Southeast Nigeria, came from the Middle East, probably Mecca. Bayajidda was believed to have married the daughter of the queen of Daura, whom she had saved from a sacred snake. Between them, they had seven children who eventually became the kings of the seven pre-Islamic Hausa states, mentioned above, around 500–700 CE. In pre-Islamic Hausa, the practice of traditional religion was widespread. However, the entire Hausaland was soon to be converted to Islam through the efforts of the Fulbe Jihadist, 'Uthman dan Fodio. Before 'Uthman dan Fodio brought his brand of Islam to Hausaland, many parts of the ancient civilization had already been converted to Islam as early as the 12th century. Old Hausaland was part of the Kanem-Bornu Empire, the last empire of the Western Sudanic Empires, located around the Lake Chad region. Native Hausa-speaking people, who claimed blood relations to the **Kanuri** people of the Old Bornu Empire, founded the majority of the Hausa states. The states in old Hausaland were of two distinct groups. The first group was the Hausa Bokwoi states, and the second group was the

Hausa "Bonza" states, each comprising of distinct ethnic groupings. The Bokwoi states comprised of lesser tributary states of Daura, Gobri, Zaria, Katsina, Kano, Rano, and Bilma, while the Hausa "Bonza" states comprised of Ilorin, Yauro, Jukum or Karorofa, Zamfara, Nupe, and Yuri. By the turn of the 19th century, most of these states had been converted to Islam and were ruled under Islamic civil and penal codes.

Considered a pagan state, most subjects of the old Hausaland were traditional worshipers of idols who fought vigorously against conversion to Islam. Early attempts by Islamic scholars to propagate Islam in Hausaland failed because of the traditional belief among Hausa people that equated the authority of their chiefs to those of the ancestors. In many instances, paganism was widely embraced by several Hausa lesser states whose rulers were able to keep Muslim preachers at bay. However, by the late 18th century, a significant population of Fulbe-speaking people had migrated to Hausaland where they lived under the magnanimity of Hausa rulers who chose to maintain friendly relations with the Islamic community. One of those Fulbes who migrated to Hausaland was 'Uthman dan Fodio, whose family migrated to Hausaland from the lower part of Futa Jalon, where they settled among the growing Fulbe speakers around the Gobri area. As a young man, 'Uthman dan Fodio took up Qur'anic studies under the direction of leading scholars in Gobir. But his emphasis on the second *jihad* in his Friday's sermons caught the attention of **Tuareg** Muslims, who were soon to form the bulk of his holy warriors.

In an attempt to suppress 'Uthman dan Fodio's militancy, the *Sultan* of Gobir mounted an attack on his followers with the sole purpose of eliminating him and his Qadiriyah (a Sufi brotherhood) views from the *Sultanate* of Gobir. But he failed to displace 'Uthman dan Fodio and his followers. Henceforth, 'Uthman declared himself the new ruler of the Emirate of Sokoto appointing his son in-law (the husband of his first daughter, Nana Asmau) as the *Waziri* (war commander), and his brother, Abdulahi, as the *Galadima*. From the Emirate of Sokoto, Uthman was able to pursue his ambition of converting nonbelievers in Hausaland, and beyond, to Islam. By 1807, most parts of Hausaland had been converted to radical Islam.

Muslim woman from the Hausa people wears a modesty garb called a Ijbab or hijab. (Smandy/Dreamstime.com)

Unlike their Yoruba and **Igbo** neighbors to the south, Hausaland is highly centralized with a remarkable degree of social stratification. Occupational mobility is limited, and social position in the Hausa society is largely determined by birth and wealth. The Hausas are organized into patrilineal groups and marriage type is exogamous, meaning that one has to marry outside of one's clan. Endogamous or in-group marriage is absolutely forbidden. Like the Yorubas, the Hausa (either Muslim or pagan) are polygamous, and a man is allowed to marry more than one wife. The basic family unit is the compound comprising of patrilocal extended family. Once a male child is married, he is expected to bring his wife to his father's compound, where he is allocated a living quarter (a small hut). The patriarch of the compound is usually the eldest male member, most often the grandfather, who wields unbridled authority and power over all members of the unit. In Islamic Hausaland, gender segregation is the norm and women are often restricted into the remote corners of the compound where they are only accessible to their husbands. Visiting members of other clans, and other unrelated male siblings, are strictly forbidden from the female quarter. Amongst Muslim Hausa women, the wearing of *Ijbab* (*hijhab* in Arabic meaning head scarf) is common, and they must cover their bodies to avoid notice by men. In some instances, a Muslim wife must be accompanied to the market by a male member of the compound, most often the husband's brother. A woman can be stoned to death for committing adultery, while a man who engaged in sexual intercourse with another man's wife could be subject to public be-heading or flogging.

Hausaland has a very complex and centralized system of governance. At the apex of power is the emir, who is selected from amongst the royal princes by the council of *Mullah*s or *Mallamai*, in Hausa language. These are Islamic clerics who based their choice not on age but on the commitment to Islam, and rights of origin. The emirs, because of their royal and lineage connections, wield absolute power over the subjects under their jurisdiction. They are responsible for both civil and judicial administration with the support of the *Waziri*s and *Galadima*, who are both in charge of native administration and military service. As a result of the accommodation with the British rulers at the onset of colonial administration, the northern protectorate was allowed to maintain its Muslim law or *Shari'ah* code under which citizens are tried following the procedure laid down in both the Qur'an and the Hadith, the two most important documents of the Islamic religion. At the village level, the chiefs are responsible for local administration and are responsible for the collection of tributes or taxes (corvee). The majority of Hausa-speaking people are either pastoralists or farmers, and their surplus produce is extracted to support the elaborate system of fiefdom. The chiefs are also responsible for the task of sanitation, maintenance of a civil defense force, and recruitment of young men for military service within the emirate.

In 1914, the northern protectorate (Hausaland) was merged with the three other British protectorates in the south (East,

West, and Lagos protectorates) to form modern Nigeria. In 1960, Nigeria became independent from British rule, and the first elected president of the federation was Alhaji (Sir) Abubarka Tafawa Balewa, a Hausa politician; while another Hausa, Alhaji Ahmadu Bello, one of the descendants of Uthman dan Fodio, became the first governor of Hausaland. Unfortunately, both were killed in the bloody military coup of 1966, which eventually led to the prolonged civil war that lasted from 1967 to 1970. Both Sir Tafawa Balewa and his Royal Highness, Alhaji Ahmadu Bello, the *Sardauna* of Sokoto, were champions of Nigerian freedom from British rule, and they are both remembered today as great historical figures in Hausaland. Most of the political authorities of the emirs have now been replaced by a regional civil administration headed by an elected state governor.

Pade Badru

Further Reading

Adamu, M. *The Hausa Factor in West African History.* Ibadan: Oxford University Press, 1978.

Badru, P. *Imperialism and Ethnic Politics in Nigeria, 1960–1996.* Trenton, NJ: Africa World Press, 1998.

Badru, P. *The Spread of Islam in West Africa: Colonization, Globalization and the Emergence of Fundamentalisms.* New York: Edwin Mellen Press, 2006.

Barkindo, B. M. "Growing Islamicism in Kano City since 1970: Causes, Firms and Implications." In *Muslim Identity and Social Change in Sub-Saharan Africa*, edited by L. Brenner. Bloomington: Indiana University Press, 1993.

Bruce-Lockhart., James R., ed. *Clapperton in Borno: Journals of the Travels of Lieutenant Hugh Clapperton, R. N, from January 1823 to September 1824.* Cologne: Westafrikannisce studdien 12, Cologne. Rudiger Koppe, Verlag, pp. 239, DEM 52, 1966.

Bruce-Lockhart, J., and Wright, John (eds.). *Difficult and Dangerous Roads: Hugh Clapperton's Travels in Sahara and Fezzan (1822–25).* London: Sickle Moon Books, 2000.

Clapperton, H. *Journal of a Second Expedition into the Interior of Africa from the Bight of Benin to Soccatoo.* Philadelphia: Carey: Lea and Carey, 1829.

Clapperton, H. *Into the Interior of Africa: Record of the Second Expedition 1925–1927*, edited by Jamie Bruce Lockhart and Paul Lovejoy. Leiden: Koninklyjke Brill N.V, 2005.

Greenberg, Joseph H. "Islam and Clan Organization among the Hausa." *Southwestern Journal of Anthropology* 3 (1947): 193–211.

Hisket, M. *The Sword of the Truth: The Life and Times of Shehu Usman Dan Fodio.* New York: Oxford University Press, 1973.

Jibrin, I. "Religion and Political Turbulence in Nigeria." *Journal of Modern African Studies* 29, no. 1 (March 1991): 115–36.

Last, M. *The Sokoto Caliphate.* London: Routledge, 1967.

Loimer, R. *Islamic Reform and Political Change in Northern Nigeria.* Evanston, IL: Northwestern University Press, 1977.

Mabera, Y. H. *The Islamic Shari'ah Law in the Light of the Bible.* Lagos, Nigeria: Al-Balagh Press, 1999.

Miles, W. F. S. *Hausaland Divided: Colonialism and Independence in Nigeria and Niger.* Ithaca, NY, and London: Cornell University Press, 1994.

Shaw, Flora L. *A Tropical Dependency: An Outline of the Ancient History of the Western Soudan with an Account of the Modern Settlement of Northern Nigeria.* London: J. Nisbet & Co., 1905.

Smith, Michael G. *The Economy of Hausa Communities of Zaria*. London: Her Majesty's Stationary Office, 1955.

Herero

The Herero and related peoples are among the main ethnic groups in Namibia and represent about 7 percent of the total population, or about 100,000 people. The Herero, Himba or Ovahimba, Tijimba, and Mbanderu all speak a common language usually called Herero. The Herero language belongs to the western branch of the Bantu family and seems to have linguistic connections to the **Ovambo** and the **Luba-Lunda** of central Africa.

The Herero and other related peoples raised cattle and migrated from around the Lakes Region of Central Africa in southern Zambia in the 16th century. During their migration, the Herero abandoned agriculture and concentrated on cattle as their main economic base. Initially, they were able to push the **Khoisan** peoples they encountered out of the grazing areas of the Namibian Highlands until they met the Nama Khoikhoin, who were able to access guns from European traders in the Cape Colony. Herero expansion was halted and they even lost some lands to the Nama. Their rather isolated location allowed them to escape enslavement by **Arabs** and **Swahili** from East Africa or Portuguese from Angola. They were not contacted by Europeans until the end of the 19th century, when Germany took the area as part of their colony Südwest Afrika.

The Herero are patrilineal and were either nomadic or seminomadic pastoralists. As a result, their settlement pattern tended to be small, extended family units called *ozonganda* rather than the large intense settlements of agriculturalists. The *ozonganda* is headed by a male and his wives, children, and his unmarried sisters live in it. Cattle play a major role in Herero life and are the measure of a man's wealth. Large herds are common and one man may own over 1,000 head of animals. Herero, like other cattle people in Africa, generally did not eat their animals, but today many are commercial livestock producers.

Following the rinderpest plague and conflict with the Germans, most of their cattle either were lost to the Europeans or died of disease. Cattle formed the basis of their traditional religion, and without their cattle, many Herero converted to Christianity. In addition, cattle lost their sacredness, opening the way for commercial ranching. The Himba are the only part of the Herero who have maintained their cultural purity and represent the traditional belief system. The Himba are well known for their leather and metal bead items, especially of jewelry, which has become an item of tourist interest.

The Herero resisted German control, and in 1904 to 1905, they rose in a bloody revolt that resulted in the death of 75 percent of the Herero people. War began over land rights and Germany's General Lothar von Trotha's strategy was to not only defeat them, but to exterminate them. He drove the Herero into the desert and denied them access to water. Those who were captured were put in concentration camps. To further the defeat of the people, captured women were forced to remove

A Herero woman with her child wears a traditional Herero headdress. This style was adopted from German colonial women in the 1890s. (Shutterstock)

in women's clothes, which were an adaption of what was worn by German colonial women of the 1890s. It consists of a long dress or skirt reaching to below the ankles, a high-buttoned shirt or top with long sleeves and a headdress made of cloth that comes to two side points looking a bit like horns. The Herero played a major role in the founding of the South West People's Organization (SWAPO), which fought for Namibian independence. Once Namibia gained independence, Herero have pushed the Germans for compensation for the 1904–1905 genocide, and though the German government did offer a public apology in 2004, they have refused to pay any compensation. In 2008, the Namibian ambassador to Germany demanded the return of Herero skulls collected by German institutions during the 1904–1905 war.

John A. Shoup

the flesh from the skulls of those killed so they could be shipped back to Germany for scientific purposes. Those who could, fled across the border into British-controlled Bechuanaland (modern Botswana) where they survived by hiring themselves out as farm laborers mainly on Batswana-owned farms. The Himba in their remote isolation were left more or less undisturbed until recent decades, when their pastoral lifestyle was intruded upon by Namibian resistance groups.

In the 1920s, a form of Herero "nationalism" developed in the creation of a "national" dress as well as in political terms. National Herero dress is best seen

Further Reading

Beckwith, Carol, and Angela Fisher. *African Ceremonies*. New York: Harry N. Abrams, Inc., 2002

Collins, Robert O. *Africa: A Short History*. Princeton, NJ: Markus Wiener Publishers, 2008.

Gewald, Jan-Bart. *Herero Heros: Socio-Political History of the Herero of Namibia*. Athens: Ohio University Press, 1999.

"Herero." http://www.flw.com/languages/herero.htm (accessed May 28, 2010).

"The Herero People: An Overview of Namibia's Population." http://www.namibian.org/travel/namibia/population/herero.htm (accessed May 28, 2010).

Newman, James. *The Peopling of Africa: A Geographic Interpretation*. New Haven, CT: Yale University Press, 1995.

Sarkin-Hughes, Jeremy. *Colonial Genocide and Reparation Claims in the 21st Century:*

The Socio-Legal Context of Claims under International Law by the Herero against Germany for the Genocide in Namibia, 1904–1908. Westport, CT: Praeger, 2008.

Zimmerman, Andrew. *Anthropology and Antihumanism in Imperial Germany.* Chicago: University of Chicago Press, 2001.

Hutu

The Hutu, also known as Abahutu, Bahutu, and Wakhutu, comprise the majority population of both Rwanda and Burundi, numbering over 6 million people or 85 percent of the population of both countries. The Hutu share the same Bantu languages with their **Tutsi** neighbors called Kinyarwanda or Kirundi. Hutu and Tutsi share a long history together, but with colonization, differences between them became more pronounced and developed into political identities. Scholars note that a strong economic distinction between Tutsi and Hutu developed in the later half of the 19th century, when a form of unequal contract between patrons and clients developed, called *uburetwa*, giving patrons even more control over clients including required days of labor for the patron under threat of having their lands taken from them. This system of exploitation helped solidify social and economic classes, making it even harder to cross class lines.

The Hutu moved into the highlands in the Lakes Region of Central Africa in the 10th century; part of the expansion by Bantu speakers into the African Great Lakes. The settled agriculturalists cleared much of the forest lands to make more areas available for agriculture, building materials, firewood, and charcoal for iron smelting. As a result, they also opened more lands for grazing, which encouraged cattle pastoralists—ancestors of the Tutsi—to begin moving into the same areas. From the 12th to the 14th centuries, much of what is known today as Uganda was ruled by the Kingdom of Kitara, while in the Lakes Region, numerous chiefdoms and small states ruled over rapidly growing populations. These smaller political units remained until the formation of the first Tutsi kingdom in the 17th century. The first kingdom, that of Nyiginya, was relatively small, and the "conquest" of Hutu kingdoms progressed slowly as much through establishing client relationships as actual military conquest. The last Hutu chiefdom was brought under Tutsi control in the late 19th century.

Cultural life changed with the arrival of cattle herders. Cattle herders imposed social categories based on cattle ownership, and marriage required an exchange of cattle as part of the bride price. The agriculturalists were placed in a socially inferior position as clients of their cattle-owning social superiors. Prior to European colonization, it was possible to move between categories of Hutu and Tutsi. Tutsi kings owned large herds that were spread out among clients (the position of cattle herder was passed down through generations), and kings used gifts of cattle as reward for service. The patron/client relationship formed the basis of Tutsi/Hutu relationships. The patron or *shebuja* and client or *garagu* were bound together in a system called *ubuhake*, which comes from cattle terminology dealing with calving. The client was given protection "as if he was a calf in the womb of his mother" in exchange for services including part of the crops (Vansina, 47). It was an unequal contract, though, stipulating that should the patron decide to end the contract, the client was forced not only to return the cattle of the patron, but to relinquish all of those the client had been able to obtain or produce as well. Later, other forms of unequal contracts were instituted by the cattle- and landowning Tutsi, which helped form class identities and thus the two "ethnicities" as observed by European colonial authorities.

In the past, Hutu were able to gain positions of power, particularly in the military where by 1800, a number of the army commanders were Hutu. A Hutu could become a Tutsi through favor of a king and would go through a ceremony called *guhutura*, meaning "to shed Hutu status." Intermarriage was common, especially between Hutu men and Tutsi women, though the children would take the identity of their father. Marriages between Tutsi men and Hutu women were less common—it was easier for women to marry down than to marry up. Intermarriage was more common in the southern districts of Rwanda than in the north. Poverty could cause a Tutsi to become a Hutu, and even those of high birth such as cousins of the king could lose their Tutsi status and become Hutu.

The Germans incorporated both kingdoms of Rwanda and Burundi in the late 19th century in their East African colony and held them until 1916, when they lost them to the Belgians. Belgian authority was recognized by the League of Nations in 1923. The Europeans brought with

them the European need to make sense and order out of local institutions, and they created ethnic categories. The economic basis for the Tutsi and Hutu as groups did not fit into colonial constructs of ethnic categories. The colonial authorities were drawn to the romantic figures of the cattle-owning Tutsis, who were characterized as tall, lighter skinned (and therefore perhaps of Hamitic rather the African Bantu origins and it was fantasied they were descendants of Ancient Egyptians), with narrower noses and thinner lips—again, more "European." Tutsi were warriors, while the Hutu were farmers. The Hutu were characterized as short, dark, and with broad noses and wide lips, thus clearly of African/Bantu origins. Colonial stereotypes became ingrained not only in the minds of the colonial authorities, but also among the local people as social classes hardened.

The Hutu of Rwanda, through Christian missionaries, became educated and, before independence, began demanding equal political rights. Their demand for democracy caused a change in who the colonial powers backed; from the Tutsi to the Hutu. In 1957, a group of Hutu intellectuals published the Bahutu Manifesto, calling for democracy and the end of Tutsi (who accounted for only 15 percent of the population) domination. The Tutsi elite responded by saying that the traditional patron-client relationship was the proper one, and that the Hutu should not expect to share power. The Rwandan Revolution erupted in 1959, and thousands of Tutsi died and around 200,000 fled to nearby countries. The last Tutsi king was among the dead, and, in 1961, the Hutu and

Belgians officially ended the Kingdom of Rwanda. In 1962, the country became independent.

The Hutu of Burundi were not able to put an end to Tutsi domination. In 1961, the Kingdom of Burundi separated from the joint Rwanda-Burundi colonial authority and, in 1962, became the independent Kingdom of Burundi. The Tutsi dominated the military, but the king announced that the country would become a constitutional monarchy and give political representation to the Hutu. However, the king refused to install the elected Hutu prime minister, which provoked a Hutu uprising. The response was the mass killing of Hutu, especially intellectuals. The uprising failed, but caused a military coup that ousted the king. In the 1970s, another Hutu rebellion resulted in the death of 200,000 Hutu, and another 100,000 fled to neighboring countries. Again in the 1990s, Hutu-Tutsi violence in Burundi caused some 700,000 people (both Tutsi and Hutu) to flee. Attempts at political settlement in Burundi began in 2003, and the past two elected presidents have been Hutus.

In Rwanda the mass exodus of Tutsi in the Rwanda Revolution began a diaspora population living mainly in Uganda. Tutsi rebel forces launched several cross-border raids with minimal effect, but in 1963, they were able to overpower a Hutu military base, collect modern weapons, and speed on toward the capital before they were defeated. The invasion sparked a killing of approximately 10,000 Tutsis. The president was ousted and the Hutu general Juvénal Habyarimana became the new president in 1973.

Habyarimana formed the *Mouvement révolutionnaire pour la developpement* (MRND) in 1975 and imposed a strict quota of 9 percent on Tutsis in all jobs, both public and private sectors, as well as in schools for all ages. Tutsis were barred from becoming officers in the military, and Hutu soldiers could not marry Tutsi women. In 1991, the "Hutu Ten Commandments" set out a program of complete separation of the two peoples, and any Hutu who broke any of the commandments would be considered a traitor. The MRND formed a youth wing called the *Interahamwe*, meaning "those who work together," and a youth militia called *Impuzamugambi*, meaning "those with a single purpose," centered around Habyarimana's powerful wife Agathe Kanzinga and her clique. Despite the open discrimination of the Rwandan government, Habyarimana was supported by France, as it saw its influence in Africa in danger with the growing power of the Anglophone Tutsi Rwandese Patriotic Front (RPF).

Habyarimana was forced to deal with the power presented to him by the Tutsi diaspora, but, at the same time in 1993, Habyarimana and the "Hutu Power" clique, including his politically powerful wife Agathe Kanzinga, prepared behind-the-scenes plans for the "cleansing" of Tutsis in Rwanda. *Interahamwe* were trained and organized to set about the killing of Tutsis; arms were stored, and lists of names and addresses of Tutsis and Hutu moderates were compiled. In 1994, when Habyarimana's plane was shot down returning from signing the peace accords with the Tutsi Rwandese Patriotic Front (RPF), the killings began, and in 100 days,

Hotel Rwanda and Shake Hands with the Devil: Rwandan Genocide in Film

The 1994 genocide in Rwanda of Tutsis and moderate Hutus was the basis for two major films, one American and the second Canadian. The American film, *Hotel Rwanda*, released in 2004, is based on the real story of hotel manager Paul Rusesabagina, who protected 1,268 Tutsi and moderate Hutu who sought refuge at Hôtel des Mille Collines, owned by the Belgian airline Sabena. The real Paul Rusesabagina served as a consultant for the film, which was shot in Rwanda and South Africa. Paul had never been attracted to radical Hutu Power politics, unlike his longtime friend Georges Rutaganda, one of the leaders of the *Interahamwe* militia.

In the movie, Paul makes use of the friendship he had cultivated with General Augustin Bizimungu to help protect the hotel. The UNAMIR commander, Colonel Oliver (based on the real UNAMIR commander, Canadian general Roméo Dallaire), also provides protection, but the UNAMIR forces are under strict orders from New York to not engage the *Interahamwe* or the Rwandan army. Eventually, the United Nations is able to move all 1,268 people to safety behind rebel lines.

Shake Hands with the Devil chronicles the story of General Roméo Dallaire and the UNAMIR mission to Rwanda. The 2007 film is based on the book with the same title written by General Dallaire (published in 2003). The book won Canada's Governor General's Literary Award for best nonfiction work in 2004. The film's screenplay was cowritten by Dallaire, who also helped coach actor Roy Dupuis, who played him on screen. Like *Hotel Rwanda*, many of the scenes were filmed in Rwanda on the actual sites where events took place. The film has played at international film festivals and been released worldwide via satellite channels.

between 500,000 and 800,000 Tutsis and moderate Hutus were killed by the Rwandan army and the *Interahamwe* militias.

The RPF successfully defeated the Rwandan army and pushed the Hutu government into nearby Zaire (Congo). Habyarimana's widow and her inner circle were given French assistance and were among those evacuated from Kigali by the French military during the United Nations–brokered evacuation of "White non combatants." The *Interahamwe* spread fear of Tutsi reprisals to Hutu civilians, and nearly 1.7 million people fled to Zaire.

The new government in Rwanda is attempting to reconcile Hutus and Tutsis. About 130,000 Hutu have been arrested and are awaiting trial in Arusha, Tanzania, at the hands of an international tribunal. Many of the Hutu who fled to Zaire (Congo) have returned, only to find their houses occupied by returned Tutsis. The presence of over 1 million Hutu refugees

Hutu refugee children carry water containers during the civil war in 1994. (MSGT Rose Reynolds/U.S. Department of Defense for Defense Visual Information Center)

in the eastern region of Zaire caused further problems and the eventual downfall of Zaire's president Mobutu. Hutu power groups were able to establish a state in exile in Kivu province, including recruiting and training an army. Hutu were involved in the Congolese civil war from 1994 to 1998, and many Hutu remain refugees in eastern Congo.

John A. Shoup

Further Reading

Adekunle, Julius O. *Culture and Customs of Rwanda*. Westport, CT: Greenwood Press, 2007.

Berkeley, Bill. *The Graves Are Not Yet Full: Race, Tribe, and Power in the Heart of Africa*. New York: Basic Books, 2001.

Dallaire, Roméo. *Shake Hands with the Devil: The Failure of Humanity in Rwanda*. Cambridge, MA: Da Capo Press, 2005

Meredith, Martin. *The Fate of Africa: A History of Fifty Years of Independence*. New York: Public Affairs, 2005.

Twagilimana, Aimable. *Hutu and Tutsi*. New York: Rosen Publishing Group, Inc. 1998.

Vansina, Jan. *Antecedents to Modern Rwanda; the Nyiginya Kingdom*. Madison: University of Wisconsin Press, 2004.

Igbo

The Igbo or Ibo ethnic group occupies the Lower Niger Basin in the area now known as southeastern Nigeria. Before amalgamation in 1914, the Igbo (Ibo) were organized into several decentralized patriarchal units without a hierarchical political structure that characterized the social structures of their neighbors to the north and southwest, the **Hausa** and the **Yorubas**. Igbo people are culturally homogenous, and members are united by one language with minor local dialectic variations. There are two types of Igbo people, the Upland Igbo and the Lowland Igbo, the majority of whom still live in rural settings. In all of Africa, the Igbo ethnic group is credited for having the most democratic political system because of a clear absence of the chieftaincy system until the British invaded the area toward the end of the 19th century. In a desperate search for leaders, the British colonial officials imposed upon the Igbo a system of warrant chiefs whereby noted Igbo merchants, who had collaborated with the British officials, were appointed warrant chiefs to rule on behalf of the British Crown. Today, Igbo people number between 15 million and 20 million people, depending on which census one relies on.

In some oral tradition, the Igbo were supposed to have migrated from southern Africa, probably a breakaway band of the Zulu (**Nguni**) or another Bantu ethnic group. They originally settled in the confluence of the Niger-Benue River before migrating southward toward the Lower Niger Basin. Other oral traditions state that Igbo migrated from Egypt, passed through the Sudan, and headed southward to their current location in the Lower Niger Basin much like the stories of the Hausas and Yorubas of the same country. However, more recent historical evidence suggests that the majority of the Igbo people, especially those in large cities like Onitsha, the nerve of Igbo culture, migrated from the ancient city of Benin in the 16th century during the reign of *Oba* Esigie of Benin, who ruled his people from 1504 to 1550. It was at this time that the first contacts with the Portuguese were made. This suggests that most Igbo were originally part of the **Edo** ethnic group in present-day midwestern Nigeria, and most probably related as well to the Ibiobio speaking people, which are considered to be the closest Igbo neighbors.

The Igbo have a vibrant culture that many are proud of today and it is often displayed in their elegant mode of dress, characterized by a flowing gown, a red or black hat, and a walking stick. In many parts of Igboland, the patrilineal extended family system is the norm; however, there are pockets of matrilineal groupings in which women dominate all aspects of society. Polygamous marriage is widely practiced with a man having more than one wife; though there is no evidence of a woman having more than one husband. Most Igbo live under an extended family unit, which may include generations of related siblings. Before embracing Christianity, Igbo practiced a unique form of traditional African religion, which may equate to ancestor worship. The main God is known as *Chuckwu*, whom the entire village worships, and it is widely recognized as the universal being, the creator. There are also other lesser gods called *"Umuagbar,"* and below these are the *"Ndi Ichie"* or spirits of the ancestors. Some Igbo subgrouping also worships their personal god called *chi*. An Igbo man carries his *chi* in his pocket on his way to sell his wares in the market. If he returns with all his wares sold, he pours a drink of gin or palm wine as a libation to his lesser god (*chi*); but if he returns home without a good amount of sale, he throws the *chi* out of the window and replaces it with another one. He settles on the one that brings him personal fortune. The Igbo people are more practical in their belief system; if the god does not provide, there is no need to worship such a deity.

The traditional Igbo society was probably the most democratic society in sub-Saharan Africa, with the village assembly being the basis of civil governance where ordinary citizens could have their say. But with the appointment of the Warrant Chiefs by the British during the early phase of colonization, this democratic decision-making process was abolished and replaced by a British-style customary system of civil administration dominated by the emerging elite, most especially the warrant chiefs and the Igbo merchant class. At the village level, the king or *Eze*

rules his people with the assistance of "red-hat" chiefs decked in local red beads indicating their ranks. The Council of Elders also serves in an advisory capacity to the king and, together with the beaded chiefs, maintains order and stability in the village. However, with the advent of colonization, the traditional social structure of Igbo society is increasingly giving way to a modern way of life, with Christianity replacing the old traditional belief system which is well described in Achebe's novel *Things Fall Apart* first published in 1958.

One of the most legendary personalities in Igbo modern history was Dr. Nnamidi Azikiwe, who was born in the northern Nigerian town of Zunguru on November 16, 1904. Azikiwe attended the Lagos Methodist Boys' High School before proceeding to Lincoln and Howard universities in the United States. While in the United States, he met leading African American scholars and social activists like Dr. W. E. B. Du Bois, who encouraged him to attend the second Pan African Congress in Manchester in 1949, where the main issue of the conference was decolonization. Azikiwe returned to Africa first to Accra, Ghana, in 1934 to become the editor of the *African Morning Post*, a platform he used to promote his anti-colonization views. When Nigeria was granted independence in 1960, Azikiwe became the first president of the country; a position he held before the first military coup of 1966. With the coup came the Biafra war, under the command of a young Igbo officer, Colonel Odumegwu Ojukwu. The war brought much suffering to the Igbo and nation, and as a group, they suffered the worst calamity of their recent history. By the time the war ended in 1970, nearly 3 million Igbo people had been slaughtered by federal forces led by Hausa, Fulani (**Fulbe**), and Yoruba generals. The Biafra war is perhaps the first case of ethnic genocide in Africa, and possibly the most brutal.

Pade Badru

Further Reading

Achebe, Chinua. *Things Fall Apart*. London: Heinemann, 1958.

Afigbo, A. E. *Ropes of Sand: Studies in Igbo History and Culture*. Ibadan and Oxford: Ibadan University Press and Oxford University Press, 1981.

Amadiume, Ifi. *Afrikan Matriarchal Foundations: The Igbo Case*. London: Karnack House, 1987.

Amadiume, Ifi. *Male Daughters, Female Husbands: Gender and Sex in an African Society*. London: Zed Books, 1987.

Anyanwu, U. D., and J. C. U. Aguwa, eds. *The Igbo and the Tradition of Politics*. Enugu: Fourth Dimension, 1993.

Arinze, F. A. *Sacrifice in Ibo Religion*. Ibadan: Ibadan University Press, 1970.

Basden, G. T. *Niger Ibos*. London: Frank Cass, 1966.

Cole, Herbert, and Chike Aniakor. *Igbo Arts: Community and Cosmos*. Los Angeles: University of California, Museum of Cultural History, 1984.

Forde, D., and G. I. Jones. *The Ibo and Ibibio-Speaking Peoples of South-Eastern Nigeria: Ethnographic Survey of Africa*. London: Stone & Cox, 1962.

Green, M. M. *Ibo Village Affairs*. New York: Praeger, 1947.

Hodder, B. W. *Markets in West Africa: Studies of Markets and Trade among the Yoruba and Ibo*. Ibadan: Ibadan University Press, 1969.

Horton, R. "Stateless Societies in the History of West Africa." In *History of West Africa*, edited by J. F. Ade Ajayi and Michael Crowder, vol. 1, 72–113. London: Longman, 1976.

Isichei, Elizabeth. *A History of the Igbo People*. New York: St. Martin's Press, 1976.

Isichei, Elizabeth. *Igbo Worlds: An Anthology of Oral Histories and Historical Descriptions*. Philadelphia: Institute for the Study of Human Issues, 1978.

Leith-Ross, Sylvia. *African Women: A Study of the Ibo of Nigeria*. London: Faber & Faber, 1939.

Metuh, E. I. *God and Man in African Religion: A Case Study of the Igbo of Nigeria*. London: Chapman Press, 1981.

Njoku, John E. Eberegbulam. *The Igbos of Nigeria: Ancient Rites, Changes and Survival*. New York: Edwin Mellen Press, 1990.

Nsugbe, Philip. *Ohaffia: A Matrilineal Ibo People*. Oxford: Clarendon Press, 1974.

Nzimiro, Ikenna. *Studies in Ibo Political Systems*. Berkeley and Los Angeles: University of California Press, 1972.

Ohadike, D. C. *Anioma*. Athens: Ohio University Press, 1994.

Onwuejeogwu, M. A. An *Igbo Civilization: Nri Kingdom and Hegemony*. London: Ethiope Publishing, 1981.

Uchendu, V. C. *The Igbo of Southeast Nigeria*. New York: Holt, Rinehart & Winston, 1965.

Ijaw

The Ijaw, also called Ijo, Ejo, Izon, Ezon, Ejon, Uzon, or Ujon from the name of the founding ancestor Ujo or Ojo, appear to be one of the oldest populations living in the Cross River/Niger Delta region of Nigeria and claim to have lived in their current location for over 7,000 years. Their language has no immediate cognates, which helps support the idea that they speak a unique language called Izon and belong to the Ijoid family of the Niger-Congo phylum, some Ijaw claim they originated in Upper Egypt while others say in South Africa. They number over 14 million people, or 10 percent of Nigeria's population, and are broken up into a number of subgroups, including the Ibanji, Okrika, Kalabari, Nemba, Akassa, and Defka.

It appears that the Ijaw have lived in the Delta region before the fifth millennium BCE, and they were able to keep a separate identity because they lived where the agriculturally dependent Bunue-Kwa groups were unable to penetrate. Ijaw economics were based on fishing; they dried and salted fish for trade with agriculturalists for yams and other goods. In addition, the Ijaw had direct access to the sea and also traded sea shells as ornamentation and salt to inland group.

In the 12th century, a number of states grew, and by the 16th century, the Ijaw formed a number of powerful kingdoms with strong central rule. In the 15th century, they came into contact with European traders and became involved as middlemen supplying slaves.

Around 95 percent of Ijaw are Christians today, but the remainder follows the traditional religion. Traditional religion involves both ancestor worship and water spirits, or *owuamapu*, who do not share form or emotions with humans. Ancestral sprits watch over the living and, in honor of them, bits of food from a meal are offered. In addition, traditional religion has divination as part of its practice. It is noted that some of the traditional practices of the Ijaw are similar to those of the **Igbo** in elaborate wooden carvings, dance, masks, and music.

British colonization of the Ijaw took place between 1884 and 1894 as different states were forced to agree to be British protectorates. It took until 1902 to bring the whole of the Delta area under British control with the defeat of the Igbo. Many of the Ijaw converted to Christianity and sought better jobs through education.

Nigeria became independent in 1960 and became a republic in 1963. The crisis of the Biafra War from 1967 to 1970 greatly impacted all of the southern part of Nigeria, though the Ijaw did not support the Igbo attempt for independence. Ijaw "rebellion" began later with the discovery of oil in their part of the country. Feeling denied most of the financial benefits of the oil monies, they have become embroiled in conflict with the government. While they are able to take advantage of higher-paying jobs, they have not seen the social improvements they would like. The conflict has escalated with Shell Oil rigs and Shell employees being taken over or kidnapped by Ijaw militants. A major issue the Ijaw see is the environmental damage caused by oil exploration and pumping stations, which impacts fishing and other aspects of their livelihood. In 2010, Dr. Goodluck Jonathan, himself an Ijaw, was sworn in as the acting president of the republic in response to further threats of violence on the part of Ijaw youth.

John A. Shoup

Ijaw women protest the deal Chevron offered their people for oil exploration in their lands in July 2002. (AP/Wide World Photos)

Further Reading

Ehret, Christopher. *The Civilizations of Africa: A History to 1800*. Charlottesville: University Press of Virginia, 2002.

Falola, Toyin. *Culture and Customs of Nigeria*. Westport, CT: Greenwood Press, 2001.

"Ijaw and Ibo Beliefs: Self, Soul, and Afterlife." http://www.meta-religion.com/World _Religions/Other_religions/ijaw_and_ibo _beliefs.htm (accessed May 28, 2010).

"Ijaw History." http://www.ijaw-naa.org/ijaw/ home.htm (accessed May 28, 2010).

"Ijawnation." http://www.ijawfoundation.org/ people.htm (accessed May 28, 2010).

"Nigeria: Swear-in Jonathan or Leave Our Oil, Ijaw Youths Declare." AllAfrica.com. http://allafrica.com/stories/201001261053 .html (accessed May 28, 2010).

Olson, James. *The Peoples of Africa: An Ethnohistorical Dictionary*. Westport, CT: Greenwood Press, 1996.

"Warri City and the Western Niger Delta Crisis." http://www.nigerdeltacongress .com/warticles/warri_city_and_the_western _niger.htm (accessed May 28, 2010).

Isoko

The Isoko, also called Urhoba, Biotu, Igabo, and Sobo, live in the northwestern edge of the Niger Delta region in Nigeria. Sobo and Igabo are both pejorative terms, and Biotu is the **Ijaw** word for them meaning "interior people." Though in Izon, the language of the Ijaw, the word Biotu is not a pejorative, the Isoko consider it to be so. They number 423,000 people. Their language is called Isoko and it belongs to the Kwa group of the Niger-Congo phylum. They hold that they descend from people from the Benin Kingdom, but this is disputed by scholars.

The Isoko live from fishing and the production of palm oil as well as farming cassava, maize, beans, and peanuts. Isoko society is patrilineal and each homestead is headed by a male and each homestead occupies a ward in a traditional village. Villages are compact numbering usually around 500 people. Society, both men and women, are divided into age grades with specific tasks for each grade. In addition, each village is autonomous. The majority of the Isoko today are Christians.

Since Nigerian independence in 1960, the Isoko have mixed with other peoples in the Niger Delta area such as the Ijaw. Nonetheless, they have strived to maintain their own identity. In recent years, the Isoko have ventured widely from their home region, working throughout Nigeria as small commercial entrepreneurs despite the fact that their own home region is nearly all rural.

John A. Shoup

Further Reading

Falola, Toyin. *Culture and Customs of Nigeria*. Westport, CT: Greenwood Press, 2001.

"Isoko." http://www.ethnologue.com/show _language.asp?code=iso (accessed May 28, 2010).

J

Jews

The word Jew refers to an ethnicity as well as to a religion, and historically, non-Jews such as **Berbers** in North Africa have converted to Judaism assuming with their conversion the idea of a common origin and common historical experience. Jews speak a wide range of languages for their daily interactions, and until the creation of the Zionist movement and the attempt to create a Jewish homeland in Palestine in the late 19th and early 20th centuries, Hebrew was a literary and liturgical language rarely spoken outside of religious discourse. Hebrew belongs to the Northwest family of Semitic languages of the Afro-Asiatic phylum. Most of the other languages of this group, such as Canaanite, are no longer spoken with the exception of Aramaic; **Arabic** belongs to the West Semitic family, and though it shares many similarities to Hebrew, the two languages are not closely related. Modern Hebrew was created to be a national language shared by all Jewish immigrants to Palestine and then, after 1948, to the state of Israel. It differs from Classical Hebrew in pronunciation, some vocabulary, and in some grammatical points. Modern Hebrew is spoken by nearly 6 million people in Israel, while another 200,000 speakers are mainly in North America and Europe. According to the Jewish Agency for Israel in 2007, there were 5.5 million Jews in Israel and among the Middle Eastern and African countries with Jewish populations; Turkey has 17,800, and South Africa has 72,000 Jews. Other Middle Eastern and North African countries such as Syria, Iran, Tunisia, and Morocco have small minorities of generally less than 5,000 each.

The term Jew in Western European languages originates from the Latin *Iudaeum* meaning the inhabitants of Judea, which refers to the land of the tribe of Judah or *Yehuda* in Aramaic—thus the terms *Yahud/Yahudi* for "Jewish" in other Semitic languages such as Arabic. The term has come to mean the followers of the religion of Judaism. The term *Hebrew* or *'ibri* is used today to refer to the language and to the ancient Hebrew people who established the First Kingdom in Jerusalem (1005/1004–930 BCE).

According to Jewish, Christian, and Islamic accounts, the Hebrews descend from the Patriarch Abraham/Ibrahim through his wife Sarah, while the Arabs descend from him through the Egyptian bondwoman Hagar/Hajar. Relations with Egypt were significant, and among the social practices borrowed from the Egyptians was male circumcision, which is a widely practiced custom in Africa.

Following their long sojourn in Egypt, the Hebrews established themselves amidst older populations in today's Jordan and Palestine-Israel, and remained a loose confederation of pastoral tribes who eventually began to take up agriculture. Eventually, the tribes were brought under the command of one leader, first Saul, and later David (1005/1004–930 BCE). Moroccan Jews believe the earliest Jewish settlements in Morocco date from the time of King Solomon (970–930 BCE), who sent trading missions as far as to the Massa River in Morocco's Sus region. Some scholars note that Jews helped in the founding of Carthage in 814 BCE. The First Kingdom was short-lived and, upon the death of Solomon in 930 BCE, it was divided into the northern Kingdom of Israel and the southern Kingdom of Judah. The two kingdoms frequently fought, and Judah did not come to the aid of Israel when it was overrun by the Assyrians in 772 BCE. The Assyrians took large numbers of Jews as prisoners and deported them to Mesopotamia. Judah was destroyed by the Babylonians in 587–586 BCE, and large numbers of Jews again were taken prisoner and brought to Mesopotamia. Some Jews escaped west to Egypt and North Africa and the *Ghriba*, or "The Marvelous" Synagogue on the Island of Jerba off the southern Tunisian coast, is said to date from 587 BCE. According to local legend, a door from the First Temple was built into its walls. It is the oldest continually used synagogue in the world.

The Babylonian Exile came to an end with the Persian conquest of Babylon in 538 BCE by Cyrus the Great. The Persians were relatively tolerant rulers and allowed the Jews to return to Palestine and even to rebuild the Temple in Jerusalem. Another was built in Elephantine Island (near Aswan) in Egypt. It was during the Babylonian Exile and the subsequent Persian period that the Torah was consolidated between written and oral traditions.

The Persians were in turn conquered by Alexander the Great in 333 BCE. The Greek Period (333–37 BCE) is one of conflict between Greek Hellenism and Judaism. Palestine fell under the control of the Ptolemys in 301 BCE, and Jewish society began to split between the *Hasidim*, or pious ones, and the more liberal Hellenists. The clash within Jewish society erupted when the Ptolemys lost control of most of Palestine to their rivals, the Seleucids, the Greek rulers of Syria. Jews rose in a revolt lead by Judas Maccabeus, which was successful in pushing out the Seleucids and establishing a separate state ruled by the Jewish Hasmonaean dynasty. Beset by dynastic quarrels, the Hasmonaeans contributed to the continued divisions in Jewish society, with a number of its rulers embracing Hellenism. The internal feuding ended when the Roman general Pompey captured Jerusalem in 63 BCE. The Hasmonaeans remained in power under a Roman protectorate until 43 BCE, when the first of the Herodian dynasty was made governor of Judea by the Romans. Three successive Jewish revolts were crushed and the last, the Bar Kokhba Revolt in 132 CE, resulted in mass destruction of Jerusalem including the Temple and banishment of Jews from Jerusalem, which was renamed Aelia Capitolina.

Jews spread through much of the Roman Empire, with the largest numbers in Syria, Anatolia, and Italy. During the Roman period, the Mishna and the Talmud were codified and became the main body of religious teachings for Jews, who were now mainly minorities living among non-Jews. Jews had long been in Egypt and

North Africa as well as in Persia, Ethiopia, the Hijaz, and Yemen. Frescos on the wall of the synagogue at Dura-Europus in eastern Syria built in 245 shows the combination of Hellenistic traditions with Persian elements.

In the late fourth century, the Himyari kings of Yemen converted to Judaism and, in 524, King Dhu Nuwas, in his religious zeal, ordered the killing of the Christians in Najran for refusing to convert to Judaism. The harsh treatment of Christians by Dhu Nuwas caused the Christian king of Ethiopia to intervene, and an Ethiopian army conquered Yemen in 525.

The Prophet Muhammad was greatly affected by Judaism and, at first, he had a very favorable attitude toward both Jews and Christians, whom he saw as part of the same community as Muslims. Four Jewish tribes lived in Madinah and formed a large part of the population. Originally, the direction for Muslim prayer was toward Jerusalem, but within the first year of being in Madinah, the direction was changed towards Makkah, and the role of the Ka'abah being originally built by the Patriarch Abraham/Ibrahim as the first place of worship to the one God overrode the importance of Jerusalem (*surah* 2:142–150 *Surat al-Baqarah*). Initially, Muhammad had no interest in building a new religion, but to restore the religion of the prophets of old; however, rejection by the Jews of Madinah caused him to start a separate identity. Following Muhammad's victory over the Makkans at the Battle of Badr in 624, he began to turn his attention to the Jewish tribes in Madinah. The first to be forced to leave were the Qaynuqa', who were the most vocal in their criticisms of him. The next to be forced to leave were the Bani al-Nadir who, though not in league with his opponents from Makkah, were openly happy about Muhammad's defeat at of the Battle of Uhud in 625. Following the defeat of the Makkans at the Battle of the Trench in 627, Muhammad turned on the last Jewish tribe of Madinah, the Qurayzah, who, upon suspicion of helping the Makkans, were not treated as the others; the men were put to death and the women and children became slaves.

Generally speaking, the Prophet did not require Jews and Christians living in the Arabian Peninsula to convert to Islam. Prior to his death in 632, he led an expedition to Tabuk and made agreements with local Christian and Jewish leaders in southern Jordan that were the models for conditions of surrender during the early Islamic conquests of Byzantine and Persian lands.

Jews, along with Christians and Zoroastrians, were *ahl al-Kitab* or People of the Book (a divinely revealed religion) and *ahl al-Dhimmah* or People of the Pact—protected by the Islamic state. Muslim rulers allowed Jews their own courts, and Jewish communities had their own leaders who were responsible to the state. The *Khalifah* 'Umar ibn al-Khattab (634–644) permitted Jews to once again live in Jerusalem, the first time since the Bar Kokhba Revolt. The Muslim Umayyads of Spain (756–1031) created the "Golden Age" in Jewish history, during which all three religions lived in relative peace and combined to produce some of the highest achievements in medieval culture. Baghdad,

Damascus, Aleppo, Cairo, Qayruwan, and Fez became important seats of Jewish culture, and Jewish merchant families spread from China to northern England as attested to by the Genizah documents from Cairo. Jews were important to the trans-Saharan trade, and Jewish communities were found in the major oases such as Sijilmassa (in Morocco) and Touat (in Algeria), and in towns and cities in the Sahel such as Timbuktu.

The 12th-century Jewish traveler Benjamin of Tudela records the fairly large Jewish communities he encountered in Muslim Turkey, Syria, Palestine, and Iraq. For example, Baghdad had a population of 40,000 Jews, 28 synagogues, and 10 academies for the study of Jewish texts. These communities were large compared to his figures for the largest Jewish communities in Christian lands, of which none totaled more than 600 Jews.

Jews were subject to occasional outbreaks of anti-Jewish sentiment in the Islamic world. Mamluks of Egypt (1250–1517) imposed certain restrictions during periods of crisis in the 14th century as did some of the more orthodox dynasties in North Africa. Nonetheless, many Jews sought refuge in Islamic countries after expulsions from Europe. Following the conquest of Muslim Granada in 1492, some 150,000 Jews left to find refuge in Morocco and Ottoman lands.

Jewish cultural life under Islam has produced a number of major personages. Allowed to practice their religion, Jews developed art, architecture, science, and philosophy, as well as religious discourse. The Umayyad period in Muslim Spain allowed a flowering of Jewish culture,

and a number of Jews rose to important positions in the royal courts. Their knowledge of both Arabic and Hebrew allowed them to use the languages interchangeably, using one script to write in the other. Jews in Muslim Spain were scholars, scientists, poets, and translators. One of the most famous of these scholars was Musa bin Maymun or Moses Maimonides (1138–1204), who was born in Cordoba, lived for some time in Fez, and died in Egypt. The works of Maimonides were translated into Latin between 1220 and 1250 at the famous school of translation established by Archbishop Don Raimundo in Toledo.

Jewish mysticism or the Kabbalah grew during the 16th century under Ottoman protection. Jewish mysticism was influenced by Sufism or Islamic mysticism and it is noted that it is difficult to study the Kabbalah without knowledge of Sufism. The town of Safad in Palestine played an important part, and in 1524, a *yeshiva* was founded for the study of Jewish mysticism. A number of Jewish messianic movements occurred in Islamic countries; in Persia, Kurdistan, Yemen, and Morocco, but the most influential of them began in 1665 led by Shabbetai Zevi. Born in Izmir in 1626, Shabbetai Zevi studied the Kabbalah and began a movement that eventually gained him the notice of the Ottoman authorities. He died in 1676, and he had created an important influence on Jews not only in the Ottoman Empire, but through his teachings, Jews in Europe as well.

Jews played a major role in the professional crafts, especially in making silver and gold jewelry. Among the **Tuareg**, the professional crafts class or *inaden* claim to descend from David or *Nabi Da'ud*. Similar claims have been made about other populations in the Sahara and West Africa. Dr. Labelle Prussin has studied the similarities in design and production methods of West African craftsmen with those from North Africa and Yemen, where Jews dominated the crafts; and though there is a good deal of similarity, including use of numerical combinations that are used in the Kabbalah, it is difficult today to establish definite links. In addition, in certain parts of West Africa, people claim to either descend from or can point out wells dug by the Bani Isra'ila or the Sons of Israel. In addition, the Islamic holiday marking the end of the *Haj* and commemorating Ibrahim's willingness to sacrifice his son Isma'il in the Islamic tradition is called *Tabeski* in most West African languages, which is a Berberized version of the Hebrew word *Pesakh* or Passover.

In Morocco, Jews living in large cities generally lived in a special neighborhood called a *mallah*. The first *mallah* was built in Fez during the 15th century under the Marinds (1216–1510), who compelled the Jews to move next to the newly built royal palace in 1438. The *mallah* in Fez remained the only such special district for Jews in Morocco, but under the 'Alawi dynasty (1661–present) most Moroccan cities had similar neighborhoods. When *Sultan* Sidi Muhammad bin 'Abdallah (1757–1790) built the port city of Essaouira in 1760, a special quarter was built for Jews, and 40 percent of the city was Jewish. The Maliki *'ulama'* of Morocco had declared that direct commerce with a Christian was not possible for Muslims, and money

The Mellah or Jewish section of the Fez displays the usual balconies on the front of houses that set Jewish homes apart from Muslim ones, with no such outside openings to the street. Today most of these homes are occupied by Muslims who have recently come into the city from the countryside, and they have modified them by blocking off the balconies. (John A. Shoup)

made in such a transaction was forbidden or *haram*. The money could be made clean or *hilal* only if it passed first through the hands of a Jew. Jews became increasingly important to the Moroccan state and certain Jewish families became the *Tujjar al- Sultan* or the Sultan's Merchants, who represented the state in any commercial dealings with non-Muslims and, in some cases, served as ambassadors in non-Muslim countries.

Nearly all of the Jews in the Middle East and North Africa belong to the Sephardic tradition. Rabbinism and Karaism are both

Bukharian Jews (originally from Central Asia) celebrate a family event at the Wailing Wall in Jerusalem. (John A. Shoup)

found among them, and Damascus used to be a major center for Karaism. In the liturgy used, both the Babylonian and the Palestinian rites are found, but in much of the Arab East, the Babylonian rite was more common. Moroccan Jews have continued practices such as visitations to saints' shrines called *mimuna* after Passover in Israel as part of maintaining community identity. Since the 1970s, other "Oriental" Jewish communities, such as the Iranian, have also begun to celebrate their own communities' cultural practices as part of their emerging identity within Israel.

Modern history begins with the *Tanzimat* or Reform Movement in the Ottoman

Empire during the 19th century. The Ottoman *Sultan*s 'Abd al-Majid I (1839–1861) and 'Abd al-'Aziz (1861–1876) embarked on a policy of reforms between 1839 and 1876. In 1839, the *Hatt-i Sharif* recognized equal rights of property, life, and honor for Jews and Christians with Muslims, and in 1856, the *Hatt-i Humayun* gave full equality for all non-Muslims in the empire, including the right to serve in the army. Opposition to the reform provoked the brief war in Lebanon between Maronite Christians and Druze, and upon his assumption of the throne in 1876, *Sultan* 'Abd al-Hamid II suspended parliament and slowly began a process of dismantling the reforms.

Jewish emigration from the Arab provinces of the empire began in the 19th century. Syria's economy was badly affected by the opening of the Suez Canal and did not recover until in the postindependence period. Large numbers of Syrian Jews relocated to Latin America before World War I. Egypt's economy grew because of British interests in cotton, and even some Jews from Italy moved to Alexandria, where the Egyptian Stock Market was located. Jews in Egypt were important part of the *khawajah* or non-Egyptian society that emerged in Alexandria, which also included Greeks, Maltese, and others who were more European than Arab in culture. In Egypt, Jews spoke Arabic as well as English and French, and several of the major film stars of the 1930s and 1940s were Jewish, such as Layla Murad and Bishara Wakim.

The rise of Zionism in the 19th century at first did not affect Jews in Muslim countries. However, following the defeat of Turkey in World War I and the establishment of European mandates over much of the Middle East, the clash between Jewish nationalism in the form of Zionism and Arab nationalism did greatly affect them. The Jewish population of Palestine in 1880 is estimated to have been 24,000 at most, and by 1918, they numbered 56,000, most of whom were mainly European Jews. As early as 1920, Arab Palestinians rioted over the numbers of European Jews arriving. Arab protests continued through the 1930s and erupted into a full-fledged revolt against the British in 1936. By 1936, Jews numbered close to half a million, making them about a third of Palestine's population.

Following World War II, it was clear to many Jews in Europe that the survival of Jews as a people meant this could be achieved only with a Jewish state. The Holocaust strengthened Zionism's call for a Jewish state in Palestine, and in 1948, Israel declared its independence just as Great Britain's mandate ended. The new Israeli army defeated the Egyptians and Syrians, but was unable to dislodge the Jordanians from Jerusalem and the West Bank. Jews in Arab countries generally suffered from official and unofficial discrimination as a result, and large numbers left for Israel. In Egypt and Iraq, both with large Jewish populations, nearly all of their Jews left soon after 1948. Although official policies in Tunisia, Algeria, and Morocco have not generally discriminated, unofficial practice and anti-Jewish sentiment by people have encouraged Jews to emigrate, many going to Israel. In Morocco, those who could afford to do so have emigrated to France, Canada, and the United States, while the poorer have gone to Israel, especially following the 1967 Arab-Israeli War. Today, Morocco has about 5,000 Jews, and 260,000 have immigrated to Israel. Syria imposed emigration restrictions on Jews, allowing them to leave if they had visas to countries other than Israel, but, following the 1990–1991 Gulf War, the Syrian government relaxed its restrictions, and most of its remaining 5,000 Jews left.

The Israeli government organized Operation Magic Carpet to bring most of Yemen's Jews to Israel between 1949 and 1950. British and American transport planes flew from British-controlled Aden to bring to Israel 49,000 Jews from both North and South Yemen. Only a few hundred Jews remain in Yemen today. The Falasha of Ethiopia were also airlifted to Israel in 1984. Their status as Jews was not recognized by Israel until 1973, when the Sephardic chief rabbi finally declared them to be Jews. There are other Jewish communities in Africa, with South Africa having the largest, but most of these are a result of European colonial history and are not indigenous, African Jews. The exception is the **Lemba** in southern Africa, who recently developed a Jewish identity based on the work of the British scholar Tudor Parfitt.

John A. Shoup

Further Reading

Bernus, Edmond. "The Tuareg Artisan: From Technician to Mediator." In *Art of Being Tuareg: Sahara Nomads in a Modern World*, edited by Thomas Seligman and Kristyne Loughran. Los Angeles: UCLA Fowler Museum of Cultural History, 2005.

Buhl, F., et al. "Muhammad." In *Encyclopaedia of Islam*, 2nd ed., CD-ROM.

Darwish, Mustafa. *Dream Makers on the Nile: A Portrait of Egyptian Cinema.* Cairo: Zeitouna Book, American University in Cairo Press, 1998.

De Lange, Nicholas. *Atlas of the Jewish World.* New York: Facts on File, 1988.

Eickelman, Dale. *The Middle East and Central Asia: An Anthropological Approach.* 3rd ed. Upper Saddle River, NJ: Prentice Hall, 1998.

"Hebrew." http://www.omniglot.com/writing/hebrew.htm (accessed January 6, 2010).

Hunwick, John O., and Alida Jay Boye. *The Hidden Treasures of Timbuktu: Rediscovering Africa's Literary Culture.* London: Thames and Hudson, 2008.

Jewish Agency for Israel. http://www.jewishagency.org/JewishAgency/English/home (accessed January 6, 2010).

Maisel, Sebastian. "Najran (Region)." In *Saudi Arabia and the Gulf States Today: An Encyclopedia of Life in the Arab States*, edited by Sebastian Maisel and John A. Shoup. Westport, CT: Greenwood Press, 2009.

Novaresio, Paolo. *The Sahara Desert: From the Pyramids of Egypt to the Mountains of Morocco.* Cairo: American University in Cairo Press, 2003.

Prussin, Labelle. "Judaic Threads in the West African Tapestry: No More Forever?" Draft of the article published in *Art Bulletin* (2006).

Roaf, Michael. *Cultural Atlas of the Mesopotamia and the Ancient Near East.* New York: Facts on File, 1990.

Ross, Eric, John Shoup, Driss Maghraoui, and Abdelkrim Marzouk. *Assessing Tourism in Essaouira.* Ifrane, Morocco: Al Akhwayan University, 2002.

Schroeter, Daniel. "Royal Power and the Economy in Precolonial Morocco: Jews and the Legitimation of Foreign Trade." In *In the Shadow of the Sultan: Culture, Power, and Politics in Morocco*, edited by Rahma Bourqia and Susan Gilson Miller. Cambridge, MA: Harvard University Press, 1999.

Shamir, Ilana, and Shlomo Shavit, eds. *Encyclopedia of Jewish History: Events and Eras of the Jewish People.* New York: Facts on File, 1986.

Shoup, John. *Culture and Customs of Syria.* Westport, CT: Greenwood Press, 2008.

Smith, G. R. "Yaman." In *Encyclopaedia of Islam.* 2nd ed., CD-ROM.

Zafrani, H. "Mallah." In *Encyclopaedia of Islam.* 2nd ed., CD-ROM.

K

Kalenjin

The Kalenjin are a **Nilotic** people composed of several subgroups, the Kipsigi, Nandi, Keiyo, Tugen, Pokot, Marakwet, Endo, Sabaot, Terik, and Okeik, who mainly live in Kenya, Uganda, and Tanzania. The name Kalenjin for both the people and their language was adopted in the 1940s and means "I tell you." The Kipsigi and Nandi are the two largest of the subgroups and, in total, the Kalenjin number some 4 million people, making them the fourth-largest ethnic group in Kenya or 12 percent of the total population. The Kalenjin language belongs to the Southern Cushitic group and there are a number of dialects that are not easily intelligible.

The Kalenjin originally came from the region around the northern tip of Lake Turkana and began moving south along the eastern side around 500 BCE. They introduced a new form of age sets and expanded that of the warrior period, which gave the Kalenjin a decisive military strength over their neighbors. The Kalenjin, like many other Nilotes, were cattle people, and they either absorbed or pushed out those they found living in the highlands to the east of Lake Victoria. Among the hunter-gatherer populations they absorbed are the Okeik, who began making a type of pottery named after them, which was traded in much of East Africa.

Bantu peoples arrived in East Africa in waves between 500 and 1000 and were not able to dislodge the Kalenjin. Around 700 CE, Bantu cultivators added crops such as banana that were able to be grown in the highland areas, challenging Cushite control. The Kalenjin were able to resist Bantu challenges and generally Bantu moved around them. The Bantu also brought with them iron tools and weapons, but the Kalenjin did not adopt iron weapons until after the eighth century.

Between 800 and 1000, the Kalenjin expanded and became involved in commercial exchange with Bantu peoples. Their influence was such that many others adopted their traditions, including their age grade system. Pastoral products, such as animal skins, were traded for agricultural goods that the Kalenjin did not produce themselves.

The Kalenjin were not greatly threatened until the arrival of another Nilotic people, the Maa, ancestors of the Massai, in the 16th century. Some Kalenjin, pressed by the Maa, became Maa in identity and language. In the 17th century, the spread of agriculture among the Marakwet seems to have occurred, with forests being cleared and terraced fields with irrigation systems built. Some of the Kalenjin seem to have been absorbed by the Bantu Luyia. Nonetheless, the Kalenjin remain the largest Southern Cushitic group today.

The Kalenjin are mainly pastoralists, and cattle play a major role in their lives. Cattle and their products give clothes, food, and even housing to the people.

Age Sets

Age sets or age grades are a way of organizing society in many African cultures. They usually start with a form of coming-of-age ceremony, which for boys can involve circumcision. All boys or girls born within the span of several years go through the ceremonies together and, subsequently, go through all stages of life together. Age sets are a way of solidifying the group as a whole by providing an alternate to family ties. Age sets cross-cut kinship lines and frequently form a stronger basis for relationships than kinship. In southern Africa, age sets served as the basis for military regiments organized by the Zulu King Shaka.

The age sets of the Nilotic peoples, such as the Maasai, were borrowed by other non-Nilotes such as the Bantu Kikuyu. The Maasai, Kalenjin, and others divide society into age groups and have mass celebrations to mark the move from one level to another. The Kalenjin and other Nilotes during their migrations south modified their age sets, reducing the total number from eight to two important stages. Both boys and girls are children until around age 15; the boys are brought together, circumcised, and after a period of healing, become *muren* or warriors. The warriors mark their status with elaborate beadwork and wear their hair long, braided or twisted, and smeared with red clay. They stay in the warrior stage for around 15–20 years before they go though the next stage-of-life ceremony. The warriors are brought together and a special ceremony, called *eunoto* by the Maasai, is held. The warriors' elaborate coiffeurs are shaved off by their mothers and they are initiated into adulthood or elder status called *payyan*. Their beads and spears are replaced with a cloak and a walking stick, and as men, are allowed to marry.

Traditional homes are built of brush and cattle dung. *Mursik* or fermented milk is one of their main foods. Cattle raiding played, and still plays, a major role in Kalenjin life and in their social organization. Young men or warriors called *muren* developed in order to protect their own cattle herds as well as be a ready group to raid those of others. The *muren* stage lasts between 10 and 15 years before each warrior goes through a ceremony that marks the end of this stage and the beginning of the next age grade as an elder or *payyan*.

Most Kalenjin claim they are either Christians or Muslims, but their traditional religion plays a significant role in their lives. Their traditional religion is monotheistic and has a powerful god/goddess called *Asis* or *Cheptalel*, who is associated with the sun. The word *asis* means both "god" and "sun," and some have speculated an Egyptian origin for the Kalenjin noting that Isis, one of the main gods of ancient Egypt, is close to *Asis*. Prayers to *Asis* are given before sunrise. Under *Asis* is *Elat*, who though not a god, controls thunder and lightning. In addition, there are the *oyik* or spirits of the dead who can interfere with human life. There are diviners or *orkoik* who can contact the spirits and find out what they want and what needs to be done to set things right, often in the form of an offering of meat or beer. Christian missions did not appear in the region until 1933, mainly because the region where the Kalenjin lived did not attract many British families. Today some 44 percent of the Kalenjin are Christians.

Kalenjin identity grew in the 1930s and 1940s as much as a means to separate themselves from other groups such as the **Kikuyu**. During World War II, the radio announcer John Chemallan signed off his segment with the phrase "*kalnejok*," the plural form of *Kalenjin*, and was picked by students in high schools. The movement was backed by the British authorities to foster anti-Kikuyu sentiment during the Mau Mau revolt.

Following Kenyan independence in 1963, politics have been dominated by the Kikuyu and the **Luo** to the exclusion of other ethnicities. The Kalenjin have been able to make a name for themselves as great long-distance runners, and since the gold medal for the 1,500-meter race in the 1968 Olympics was won by Kalenjin Kip Keino, Kenya has won 38 other long-distance medals, of which Kalenjin have won 75 percent. In addition, President Daniel Arap Moi, who governed from 1978 to 2002, was a Kalenjin.

John A. Shoup

Further Reading

Ehret, Christopher. *The Civilizations of Africa: A History to 1800*. Charlottesville: University Press of Virginia, 2002.

"The Kalenjin Peoples of Kenya." http://www.orvillejenkins.com/profiles/kalenjin (accessed May 28, 2010).

"The Kalenjin Tribe (Kenya)." http://www.kenya-advisor.com/kalenjin-tribe.html (accessed May 28, 2010).

Newman, James. *The Peopling of Africa: A Geographic Interpretation*. New Haven, CT: Yale University Press, 1995

Sobania, N. W. *Culture and Customs of Kenya*. Westport, CT: Greenwood Press, 2003.

Kamba

The Kamba, Akamba, or Wakamba (in plural) are one of the largest ethnic groups in Kenya, numbering 2.5 million people or 11 percent of the total population of the country. Their language is called Kakamba, and it belongs to the Bantu group. The Kamba and other Bantu peoples of the region absorbed earlier Cushitic people, who have left influences in loanword to the language as well as in oral traditions and irrigation works.

The Kamba originated with the Bantu peoples who pushed into Kenya in the fifth century CE and subsequently expanded, especially where they were able to grow crops such as bananas. Sometime in the 16th century, the Kamba encountered the Maa, a **Nilotic** people and ancestors of the modern Maasai/Masai, who recently arrived. Some Kamba sought refuge with the **Chagga** on the slopes of Mount Kilimanjaro, while others moved southward into tsetse fly–infested regions, where the cattle-breeding Maa did not want to go. By the late 17th century, most Kamba relocated to the arid woodlands in the Chyulu Hills, where they were able to succeed by using the various farming skills such as irrigation methods and terracing. By the 18th century, the Kamba had become middlemen between the **Swahili** and **Arab** merchants on the coast and those people who lived further inland. In the late 18th century, they lost control over part of the trade to the Doe in what is today known as Tanzania. The Kamba became expert traders in much of Kenya, as well as farmers and cattlemen.

Today most Kamba are Christian, but their traditional religion was very similar to that of their neighbors, the **Kikuyu**. They believed in a single, powerful creator god as well as number of other spirits who could be contacted through mediums.

The Kamba were organized into a number of patrilineal clan territories called *utui* governed by councils of elders. Society was divided into age grades, but they generally did not go through the elaborate age grade ceremonies such as those of the various **Nilotic** peoples or the Kikuyu. Nonetheless, the Kamba are one of the few peoples in Kenya who still practice female circumcision.

The Kamba were among the first people encountered by European explorers to East Africa, and their name of Mount Kenya (*Kinyaa*) was recorded for the mountain and subsequently, became the name of the country. Due to their experience as traders, they had a vast knowledge of the country, and Europeans hired Kamba to be both guides and porters for their explorations inland. Kamba lands were not of interest to most Europeans, at least not initially, because they were generally arid and not as productive as other

areas. Kamba resisted the railway the British intended to build since it would seriously damage their trade with more distant people, and in 1896 to 1897, a military expedition was sent to defeat them and place them on native reserves.

The Kamba were quick to recognize the value of education brought by missionaries and, because of their own reliance on trade, they were able to reconcile economically. The British tried to ban traditional religion. The Kamba traditional gathering, called a *wathi*, was forbidden, and the British chopped down a number of the Kamba's sacred trees in their attempt to stop traditional practices.

During World War I, the Kamba did not want to serve in the British army's Carrier Corps, and various means were used to try to avoid service, including abandoning entire villages; but by the end of the war, over three-fourths of all Kamba men had served in the army. Following the war, the Kamba did serve in both the police and in the King's African Rifles, but poor treatment of Africans, especially when white colonists tried to have their herds reduced, brought about fast response. The Kamba mobilized a large group of people who eventually got the attention of the colonial governor, who backed down on the plan to force them to give up large numbers of their herds.

Following World War II, Kamba saw no improvement of their condition, and when in the 1950s the Mau Mau Rebellion began, many Kamba joined. It was estimated that in one of the main Kamba towns, Machakos, as many as 2,000 people had taken the Mau Mau oath. The oath was taken in the name of the traditional god, and each person who took the oath vowed on pain of death to never reveal anyone else who was part of the movement. Many of the Kamba who joined the movement worked for the railway and controlled the railway men, and many others were members of the King's African Rifles. Despite their ability to shut rail service with strikes, few strikes were ever called during the conflict. The rebellion was defeated by 1956, but it did result in Kenya's independence in 1963. Kenya became a republic in 1964. The Kamba have generally prospered as urban professionals and merchants.

John A. Shoup

Further Reading

Ehret, Christopher. *The Civilizations of Africa: A History to 1800*. Charlottesville: University Press of Virginia, 2002.

Sobania, N. W. *Culture and Customs of Kenya*. Westport, CT: Greenwood Press, 2003.

www.bluegecko.org/kenya/tribes/kamba/history2 (accessed June 1, 2010).

www.flw.com/languages/kamba (accessed June 1, 2010).

www.kenya-advisor.com/kamba-tribe (accessed June 1, 2010).

Kanuri

The Kanuri, whose presence in the Lake Chad area goes back 1,000 years, make up the core ethnic group of the Emirate of Bornu (Bornou, Borno), in what is now northeastern Nigeria. Along with the **Tubu** and related groups, they belong to the Nilo-Saharan language family, stretching through Chad from eastern Niger to the Darfur region of western Sudan. The Kanuri, who now number nearly 4 million in Nigeria, Chad, Niger, and northern Cameroon, are closely related to a number of groups of eastern Niger, and especially to the Kanembu, centered north of Lake Chad, who represent the original stock from which the Kanuri developed.

Deeply implicated in both interregional and trans-Saharan trade, the Kanuri developed a complex, commercialized economy. While a mixture of agriculture and livestock production provided the bulk of local subsistence, most Kanuri were settled in towns and villages, where craft specialization and weekly markets also flourished. Bornu was an exporter of slaves and ivory, cloth, and leather goods, importing salt from the Sahara and manufactured goods from as far away as North Africa and Europe.

Kanuri origins can be traced to the kingdom of Kanem, which took shape along the northeastern shores of Lake Chad toward the end of the first millennium CE. The Maguni Sefuwa clan, from whom the Kanuri trace their ancestry, constituted the ruling dynasty of Kanem. The kingdom, which developed as a terminus of the trans-Saharan trade route via the Kawar oases to Libya, soon adopted Islam and developed ties with Egypt and other North African states.

After a period of rebellions and invasions in the 13th and 14th centuries, however, the *Mai* or king of Kanem and his supporters were obliged to flee, founding the new state of Bornu southwest of Lake Chad. Bornu soon recovered, reasserting its control over both Kanem and the trans-Saharan trade, and resisting the expansion of the **Songhay** Empire to the west.

The fall of Songhay—invaded by Morocco in 1591—destabilized the region, opening Bornu to **Tuareg** and Tubu raiding from the northwest. At the same time, Islamic *jihads* (holy wars) were displacing old ruling groups all along the Sahel. In the **Hausa** states west of Bornu, Islamic reformers, with a strong Fulani (**Fulbe**) ethnic base, were taking power, creating the new Caliphate of Sokoto. In the early 1800s, the *Mai* of Bornu himself was twice driven from his capital by Fulani forces, each time recovering thanks to the support of the *Shehu* (local pronunciation of the **Arabic** word *Shaykh*), the Kanembu leader of Bornu's parent state and vassal, Kanem. The balance of power had changed, however, and it was now the *Shehu*, who settled in a new town near the *Mai*'s old capital, who wielded effective authority. By the mid-19th century, the new Al-Kanemi dynasty took formal control.

Kanuri social and cultural life has tended to be dominated by the pervasive influence of Islam, on the one hand; on the other, the political hierarchies that have been such a salient focus of Kanem-Bornu over the centuries. At the apex of the Bornu system was the *Mai*, surrounded by his royal kin and the *Koguna*, a ruling elite of free and slave titleholders. These officials were given landed estates for their support, from which they raised taxes, in turn, and supplied horses and troops for the *Mai*'s annual military campaigns. Warfare was necessary to supply the state both with slaves for local service or export, and with tribute from conquered towns and vassal states.

Trade and warfare encouraged an accumulation and centralization of resources, underwriting elaborate court ceremonial as well as extensive redistribution in the form of gifts of clothing and other goods at the time of various religious holidays and other festivities and ceremonies. From the ordinary household to the royal court, considerations of prestige, channeled through omnipresent patron-client hierarchies and the circulation of goods, were at the heart of Kanuri social life. The *Mai*—and later the *Shehu*—was also the "Commander of the Faithful" or *Amir al-Mu'minin* (a title also held the by Moroccan king yet today), helping support numerous Islamic schools and influential clerics.

Kanuri society is divided into three main classes. The large, extended family of the *Shehu* is the highest level, then the commoners, and in the past, slaves were at the bottom of the social scale. In the past, slaves were able to rise to powerful political positions and were given land grants by the *Shehu* or the *Mai*. Unlike most African peoples, the Kanuri are less concerned with kinship, meaning that specific lineage has little socially ascribed meaning. Many Kanuri were, and are, farmers and trade with Fulani and Shuwa Arab pastoralists for dairy products. In addition, Kanuri are well-known traders and today are involved in trade between Chad and Bornu State in Nigeria and beyond.

In the 19th century, under the new Kanembu dynasty, centralization was increased, the standing army expanded, and Islamic orthodoxy (including the application of *Shari'ah* law) intensified. In 1893, however, Bornu was invaded and occupied by a *Jihadi* warrior, Rabeh, who attacked and enslaved even Muslims in the name of reform. In any case, in Bornu as in other Sudanic states, there had been an immense expansion in the local use of slaves, who constituted from a third to a half of local populations by the end of the century.

The French, Germans, and British moved into the region in the early 1900s. Rabeh was defeated, and the *Shehu* of Bornu—in exile in Kanem—was reinstated. The British persuaded the *Shehu* to return to Bornu, where a new capital was developed at Maiduguri. The system of indirect rule allowed the reconstitution and gradual modernization of Bornuan political hierarchies, while the development of peanut exports provided a new source of revenues to replace those of the traditional long-distance trade.

Bornu's recent history has been more turbulent. Starting in the 1950s, a new Kanuri nationalism developed, calling for a reunification of the old Kanem-Bornu territories. Secessionist demands revived in the 1970s, and in 1976, a separate Borno State was created within the federal Nigerian system. Nationalist demands, spreading to include the Kanembu, revived in the 1990s; in 2000, along with 11 other northern Nigerian states, Borno expanded the application of *Shari'ah* law to the criminal domain.

K. P. Moseley

Further Reading

Cohen, Ronald. *The Kanuri of Bornu*. New York: Holt, Rinehart & Winston, 1967.

Collelo, Thomas, ed. *Chad: A Country Study*. Washington: GPO for the Library of Congress, 1988. http://countrystudies.us/chad/ (accessed May 25, 2011).

Falola, Toyin. *Culture and Customs of Nigeria*. Westport, CT: Greenwood Press, 2001.

Lovejoy, Paul E. *Transformations in Slavery*. Cambridge: Cambridge University Press, 1983.

"Nigeria's Borno State Adopts Sharia." http://news.bbc.co.uk/2/hi/africa/887355.stm (accessed May 25, 2011).

Khoisan

Khoisan refers to the Khoikhoin and San peoples who live in southern Africa. The term Khoisan was coined in 1928 by Leonhard Schultze and is more acceptable to both peoples than the older terms Hottentots (from the Dutch word meaning stutters from hearing the click sounds in their language) for Khoikhoin and Bushmen for San. In Botswana, the *Setswana* name *Basarawa* (*Mosarwa* in singular) is frequently used. The numbers of Khoisan speakers today is rather small—around 50,000 in Botswana, 33,000 in Namibia, 8,000 in Angola, 4,500 in South Africa, and 2,000 in Zambia and Zimbabwe. Khoisan also refers to their language, which includes a number of click sounds, some of which have been borrowed into Bantu languages such as *isiZulu*, *isiXhosa*, *Sesotho*, and *Setswana*.

The Khoisan were once spread throughout southern and much of eastern Africa. It is believed that the San, at least, are the oldest inhabitants of southern Africa, stretching back more than 12,000 years ago, though some have tried to connect them to fossil remains of more than 40,000 years ago. The Khoikhoin or

While the San are best known for living in the Kalahari Desert, they once inhabited the entire region of southern Africa. Some, such as these men, live in the great inland Okavango Delta in Botswana. (John A. Shoup)

Khoehoe seem to have emerged from the San and changed their main economic life from hunting and gathering to pastoralism some 2,300 years ago, and at least 2,000 years ago, they had reached the Cape of Good Hope.

The arrival of the Bantu peoples sometime in the third to fourth centuries CE put the new arrivals into conflict with both the San and the Khoikhoin. Bantu farmers and stockmen did not take kindly to San killing their valuable cattle or foraging their crops. Khoikhoi pastoralists competed for important grazing areas, and the Bantu were often hostile to Khoisan peoples. Rock art made by the San show them in conflict with the larger, spear-carrying Bantu. By the arrival of the Europeans in South Africa, Khoisan were already displaced or being displaced by Bantu farmers. Many Khoisan sought refuge in the less productive mountains (such as the Drakensburgs and Malotis) or in the more arid areas where settled farming is more difficult.

Most San have retained their traditional religion, which centers on a supreme god who is both great and good. He is the father of the moon and the sun, though the moon plays a greater part in ritual life; curing/trance dances occur most often at night during a new and full moon. San curing/trance dances are still held as people try to adjust to the difficulties of modern life. In the trance dances, the person able to deal with spirits (similar to a *shaman*) begins with a slow circling dance around the women, who are seated at a central fire. The women sing in high falsettos and clap. The men form a ring around the outside and sing in lower ranges in harmony with the women. The men both stomp as they dance and also clap their hands to give a syncopated rhythm to the dance. The spirit medium goes into a trance, and his eyes roll back into his head. He takes on the illness of the person to be cured and shouts out of himself the spirit which caused the illness. In doing so, he may suffer nosebleeds as his body stiffens and he throws his stiffened arms behind him. In rock art, representations of healing ceremonies are easy to pick out since they show one or more figures in the stiffened position, arms behind them, bleeding from the nose.

Rock art in southern Africa is the product of mainly San peoples, and in recent years archeologist and anthropologists have developed a great appreciation for the insights into San life provided by the paintings. Some of the sites, such as those at Tsodilo Hills in Botswana, are still visited and retouched by San. In 2001, Tsodilo Hills was declared a UNESCO World Heritage Site.

There are no San still living as their ancestors did before European contact. Claims to this effect for the international release of the South African film *The Gods Must Be Crazy* have proven to be untrue. By the 1960s, all San were in contact with modern nation-states, and Botswana and South Africa had programs to settle San and teach them to farm. White and Bantu farmers closed off important food-gathering areas as well as important water sources, interrupting San seasonal gathering patterns. In the 1960s and 1970s, San bands were left with no food or water sources, and some died of starvation or thirst. San became low-paid farm workers, with little to hope for continuing their traditional life style. In the 1980s, John Marshall took over a failed San project and turned it into a successful cattle project for them. The idea was to integrate cattle ranching and traditional use of the region in the north of Namibia. The project was initially objected to by both **Herero** ranchers and the Namibian government. Despite attempts to close the project, international organizations such as Oxfam began to provide needed financial aid and international notoriety.

Some San now make money by selling traditional San decorations made from leather, glass beads, and ostrich shell. Several cooperatives and income-generation projects help market their work in Botswana, Namibia, and South Africa. In some instances, the money made from sales of San craft are more than the salaries offered to San by white and Bantu farmers and ranchers.

Most Khoikhoin have lost touch with their pre-contact traditions and have converted to Christianity. The Khoikhoin were heavily influenced by the Dutch settlers from the Cape of Good Hope and rapidly adopted both the horse and the gun. Although many Khoikhoin became servants to Trek Boer farmers, those who remained free, such as the Griqua, established their own independent areas in the early 19th century, defeating Bantu peoples. The Griqua were themselves eventually absorbed into the **Afrikaner** Orange Free State. Others, such as the Nama in Namibia, were able to expand at the expense of Bantu and San again using the gun and the horse.

Khoikhoin from around the Cape region came into contact with Europeans starting with the arrival of the first Portuguese explorers in the 15th century. With the Dutch settlement in Cape Town in 1652, many were forced into labor for the Dutch freehold farmers and within a century had been absorbed into the emerging mixed race Cape Coloreds (**Creole**). Afrikaner expansion into the interior was greatly facilitated by Khoikhoin labor.

By the 19th century, pressures from both Bantu and European farmers for land had pushed into more and more isolated and unproductive areas. The Afrikaners thought of them as "vermin" and organized hunting parties to exterminate them. In the 20th century, surviving San have struggled to maintain their ancestral lands from encroaching needs of Bantu and white governments. In 2006, the San in Botswana won their court case to be allowed to return to their homeland in the Central Kalahari Game Reserve, and in 2008, the UN Human Rights Council criticized Botswana for selectively not allowing some of the San to return.

John A. Shoup

Further Reading

Afolayan, Funso. *Culture and Customs of South Africa*. Westport, CT: Greenwood Press, 2004.

Barnard, Alan. *Hunters and Herders of Southern Africa: A Comparative Ethnography of the Khoisan Peoples*. Cambridge: Cambridge University Press, 1992.

Collins, Robert O. *Africa: A Short History*. Princeton, NJ: Markus Wiener Publishers, 2008.

Denbow, James, and Phenyo Thebe. *Culture and Customs of Botswana*. Westport, CT: Greenwood Press, 2006.

Guenther, Mathias. *Tricksters and Trancers: Bushman Religion and Society*. Bloomington: Indiana University Press, 1999.

Hewitt, Roger. *Structure, Meaning, and Ritual in the Narratives of the Southern San*. Johannesburg: Wittwatersrand University Press, 2008.

Schapera, I. *The Khoisan Peoples of South Africa: Bushmen and Hottentots*. London: Routledge Kegan Paul, 1960.

Shostak, Marjorie. *Nisa: The Life and Words of a !Kung Woman*. Cambridge. MA: Harvard University Press, 2000.

Shostak, Marjorie. *Return to Nisa*. Cambridge, MA: Harvard University Press, 2002.

Thompson, Leonard. *A History of South Africa*. New Haven, CT: Yale University Press, 1995.

"Tsodilo." http://whc.unesco.org/en/list/1021 (accessed November 22, 2009).

UNHCR–Refworld. http://www.unhcr.org/refworld/country,,,,BWA,456d621e2,4a6452ccc,0.html (accessed November 22, 2009).

Kikuyu

The Kikuyu are the single largest group in Kenya and number some 5 million or around 20 percent of the total population of the country. The Kikuyu speak a Bantu language also called Kikuyu and are closely related to the Embu, Meru, **Kamba**, and Mbeere, who also seem to come from the same Bantu stock as the Kikuyu. *Kikuyu* is the **Swahili** pronunciation of the more correct *Gikuyu* or *Agikuyu*, as they call themselves.

Bantu peoples began moving into East Africa sometime before 500 CE and first

The Kikuyu are the largest ethnic group in Kenya and arrived there during the 15th century. (Library of Congress)

occupied the more lush highlands skirting around Lake Victoria. The Kikuyu have occupied the same area in Kenya long enough for their traditional religion to say that their god *Ngai* or *Mogai* placed them where they are. The Kikuyu believe that *Ngai* had three sons, one of whom was named Gikuyu, who married the woman Moombi, who was provided by *Ngai*. Moombi bore Gikuyu nine daughters, who founded the nine main clans of the Kikuyu.

It seems that the Kikuyu arrived in their current homeland in the 15th century and combined settled agriculture with animal husbandry. By the end of the 1600s, the Kikuyu and other closely related Bantu peoples had settled on the slopes of Mount Kenya and the nearby highlands. Kikuyu had generally good relations with the **Nilotic** Maasai. The Maasai provided leather for the market and, in exchange, wanted iron weapons and gourds for containers. The Maasai expanded in the 18th century, and the Kikuyu adopted Maasai weapons and fighting strategies, making them one of the strongest groups in the Kenyan Highlands.

In the 19th century, Europeans arrived in large numbers, and Kenya officially became British in the Berlin Conference of 1884—which included only European powers. Germany was awarded the territory to the south, then called German East Africa and later Tanganyika. Germany lost its African colonies in World War I to Great Britain, France, and Belgium, and Tanganyika became British. The British began "opening up" lands for European farmers in the first decades of the 20th century, and the area of the Kikuyu were of special interest to those who wanted to establish coffee plantations. The Kikuyu were removed (often by force) and settled in poor, infertile areas, but often became labor for the new European farms. A new form of identification document was required for all East African men, locally called the *kipande*, which stated the name of their employer and even how much they were paid. It was illegal to not carry the *kipande* and, in essence, it was illegal to move around outside of "Native" reserves and not have a European employer.

Kikuyu life was centered on settled villages scattered along the highlands. Family compounds called *Shamba* produced a variety of agricultural goods. Introduction of crops such as bananas, maize, potatoes, coffee, and tea transformed the Kikuyu, and they have a reputation for being "driving, opportunistic, and industrious" (Olson, 286).

Coming-of-age ceremonies were held for both boys and girls, and this included female circumcision. These ceremonies helped form an age set as well as age set obligations among those who go through the process together. Both boys and girls are circumcised, and it is noted that some 50 percent of all women in Kenya today are circumcised. Circumcision is a visible difference between the young, inexperienced members of society and those who are now adults. Female circumcision is still practiced today among the Kikuyu, though there is growing opposition to it not only in Kenya, but in other parts of Africa. The girls are circumcised by other women, and among the Kikuyu, a more severe version is practiced. The wound may be bound together by binding the legs together for up to 40 days.

The Kikuyu were exposed to Christian missionaries starting in the early 1900s, and as a result, most are today Christians. A small minority of Kikuyu still adheres to the traditional religion, but perhaps the larger number follows their own form of Christianity that combines traditional belief with Christianity.

The Kikuyu did not develop a strong, central political organization, but instead remained clan-based, with the nine main clans each forming a sense of unity. In addition to the clans, there are age sets called *riika* for both boys and girls. Villages were managed by a council of nine elders who represent different age set groups. Members of the village council hold office between 20 and 40 years before another member is elected. Above the village council was a district council, and each village elected one member who acted as a legal court.

The Kikuyu were recruited to work for the British army in World War I as "carriers"; that is, carrying goods to and from the battlefield and performing other menial jobs for British soldiers such as digging latrines. In 1920, the Kikuyu Central Association was formed to deal with the discrimination suffered by Kikuyu soldiers. Again in World War II, Kikuyu fought for the British, and following the end of the war, Kikuyu soldiers were again ignored by the colonial authorities. As a result, the Kikuyu formed an anticolonial movement called *Mau Mau*, which committed a number of violent acts starting in 1952. Between 1952 and when the movement was brought to an end in 1956, around 13,000 Africans had been killed, mostly among the Kikuyu. However, among the Mau Mau leadership was a young Kikuyu, Jomo Kenyatta, who would emerge as Kenya's leader for independence.

Independence came in 1963 and the mainly Kikuyu Kenya African National Union (KANU) won most of the seats. Jomo Kenyatta became the first elected president in 1964. The Kikuyu's proximity to the national capital of Nairobi and to British farmers led them to be among the most educated of Africans in Kenya. The Kikuyu held most government posts and dominated the government until Kenyatta's death in 1978. Daniel Arap Moi tried to take Kenya along the lines of a single-party state, which was opposed by most Kikuyu; and in 1986, Moi tried to remove

Kikuyu from his government in what was called the "Mwkenya Conspiracy."

Kikuyu continue to dominate the government today, and the current president, Mwai Kibaki, is a Kikuyu. His main opponent in the 2002 elections was Jomo Kenyatta's son Uhuru Kenyatta. Wangari Maathai, an internationally known and respected environmentalist and activist, is also a Kikuyu, and between 2003 and 2005, she served in the Kibaki's government. In 1999, former Mau Mau members announced they would pursue the British government for human rights abuses during the uprising. In 2006, they brought the suit before the British High Court, but no ruling was made as of 2011.

John A. Shoup

Further Reading

Ehret, Christopher. *The Civilizations of Africa: A History to 1800*. Charlottesville: University Press of Virginia, 2002.

Jenson-Elliot, Cynthia. *East Africa*. San Diego, CA: Lucent Books, Inc., of the Gale Group, 2002.

"Mau Mau Veterans Lodge Compensation Claim against UK." http://www.guardian.co .uk/world/2009/jun/23/mau-mau-veterans -compensation (accessed May 1, 2010).

Newman, James. *The Peopling of Africa: A Geographic Interpretation*. New Haven, CT: Yale University Press, 1995.

Sobania, N. W. *Culture and Customs of Kenya*. Westport, CT: Greenwood Press, 2003.

Stokes, Jamie. "Kikuyu (Gkuyu)." In *Encyclopedia of the Peoples of Africa and the Middle East*. New York: Facts on File, 2009.

Kongo

The Kongo (Bakongo) are among the largest ethnic groups in Central Africa and the largest ethnic group in the Democratic Republic of Congo. The Kongo are located along the Atlantic seaboard of Congo Brazzaville, Democratic Republic of Congo, and Angola and at the end of the 20th century, they were estimated to number over 10 million. Their language, Kikongo, is a Bantu language and is composed of some 50 dialects. One such dialect, Kileta, is used as a common language for both Kongo people and non-Kongo people as well as **Lingala**, a trade language along the Congo River.

The Kongo people began to form into a kingdom sometime in the 13th or 14th century. There is a debate over where the Kingdom of Kongo first began, either along the Congo River along the Malebo Pools or around the current city of San Salvador in northern Angola. Whether the initial move toward a unified state began in one place or another, a number of smaller kingdoms were unified under the leadership of Lukeni Nimi, who allied himself with the Mwisikongo people to gain control over the trade in copper. Lukeni Nimi took the title of *Manikongo*, or king of the Kongo, and he and his successors built a strong state. The Kongo controlled not only trade in copper, but also *nzimbu* shells that were used as the currency in the region until the 16th century.

The Portuguese arrived in 1482, and by that time, the Kongo were a strong and flourishing kingdom. The *Manikongo* lacked an ideological base for his authority and ruled over a decentralized state with a number of others claiming local title as *mani*. The Portuguese brought Christianity, which both they and the *Manikongo* used to their advantage.

Christianity brought with it a host of saints or spirits to rival those of the traditional religion, and the *Manikongo* Mbcmbe a-Nzinga converted to Christianity and sent his son to Portugal for education. The prince converted to Christianity and came to the throne as King Alfonso I in 1506, ruling until 1543. Since that time, all subsequent kings of Kongo have been Christian.

The Kongo state was slowly undermined by the actions of the European traders and by those of its own client states that opened up direct trade with Europeans. The *Manikongo* had to deal with both internal problems, such as the invasion by the Jaga (or identified as the **Ovimbundu**) in 1568, and other issues, such as playing the Dutch against the Portuguese. In exchange for Portuguese assistance against the Jaga, the king was forced to allow the Portuguese seizure of Luanda Island, and in 1576, the Portuguese established the colony of Angola on the mainland. In addition, Portuguese soldiers who were sent to assist against the Jaga stayed and married locally, forming a new Luso-African class called *Pombeiros*, engaged primarily as merchants.

The slave trade grew in the 16th and 17th centuries, and various provinces or dominated kingdoms were able to break loose from the central state and engage in direct trade. Ndongo and Matamba both seceded from the kingdom and grew to economically rival Kongo. The increase in warfare helped bring more slaves to the coast, and the mixed-race Luso-Portuguese acted as the main traders. In 1665, the Portuguese defeated the army of the *Manikongo*, and the kingdom

fragmented with French, Portuguese, and later Belgian colonists able to gain control of the territory.

The majority of Kongo are at least nominal Christians, but many belong to local denominations that combine African concepts with Christianity. In 1705, Beatrice Kimpa Vita was a Kongo prophetess who tried to restore aspects of the traditional religion, and in 1921, Simon Kimbangu also taught a combined version of Christianity and local religion, which still has a strong following of Kimbanguist today. Kimbanguist religion played a major role in Kongo resistance to domination by the Belgians.

Local religion consisted of animist beliefs, ancestral spirits, and magic, all of which were among the beliefs that survived conversion to Christianity. Nail fetishes or *nkondi* are among the items produced, which are wooden statues that are pounded with a number of nails and can be "activated" by the owner or a diviner specialist called an *nganga*. The statues are only statues, the reason they can be sold on the art market and to tourists, until a diviner or owner, using spells, is able to make them operational and come "alive." There are different types of *nkondi*; those of a male with a spear who represent punishment, a woman and child who represent gentleness, and a dog who mediates between the living and the dead. Such statuary is now considered to be art and sought after by collectors in Europe and North America.

Kongo were matrilineal, yet political leadership was in the hands of local headmen who had limited authority. Headmen were responsible to chiefs and on up the line to the king of *Mani*. Before the final subjugation of the Kongo in 1900, the *Manikongo* had authority over a number of semi-independent kings—each called a *mani*—who recognized his power. The loose federation of the political structure was both a strength and a weakness of the system. The traditional leadership, though it still exists in the rural regions, has lost much of its political power.

The various Kongo kingdoms were finally subjugated by the French (Brazzaville), Belgians (Democratic Republic of Congo), and Portuguese (Angola) by 1900. King Leopold of Belgium ruled the Congo Free State from 1885 to 1908 until his massive abuses of the indigenous peoples were exposed and he was forced to turn the colony over to the Belgian state. In 1910, the new colonial authority for the Belgian Congo recognized chiefs as agents of the state, and the right to appoint chiefs went to the hands of the colonial power. The colonial authorities began to create chiefdoms that had not existed before, and in 1921, no more were allowed to be recognized.

During the colonial period, over 64 million hectares or 160 million acres were set aside for private companies to exploit in the Belgian Congo. A system of forced labor was put in place, and local people lost their rights to hunt, farm, fish, or gather from these lands. Forced labor was justified as a means of tax collection, and all Congolese were required to serve 60 days a year in time of peace and 120 days a year in times of war on government lands.

Kongo people led the movements for independence in the French and Belgian Congos and in Angola. The *Association des Bakongo* in Belgian Congo and the *Frente Naconal de Libertacao de Angola* were active in the independence movements and into the postindependence period. Today the Kongo are among the better educated in all three countries and represent many of the urban professionals. In the countryside, Kongo are mainly farmers, and little of their former political organization is evident.

John A. Shoup

Further Reading

Bacquart, Jean-Baptiste. *The Tribal Arts of Africa: Surveying Africa's Artistic Geography*. New York: Thames and Hudson, 2000.

Ehret, Christopher. *The Civilizations of Africa: A History to 1800*. Charlottesville: University Press of Virginia, 2002.

Meredith, Martin. *The Fate of Africa: A History of Fifty Years of Independence*. New York: Public Affairs, 2005.

Mukenge, Tshilemalaema. *Culture and Customs of the Congo*. Westport, CT: Greenwood Press, 2002.

Newman, James. *The Peopling of Africa: A Geographic Interpretation*. New Haven, CT: Yale University Press, 1995.

Oyebade, Adebayo. *Culture and Customs of Angola*. Westport, CT: Greenwood Press, 2006.

Tishken, Joel E. "Central Africa: Peoples and States." In *Africa Volume 1: African History before 1885*, edited by Toyin Falola. Durham, NC: Carolina Academic Press, 2000.

Vansina, Jan. *Paths in the Rainforests: Toward a History of Political Tradition in Equatorial Africa*. Madison: University of Wisconsin Press, 1990.

Kuba

The Kuba (Bakuba plural) number between 200,000 and 250,000 people and are composed of between 16 and 18 different peoples who all speak the same Bantu language called Bakuba. The Bushoong or Bushongo formed the political heart of the Kuba, while other groups such as the **BaTwa** (a **Khoisan** people), **Lele**, and Njembe or Ngeende were included as Kuba, but did not participate in governance above the regional level. They live in the Kasai region in the southern Democratic Republic of Congo.

The Kuba originated in the 16th century when various proto-Kuba people moved into the region between the Kasai and the Sankuru rivers. They encountered the Kete and Twa, whom they began to absorb. In the 17th century, the dominant Bushongo, or "people of the throwing knives," began to arrive and defeated other rivals. The Bushongo established a divine kingship, or *nyim*, and an imperial order/rule or *matoon* around the semi-mythical founder of the dynasty Shyaam aMbul aNgong. Those who were dominated by the Bushongo were *bubil* or affiliated chiefdoms. The arrival of new food crops such as cassava and maize from the Americas allowed their economy to thrive, and its aristocrats supported artisans producing a high tradition of arts in raffia cloth, wood carving, and metal. Their location, on the edge of the rain forest, woodlands, and savanna, gave them a wide range of products for trade. Twa skills as hunter-gatherers originally were used as a source of items such as honey and animal hides, since the Kuba were themselves fishermen and farmers. The Twa lost their independence to Kuba chiefs as they became a more vital part of the local economy.

The Kuba were in the position to control a good deal of the trade networks and lacked little themselves. Ivory was one of the main trade items controlled by the Kuba, but the Portuguese and Luso-Africans were used to exchanging European cloth for it. The Kuba produced their own cloth and generally refused to exchange ivory for items other than slaves and cowrie shells. As the 19th century progressed, ivory became less and less available from other sources in eastern Angola such as from the **Chokwe**. The Kuba developed a "stranglehold" over ivory and they banned hunting by those other than themselves. Initially, most of the trade was with the Portuguese in Angola, and the Kuba would most likely have become part of the Angola colony if, in 1884, the Belgian king Leopold II had not claimed the region as part of the Congo. The 1885 Berlin Conference awarded Leopold the Kasai region, and it became part of the Belgian Free Congo.

Initially, the Kuba were able to enforce a policy of isolation against the encroachments of Europeans. In the past, they had allowed a small number of Portuguese and Luso-African traders to set up posts in some of their markets, but did not allow them to become a permanent presence in the kingdom. The Portuguese, like the **Arabs** and **Swahili** traders, came as caravan traders and did not stay. The Belgians were unable to control the Kuba until after 1910, when a state post was finally built in the royal capital. The Belgians were assisted by the local chief they called "Zappo Zap" (Nsapu Nsapu) and his son, whom they also called Zappo Zap.

Kuba art was recognized as superior to many others and was immediately noted for being one of the most "developed" in Africa. As part of a "national" identity, Kuba art, architecture, dance, religion, and language was promoted by the kingdom. The different ethnic groups who formed the Kuba then had a single cultural development and identity. Much of the art was produced for the aristocracy, who used it to denote social rank, as well as for export. In fact, almost from the first contact with Europeans, Kuba art has been collected for its beauty, and has been compared to that of "pharaonic Egypt, to Augustan Rome and to imperial Japan" (Binkley and Darish, 7).

The Kuba produced various masks used in ceremonies, such as for *ngesh* or nature spirits and *makanda* initiation rites. Among the most spectacular is the *Mawaash a Mbony*, worn by Kuba kings during trials, which represents Woot, the founder of the Bushongo. The *Mukenga* mask closely resembles the *Mawaash*, and both masks have a long trunk to recall the elephant, which to the Kuba represents the power of the king.

The *ndop* or king figures are another developed art. These are carved wooden figures, and each represents a past king identified by his animal totem. Other carved items include drinking cups, lidded boxes, smoking pipes, drums, and nearly all daily items that are carefully engraved and many are covered in cowrie shells.

Personal dress is another form of Kuba art. Raffia cloth made from palm fiber is spun and then woven into cloth by men on single-headed looms. The cloth is then given to women who appliquéd, tie-dyed, beaded, and/or embroidered the piece depending on its intended use. The cloth is still made and exported to Europe and North America, where it is bought mainly by collectors of African art. Other aspects of personal dress such as elaborate raffia belts are decorated with beads and cowrie shells. Rank can be determined by other aspects of dress, such as carrying a large blade of copper, iron, or brass that signifies status. Western demand for Kuba art is such that it has now put constraints on what can be produced and sold, since Western consumers want what is identifiable as "traditional" pieces.

Kuba political structure reflected the different ethnic groups that formed the kingdom, and the provinces represented the ethnicities. At the village level, a council of elders from the different clans, and thus every clan, had the right to participate in politics. In larger communities, each of the different residential areas also had its own council. Each of these communities selected a representative to the higher council up to the level of the province. At the province level, the chief was principal chief of the ethnic group and the paramount chiefs of the Bushongo clans elected the king, who served with divine authority. Divine right of the Kuba kings helped unify the people, as did his army and common administration.

In 1901, the Compagnie du Kasai was formed and given the monopoly over ivory, rubber, and other raw materials of the region. Fairly soon after its formation, company greed and the start of a Presbyterian mission fomented rebellion through the use of a charm called *Tongatonga*. The charm was for collective protection for the community from the exploitation by the company and others. The rebellion was ended by 1909, but by then the Belgian Free State was turned over to the Belgian state to manage.

The Kuba experienced a significant loss of life during the colonial period. Population figures for the precolonial and colonial periods are difficult to reconcile; nonetheless, people either fled the area or succumbed to epidemics due to the colonial opening of the region—the colonial regime recorded a total of only 150,000 people in 1920. Both the conquest from 1899 to 1900 and the revolt of 1904–1905 caused a good deal of damage and loss of population.

The Kuba polity was able to survive the colonial period and even regained some of the lands it had lost when, in 1910, the Belgian law on chiefdoms was established. The Kuba were able to take advantage of indirect rule, given the political structure was better intact than elsewhere in the colony. Nonetheless, Kuba society needed a means to try to reestablish a sense of peace or *poloo* with the spirit world, and in 1924 the Lakosh cult began. Named for one of the *ngesh* spirits who it is believed revealed it, the Lagosh belief spread rapidly beyond the Kuba area. Lagosh was replaced in 1950 with a new, similar cult, Miko miYool. These tradition-based religions have a greater appeal than Christianity to the Kuba, and few today have converted.

Following independence in 1960, the Kuba formed the state of Kasai and tried to break from the control of Kinshasa in 1961, but they were forced to return. The Kuba Kingdom has endured civil war and, although greatly replaced by civil servants from the central government, there is still a king, Kwet aMbweky III, who has ruled since 1969.

John A. Shoup

Further Reading

Bacquart, Jean-Baptiste. *The Tribal Arts of Africa: Surveying Africa's Artistic Geography.* New York: Thames and Hudson, 2000.

Binkley, David, and Patricia Darish. *Visions of Africa: Kuba.* Milan: 5 Continents Press, 2009.

"Kuba Information." http://www.uiowa.edu/~africart/toc/people/Kuba (accessed June 1, 2010).

Mbajekwe, Patrick U. "East and Central African in the Nineteenth Century." In *Africa Volume 1: African History before 1885*, edited by Toyin Falola. Durham, NC: Carolina Academic Press, 2000.

Mukenge, Tshilemalaema. *Culture and Customs of the Congo.* Westport, CT: Greenwood Press, 2002.

Vansina, Jan. *Being Colonized: The Kuba Experience in Rural Congo, 1880–1960.* Madison: University of Wisconsin Press, 2010.

Vansina, Jan. *Paths in the Rainforests: Toward a History of Political Tradition in Equatorial Africa.* Madison: University of Wisconsin Press, 1990.

Weston, Bonnie E. "A Kuba Mask." http://www.randafricanart.com/kuba_Mukenga (accessed June 1, 2010).

Kurds

The term Kurdish refers to an ethnolinguistic group of the Iranian branch of the Indo-European language family. The majority of Kurdish people today inhabit a geographic region known as Kurdistan, which extends into Turkey, Iran, Iraq, and

Syria; a sizeable community of Kurds inhabit the Near East, and to a lesser extent in Russia and Armenia; a global diasporic community exists as well. It is difficult to say with precision, but it is estimated that there are approximately between 20 million and 36 million Kurds today. The term "Kurd" is thought to be a derivative of "Carduchii," an ancient people who are recorded in the writings of Xenophon and Strabo; it is clear that in the medieval period, the meaning of the term "Kurd" was somewhat ambiguous, perhaps referring to a people with a nomadic lifestyle. The Ayyubid dynasty (1169–1260, mainly in Egypt and Syria) was of Kurdish descent; prominent Kurdish leaders include the 12th-century *sultan* Salah al-Din (Saladdin), and, in the 20th century, 'Abdullah Öcalan, founder of the PKK (Parti Karkeren Kurdistan or Kurdistan Workers Party).

As noted above, the Kurdish people are thought to be descended from the Carduchii (perhaps the Kardoukhi) described by Xenopohon and the Kardakes described by Strabo; Strabo states that "Karda" means "warlike" or "manly"—this is perhaps paralleled by the Assyrian term *qardu* or "strong." An Iranian people by language, the Kurdish people are ethnically diverse due to intermarriage with other ethnic groups with which they have come into close contact; given the vast territory that Kurdistan covers, this would suggest intermarriage with such peoples as **Arabs**, **Armenians**, **Persians**, and **Turks**.

The Kurdish language is divided into three main groups: Kurmanji (northern); Sorani (southern); and such southeastern dialects as Sine'i, Kermanshahi, and Leki.

While Kurdistan was initially ruled as a series of independent Kurdish princedoms in the classical and early medieval eras, those princedoms were later reduced to feudal vassals of the Ummayad *Khalifahs* (661–750); this was reinforced later by the Ottoman Empire (1281–1924).

Kurdish lifestyle is difficult to generalize, as the Kurds are not confined to a single political state. The Kurdish economy is in part based on agriculture, and Kurdistan is partially arable; peasant farming and pastoral nomadism have been widely practiced in the past, with such major crops being wheat and other grains, and vegetables; fruit and nut trees are widely found in Turkey, Iran, Iraq, and Syria. In recent years as the nomadic tribes have been encouraged to settle, pastoral nomadism has greatly declined in favor of sedentary types of economy. While the Kurdish towns used to produce crafts and goods, international trade has made this increasingly difficult, as foreign products are often cheaper and more readily available than those of traditional make. Kurdish life is very much structured by a dependence upon land, family, and clan; marriage within the clan system is preferred, and the *agha* (chief) of the clan has considerable authority over the lives of those within the clan. In general, Kurdish society encourages the celebration of festivals marked by traditional song and dance, without gender segregation; however, some of the Kurds along the Iran-Iraq border practice extreme forms of gender segregation. Further, both traditional and modern outdoor field sports are commonly practiced by Kurdish youth, both boys and girls.

Rugged mountains in Kurdistan protect it from invasion. (Salajean/Dreamstime.com)

The majority of Kurds are Sunni Muslim of the *Shafi'i* school of jurisprudence; this distinguishes them from the Turks and some Arabs of neighboring territories, who are of the *Hanafi* school. The Kurds in Iran, however, are mostly Shi'ite. A minority of Kurds also belong to such religious movements as the *Ahl-i-Haqq* (People of the Truth) and the Yezidi, which began as a Sunni sect but has diverged to the point that it is no longer considered to be Muslim. Likewise, a very small minority of Kurds practice Judaism and Christianity. *Sufism*, especially the Qadiri and Naqshbandi orders are especially popular in Kurdistan, and the *shaykhs* of these orders wield considerable social and political influence. Religion (especially Islam) has played an important role in defining Kurdish identity, especially in terms of differentiating them from Turkish and Arab neighbors.

Unlike other ethnic groups in neighboring regions such as Turkey and Iran, the Kurds have never had a political state of their own, but rather, Kurdistan overlaps several countries. This, coupled with the strategic importance of the area, has made Kurdistan coveted by its neighbors, and yet its rugged mountain terrain has served to shield it from invasion. Given the vast size of Kurdistan and the fact that the Kurds inhabit different countries, there has been no real idea of Kurdish unity or independence until the 19th century, when several tribal chieftains and Muslim *shaykhs* began to rebel against Ottoman authority. In the mid-to-late 20th century, Iraq and Turkey had especially tense relationships with the Kurds, as both nations were reluctant to recognize the Kurds as a separate ethnic group. In Iraq, the Kurds faced violent opposition in their struggle for recognition and independence, and Iraq was strongly condemned internationally in 1987–1989 for its use of chemical weapons against Kurdish settlements. In Turkey, Mustapha Kemal Atatürk tried to appeal to the Kurds during the early stages of the republic, but later abandoned this approach in favor of hard-line Turkish nationalism. In response, the PKK (Kurdistan Worker's Party) arose in the mid-20th century, under the leadership of 'Abdullah Öcalan. In the 1970s and 1980s, the movement became an armed conflict, causing some international unrest as Syria supported the PKK, which greatly strained relations between Turkey and Syria. The armed insurgence of the PKK ceased only in 1999 with the recent arrest of Öcalan; since then, Öcalan has openly renounced violence and called for a peaceful political solution to the issue of Kurdistani sovereignty.

Connell Monette

Further Reading

Abazov, Rafis. *Culture and Customs of Turkey.* Westport, CT: Greenwood Press, 2009.

Barkely, H., & G. Fuller. *Turkey's Kurdish Question.* Lanham, MD: Rowman & Littlefield, 1998.

Bois, Th. "Kurds, Kurdistān." In *Encyclopaedia of Islam Online*, 2010.

CIA World Factbook. January 2010. http://www.cia.gov/library/publications/the-world-factbook/ (accessed May 25, 2011).

Daniel, Elton L., and Ali Akbar Mahdi. *Culture and Customs of Iran.* Westport, CT: Greenwood Press, 2006.

Jwaideh, W. *Kurdish National Movement: Its Origins and Development.* Syracuse, NY: Syracuse University Press, 2006.

Kent, R. *Old Persian: Grammar, Texts, Lexicon.* 2nd ed. New Haven: Oriental Texts Society, 1953.

Manady, A. *The Kurdish Political Struggles in Iran, Iraq, and Turkey.* Laham: University Press of America, 2005.

Marcus, Aliza. *Blood and Belief: The PKK and the Kurdish Fight for Independence.* New York: New York University Press, 2007.

Natali, D. *The Kurds and the State: Evolving National Identity in Iraq, Turkey, and Iran.* Syracuse, NY: Syracuse University Press, 2005.

Shoup, John. *Culture and Customs of Syria.* Westport, CT: Greenwood Press, 2008.

Van Bruinessen, M. *Agha, Shaikh, and State: The Social Structures of Kurdistan.* London: Zed Books Ltd., 1992.

L

Lebou

The Lebou are one of Senegal's smallest ethnic populations and are found primarily in and around the capital city of Dakar. They are the original inhabitants of the Cape Verde peninsula and have thus become an important economic force in the country, despite their small numbers. Lebou number only around 50,000, mainly in Dakar and the two nearby villages, now part of the greater Dakar area, Yoff and Cambérène. The Lebou speak a form of **Wolof**, but it is a distinct version and not a dialect of the language.

The Lebou resisted the Portuguese and later the French, keeping their independence from European control for centuries. In 1444, the Portuguese established themselves on the island of Gorée, and the Lebou inhabitants were forcibly removed. The Lebou won their independence from the Kingdom of Kayor in 1790 and became a small, federal republic ruled by a Muslim religious lineage, the *serins* of Ndakarou. Today, the Senegalese government still recognizes the *serin* as the titular head of the Lebou people.

The Lebou form the main base for the Layène Sufi Order founded in Seydina Limmamou Laye in the late 19th century. The Layène Order has close links with the spiritual importance of 'Issa (Jesus) and several of the orders leaders have either the name of 'Issa or aspects of his spiritual presence in their names. The Layène Order founded the nearby village of Cambérène, next to Yoff, where Seydina 'Issa Rohou Laye established an important shrine in 1914. There are a number of special celebrations held by the order, such as the celebration of Christmas (December 25), at their Cambérène shrine.

Some Lebou remain fishermen along the coast, the traditional form of subsistence for the villages of Yoff and Cambérène; but, they are also among Dakar's major property owners. Lebou secured title to lands during the French colonial period and many have subsequently become very wealthy as Dakar developed into the main administrative center for the country. As neighborhoods developed, the Lebou engaged in friendly rivalry through sponsoring traditional wrestling matches or *mbapat*. Wrestling is more part of rural Senegalese life, but the Lebou began to sponsor matches in the 1920s. Matches were reborn in Senegal in the 1990s with the irreverent *Bul Faale* or New Generation movement in Dakar and today matches take place at major stadiums.

The modern period for the Lebou was ushered in by French occupation of Dakar starting in first half of the 19th century, especially after the abolition of slavery throughout the French empire in 1848. In 1872, the French recognized both Gorée and St. Louis (on the mouth of the Senegal River) as *communes* or municipalities, and in 1880, French traders in Rufisque also gained the status of a *commune*. In 1887,

Iconography in Senegal helps identify the owner of a shop or business with the Sufi Brotherhood he or she belongs to. This portrait of the Layene Brotherhood in Yoff shows the owner is a member of the order, which is exclusively Lebou in membership. (John A. Shoup)

Dakar was detached from Gorée and became its own municipality, and in 1902, Dakar became the capital of the new Afrique Occidentale Française. The Lebou emerged as both politically and economically powerful during the French colonial period by making sure their land claims were given official French recognition. Intermarriage with powerful Wolof families has happened and continues to happen; nonetheless, strong Lebou identity remains.

John A. Shoup

Further Reading

"Cambérène." http://www.aui.ma/personal/~E.Ross/camberene.htm (accessed May 1, 2010).

Olson, James. *The Peoples of Africa: An Ethnohistorical Dictionary*. Westport, CT: Greenwood Press, 1996.

Ross, Eric. *Culture and Customs of Senegal*. Westport, CT: Greenwood Press, 2008.

Stokes, Jamie. "Lebu." In *Encyclopedia of the Peoples of Africa and the Middle East*. New York: Facts on File, 2009.

Lele

The Lele belong to the different ethnicities that make up the **Kuba** and inhabit the lower Kasai region of the Democratic Republic of Congo (formerly Zaire). They are a Bantu-speaking people numbering between 20,000 and 30,000 people. The Lele are referred to by a number of terms and spellings, including Bashileele, Bashilele, Bashilyeel, Batsilele, Leele, Schilele, and Shilele.

As one of the non-Bushongo Kuba provinces, the Lele had their own *nymi* or king/paramount chief with limited authority. He ruled over a number of villages that were organized by product; villages that made palm wine and others of sculptures, while women did most of the agricultural work. Lele woodcarving, though similar to other Kuba work, made use of well-defined human heads in their pipe bowls, and the palm wine cups had distinctive zigzag decoration. Villages are organized according to age sets, with the elders acting as a council and controlling most of the traditional religious practices including traditional healing. In the past, traditional healers belonged to a society called *banging*, which required an initiation. The Lele, like others in the Kuba kingdom, resisted the Belgians. Today most Lele are small farmers or work in the major cities in the Democratic Republic of Congo such as Kinshasa.

John A. Shoup

Further Reading

Mukenge, Tshilemalaema. *Culture and Customs of the Congo*. Westport, CT: Greenwood Press, 2002.

Olson, James. *The Peoples of Africa: An Ethnohistorical Dictionary*. Westport, CT: Greenwood Press, 1996.

"Tribal African Art: Lele (Bashileele, Bashilele, Bashilyeel, Batsilele, Leele, Schilele, Shilele)." http://www.zyama.com/lele/pics..htm (accessed June 1, 2010).

Lemba

Lemba, also called the Valemba, Remba, and Baremba, are a small Bantu-speaking people who live in the Belingwe region of Zimbabwe, South Africa, Mozambique, and Malawi, numbering only 70,000. The majority speak **Shona**, but generally they speak the language of the dominant group around them.

The origin of the Lemba is controversial, but the British researcher Tudor Parfitt claims he proved the Lemba are descendants of ancient **Jews** through DNA testing of Lemba, Yemeni Arabs, and Jews. They also may be descendants of Muslim traders from the African coastal cities that grew up to trade with Great Zimbabwe. Personal names also indicate a more likely **Arab** origin than Jewish.

The Lemba are today Christians, but they do have a number of traditional practices such as strict monotheism, food restrictions, and keeping one day holy for their God, all practices that are similar to Judaism. Many of these customs are also shared with Muslims and Jews, such as ritual slaughter of an animal, not eating pork, and male circumcision. In addition, Lemba women wear long sleeves, dresses, and headscarves similar to Muslim women.

The Lemba are a small community engaged in crafts such as weaving, pottery, and iron working. The research into their origins by Tudor Parfitt has given rise to a strong sense of Jewish identity since 2003.

John A. Shoup

Further Reading

Afolayan, Funso S. *Culture and Customs of South Africa*. Westport, CT: Greenwood Press, 2004.

Insoll, Timothy. *The Archeology of Islam in Sub-Saharan Africa*. Cambridge: Cambridge University Press, 2003.

Olson, James. *The Peoples of Africa: An Ethnohistorical Dictionary.* Westport, CT: Greenwood Press, 1996.

Owomoyela, Oyekan. *Culture and Customs of Zimbabwe.* Westport, CT: Greenwood Press, 2002.

Parfitt, Tudor. "Constructing Black Jews: Genetic Tests and the Lemba." http://eprints.soas.ac.uk/4580 (accessed November 21, 2009).

Tyrrell, Barbara, and Peter Jurgens. *African Heritage.* Johannesburg: Macmillan South Africa, 1986.

Lingala

Lingala is a Bantu trade language or commercial *lingua franca* that emerged along the Congo River in the 19th century. It began in the middle region of the river, around where Kinshasa and Brazzaville, the modern capitals of Congo and Democratic Republic of Congo (formerly Zaire) would be built, and it is spoken by over 10 million people. One of the four major languages of the Democratic Republic of Congo, it is used in broadcasts by Radio Télévision Congolaise and is one of the main means of communication in the army and other official organizations. It is seen as the language of urban and modern life and is the main language used in modern music, particularly for what was called *Lingala Jazz, soukous* and *sundama.*

Lingala was chosen as the main language for the dance music called *soukous.* *Soukous* grew from Congolese rumba that was popular in much of Africa from the 1940s through the 1960s. Congolese rumba developed a local sound, but was primarily borrowed from the Afro-Caribbean rumba that found its way back to Africa in the 1940s. Latin American music with strong and noticeable African origins, such as rumba, became popular in the 1940s with Western audiences. The popularity of rumba, and other Cuban or Dominican dances, was such that local bands emerged in many of the European African colonies who performed at night clubs and bars. Some even attempted to sing in Spanish, but oftentimes it was more like trying to imitate the sound of Spanish rather than actually singing the words.

In the 1960s, a new sound was developed as part of the break with the colonial past. The first group to typify the new sound was OK Jazz, which had first been a popular rumba band. Borrowing from Congolese popular music, they blended instruments such as the *likembe* or thumb piano and the acoustic guitar; a fusion occurred, and *soukous* was born. The New Wave developed in 1970 with the group Zaiko Langa Langa among the leaders. Their group's leader, Nyoka Longo, stated that the music is "like a fetish. People don't understand the effect of our music has on them. But they have to dance." (Ewens, 141). Among the new stars was Papa Wemba, who started the *Sapeur* movement. This movement took its name from the Society for Ambiencers and Persons of Elegance, where being dressed in the best fashions was taken up by the youth in cities like Kinshasa or *kinois* as they are called.

Soukous was also embraced by youth in other African countries and in Europe, where a new, reformed version of the dance music was started by Congolese living in Europe and called *kwasa kwasa* from the phrase that is repeated in many of the songs. *Kwasa* comes from the French phrase *qua ca* or "like that." Among the most successful was Kanda Bongo Man, a "one-man band" who cut back on the large stage bands of Congolese *soukous* (Ewens, 154). Although *kwasa kwasa* was extremely popular, the quick commercialization of this format brought an end to its popularity, though Kanda Bongo Man himself has remained popular.

Soukous, though still internationally popular, was eventually replaced by the new dance craze in Congo, the *sundama*. *Sundama* groups, like Swede Swede, were large, but the lead singer was the most important member of the group. The musicians borrowed from the traditional styles of the Mongo people of the Equatorial region of the country. Along with the Western set of drums, they included the *lokole* or slit long drum, which gave a "ragged" sound to the music. *Sundama* groups performed with Caribbean *zouk* bands and have added to the round of African and African diaspora influences in music.

John A. Shoup

Further Reading

Ewens, Graeme. *Africa O-Ye! A Celebration of African Music*. London: Guinness Publishing, 1991.

Eyre, Banning. *Africa: Your Passport to a New World of Music*. Los Angeles: Alfred Publishing, 2006.

Graff, Folo. *African Guitar Styles*. Ontario, CA: A. D. G. Productions, 2001.

Mukenge, Tshilemalema. *Culture and Customs of the Congo*. Westport, CT: Greenwood Press, 2002.

Tenaille, Frank, and Akwe Betote. *Music Is the Weapon of the Future: Fifty Years of African Popular Music*. Chicago: Lawrence Hill Books, 2002.

Lozi

The peoples of the Lozi kingdom, also known as "Barotse," center along the upper Zambezi River floodplain in Zambia's Western Province, with additional populations in eastern Angola, Namibia's Caprivi Strip, northwestern Zimbabwe, and northern Botswana. Historically, the region was known as "Barotseland." Lozi identity is fluid and includes members from 25 linguistically distinct groups whose degree of participation varies on a community and individual basis. The *lingua franca* is Silozi, a **Sotho**-based language that reflects the region's integration of southern and central African influences. "Rotse" or "Barotse" is a colonial-era Sotho-ized pronunciation of the currently preferred "Lozi." Today, Lozi number over 800,000.

Lozi royalty trace their roots to princess Mbuyu (also known as Mbuywamwambwa) who broke from the **Lunda** kingdom of Mwata Yamvo in Congo in the 17th or 18th century. All subsequent kings, known as *Litunga*, derive their authority from coronation rites held at her grave. Some legends suggest attempts to strengthen Lozi dynastic claims by asserting that the royalty have lived along the Zambezi since time immemorial and trace their descent to Nyambé, or God, who coupled with female ancestor Mbuyu. Until the 1830s, the royalty were known as Luyana

Lozi men paddle the royal barge carrying the Litunga of Barotseland during the annual boat pageant, "Kuomboka." (AP/Wide World Photos)

or Luyi. In 1840, a Sotho leader named Sebituane assumed control until his death in 1860. "Lozi" or "Rotse" refers to the Sotho-Luyana blend that followed. Lozi identity, as it is understood today, emerged during the reign of Barotseland's legendary king Lewanika (r. 1876–1916), who negotiated with the British South Africa Company to establish Barotseland as a protectorate and not a colony.

Lozi are perhaps best known for their annual boat pageant, *Kuomboka*. Each year as the waters of the Zambezi rise, the Lozi king (*Litunga*) leads a procession of elaborately decorated barges across the flooded plain to high ground. The *Litunga lya Mboela* (Queen of the South) also performs *Kuomboka*, which translates "to get out of the water." Rich in costumes, performances, and music, this annual event celebrates the diversity within the region and attracts international audiences. It is balanced by the smaller return trip, *Kufuluhela*.

Lozi are also widely recognized for their elaborate manners that include kneeling and clapping in greeting. Lozi have also marketed their identity internationally with art forms, most notably carved wooden bowls featuring animal motifs on the lid and baskets woven from the root of the *Mukenge* tree, and they maintain their wealth in cattle.

Missionaries have had long-standing relationships in the area, dating back to the travels of David Livingstone, and today the vast majority of Lozi are Christian.

Lozi maintain a traditional court or *kuta* system known as the Barotse Royal Establishment. All kings since 1916 have descended from Lewanika. In 1964, *Litunga* Sir Mwanawina signed the Barotseland

Agreement that joined Barotseland with Northern Rhodesia to form Zambia. His successor, Mbikusita Lewanika II was a founder of the Africa National Congress, and his children Akashambatwa and Inonge hold prominent national and international political roles.

Karen E. Milbourne

Further Reading

Caplan, Gerald. *The Elites of Barotseland, 1878–1969: A Political History of Zambia's Western Province*. Berkeley and Los Angeles: University of California Press, 1970.

Gluckman, Max. *Economy of the Central Barotse Plain*. Manchester: Manchester University Press for the Rhodes-Livingstone Institute, 1941.

Mainga, Mutumba. *Bulozi under the Luyana Kings: Political Evolution and State Formation in Pre-Colonial Zambia*. London: Longman, 1973.

Milbourne, Karen. "Collecting and Projecting Identity: Barotseland's Arts in International Arenas." *Collections* 4, no. 1 (2008): 85–100.

Milbourne, Karen. "Craft and Creativity: Artists and Missionary Outreach in Barotseland." *Museum Anthropology* 24, no. 1 (2000): 42–56.

Milbourne, Karen. "Diplomacy in Motion: Art, Pageantry and the Politics of Creativity in Barotseland." PhD diss., University of Iowa, 2003.

Prins, Gwyn. *The Hidden Hippopatamus: A Reappraisal in African History, the Early Colonial Experience in Western Zambia*. Berkeley and Los Angeles: University of California Press, 1980.

Luba

The Luba or Baluba are one of the largest single ethnic groups in the Democratic Republic of Congo (former Zaire), numbering over 5.5 million and inhabiting the southern Katanga, Kasai, and Maniema regions. They speak a Bantu language called Ciluba or Tshiluba and are closely related to the **Lunda**. Around 12 percent of Luba are Muslims, due to contacts with **Swahili**-speaking peoples in the past century, while the remainder are nominally Christians observing many of their traditional religious practices.

Origins of the Luba can be traced back to the eighth century with the emergence of small, agricultural states in the Katanga region. The Upemba Depression produced important items, but most important was copper that was used as both a currency and a marker of social status. In addition, the abundance of fish allowed the population to grow. The growth of the small states provoked conflict with each other over vital resources, which caused a quick militarization of them. The most powerful of the state, called Luba, was based around Lake Kisale, whose leadership was taken over by a people from the north called the Songye. Among the important changes brought by the Songye was the change to a matrilineal system of descent. The Luba kingdom is called the First Luba Empire or the Kingdom of Upemba that lasted from around 1100 to 1450. It has been noted that there were in fact four states that did not combine into one but, from time to time, verged on empire status. Luba influence was such that other kingdoms claimed real or fictive claim to Luba origins.

By the 16th century, the Luba had formed a powerful, centralized state with the leader or *mulopwe* not only the secular ruler, but also the religious head as well.

This is the Second Luba Empire that would last until the 19th century. The *mulopwe* was assisted by a number of ministers with specific duties who also ruled the various provinces of the kingdom, thus keeping the government confined to a very small number of aristocrats. Starting around the beginning of the 17th century, various disgruntled Luba aristocrats struck out and formed their own political entities beyond the Luba Kingdom, including the Lunda, which was founded by such a Luba aristocrat called Chibinda Ilunga.

The Luba Kingdom expanded and took over other peoples as tributaries or *mukonso* rather than as equals. The central state did not see the necessity of providing for the provinces, which was one of its main weaknesses. The Luba Kingdom lasted until it was confronted by the Belgian colonial authorities in the 1880s as well as by the growth powered by the **Chokwe** state. The Luba actively resisted the Belgians between 1907 and 1917, but were eventually defeated.

The Luba are generally matrilineal, though some groups are patrilineal, and the role of women in society is important. The importance of women is reflected in a number of cultural ways including Luba art, which often depicts women. The Luba are farmers, but the shallow soils in tropical areas need time to recover from cultivation. Nonetheless, they produce crops of cassava, maize, millet, sorghum, bananas, and tobacco and keep small stock such as pigs, poultry, goats, and sheep.

Following its defeat in 1917 by the Belgians, the kingdom fell apart, and the current situation of numerous chiefdoms emerged. The chief is selected based partially on seniority of descent and partially on a rotation system that allows all families the chance to exercise rule. Lineages that are not local, that is founded by a foreigner—refugees or prisoners of war—are excluded from the chieftainship, but are represented in the council. In addition, another factor became more important starting in the colonial period: wealth. Only those families with enough financial means could qualify for the role of chief. It has been noted that the colonial authorities frequently agreed to candidates who were willing agents of colonialism as well. Today, wealth still is an important factor in selecting a chief.

Following independence in 1960, the Katanga province rose in rebellion and, between 1960 and 1963, set up an independent state. The province was brought back into Congo (then Zaire) in 1965 when the national army defeated the rebels. Most of the Luba did not support the rebels and even provided troops to fight them. The secessionists were led by a member of the Lunda aristocracy, and the Luba have generally not supported subsequent rebellions in 1977 and again in 1984.

John A. Shoup

Further Reading

Collins, Robert O. *Africa: A Short History.* Princeton, NJ: Markus Wiener Publishers, 2008.

Lamphear, John, and Toyin Falola. "Aspects of Early African History." In *Africa*, 3rd ed., edited by Phyllis M. Martin and Patrick O'Meara. Bloomington: Indiana University Press, 1995.

"Luba Information." http://www.uiowa.edu/~africart/toc/people/Luba (accessed June 10, 2010).

Mukenge, Tshilemalaema. *Culture and Customs of the Congo*. Westport, CT: Greenwood Press, 2002.

Tishken, Joel E. "Central Africa: Peoples and States" in *Africa Volume 1: African History before 1885*, edited by Toyin Falola. Durham, NC: Carolina Academic Press, 2000.

Lulya

The Lulya or Luhya (Buluhyia, Abaluyia plural) are a Bantu people and are the second largest population in Kenya after the **Kikuyu**, numbering 5.3 million or 14 percent of the population of Kenya. Their language, called oluLuhya, is shared by 16 to 18 subdivisions in Kenya and another 4 in Uganda, including the Isukka, Idakhos, Kabra, Nyala, Tsotso, Wanga, Marama, Kisas, Nyore, Margoli, Tirilis, Bakhayo, Tachoni, Marach, Samia, and Bukusus. A minority of Luhya live in Uganda and Tanzania, but the majority live in Kenya.

The Luhya have a number of different origins and migrated to their current location in the 15th century. They seem to be descendants of Bantu peoples from around the Lakes Region, but also have **Kalenjin** and Maasai ancestors. Their own legends state that they migrated from *Misir* or Egypt. They remained a decentralized group and did not develop a collective identity until recently. However, it is believed that the different ethnicities coalesced into a single group in the 17th century, with the language serving as the main means of group identity. OluLuhya has been spoken for some 500 years, and the different dialects are all mutually intelligible. Most Luhya are Christians today, but many of their traditional beliefs, such as in witches, remain. The Wanga subgroup of the Luhya, unlike most of the other Luhya groups, did develop into a kingdom influenced greatly by the nearby **Ganda**. In 1883, the first European passed through their land and met with the Wanga king Nabongo Mumia.

The Luhya live in an arid area, and generally those in more arid areas raised cattle, while those in better-watered southern areas raised crops such as millet and maize. The importance of livestock to their culture is evidenced in the marriage bride price, which is paid in cattle, sheep, and goats. Marriage must be from a clan not related to the groom's clan, and even today, out-of-clan marriages are a necessity. Even though most marriages are still arranged by families, both men and women are allowed to take lovers. Families are patriarchal, and men are allowed to take a number of wives. The first wife is responsible for managing the various members including any subsequent wife the head of household may marry.

The Luhya also practice male circumcision, which marks a boy's entry into adult life. Boys are circumcised between the ages of 8 and 15 during an event that takes place once a year. It can be delayed up to five years; afterwards, the boys are then put into age sets. Traditional bullfights are still held once a year and have become a major tourist attraction. Another aspect of tourism is the making of "Wanga dolls" and "Wanga packets" (often spelled pakets), which are supposed to have charms or help in a person's life. Both the dolls and packets seem to be a cross between West African *voodoo* and the Wanga belief in witches and have become popular with

North American clients. It is possible to purchase both the dolls and the packets online.

Luhya lands were expropriated for colonial farms, and the Bukusus in particular resisted engaging in numerous battles to regain their lands. However, the Wanga and Kabra collaborated with the British and worked on colonial farms. In 1902, the British split Luhya lands in half when the boundary between Kenya and Uganda was agreed upon.

Following colonization, sugar cane was introduced as a cash crop, and today the Luhya produce nearly all of Kenya's sugar. Along with sugar, crops of wheat and maize are also produced. A good number of Luhya still live in their traditional home region, and the Bukussus have been able to retain much of the precolonial life, but more and more young people are moving to Kenya's major cities for work.

John A. Shoup

Further Reading

"The Luhya of Kenya." http://www.orville jenkins.com/profiles/luhya (accessed June 10, 2010).

"Luhya Tribe." http://www.enhols.com/kenya _safari/people/luhya (accessed June 10, 2010).

"The Luhya Tribe." http://www.kenya-advisor .com/luhya-tribe.html (accessed June 10, 2010.

"The Luhya Tribe." http://www.kenya -information-guide.com/luhya-tribe (accessed June 10, 2010).

Sobania, N. W. *Culture and Customs of Kenya.* Westport, CT: Greenwood Press, 2003.

Stokes, Jamie. "Luyia." In *Encyclopedia of the Peoples of Africa and the Middle East.* New York: Facts on File, 2009.

Lunda

The term Lunda covers a number of peoples who once lived in the Lunda Empire as well as to those who adopted a government influenced by the Lunda Empire. In general, the Lunda are a Bantu people who speak Cilunda or Kilunda and are found today in the Democratic Republic of Congo, Angola, and Zambia. They number over 1.5 million people, and nearly one-half lives in the Katanga province of Congo, one-third live in Angola, and the rest live in Zambia. They are called Rund or Runda as well, as individual groups took the names of their leaders such as the Kazembe.

The Lunda began as several small states in the Nkalaany Valley in the Upper Kasai River in the 16th century. **Luba** ideas of government spread into the Lunda area and, in the early 17th century, a Luba prince named Kibinda Ilunga left the Luba when passed over for a political position and married the Lunda leader, the woman Lueji. Kibinda or Chibinda introduced Luba governing principles, which were further refined and implemented by his descendants, named Lusengi and Naweji. It has been noted that three of Queen Lueji's brothers, not content with the Luba prince Kibinda taking charge of the chiefly symbols of the royal bracelet, bow, and drums, left with followers and established other Lunda polities to the south.

The Lunda embarked on expansion by military conquest or by domination, and by the 18th century, the kingdom was flourishing. Much of the wealth of the Lunda Empire was based on trade with the Portuguese from Angola and with the **Arabs** and **Swahili** traders from East

African port cities and Zanzibar. Trade for salt, copper, ivory, and slaves brought in cloth, cowrie shells and other items.

The success of the Lunda was in the invention of the position of the *Mwaant Yaav* or king, a term invented by Kibinda's grandson Naweji. Unlike that of the Luba or other king positions in much of the region, the *Mwaant Yaav* of the Lunda embodied the dual principles of positional succession and perpetual kinship. That is, the person who became the *Mwaant Yaav* automatically inherited the kinship of his predecessor, and he and his own kinsmen became kinsmen with those of the previous king "with the same mutual rights and obligations forever" (Mukenge, 17). Conquered chiefs kept their positions as leaders of their people as the *Mwaant a Ngaand* or owner of the land, meaning that the land still belonged to the original owners. Taxes were collected by a special militarized chief called the *Kawata*, who ensured as well that the king's messages were delivered.

In the 18th century, the semi-independent kingdom of Kazembe was established when the ruling *Mwaant Yaav* Muteba awarded the eastern expansion of the Lunda Empire to Ngonda Bilonda as *Mwaant Kazembe*. By the turn of the 19th century, the new Kazembe kingdom was the heart of trade both to the Atlantic via Portuguese and Luso-African traders and to the Indian Ocean via Arab and Swahili traders. The Lunda Empire eventually broke up in the late 19th century due to internal conflicts and the mounting pressure of the **Chokwe**.

The Lunda were and are primarily farmers living in compact villages. The land in the region is typical of tropical soils, being light and needing time to recover from cultivation. In order to not overuse the soils, a system of shifting agriculture was developed, producing crops of millet and sorghum and later also maize and cassava. Cash crops of sunflowers and pineapples were introduced by the European colonial authorities. Women did most of the cultivation, and men both hunted and fished. Lunda skills in fishing have been exploited with the recent introduction of fish farming.

Most Lunda converted to Christianity in the 20th century, and Christian missionaries made use of their traditional belief in a supreme being called *Nzambi*. Nonetheless, many Lunda hold to several of their traditional beliefs, particularly to the idea that their ancestors can punish or reward them. The Lunda in Zambia celebrate *Mutomboko* or crossing the river, which marks the day that they defeated the Bwile and Shila and established the Kazembe kingdom. The celebration is held in the old royal capital, and the king himself dances.

The Lunda are matrilineal or patrilineal, depending on the group. In some instances, a person counts both lines as equally important. Because the Lunda have incorporated a number of different conquered peoples, they do not have a single form of descent, but it is likely that the original core Lunda population was matrilineal.

The Lunda were colonized by the end of the 19th century by three different powers, the British in Zambia, the Portuguese in Angola, and the Belgians in the Congo. In each of these, the Lunda have had a somewhat different experience. In Zambia, the Lunda remained a cohesive group and were able to maintain a good deal of their traditional culture. They did not generally move to the mining areas of the country. In the Belgian Congo, the Lunda resisted and, following World War II, founded CONAKAT, a powerful political organization whose main purpose was to counter Luba and Chokwe politicians.

When Congo gained its independence in 1960, the Lundas opted for their own independence and rose in rebellion. From 1960 to 1963, the Katanga province was outside main government control, and the mainly Lunda rebels were not finally defeated until 1965. The Lunda have risen again in 1977, 1978, and 1984. In 1993, Katanga again declared its independence, and the governor was arrested by troops from the central government in 1995. The violence increased, and it has calmed down only with the release of the governor from jail in 2003.

John A. Shoup

Further Reading

Ehret, Christopher. *The Civilizations of Africa: A History to 1800*. Charlottesville: University Press of Virginia, 2002.

Lamphear, John, and Toyin Falola. "Aspects of Early African History." in *Africa*, 3rd ed., edited by Phyllis M. Martin and Patrick O'Meara. Bloomington: Indiana University Press, 1995.

"Lunda Information." http://www.zyama.com/Iowa/Peoples/Lunda%20People.htm (accessed June 10, 2010).

Mbajekwe, Patrick U. "East and Central Africa in the Nineteenth Century." In *Africa Volume 1: African History before 1885*, edited by Toyin Falola. Durham, NC: Carolina Academic Press, 2000.

Mukenge, Tshilemalaema. *Culture and Customs of the Congo*. Westport, CT: Greenwood Press, 2002.

Taylor, Scott. *Culture and Customs of Zambia*. Westport, CT: Greenwood Press, 2006.

Wills, A. J. *An Introduction to the History of Central Africa: Zambia, Malawi, and Zimbabwe*. Oxford: Oxford University Press, 2002.

Luo

The Luo or Lwo are a **Nilotic** people and are the third-largest ethnicity in Kenya, making up 13 percent of Kenya's population. The Luo number over 3 million and are found in western Kenya, near Lake Victoria, as well in Tanzania, Uganda, and southern Sudan. The Luo language, Dholou, belongs to the same Nilotic group of languages as the **Acholi** of Uganda and the Shilluk of Sudan.

The Luo originated in the southern part of Sudan, south of the Sinnar Kingdom and along the Bahr al-Ghazal watershed. The Ocholo Kingdom united a number of Luo-speaking people in the 14th century with a sacred ruler. The Luo lived along the Nile and had a varied diet from crop cultivation as well as raising cattle. In the 15th and 16th centuries, the Jyang or Dinka (**Nilotic**) began to expand into the Ocholo Kingdom about the same time as the southern Luo began to migrate south into what is today Uganda.

The Luo migration from Sudan to Kenya lasted over the past 400 to 500 years. Their migration was prompted by the redistribution of grazing lands in southern Sudan by the Dinka and Nuer (**Nilotic**). The Luo began a slow movement with their cattle "setting up temporary camps among the way" (Newman, 164). The Luo were well organized and established several kingdoms along their migration route, both among Bantu farmers and other Sudanic peoples who had migrated earlier. The Bito clan of the Luo established control over the Bantu Nyoro, the Hinda clan did much the same over Bantu speakers on the western side of Lake Victoria, and the Hima clan, pushing further south, founded the **Tutsi** kingdoms of Rwanda and Burundi. There is some dispute among scholars about the influence of the Luo and the royal traditions of the interlacustrine or Lakes Region, which stretches from Lake Turkana in the north to Lake Malawi in the south. Some have postulated that the Luo brought many of the concepts with them, while others note that pre-Luo Bantu peoples had many of the same customs and symbols of royalty.

The Luo are patrilineal, and many families are polygamous. In fact, around 30 percent of households are polygamous today. The practice of multiple wives seems to have grown with the need to have all adults married. Husbands pay a bride price, and the woman does not sever connections with her own lineage, but maintains close relations with her brothers. The bride price goes to the woman and is a means by which she can maintain her own kin ties and her own sources of wealth.

The Luo do not practice circumcision as a means of noting the rite of passage for either a boy or girl. Instead, Luo mark the passing from childhood into adulthood by knocking out the bottom six front teeth. Some have speculated the practice made them less attractive to slavers. Traditionally, girls spent their teen years in the company of other girls minded by elder women in separate sleeping huts.

Both the Anglican and the Roman Catholic churches have missions in Kenya's Luoland, and a large number of people have converted. Nonetheless, the Christianity practiced by the Luo includes a good deal of their pre-Christian belief system. In 1912, the first independent church, the Nomiya Luo Church, was founded. The traditional belief system does have a supreme being who is referred to by a number of names that indicate his powers, including *ruoth* or "the king," which helped Christian missionaries identify the Christian god, and especially Christ as king of Heaven, with that of the Luo. In addition to a supreme god, the Luo believe in a number of other spirits or *jouk*, which means shadow. Most of these spirits cause mischief or harm if they are not properly respected and/or remembered.

Luo expansion continued until the late 19th century, when they encountered the British. The Luo, like other "natives" in Kenya, suffered loss of lands to white farmers and ranchers. During the colonial period and after independence, the Luo have remained isolated from national politics. Their area of country is generally less developed than others, and a good portion of women are illiterate. A disproportionate number of Luo suffer from HIV, and infant mortality and food shortages are, unfortunately, all too common. The water supply is contaminated with a number of waterborne diseases in much of Kenya's Luoland. In addition, tourism and tourist dollars are funneled to Lake Victoria and generally bypass the Luo. Anger over these problems bubbled to the surface with elections in 2007 and 2008 between Raila

An American Luo: President Barack Obama II

American president Barack Obama is the first African American to be president of the United States. His mother, Stanely Ann Dunham, is from Wichita, Kansas, and his father, Barack Obama Sr. is from Nyang'oma Kogelo, Kenya. Obama Sr. was in the United States as a foreign student, and Barack Obama Jr.'s parents met in a Russian language class at the University of Hawaii and married in 1961. Obama Sr. went on for a degree at Harvard University, and in 1964, the two divorced.

In 1988, Barack Obama made a trip to Kenya, where he met for the first time a number of his father's relatives. As part of his experience in his father's culture, he was asked to wear traditional clothes, and some of those photos made it into the American media during the 2008 presidential race.

When he won the 2008 American presidential election, many in Africa celebrated the victory. In Kenya, people thought of him as one of their own. Though American born and with an American mother, Africans saw him as an African, the first African president of the United States.

Odinga and Mwai Kibaki. Odinga was supported by Luo and **Kalenjin**, while Kibaki was supported mainly by **Kikuyu**. Violence erupted after Kibaki was declared the winner in the election for president and, in the end, international mediation was needed to calm the situation. A unity government was formed with Kibaki as president and Odinga as prime minister.

John A. Shoup

Further Reading

Ayodo, Awuor, and Atieno Odhiambo. *Luo*. New York: Rosen Publishing Group, 1996.

Collins, Robert O. *A History of Modern Sudan*. Cambridge: Cambridge University Press, 2008.

Countries and Their Cultures. "Luo." http://www.everyculture.com/wc/Japan-to-Mali/Luo (accessed June 10, 2010).

Miller, Frederic, Agnes Vandome, and John McBrewster. *Luo*. Beau Bassin, Mauritius: Alphascript Publishing, 2010.

Miruka, Simon Okumba. *Oral Literature of the Luo*. East Lansing, MI: East African Education Publishing, 2003.

Newman, James. *The Peopling of Africa: A Geographic Interpretation*. New Haven, CT: Yale University Press, 1995.

Obama, George, and Damien Lewis. *Homeland: An Extraordinary Story of Hope and Survival*. New York: Simon and Schuster, 2010.

Otiso, Kefa M. *Culture and Customs of Uganda*. Westport, CT: Greenwood Press, 2006.

Sobania, N. W. *Culture and Customs of Kenya*. Westport, CT: Greenwood Press, 2003.

Lur

There are over 2 million Lur living mainly in the Zagros Mountains of western Iran, representing 1 percent of the Iranian population. Luri is their language and it is closely related to **Persian**, which is an Indo-Iranian language of the Indo-European phylum. There are two main dialect groups of Luri; Lur-i Buzurg (Greater Lur) and Lur-i Kuchik (Lesser Lur) which are further divided into regional dialects. The two names of Greater and Lesser Lur originally referred to the geographic division within Luristan (homeland of the Lur) which came into usage during the Ilkanid rule (1256–1353) in Iran. The word "Lur" means "wooded hill" in the Luri language, which may be connected to places such as Rur found in the geographical dictionary of Yaqut al-Hamawi (d. 1229).

The origin of the Lurs and the name Lur is associated with the region of Manrud located in Lesser Luristan. In 1106, a group of **Kurds** from Syria arrived and settled on lands of the Jangrawi *Atabek*. They were later joined by other tribal peoples, mainly Kurds, but also several **Arab** tribes. From these emerged the Lur tribes of today; the **Bakhtiyari**, Kuh-Gilu, Fayli, and Mamassani. Many Lur tribal groups, such as the Kuh-Gilu, are composed of various sections of Luri, Kurdish, and Arab origins.

The Jangrawi clan emerged as the leaders of the Lur and established the Khurshidi dynasty of Atabeks, who ruled from 1184 to 1597 from their capital of Khurramabad. The Lurs supported the Safavid ruler Shah Isma'il I (1501–1524) and adopted 12er Shi'ism of the State, the Lur leadership having already assumed an 'Alid genealogy, that is claiming descent from 'Ali ibn Abi Talib, the cousin of the Prophet Muhammad and husband of the Prophet's daughter Fatimah Zahrah.

Most Lur are Shi'ites, following the mainline 12er Shi'ism that became the state religion in Iran under the Safavid Shahs (1501–1722). The noted scholar on Iran, Vladimir Minorsky, states that the level of knowledge of Islam held by the Lur was so doubtful that the Qajar prince (the Qajar dynasty ruled Iran from 1779 to 1925), Muhammad 'Ali Mirza, felt he had to send a *mujtahid* (a religious scholar) to "convert" them to Islam.

Some of the Lur, mainly those of Kurdish origin, follow the heterodox Islamic sect called *Ahl-i al-Haqq* (meaning Men of Truth [God]) or *'Ali Ilahi*. It is a secretive sect that is found mainly in western Iran. It seems to have begun sometime in the 18th century, but due to the fact that it is a secretive sect, information about them is limited. It appears to combine Isma'ili or 7er Shi'ism and 12er Shi'ism, and the poems in Turkish by Safavid *Shah* Isma'il I form the important base for their belief, though this is not well understood.

Luri women are well-known weavers, and weaving by women from the main Luri tribes differs from those of the Bakhtiyari. Luri women use a horizontal looms and weave only geometric motifs, like most other "tribal" carpets (as opposed to the more sophisticated types made in Iranian cities such as Isfahan or Hamadan). Diamonds, stepped triangles, and stylized tree of life are the most common designs done in yellow, white, and light blues on a red or blue background.

In the 19th century, the Qajars were able to effectively bring most Lur, with notable exception of the Bakhtiyari, under state control; however, by the middle of the 19th century, any vestige of state control was gone. The Qajars were not able to effectively control a number of tribal areas, and it was not until the rise of the Pahlavi dynasty (1925–1979) under Reza *Shah* that a state policy of forced settlement of pastoralists was enforced.

In 1941, Reza *Shah* was forced to abdicate in favor of his son Muhammad Reza because of his pro-German politics. Muhammad Reza was, in reality, the nominal ruler of the country between 1941 and 1953 (the date of the Mussadeq coup), and many of the tribal leaders were once again able to take control of rural areas. The Lur abandoned the settlements and returned to pastoralism. Following Muhammad Reza's return to the throne after the Mussadeq coup was defeated, a vigorous autocratic rule was instigated along with a number of major reforms from 1960 to 1977. The state tried to force pastoral nomads to settle; however, many of these farms failed. Julia Huang, daughter of the well-known American anthropologist and expert on Iranian pastoral peoples, Lois Beck, notes that the Islamic governments in Iran have been less hostile to groups such as the Lur, who are able to maintain a degree of their lifestyle, including distinctive clothes, because they are seen as "authentic indigenous" Muslims, less influenced by Western culture.

John A. Shoup

Further Reading

Daniel, Elton L. and Ali Akbar Mahdi. *Culture and Customs of Iran*. Westport, CT: Greenwood Press, 2006.

Huang, Julia. "Integration, Modernization, and Resistance: Qashqa'i Nomads in Iran since the Revolution of 1978–1979." In *Nomadic Societies in the Middle East and North Africa: Entering the 21st Century*, edited by Dawn Chatty. Leiden: Brill, 2006.

Khalili, Nasser. *Islamic Art and Culture: Timeline and History*. Cairo: Cairo University Press, 2008.

Lamb, Harold. *Mountain Tribes of Iran and Iraq*. Washington, DC: National Geographic Press, 1946.

Lapidus, Ira. *A History of Islamic Societies*. Cambridge: Cambridge University Press, 1997.

Minorsky, V. "Ahl-i al-Hakk." In *Encyclopaedia of Islam*, 2nd ed., CD-ROM.

Minorsky, V. "Lur." In *Encyclopaedia of Islam*, 2nd ed., CD-ROM.

Minorsky, V. "Lur-i Kuchik." In *Encyclopaedia of Islam*, 2nd ed., CD-ROM.

Minorsky, V. "Luristan." In *Encyclopaedia of Islam*. 2nd ed., CD-ROM.

Makonde

The Makonde or Chimakonde, Konde, Maconde, and Matambwe are a large ethnic group in southern Tanzania and northern Mozambique. They are spilt by the Rovuma River and, in the past, developed distinct cultures. They speak a Bantu language called Makonde or Chimakonde, and it is spoken by over 1.3 million people. Some Makonde moved to Kenya in the 1930s for work, and other small minorities are found in Malawi.

The Makonde are closely related linguistically to the Makua-Lomwe peoples of northern Mozambique and the **Yao** of Mozambique, Tanzania, and Malawi. The Bantu peoples arrived in the region of southern Tanzania and northern Mozambique as early as 500 BCE. A group called the Mashariki Bantu peoples increased food production, used metal tools, and developed livestock raising, including sheep husbandry. When they reached the Romuva River, some proceeded down the river to the coast and on to South Africa, while others moved along a western route. By 100 CE, Bantu were firmly in place along the Romuva River. Among them were the Kusi, from whom the Makonde seem to descend.

The Makonde are matrilineal farmers raising crops of millet and sorghum as well as owning cattle and goats, though livestock have never been important economically. Hunting supplements farming. They never developed a central political authority and each village, managed by a headman, is independent of each other. Village headmen are selected through the principle of matrilineal descent.

The Makonde are well known for their art, mainly for their wood carvings. The Makonde make masks, figures, and decorative objects mainly from hardwood. Among the collectables of Makonde art are the *lipico* masks, which are very lifelike and often include human hair insets. Other objects are wooden statues generally thought to represent their ancestors. In addition, the Makonde produce a number of other daily objects with the human face, such as combs, pipes, canes, and boxes. Makonde art has become one of their main sources of income, as their work is sought by tourists as it is by museums.

The Makonde live in an isolated area and were not contacted by Europeans until 1910. Nonetheless, they were, no doubt, contacted long before by **Arab** and **Swahili** slave dealers. Today, around 80 percent of the Makonde are Muslims of the *Shafi'i* school of Sunni Islam, while the rest are Christian or cling to their ancestral religion. In Mozambique, the Makonde played a significant part in FRELIMO's (Liberation Front of Mozambique) resistance to the Portuguese.

John A. Shoup

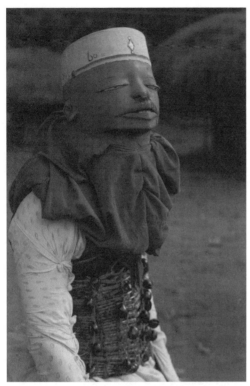

A masked Makonde dancer performs in Mozambique. The Makonde are known for their woodcarving and life-like masks. (Volkmar K. Wentzel/National Geographic/Getty Images)

Further Reading

Bacquart, Jean-Baptiste. *The Tribal Arts of Africa: Surveying Africa's Artistic Geography.* New York: Thames and Hudson, 2000.

"Makonde Information." http://www.uiowa.edu/~africart/toc/people/makonde (accessed June 10, 2010).

"Makonde—Introduction." http://www.bluegecko.org/kenya/tribes/makonde (accessed June 10, 2010).

Meredith, Martin. *The Fate of Africa: A History of Fifty Years on Independence.* New York: Public Affairs, 2005.

Ndege, George. *Culture and Customs of Mozambique.* Westport, CT: Greenwood Press, 2006.

Malagasy

The Malagasy population is composed of several major groups: the Malayo-Indonesians, whose main groups are the Merina (27%) and the Betsileo (13%), who together make up 40% of the total population; and the Malayo-Indonesian, **Arab**, and African mix called Côtiers, who make up the largest number of the of the people on the island of Madagascar today. In addition to the Merina and Betsileo, there are the Betisimiraka (15%), Sakalava (6%), and the Mehafaly or Mahafaly, who are also Malayo-Indonesians. The Malagasy language belongs to the Malayo-Polynesian group of the Austronesian language phylum and is spoken by about 17 million people on Madagascar. The standard/official form of the language is based on the Merina dialect.

Madagascar was first settled between 200 and 500 CE by migrants from what is today Indonesia, though it may have been as early as the sixth century BCE. From linguistic evidence in the Malagasy language, they apparently first settled on the East African coast, where they borrowed a number of terms from the Mashariki Bantu before moving on to settle on the island of Madagascar. The Malagasy brought with them Asian food crops that were well suited to the East African coast, such as Asian yams, taro, bananas, and sugar cane, which impacted Bantu agriculture. In addition they also brought with them the xylophone, which spread rapidly across the region and became associated with kings and chiefs. In the seventh century, Arab traders set up stations on the island, and their geographies began to indicate the island and describe its people. Between the 10th and 13th centuries, Muslims began to settle on the northern end of the island, and in 1500, the first European, the Portuguese Diego Dias, visited it.

By the 18th century, there were three kingdoms on the island: the Merina dominated the central part of the island, the Sakalava on the west, and Betsimisaraka on the east. The Merina kings Andrianampoinimerina and his son Radama I brought all of Madagascar under one kingdom for the first time at the start of the 19th century. King Radama I was able to secure recognition of his control of the whole island in 1817 from Great Britain. Initially, the Malagasy were able to keep from falling under European control, but in 1883, France invaded and tried to establish a protectorate over the whole island. The French fought two wars with the Merina Kingdom, in 1883–1885 and in 1895, before the Malagasy were defeated. In 1896, France declared Madagascar to be a colony open for French settlement, and in 1897, they deposed Queen Ranavalona III, the last Malagasy monarch.

Originally the major populations of the Malagasy lived in different parts of the country and had different economic systems. The Merina are the largest of the groups on Madagascar and number over 3 million. Merina society was divided between the free or *fotsy*, descendants of free Merina, and the *mainty*, descendants of slaves. The Merina are among the best educated of the people on Madagascar

and tend to the social and political elite. The Betsileo are very similar to the Merina. The Betsileo were mainly farmers and developed skills in rice production. They number over 1.3 million people and, like the Merina, are well represented in the professions and in the civil service.

The Betsimisaraka are the second-largest population on the island, numbering over 1.5 million people. The Betsimisaraka were concentrated along the eastern shores of Madagascar and engaged in commercial crops of cloves, coffee, and vanilla. They are divided into two main groups; the Betsimisaraka proper, and the Betanmena.

The Sakalava live on the western coast and have been open to Muslim settlers from the Comoros Islands. As a result, Islam has influenced them perhaps more than other Malagasy people. The Sakalava are both seminomadic pastoralists as well as agriculturalists. The Mahafaly or Mehafaly are also pastoralists and are of Sakalava origin. They inhabit the region between the Menarandra and Onilahy rivers, moving their flocks and herds according to the seasons.

The Malagasy groups are all joined in a cultural practice of funerary traditions. Nearly all of the Malagasy groups practice some form of what is called secondary inhumation; that is, the body of the deceased is either temporarily buried or is allowed to dry in the sun to purify before its bones are placed in an ancestral communal tomb. The tombs are marked with wooden carvings in human form, which have become collectors' items. Though each of the Malagasy peoples has slightly different customs and the wooden carvings have different representations, they share the same tradition. The current government is trying to get many of the tomb statuary back from foreign private and public collections and museums.

Around 50 percent of all Malagasy belong to their traditional religion, which focuses on spirits and the ancestors. Much of the worship is held at the communal tombs where funerary objects are used. Christianity was introduced by the Europeans in the 19th century, both by British Protestants and by French Roman Catholics. Around 10 percent of Malagasy are Muslims. Islam has had a much longer presence in Madagascar than Christianity and was brought by Arab and **Swahili** traders. The form of Islam practiced on Madagascar is Sunni Islam, the same as that on the East African coast.

During World War II, the British occupied Madagascar when it fell under Vichy French control, and in 1943, the British turned it over to the Free French. In 1946, the French bestowed French citizenship on the Malagasy, but this did not stop their drive for independence, which erupted in a pro-independence rebellion in 1947–1948. The rebellion was defeated after some 80,000 Malagasy were killed. In 1958, the French allowed a referendum in which the Malagasy people declared for an autonomous republic within the French Community. It became fully independent in 1960 and was renamed the Republic of Madagascar in 1975.

In the subsequent years, Madagascar has had a difficult time. There have been two additional constitutions, a time of military control, and disputed presidential elections. One president was convicted of corruption—in absentia—all of which has made the Malagasy skeptical about their country's political processes.

John A. Shoup

Further Reading

Bacquart, Jean-Baptiste. *The Tribal Arts of Africa: Surveying Africa's Artistic Geography*. New York: Thames and Hudson, 2000.

Brown, Mervyn. *A History of Madagascar*. Princeton, NJ: Markus Wiener Publishers, 2002.

Evers, Sandra J. T. M. *Constructing History, Culture and Inequality: The Betsileo in the Extreme Southern Highlands of Madagascar*. Leiden: Brill Academic Publishers, 2002.

"Malagasy (Fiteny Malagasy)." http://www.omniglot.com/writing/malagasy.htm (accessed June 10, 2010).

Randrianja, Solofo, and Stephen Ellis. *Madagascar: A Short History*. Chicago: University of Chicago Press, 2009.

Mande

Mande is a large language group spread throughout much of West Africa from the Niger River and the Sahara in the east to the Atlantic Ocean in the west. There are several related peoples who speak varieties of Mande, numbering 5–6 million and living in Mali, Guinea, Ivory Coast, Gambia, Senegal, Guinea-Bissau, Burkina Faso, Sierra Leone, and Liberia. The Mande language belongs to the West Atlantic branch of the Niger-Congo family, and its original home most likely is in the area near the border between modern Mali and Guinea. Most of the Mande-speaking peoples call themselves "people of Mali," for

An itinerant trader or Dyula from the country of Guinea Conakry spreads out his wares for traditional medicine in the market of Touba in Senegal. Among his wares are plant, mineral and animal parts used in traditional medicines and some will find their way eventually north to the markets in Morocco. The word "Dyula" means "trader" and historically, these Mande traders have helped spread Islam in West Africa. (John A. Shoup)

example, *Malinke*, *Maninka*, and *Man-dinka-nka/nke* being the word for "people." Other Mande speakers include the Bambara, the Soninke, the Dyula meaning "trader" (who are not the same as the **Diola** of the Casamance region of Senegal), and the **Mende**.

Mande origins are in the ancient chiefdom called Manden. The Mande founded some of the most powerful and important states in West African history. In the sixth century, the Soninke founded the first of these great kingdoms, Wagadu or Wagdugu, which the **Arab** geographers called Ghana, located in the southeast of today's Mauritania. They most likely took their group name from the title of the king or

Maghan. The Soninke had established large settlements based on intensive agriculture by 1000 BCE, which emerged into chiefdoms by 600 BCE. Wagadu emerged as the most important of these and established control over the region between the Dhahr Tishit in Mauritania to the north to the upper Senegal River in the south, basing its capital at *al-Ghabah* or the ruins at Kumbi Saleh in southeastern Mauritania under the Cissé clan. *Al-Ghabah* means "forest" in Arabic and refers to the sacred forest where the sacred rock python lived, according to Arab geographers such as al-Bakri, writing in 1067–1068.

The Kingdom of Ghana expanded and gained control over **Berber** clients in the southern Sahara, such as the city state of Awdaghust. Trans-Saharan trade with newly Islamicized North Africa became important as gold from the fields near Bambuk was traded for salt and goods from the Islamic world, such as cloth and fine pottery. The writings of Arab geographers such as ibn Hawqal in 988 provide important information about the economic, political, and social organization of the kingdom. It is most likely that the ruling elite converted to Islam, but to the *Kharaji* form of their main trading partners in Sijilmassa in Morocco. The Berber al-Murabatin (Almoravids) gained control over the trans-Saharan trade in the 11th century, which greatly weakened Wagadu.

With the weakening of Wagadu in the early 12th century, a number of small, independent Soninke states emerged to the south of the old capital. Soso, ruled by the blacksmith Kanté lineage, emerged as the most powerful. The Malian *Epic of Sundiata* portrays King Sumaworo Kanté/Sumanguru as a cruel sorcerer (sorcery has a common connection to blacksmiths who turn metal ore into tools and weapons) and an "enemy of God." The epic of Sundiata Keita has become the national epic of Mali, and it claims that the ruling family, the Keita, descend from Bilal, the Ethiopian companion of the Prophet Muhammad.

Around 1230, Sundiata was able to defeat Sumaworo and established the Kingdom of Mali. His general Taramakan Traoré conquered much of West Africa to the Atlantic coast, beginning the widespread presence of Mande peoples. In general, Malian rule took the form of vassalage, and the original ruling elite maintained local power, but paid taxes and recognized the authority of the Malian king. Thus, Sundiata took the title of *Mansa*, meaning "King of Kings," which his descendants continued to use. The Keita rulers moved the capital from its original spot in Kangaba (Kaba) south of Bamako to Timbuktu on the Saharan side of the Niger River in order to better control the trans-Saharan trade. The height of power of Mali was during the rule of *Mansa* Musa (1312–1337), when 24 kingdoms were under his authority. *Mansa* Musa made the pilgrimage to Makkah, and though he was not the first king of Mali to do so, his pilgrimage became legendary. He spent so much gold in Cairo that its market price fell and remained low for several years after he departed.

Mali remained rich and powerful into the 15th century, when the **Songhay** king broke Mali's control and was able to take the province of Mema. The Songhay were based in their capital of Goa further east along the Niger River, and in 1469, their king Sii or Soni 'Ali Beeri conquered Timbuktu. The Kingdom of Mali broke up into numerous small states centered on major cities such as Segu and Nioro. The Mende of Sierra Leone were expelled from the Kingdom of Mali sometime before its fall and, by 1540, had established an independent state in the Cape Mount area of present-day Liberia.

The Mande peoples are mainly Muslims belonging to the *Maliki* Sunni school of jurisprudence. Islam seems to have been introduced by Arab and Berber traders from North Africa and Andalusia in the eighth or ninth centuries first to Wagadu. Some speculate that the first conversions among the ruling elite of Wagadu

Epic of Sundiata Keita

The epic of Sundiata Keita is the national epic of the Mande and is one of the most important sources of West African history and culture. The epic has passed down through the *jeli* or griot from one generation to the next, with small adjustments being made to the events. Nonetheless, the main events and the order have not been altered from the time of its original composition by *jeli* Balla Fasséké, to the present.

The first major attempt to write down the epic was done by the historian Djibril Tamsir Niane. He was able to persuade *jeli* Mamoudou (Muhammad) Kouyaté to tell him the story, which he translated into French as *Soundjata, ou l'Epic Mandingue*. The French version was published in 1960, and only one other version was similarly recorded in Kita, Mali in 1968. Many *jeli* did not like the idea of the story being recorded and therefore becoming stiff and unchanging.

The epic traces the noble origins of Sundiata's ancestors on both his mother's and father's sides. Sundiata, as a child, had to seek protection from the ruler of Sosso, grows to a man, returns, and defeats the blacksmith king of Sosso, Soumaoro. Soumaoro is a powerful magician, and his final defeat is due to the faithful *jeli* Balla Fasséké's ability to gain access to the room where all of Soumaoro's magic is stored. Once secure as the king of Mali, Sundiata issued the *Kouroukan Fouga*, composed of 44 articles and thought to be the world's oldest modern constitution. In the Republic of Guinea, a commission of *jeli*, including collaboration with some from Mali, set down an authoritative version of the *Kouroukan* in 1998.

were to *Kharaji* Islam, which was the most dominant type of Islam in Sijilmassa, the main trading partner in the trans-Saharan trade. The rise of the *Maliki* Sunni al-Murabatin (Almoravids) among the Sanhaja Berbers brought an end to *Kharaji* domination. The al-Murabatin took Wagadu's Berber dependency of Awdaghust in 1054 and captured Sijilmasa in 1053, thus gaining control over both sides of the trans-Saharan trade. In 1076, they were able to sack Wagadu's capital city and greatly weakened the state. With the success of the al-Murabatin, *Maliki* Sunni Islam spread in both North and West Africa as the only form of Islam.

Traditional religion remained the religion of the masses for several centuries following the conversions of the ruling elite. The capital of Wagadu was called *al-Ghabah* or forest, for the sacred forest presided over by priests where the sacred serpent *Bida* lived. Sacred objects were stored in the grove as well, some of them perhaps masks meant to produce fear and awe among the population. In the traditional religion, blacksmiths held an important place due to their ability to change matter into other forms (rock or ore into tools and weapons). The conflict between the sorcerer, blacksmith Sumaworo Kanté, and Sundiata Keita can be seen as the conflict between the pre-Islamic belief system and the emerging more Islamicized society. It was important for Sundiata to be connected to Bilal, a companion of the Prophet Muhammad, to reinforce his position as the champion of Islamic Mande society. Many pre-Islamic customs and beliefs remained widespread in all levels of society until the rise of the Jihadist states in the 18th and 19th centuries.

The Mande have a rich cultural life with strong class divisions similar to castes that exist yet today The basis for class division is landownership and farming, landowners (*Horonw*) being "free"; and those who were not allowed to own land, such as specialized craftsmen (*nyamakala*), who form a second class in society. The craftsmen are able to change one substance into another form, and thus were assumed to use magic. The bottom of society was the class of slaves (*jon*). At the heart of pre-Islamic Mande society were the hunters, who had a mystical connection to natural forces and pre-Islamic concepts of family totems (*tana*). Hunters formed a second type of social organization not based on lineage, but on secret societies (*ntomo*) that require initiation for a chosen membership. Among the recently Islamized Bamana, *ntomo* masks are still made and worn in various celebrations—marking a boy's circumcision, for example—and youth associations. *Ntomo* masks of the *Komo* society have the power to destroy sorcerers and protect communities. In some instances, these are mixed with

Islamic figures such as Sidi Ballo, whose masqueraders wear bird masks. Some theorize that hunters, once the warriors, lost political control to horse riders, the ancestors of the *horon*, thus establishing the Mande class division and the domination by the *horon*. An important aspect of this social division among the Mande is the *senankuya* or joking relationship between particular families that allows joking and ridicule from a social inferior. In the epic of Sundiata, Sundiata himself gives his *jeli* Balla Fasséké and his descendants of the Kouyaté family the right to joke with and ridicule the Keita.

Important to the *horon* were the *jeli*, who served as praise singers but also as oral historians and genealogists. The *jeli* Balla Fasséké plays an important role in the epic of Sundiata Keita, and his descendants, the Kouyaté, remain connected to the Keita today as their musicians. The *jeli* developed a rich corpus of music as well as musical instruments including the *bala* or *balafon* (xylophone), the *kora* (21-string harp), *donso ngoni* (hunter's harp), *nkoni* (lute), and a wide variety of drums. The long tradition of court music has made countries such as Mali major producers of music for centuries. New forms of music based on older traditions such as *Wassalu* have wide followings not only among the Mande peoples in West Africa, but worldwide. Names such as Salif Keita, Mory Kanté, Amy Koité, Kandia Kouyaté, Oumou Sangare, and Toumani Diabaté are nearly as familiar to Europeans and North Americans as they are in Mali or Guinea. Moray Kanté's song "*Yeke Yeke*" remains the single largest African hit both inside and outside of Africa.

Following the collapse of Mali in the 15th century, a number of states emerged and Mande often formed the ruling elite over other ethnic groups such as the *Gelwaar* rulers of the **Sereer** kingdoms of Siin and Saalum in Senegal. In Liberia, the Mende spread from their base around Cape Mount in the 17th century and came into conflict with the **Temne** and eventually gained control over much of what is today Sierra Leone. Mande or Mande-controlled states in West Africa were slowly conquered by the British or the French starting in the second half of the 19th century. In 1881, Samori Touré established a state in northern Guinea and Côte d'Ivoire in an attempt to revive the power of the Kingdom of Mali, which was called the Second Mandinka Empire. It finally fell to the French in 1889. The Mende in Sierra Leon were defeated by the British in 1898. The European conquest of West Africa was complete by 1900. Samori's descendant, Sekou Touré, led the independence movement in much of West Africa and, in 1958, Guinea (Conakry) became the first colonial possession to become an independent West African state. Keen to revive the cultural legacy of the Kingdom of Mali, he launched a government-sponsored program that brought large numbers of leading *jeli* to Guinea.

Touré became a dictator imposing a one-party state system and closing Guinea to much of the outside world. His economic policies caused massive poverty, and any political opposition was crushed. When he died in 1984, the military stepped in and Colonel Lansana Conté took power. Conté remained in power until 2009, when another military coup ousted him.

Mali became independent in 1960, and its first president, Modibo Keita, claimed to descend from Sundiata Keita. Modibo Keita followed a similar political program to Touré's and was ousted in a military coup in 1968 by General Mousa Trouré. Trouré was removed in a coup in 1991, and civilian government returned in 1992. Since then, Mali has been run by elected governments that have had to deal with severe droughts, a rebellion by **Tuareg** in the north (1990–1996), and extreme poverty. Mali has had peaceful elections and handover of government by popular, democratic means since 1992.

John A. Shoup

Further Reading

Charry, Eric. *Mande Music: Traditional and Modern Music of the Maninka and Mandinka of Western Africa*. Chicago: University of Chicago Press, 2000.

Collins, Robert O. *Africa: A Short History*. Princeton, NJ: Markus Wiener Publishers, 2008.

Conrad, David C. *Empires of the Past: Empires of Medieval West Africa; Ghana, Mali, and Songhay*. New York: Facts on File, Inc., 2005.

Cornevin, R. "Ghana." In *Encyclopaedia of Islam*, 2nd ed., CD-ROM.

Doyle, Margaret, et al. *Peoples of West Africa*. New York: Diagram Group, Facts on File, 1997.

Ewens, Graeme. *Africa O-Ye! A Celebration of African Music*. London: Guinness Publishing, Ltd., 1991.

Galvan, Dennis. *The State Must Be Our Master of Fire: How Peasants Craft Culturally Sustainable Development in Senegal*. Berkeley: University of California Press, 2004.

Hunwick, John O. "Songhay." In *Encyclopaedia of Islam*, 2nd ed., CD-ROM.

Hunwick, John O. *West Africa, Islam, and the Arab World*. Princeton, NJ: Markus Wiener Publishers, 2006.

Hunwick, John O., and Alida Jay Boye. *The Hidden Treasures of Timbuktu: Rediscovering Africa's Literary Culture*. London: Thames and Hudson, 2008.

Imperato, Pascal James. *Legends, Sorcerers, and Enchanted Lizards*. Teaneck, NJ: Africana Publishing Company, 2001.

Karp, Ivan. "African Systems of Thought." In *Africa*, 3rd ed., edited by Phyllis M. Martin and Patrick O'Meara. Bloomington: Indiana University Press, 1995.

McCall, John. "Social Organization in Africa." In *Africa*, 3rd ed., edited by Phyllis M. Martin and Patrick O'Meara. Bloomington: Indiana University Press, 1995.

McNaughton, Patrick R., and Diane Perline. "African Art." In *Africa*, 3rd ed., edited by Phyllis M. Martin and Patrick O'Meara. Bloomington: Indiana University Press, 1995.

Niane, Djibril Tamsir, *Sundiata: An Epic of Old Mali*. Harlow, Essex: Pearson Longman African Writers, 1994.

Zahan, D. "Mande." In *Encyclopaedia of Islam*, 2nd ed., CD-ROM.

Mangbetu

The Mangbetu (also called Mengbetu, Guruguru, Mangutu, Mombouttou, Mongbetu, and Ngbetu) are a Central Sudanic people and their language, called Mengbetu or Nemangbetu, belongs to the Nilo-Saharan language phylum. Both the people and their language are also called Amangbetu, Kingbetu, and Mambetto. Some 620,000 people speak the language, though other sources give the number as no more than 40,000. There are six dialects of the language, of which Medje is the most widely spoken. In addition to their own language, the trade and administrative languages of **Lingala** and **Swahili** are widely known and spoken by the Mangbetu. The Mangbetu live in the northeastern part of the Democratic Republic of Congo (formerly Zaire) and are among the neighbors to the **Mbuti pygmies** and to the **Zande**.

The Mangbetu arrived in their current location in the 18th century, moving south from the Sudan, and engaged the Zande in warfare over regional dominance. The Mangbetu proper only refers to the lineages of the elite as they absorbed Bantu and pygmy peoples under their control. The elite were able to set up a strong state with a centralized authority of a king who administered in the districts through his sons. However, the slave raids of the 1870s and 1880s greatly weakened the power of the king and the Mangbetu broke up into a number of smaller kingdoms called *Sultanates* ruled by Muslim Swahili-speaking petty chiefs. The well-known Swahili slaver Tippu Tib, his son Sayfu, and their former slave/general Ngong Leteta set up slaving dependencies in the interior, far from European control. Belgian authority arrived in the 1890s and expelled the slavers, establishing instead colonial authority. Mangbetu chiefs regained some power and authority, but were themselves subjects of the Belgians rather than of their king.

Mangbetu society was, and is still, based on farming. The light tropical soils are not able to sustain their numbers, and while the women maintain most of the farming, the men fish and hunt. The Belgian demands for labor changed much of the economy to wages earned by men working even outside of their home area. In the past, men worked in commercial rubber farms, and today, many work in the lumber industry.

The Mangbetu are well known for their music and art. Their music has been recorded starting in the colonial period. They use several instruments including the finger piano and the harp, both of which are frequently finely carved and are as much pieces of fine art for their beauty as they are musical instruments. Mangbetu art depicts very realistic images of people, which some think is itself due to the influence of European art on them. Most of the examples date only from the end of the 19th century following contact with Europeans; thus there is no proof for realism in their art before that time, but it is just as likely that their art has always portrayed human figures realistically. It is always possible to immediately recognize Mangbetu pieces because of their distinctive elongated heads and funnel-shaped hairstyles.

The Mangbetu custom of elongating the head by binding an infant's head made them easily recognizable. The length of the head was given even greater emphasis because of the hairstyle that was pulled up, making a funnel. The custom only waned in the 20th century with greater exposure to the outside and is now very rarely practiced. The Mangbetu were also stigmatized by accusations of cannibalism, partially because of their practice of filing men's teeth into sharp points to give them a fierce look. Some scholars note that in the interior region of the Congo River, some peoples did practice cannibalism as a means to magically gain the power of a dead enemy by eating his flesh. It is argued today that if the Mangbetu, like other interior peoples, practiced any form of cannibalism, it was due to the unstable political and economic conditions of the 1870s and 1880s caused by the constant fear of slave raids. Europeans were informed of their cannibalism by others, and it seems very little real research was done to verify the accusation. Today, it is generally held that they did not practice cannibalism at all. However, due to the weakened condition of the people due to failed crops, raids, migrations, and the like, the entire interior population was devastated by an outbreak of trypanosomiasis or sleeping sickness in the 1880s that caused a large number of deaths.

The Mangbetu warriors were armed with spears and throwing knives. They, like the Zande, did not use bows and arrows in warfare as they were seen as Mbuti pygmy weapons and not worthy of true warriors. Once they became exposed to guns, they added guns to their weaponry, though they did not have easy access to them. **Arabs**, Swahilis, and Europeans armed with modern weapons remained militarily superior through the end of the colonial period. While the Zande, under the rule of the capable Gbudwe, was able to bring order and unity to his people, the Mangbetu had no one of equal merit to organize them. When the Belgians moved in to replace the Swahili rulers, Lewis notes, a Mangbetu chief said:

Foreigners have always deceived us. We have been the prey in succession to the Zandes, the Turks, and the Arabs. Are the Whites worth more?

No, beyond doubt; But whatever they be, our territory is today freed from the presence of any foreigners, and to introduce another would be an act of cowardice. I do not wish to be a slave to anyone, and I will fight all Whites. (Lewis, 69)

Resistance to the Belgians began in the 1890s. Given the close proximity of the Mangbetu to the border region of Anglo-Egyptian Sudan, reconquered from the Mahdi's followers in 1898, it was important to both France and Belgium to secure their control over the area. By 1892, the Belgians had defeated the remaining Muslim Swahili states, and in 1904, Great Britain and France formally agreed that the Nile and its sources would be seen as British, and that the Congo and its watershed would fall to France and Belgium; thus, the Mangbetu became subjects mainly of the Belgians. The Belgians enacted a law that organized the Congo into chieftaincies that ruled in their name to help bring down the costs of managing the colony, and the Mangbetu had enough of their original political structure in place for the Belgians to rule through the king and his deputies. Following independence, the structure did not change, and even today the Mangbetu king is recognized by the state to be a local authority, but under the direct control of the central state.

John A. Shoup

Further Reading

Bacquart, Jean-Baptiste. *The Tribal Arts of Africa: Surveying Africa's Artistic Geography*. London: Thames and Hudson, 2002.

Lewis, David Levering. *The Race to Fashoda: European Colonialism and African Resistance in the Scramble for Africa*. London: Bloomsbury, 1988.

"Mangbetu." http://www.ethnologue.com/show_language.asp?code=mdj (accessed December 20, 2010).

"Mangbetu Information." http://www.uiowa.edu/~africart/toc/people/Mangbetu.html (accessed December 20, 2010).

"Mangbetu Tribe of Africa." http://www.gateway-africa.com/tribe/mangbetu_tribe.html (accessed December 20, 2010).

Vansina, Jan. *Paths in the Rainforests: Toward a History of Political Tradition in Equatorial Africa*. Madison: University of Wisconsin Press, 1990.

Mbulu

Mbulu is the **Swahili** word for the Iraqw of Tanzania. The Iraqw, also called Mbulu, Mbulunge, Erokh, or Iraku, are a Cushitic people who live in the Mbulu district in northeast Tanzania. Their language, also called Iraqw, seems to belong to the Cushitic group of the Afro-Asian phylum, though some dispute this. They number 462,000 people, but because of their kinship system, which easily absorbs others, their numbers are growing.

The Iraqw belong to the Southern Cushites, who moved from the Ethiopian highlands south into the plains of Kenya and Tanzania between 3500 and 1000 BCE. Archeologists have named the original Cushitic culture in the furthest southern reaches to be Oldishi. The Cushitic peoples settled among the older **Khoisan** inhabitants and established close relationships with the hunter-gatherers, who provided items like wild honey, while the

Cushitic peoples were herders and cultivators. Their language has borrowed a number of words from others who have come into the region, including Eastern Cushites, **Nilotes**, and Bantu. The drier climate of the Iraqw lands made them less interesting for the expanding Bantu to turn into cultivated fields. Their main threat came much later in the 18th century with the expansion of the Western Nilotes and the arrival of the Maasai.

The Iraqw, like most Cushitic people, are patrilineal. They are independent and have not formed a central political authority. They generally live in clan-based settlements, raising livestock, cattle, sheep, and goats as well as subsistence-level maize and millet. They have held to their own religion, which recognizes the existence of different spirits and allows for others to have different gods. They believe that bad happenings are the work of evil spirits and their cosmos is "dominated by *Lo'a*, a good spirit, and *Netlangw*, a bad spirit" (Olson, 242). They believe that the soul is immortal and lives on in an afterlife which is in the same space as their own homeland, but in a different dimension. Iraqw women produce some of the "most elaborately decorated items of clothing in East Africa," though it generally has not been recognized by dealers, collectors, or tourists (Stokes, 324).

In the 19th century, the Iraqw began to expand out of their main area in the Mbulu highlands. The Maasai were weakened both by plagues of rinderpest that killed numbers of their cattle between 1880s and the 1890s, and by colonial rule. The plague occurred around the same time that Great Britain and Germany established the border between Kenya and German East Africa in 1885. The Iraqw area became part of German territory while that of the Maasai was split between the two colonial powers. As a result, the Iraqw were able to colonize some of the Maasai region in what was German East Africa and later British Tanganyika.

The Iraqw are highly suspicious of the **Swahili**-speaking government officials, and Iraqw have as little to do with them as possible. Suspicion has to do with their bad experience with government employees during the colonial period and after independence, not due to a history of slave raids. Instead, the Swahili have been associated with government, taxation, and conscription to the army since the Germans' arrival in the 19th century. The Iraqw settlements are highly individual and egalitarian, much like other pastoral peoples. The independent and segmentary nature of their culture allowed them to expand territorially in the past.

John A. Shoup

Further Reading

Ehret, Christopher. *The Civilizations of Africa: A History to 1800.* Charlottesville: University Press of Virginia, 2002.

"Iraqw (Mbulu, Mbulunge, Erokh, Iraku)." http://www.christusrex.org/www1/pater/JPN-iraqw.html (accessed June 10, 2010).

Newman, James. *The Peopling of Africa: A Geographic Interpretation.* New Haven, CT: Yale University Press, 1995.

Olson, James. *The Peoples of Africa: An Ethnohistorical Dictionary.* Westport, CT: Greenwood Press, 1996.

Stokes, Jamie. "Iraqw (Mbulu, Wambulu)." In *Encyclopedia of the Peoples of Africa and the Middle East.* New York: Facts on File, 2009.

Mbundu

The Mbundu are a Bantu people living in the north central part of Angola, including the capital Luanda, and make up about one-fourth of the population of the country, or 2,420,000 people. The Mbundu are not the same as the **Ovimbundu**, who also live in Angola and are the single largest ethnic group in the country. The Mbundu speak a Bantu language called Kimbundu, which is divided into two groups, the Ambundu and Awkauanda.

The Mbundu developed several kingdoms, and in the 15th century, the Kingdom of Ndongo fell under the powerful **Kongo** king. The Ndongo king was called the *Ngola a Kiluanje*, and from his royal title the name Angola was derived. In the later part of the 16th century, the Kongo king began to lose his power over the Kimbudu-speaking kingdoms, and by the end of the century, Ndongo no longer paid him tribute. The Kimbundu states established their own commercial ties with the Portuguese. The Portuguese established a trade station at Luanda for direct trade with both the Ndongo and the Matamba kingdoms. The Portuguese were able to establish a good deal of influence especially in the royal court of Ndongo as interest in the slave trade increased. The Mbundu also helped give rise to the Kasanye Kingdom, located a bit further inland, which arose as a staging base for trade caravans going to the interior.

Queen Nzinga (d. 1663) was a princess of the royal family of Ndongo, and under her, the kingdom expanded by taking Matamba in 1620. She abandoned her base in Ndongo and built her career in Matamba, where she was able to fend off the intrusions of the Portuguese and other African states. Despite her efforts, neither kingdom lasted long after her death, and, in 1683, Ndongo was conquered by the Portuguese. By the end of the 18th century, nearly all of the western Mbundu lands were under Portuguese control. During the 19th century, commercial sugar and coffee plantations expanded into Mbundu territory, and the Portuguese had the greatest impact on the Mbundu.

The Mbundu suffered the greatest from the Portuguese colonials, which impacted their culture. Most Mbundu are Christians, and many are well educated. The problems of assimilation—the stated policy of the Portuguese government—were such that few of those who tried to assimilate into European culture were accepted. It has been noted that only 1 percent of the African population was seen as "civilized" or "assimilated" prior to the start of the resistance in 1961.

In 1961, the armed struggle for Angola began. The Mbundu backed the Marxist *Movimento Popular de Libertacao de Angola* (MPLA), which was founded in 1956 in Luanda. The MPLA was established mainly by *assimilados* and *mesticos* who had studied abroad and who had come in contact with liberation ideas from other parts of Africa. The Mbundu played a major role in Angolan independence, and the MPLA formed the first independent government in 1975.

Angola plunged into a bloody civil war between the MPLA and its rival, *Uniao Nacional para a Independecia Total de Angola* (UNITA). The two groups fought a proxy war for the United States (supporting

UNITA) and the Soviet Union (supporting MPLA), and with South Africa (supporting UNITA) and Cuba (supporting MPLA) supplying troops. The civil war ended only in 2002 after the death of Jonas Savimbi, the head of UNITA.

John A. Shoup

Further Reading

Bender, Gerald. *Angola under the Portuguese: The Myth and the Reality.* Trenton, NJ: Africa World Press, Inc. 2004.

Oyebade, Adebayo. *Culture and Customs of Angola.* Westport, CT: Greenwood Press, 2006.

Mbuti Pygmies

The Mbuti pygmies live in the Ituri ràin forest near the border between the Democratic Republic of Congo (formerly Zaire) and Uganda. BaMbuti is the name given to the pygmies by their Bantu neighbors. It has been noted that the pygmies lost their own language and adopted that of the peoples who live close to them, the Mbuti speaking Bantu languages of the Bira and **Mangbetu**, and the Efe speaking that of the BaLese. The Mbuti, including the Efe, who are one of the three main subgroups of the Mbuti, number around 40,000 in total. The third major group is the **Aka pygmies** of the Central African Republic and Congo (Brazzaville).

Various pygmy peoples who live in Central Africa number around 200,000, and are found specifically in the Democratic Republic of Congo, Cameroon, Gabon, and the Central African Republic (the **BaTwa** are found in Rwanda and Burundi as well as the Democratic Republic of Congo). The pygmy populations appear to have developed on the fringes of the rain forest regions of Central Africa, and physical anthropologists place their origin to be about 20,000 years ago. The Mbuti and Efe are thought to be long-term occupants of the rain forests due to their extreme short stature of between 142 and 145 centimeters (4.65 and 4.75 feet) for males and 134 and 137 centimeters (4.39 and 4.49 feet) for females, making them "true pygmies"; while others are pygmoids, being taller and more likely to have intermarried with Bantu peoples, such as most likely was the case for the BaTwa of Rwanda, Burundi, and southern Democratic Republic of Congo. It is believed that though hunting techniques improved with the use of nets and snares, the protein intake of the Mbuti and Efe was limited, possibly explaining their short stature.

Two different language groups of the large Niger-Congo phylum slowly pushed south from their core areas, the Bantu and the Ubangian/Adamawa. Both were settled cultivators and both began pushing south over 3,000 years ago. The Ubangian expansion reached its limit by 2,000 years ago, but the Bantu expansion continued following the rivers and streams. The rain forest provided few resources for them and could support only a small population—rain forest soils are poor and cannot support intensive agriculture. The Bantu and Ubangian peoples developed a fear of the forest, and for them the forest is full of danger and evil. They kept close to the rivers and did not venture far into the forest, leaving it for the pygmies. The pygmies developed trade relations with the villagers, providing honey, meat, skins, and medicinal plants in exchange for pottery, iron tools and weapons, and agricultural produce. Slowly, village populations grew and the Bantu expanded further into the forest, gaining control over the pygmies. Pygmy populations lost their original languages in favor of their dominators. The relationship changed pygmy culture with the adoption of non-pygmy customs such as circumcision. The relationship is called *Bakpara*, which translates as "masters of the pygmies." A number of Bantu peoples have developed historical relations of domination over the pygmies, and in some societies, such as among the **Kuba**, pygmies have been incorporated as well into mask societies being represented by faces with large, bulging foreheads or other pygmy physical features. Though there are few differences between the three main pygmy groups who live in the Ituri forest, it is noted by Turnbull and others that some hunters use nets and snares while others, perhaps more culturally influenced by Bantu neighbors, use bows and arrows (sometimes tipped with poisons) and spears to hunt.

The central belief of the Mbuti focuses on *Molimo*, which is in essence the power of the forest, and the *Molimo* Feast is done at times of crisis. It concerns men, and women and children stay indoors during the rituals. *Molimo* also refers to a usually wooden trumpet that is used to start the singing and dancing associated with the festival. When scholar Colin Turnbull asked his Mbuti hosts what the words of their songs say, they simply replied, "The Forest is Good" (Turnbull, 83).

The Mbuti, Efe, and other pygmies have other celebrations, but most of them were introduced by their non-pygmy neighbors, such as initiation/circumcision. The initiation for boys is called *nkumbi* and is held in the villages with Mbuti boys participating with those from nearby Bantu or Ubangi villages. It is part of the domination of the Bantu and Ubangi over the pygmies, and boys may also have to suffer having their teeth filed into sharp points in addition to or instead of circumcision. For girls it is called *elima*, and once again it is held with Bantu or Ubangi villagers. There are major differences between the attitudes towards a girl's menstruation; where among the Mbuti it is a gift and cause for joy, but for the Bantu and Ubangi peoples, it is considered dangerous, and according to Turnbull, "It is not a happy coming of age" (186–87).

Since the 1960s, the Mbuti, Efe, and others have to deal with the exploitation of the forest for hunting and the search for gold by outsiders. The civil wars in Central Africa have also taken a toll on the Mbuti and the Efe, and in 2003, during the meeting of the United Nations Permanent Forum on Indigenous Peoples, Sinafasi Makelo reported that Mbuti, Efe, and other pygmies are being hunted down, the women raped, and the men killed and eaten by soldiers in the civil wars. These actions were seen as part of the deep prejudice among the non-pygmies who see the Mbuti, Efe, and other pygmies as subhuman. The cannibalism, in the past, was part of local magic traditions to gain the power of the person eaten and to gain control over the forest spirits. It is widely believed that the pygmies are able to control and use forest spirits and that ability is passed to the persons who eat their flesh.

Mbuti pygmy men prepare to hunt with nets and spears in the Okapi Wildlife Reserve outside the town of Epulu, Congo. Hunting for "bushmeat" has become a more commercial practice in recent years and is contributing to the quick decline of wild forest animals. (AP/Wide World Photos)

In addition, due to the unstable conditions of the border areas of the Democratic Republic of Congo and the rampages of militias and army units, "bush meat" or meat from wild animals has become an important source of protein, and, it is argued by those who are trying to end the trade, pygmies are considered by some to be another form of "bush meat."

International logging companies, many from Malaysia and Europe, are heavily logging the Ituri forest for valuable hardwoods. Not only are the loggers destroying the natural habitat of the pygmies, but in order to be part of the cash-based economies, pygmies work in low-paying jobs for the companies. They have been exposed to diseases brought by the loggers, such as HIV/AIDS as well as other types of contagious diseases. The noise of the logging has driven most of the natural game away, leaving the pygmies little choice but to work for the logging companies. According to a report by the World Rainforest Movement, an Efe elder is quoted as saying, "You will understand why we are called the "People of the Forest" . . . When the forest dies, we shall die" (http://www.wrm.org.uy/bulletin/118/DRC.html)

John A. Shoup

Further Reading

Bailey, Robert Converse. *The Behavioral Ecology of Efe Pygmy Men in the Ituri Forest, Zaire.* Ann Arbor: University of Michigan, Museum of Anthropology, 1991.

"DRC: Efe Pygmies Deprived of Their Homeland and Their Livelihood." World Rainforest Movement. http://www.wrm.org.uy/bulletin/118/DRC.html (accessed December 30, 2009).

Duffy, Kevin. *Children of the Forest: Africa's Mbuti Pygmies*. Long Grove, IL: Waveland Press, 1995.

Newman, James. *The Peopling of Africa: A Geographic Interpretation*. New Haven, CT: Yale University Press, 1995.

Tishken, Joel E. "Central Africa: Peoples and States." In *Africa Volume 1: African History before 1885*, edited by Toyin Falola. Durham, NC: Carolina Academic Press, 2000.

Turnbull, Colin. *The Forest People*. New York: Touchstone Book, Simon and Schuster, 1968.

Vansina, Jan. *Paths in the Rainforests: Towards a History of Political Tradition in Equatorial Africa*. Madison: University of Wisconsin Press, 1990.

Wheeler, William. *Efe Pygmies: Archers of the African Rain Forest*. New York: Rizzoli International Publications, Inc. 2000.

Mende

The Mende are a **Mande**-speaking people who live primarily in Sierra Leone and Liberia and total 1.4 million. They are the largest ethnic group in Sierra Leone and comprise one-third of the country's population.

The Mende originated in the Kingdom of Mali, but sometime in the 15th century, they began to move south, conquering others as they went. Some note they were expelled for refusing to convert to Islam adopted by Mali's elite. They were joined by another Mande-speaking people, the Mani, in the early 16th century, and by 1540, they had reached the area around Cape Mount in today's Liberia.

Most Mende converted to either Christianity or Islam in the 19th century, but their traditional religion is still strong. Traditional religious practices are still followed even by those who have converted. Traditional religion centers on the Creator called *Negwo* who is the supreme being, but he is approached through the spirits of the ancestors. There are also a number of lesser spirits called *hale*, who are contacted through special masked societies. The main societies are the *Poro* and *Sande*, who perform during major ceremonies such as circumcision and during planting seasons to help ensure abundant harvests. Other masked and secret societies include the *Humui*, which deals with sexual behavior, *Njayie* that deals with major illnesses, and *Kpa* that deals with minor illnesses.

In the 19th century, Christianity was spread from the coastal region where the British built new communities such as Freetown, established in 1787, for freed slaves both from the Americas and from captured slave ships. Islam was first introduced by Muslim traders from the interior. Islam spread quickly in the 20th century because it was seen as a form of resistance to the British.

Modern history of the Mende begins with their contact with the British and the British colonies of former slaves along the Atlantic coast. In 1807, Great Britain outlawed slaving within their empire, and in 1808, Freetown came under direct British control. Illegal slaving continued, and the slaves of the famous 1839 *La Amistad* case (and made famous again by the 1997 Hollywood film *Amistad*) were mainly Mende.

In 1896, Great Britain declared Sierra Leone a protectorate and tried to impose taxation in the form of a hut tax on the peoples of the interior. There were a number of local rebellions between 1896 and 1898, but the British and the **Creole** or Krio of the Atlantic coast were able to gain control over the territory.

In 1935, the South African company De Beer's was granted a mining concession to develop Sierra Leone's mineral wealth, mainly diamonds. When Sierra Leone became independent in 1961, political power and wealth remained in the hands of the Krio, and other ethnic groups were marginalized even though the first president of independent Sierra Leone, Milton Margai, was Mende. The Revolutionary United Front (RUF) was organized by exiles in Libya, and in 1991, they assisted Liberian rebel leader Charles Taylor in launching his civil war. The RUF quickly

---

La Amistad

The 1997 film *Amistad* is based on the real court case to decide what to do with the slaves from the Spanish coastal ship *La Amistad* in 1839 following their revolt. Importation of slaves from Africa had been banned in the United States in 1808, and only slaves born into slavery could legally be sold. The court case around the Africans on the *La Amistad* dealt with illegal smuggling of slaves from Cuba into the United States.

In 1839, 56 slaves including 4 children, led by Singbe Pieh, rebelled and tried to force the crew to return them to Africa. The ship was not built for trans-Atlantic voyages; the crew kept the ship in U.S. waters until, after some weeks, it was captured by the U.S. Navy off Long Island. The ship and the people on board were taken to New Haven, Connecticut, where they were held and tried. The trail quickly became a cause célèbre for the American abolitionist movement. The wealthy New York merchant Lewis Tappan agreed to pay for the defense of the Africans. The case likewise served as a cause for the slaveowning Southern states in the person of former U.S. vice president John Calhoun.

The case was further complicated by the claims of the queen of Spain, who evoked the Pinkney Treaty of 1795 between the United States and Spain. The sitting U.S. president, Martin Van Buren, asked the U.S. attorney general to represent Spain and hoped for a quick end to the trial. However, the judge ruled in favor of the Africans. The case was argued up to the Supreme Court, which eventually ruled in favor of the Africans in 1841. In 1842, the surviving 36 men and women were returned to Africa paid for by the American Missionary Society. Very little is known of what happened to them upon their return to Sierra Leone, but it seems that Singbe Pieh renounced his conversion to Christianity and severed contact with the American Missionary Society.

gained control over the diamond fields in Kono province in Sierra Leone, financing the movement and its ability to buy weapons. The civil war in Sierra Leone and the role of diamonds in financing it is well presented in the 2006 Hollywood film *Blood Diamond*. The Mende in the Civil Defense Force set up the *Karamjor* paramilitary forces that backed the government against the RUF. The civil war ended in 2002 with the assistance of British military intervention. At one point, over 2 million people had been made homeless, and the RUF made use of child soldiers, many of which still need to be reintegrated into society.

John A. Shoup

Further Reading

Doyle, Margaret, et al. *Peoples of West Africa.* New York: Facts on File, 1997.

Ferme, Mariane. *The Underneath of Things: Violence, History and the Everyday in Sierra Leone.* Berkeley: University of California Press, 2001.

Phillips, Ruth B. *Representing Woman: Sande Masquerades of the Mende of Sierra Leone.* Los Angeles: University of California, Los Angeles, Fowler Museum, 1995.

Woods, Larry, and Timothy Reese. *Military Interventions in Sierra Leone: Lessons from a Failed State.* Seattle, WA: CreateSpace, 2008.

Mossi

The Mossi are one of the largest ethnic groups in Burkina Faso, numbering over 6 million. The Mossi are composed of a number of different peoples, including the Gurunsi, Lobi, and Bobo, who mainly speak the More or MoreDagbani language of the Atlantic branch of the Niger-Congo phylum. The majority of the Mossi live primarily in the central part of Burkina Faso, where they make up 50 percent of the population, and also live in Benin, Côte d'Ivoire, Ghana, Mali, and Togo.

The Mossi emerged in the 15th century as invaders from northern Ghana whose use of cavalry allowed them to conquer most of the peoples in Burkina Faso. Mossi tradition states that they descend from a **Dogomba** princess and a **Mande** hunter. She gave birth to a son named Ouedraogo, who is the founder of the Mossi. The Mossi elite or *nakomsé* (meaning right to rule) descend from the horsemen who conquered settled agriculturalists. Those they defeated are the *nyonyosé*, meaning the ancient ones or the children of the earth. They are further divided and include classifications for craftsmen such as smiths and traders.

The Mossi established a number of kingdoms, though they recognized the supreme authority of the *Mogho Naba*, who ruled from his capital at Ouagadougou. The *Mogho Naba* ruled through a council of *naba* or chiefs. The Mossi were able to maintain their independence from the **Songhay**, but were defeated by the Moroccan troops who conquered the Songhay in 1591. However, the Moroccans were not able to maintain control over Mossi areas and withdrew to Timbuktu. In the 18th century, the Mossi were defeated by the rising power of the Asante (**Akans**) kingdom in Ghana.

The Mossi resisted conversion to Islam until the arrival of Dyula or Jula (**Mande**) traders from Mali in the 17th century. The Mossi maintained their traditional religion, which centers on ancestral spirits and spirits that represent the powers of nature. They are renowned for their elaborate masks, which are made primarily by the *nyonyosé* and usually used in funerals or mounted to guard crops. Mossi masks are not usually worn, but are passed down from one generation to another. There are three main types of masks, including animal and human forms representing ancestors or clan totems. In some regions, women and children are forbidden from ceremonies where masks are brought out to be viewed.

Mande-Dyula traders introduced the art of cotton and silk weaving in the 17th century, and the Mossi have become expert weavers. Weaving is a male occupation, and the cloth is dyed with indigo, producing pieces of alternating undyed white strips with blue dyed strips.

The French conquered the Mossi in 1896–1897. Conversion to Islam increased dramatically as Islam was seen as an alternate means of resistance to the Europeans. Conversion to Islam continues and Islam was part of national identity building in the postcolonial period, starting with Burkina Faso's independence in 1960 as Upper Volta. The first president of independent Upper Volta, Maurice Yameogo, was a Mossi.

John A. Shoup

Further Reading

Bacquart, Jean-Baptiste. *The Tribal Arts of Africa: Surveying Africa's Artistic Geography*. New York: Thames and Hudson, 2000.

Dibua, J. I. "Sudanese Kingdoms of West Africa." In *Africa Volume 1: African History before 1885*. edited by Toyin Falola. Durham, NC: Carolina Academic Press, 2000.

Doyle, Margaret, et al. *Peoples of West Africa*. New York: Diagram Group, Facts on File, 1997.

Olson, James. "Mossi." In *The Peoples of Africa: An Ethnohistorical Dictionary*. Westport, CT: Greenwood Press, 1996.

Skinner, Elliott. *The Mossi of Burkina Faso: Chiefs, Politicians and Soldiers*. Long Grove, IL: Waveland Press, 1989.

Wheelock, Thomas. *Land of the Flying Masks: Art and Culture in Burkina Faso*. New York: Prestel Publishing, 2007.

N

Nguni

The Nguni are one of the major divisions of the Bantu language group found in South Africa, Zimbabwe, and Swaziland and account for 60 percent of Bantu speakers in southern Africa. Today there are an estimated 24 million speakers of Nguni languages, with the single largest group being *isiZulu*, numbering at an estimated 11 million living mainly in South Africa. The second-largest group is that of the *isiXhosa* speakers, who number over 7.5 million and also live in South Africa. Northern Nguni is dominated by the Zulu, and Southern Nguni is dominated by the Xhosa. *IsiXhosa* has borrowed 15 click sounds from **Khoisan** languages, more than any other Bantu language, which indicates long contact between the Khoisan and the Xhosa.

The Nguni emerged from the Bantu peoples, who arrived in South Africa sometime in the fourth century CE. They are closely related to the **Sotho/Tswana** who moved out onto the Highveld, while the Nguni moved south and reached Natal by the middle of the 11th century. The Nguni favored dense settlement patterns and developed the distinctive beehive style of architecture still associated with the Zulu. The Xhosa were on the frontier of Nguni expansion and reached the Eastern Cape along the Fish River long before their first contact with Europeans in the middle of the 18th century. The Xhosa were eventually defeated by the British in a series of wars with the Europeans, nine in total from 1779 to 1879.

The Zulu emerged as the dominant group among the northern Nguni in the late 18th and early 19th centuries as a result of struggles between contesting chiefdoms over resources, grazing lands for their cattle, and access to Portuguese trade goods from trading posts located at Delagoa and St. Lucia bays. Shaka, founder of the Zulu state, forged the Zulu into a formidable fighting force and set out to build an empire. Those he conquered, he absorbed into the Zulu, while others fled north into Sotho/Tswana territory where they spread terror and destruction. Those under Shaka's once-general Mzilikazi became the Ndebele or Matabele of Zimbabwe, while those under Sobhuza I and then his son and heir Mswati formed the Swazi. Others fled south, seeking protection of the Xhosa, and were generally called the Mfingo meaning "refugees." They and others, such as the Thembu, Mpondo, Bomvana, and Bhaca, have been culturally absorbed into the Xhosa. The period between 1816 and 1828 is called the *Mfecane* in Nguni languages, meaning the "Great Crushing."

The Southern Ndebele or the Transvaal Ndebele are Nguni in origin, but not related to the Ndebele of Zimbabwe. They too are split between a northern and a southern group as the result of a quarrel over the leadership in the 17th century.

The Transvaal Ndebele have lived among the Transvaal Sotho for so long that they have taken up many of their customs, including their language. There are today some 500,000 Transvaal Ndebele, and they have developed their own distinct culture. Their leader Nyabela (died around the time of the Boer War in the first decade of the 1900s) served a major role in asking his people to preserve their culture.

In addition to those groups who live in South Africa and Zimbabwe, there are small scatterings of Ngoni (usually spelled with an "o") throughout the Lakes Region as far north as Kenya. They trace their origins to Natal and the Ndwandwe, who were defeated by Shaka in 1819. They fled the state-making process of Shaka, but as they moved north, their superior organization and the military reforms they had learned from Shaka that they brought with them turned their flight into invasion and conquest. Groups of Ngoni are found in Malawi, Mozambique, Zambia, Tanzania, and Kenya, and they number several hundred thousand in each country.

Traditional Zulu doctor or isangoma. Depicted in her everyday dress, she still wears distinctive markers of her profession in the beads in her hair, the beaded sash, the sash made of animal hide, and the beaded staff in her hand. (John A. Shoup)

Most Nguni are Christians, the largest percentage of who belong to the Xhosa subgroup. As a result of their defeat by the British in 1853 and the subsequent death of 80 percent of their cattle due to a lung sickness introduced by European cattle, many Xhosa turned to the prophetess Nongqawuse. Similar to the Ghost Dance among Native Americans, her prophecy foretold of a resurgence of native power and the destruction of the whites. The Xhosa were to kill all of their cattle and destroy their grain, which would free them from the devil whose servants were the whites. In a great climax in 1857, more than 400,000 head of cattle were killed, and in the subsequent starvation, 40,000 Xhosa died. In the aftermath of the Cattle Killing, the majority of Xhosa turned to Christianity. The current South African national anthem, *Nkosi Sikelel iAfrika*, is a Xhosa hymn written in 1897 by the Xhosa convert Enoch Sontonga.

Christianity had a harder time gaining ground among the Zulu. Even today, many Zulu hold to both the traditional belief system along with Christianity or belong to the syncretic Zionist Apostolic churches. Traditional belief centers on the *amatongo* in *isiXhosa* and *amadlozi* in *isiZulu*, or "spirits of the ancestors." Professional priest-diviners called *isangoma* (*izangoma* in plural) in Nguni languages are trained to understand the wishes of the ancestors. A priest-diviner must first apprentice to a working master to be trained, which can take years of hard study, though some become priest-diviners at the call of the spirits who train them in dreams. Along with being able to contact and understand the wishes of the ancestors, they also are trained in the identification of medicinal plants and how to make and prescribe medicines from them. Once an apprentice is fully trained, a ceremony is held to mark the event, and the person will take on the beading that their ancestors tell them to wear as the mark of a fully accomplished priest-diviner. Some of these are highly decorative and are worn when the person contacts the spirits, but for everyday wear, their position as a priest-diviner is usually marked with beaded bracelets, anklets, and/or beaded hair.

Nguni are among the most skilled craftspeople in southern Africa, specifically in beadwork and basket weaving. The Transvaal or Southern Ndebele use similar designs from the beadwork to paint their houses, mainly geometrics, stylized cars, buses, and the like, as well as numbers and letters, frequently made backwards. The Transvaal Ndebele are well known for elaborate costuming, developed in the 19th and early 20th centuries primarily for their women. Women mark their social status with heavily beaded front skirt panels. Young girls, before puberty, wear *ghabi* or a cache-sexe that has a small, stiff, beaded panel but is

Two older Xhosa women in southwestern Lesotho. The one is wearing a typical Basotho blanket, and the other a traditional Xhosa blanket made of cotton with black strip appliqué. Both are wearing the larger turban typical of older women. (John A. Shoup)

heavily fringed with cords and beads. At puberty, the *ghabi* is replaced with a somewhat large stiffened piece of leather covered in beads called *ipepetu*, which serves as a front panel. The bride wears a special front panel called the *jocolo* or *tshogholo*, which has five "fingers" on the lower part of the panel indicating that she is now a married woman. The bride also wears *umgaka*, a beaded headband sometimes with a beaded chin strap, a *siyaya* or beaded face veil, and an *orare* or *ngurara*, which is a beaded blanket that she wears like a shawl. Her legs, arms, waist, and neck have stacks of grass rings covered in tightly wrapped beads called *isigholmani*. In addition, Ndebele women used to wear brass rings on their legs and around their necks called *tzila* that were permanent and could not be taken off. These are now replaced with ones in plastic with Velcro attachments that are worn only on special occasions. After a woman is married, she changes to the *mapoto* or *amaphoto* for her front panel, which extends to just above her knees. In the past, these were mainly in white beads on a stiffened piece of leather, but starting in the 1960s, other colors became more readily available to the women. Today, most of the beaded items are multicolored, with a preference for dark blues, greens, purples, and black with highlights in red, orange, and white, and the leather is sometimes replaced with canvas. To mark her as a mother, the *mapoto* has loose fringes at the bottom, each fringe ending in beads. Another piece of Ndebele beadwork is the *nyoga* or "snake" that is often worn by women at weddings. The *nyoga* are long, heavily beaded pieces that hang down the back. Another spectacular piece of Ndebele beadwork is the headband with long, beaded side panels on both sides that reach to the wearer's feet or below called *milingakobe* or "long tears." Headbands used to have coins attached to them; but the South African government passed a law forbidding the use of coins in decoration, since in order to attach them, they had to be pierced, which made them no longer usable as a coin. Traditional clothing is worn today at special occasions, but Ndebele beadwork is also a form of income generation for Ndebele women

who now make pieces for the international art market.

Xhosa are also well known for their beadwork and, like the Ndebele, the different pieces worn traditionally by both men and women developed with contact with European traders. Traditional Xhosa dress developed before beads were a common trade item, and though they are known for the beauty of their beadwork, much of the traditional clothing uses buttons as well. Buttons, especially those made of mother of pearl, were highly valued by the Xhosa, and it is reported that in the late 18th and early 19th centuries, Xhosa men robbed European dressed herd boys of their buttons. The introduction of European cloth also helped form Xhosa taste, and both men and women traditionally wear large amounts of cloth decorated with buttons and black, cloth ribbons. Women developed large turbans, again decorated with buttons and beads, and those of married women are larger and more elaborate than those of young women. Triangular scarves decorated in mother-of-pearl buttons and beads, called *iqhiya*, are part of Mfingo and Mpondo women's dress. Married Mpondo women traditionally used to wear a beaded headring to indicate her married status. Xhosa prefer, yet today, white, black, and blue beads, and white originally was used more extensively for political elite and priest-diviners. The Xhosa developed distinctive pieces such as large, net-weave necklaces or *icangi*, broaches to attach blankets or *umpaso*, beaded belts or *isaziso sesinqe* or *igqesha* (with beaded tassels), arm bands, leg bands, and sashes worn by both men and women. Tobacco pipes and bags developed with the contact with Europeans. In more recent years, Xhosa beaders have made items like bowties and ties from beads and are worn at special occasions. Like the Ndebele, Xhosa beadwork has entered the international art market and command high prices.

Zulu are also famous for their beadwork, and while Xhosa are famous for their elegance and restrained use of colors, Zulu beadwork favors reds, yellows, greens, pinks, and a host of other bright colors. Durban rickshaw pullers are covered with massive amounts of beadwork in vests and large headdresses that often include painted or beaded cattle horns. There are a number of traditional beadwork pieces, some of them color coded by Shaka and his descendants, that placed wearers in particular geographic locations. That is, regional styles were invented and maintained by the regimentation of Zulu society. Like the Xhosa, white is still favored by priest-diviners. Zulu women's traditional clothing not only was highly decorated with beadwork, but different hats also decorated with beadwork came to have special meanings. The large, wide, and flat *inkehli* traditionally was woven into a woman's hair and was colored red with ochre. It is decorated with beaded pieces called butterflies stuck into to the hat. Women in various locations of Zululand traditionally wore leather skirts called *isidwaba* and capes or *isikoti* decorated in beadwork. Zulu women wear a number of beaded items that are worn to be seen from behind, such as the back panel called *umkhambathi*, which is heavily beaded and covers the leather skirt underneath it as well as a number of belts

made from woven grass and covered in bright colors such as red and green glass beads. Among the best known of Zulu beadwork are the "love letters" or *ithemba*, which became fashionable once Zulu men began to leave their home areas and work in the mines and farms in other parts of South Africa. Zulu women, left at home, could use the post office to mail the "letters," which were made as necklaces and colors and designs carrying the meaning. "Love letters" are still made and are in demand by collectors in Europe and North America.

Zulu beadwork is not as well known and not yet as sought after as those of the Ndebele. However, Zulu baskets fetch high prices in the international art market. Zulu baskets made from waxy ilala palm fibers are water tight and, in the past, served instead of breakable pottery for serving beer as well as for storage. The baskets leak a bit which helps cool the beverage inside. There are different types of baskets and each has a specific name and function. *Ukhambu* baskets have a number of shapes, but they are for serving traditional beer and can stand up to 24 inches tall (60.96 centimeters). Large *ukhambu* baskets are given even today as wedding gifts, and are a ready source of money. In addition to traditional palm and grass baskets, in recent years Zulu women have begun to make baskets from plastic-covered copper wire. Zulu women began by using pieces of wire the telephone workmen left behind and wove them into useful baskets and plates. Subsequently, others, including white South Africans, began a market demand for them and wire baskets now have an international market. Zulu baskets are internationally famous and eagerly sought after by collectors.

Xhosa

The modern history of the Nguni begins with the contact between the Xhosa and the Europeans. The Boers were unable to defeat the Xhosa in the first four wars with them, despite the fact that the Boers had guns. The Xhosa adapted to using horses and were highly mobile, not unlike the Plains peoples in North America. The situation changed when the Cape became part of the British Empire. Over the course of the first half of the 19th century, the Xhosa fought four more wars with the Europeans and were eventually defeated in the Eighth Frontier War in 1853. The Xhosa made one last attempt to regain their lands in 1877 to 1879 but were defeated, and their lands were lost to the Cape.

The Xhosa had received Christian missionaries since the early 19th century and, after the Cattle Killing in 1856–1857, most lost faith in traditional religion. The Xhosa came under the laws of the Cape, which allowed Africans access to education and the status of free citizen. The Xhosa emerged quickly from the Cattle Killing disaster as the most educated of Africans. The Christian mission schools were staffed mainly by Europeans and North Americans with liberal political and social ideals, which greatly affected their students. In 1912, the African National Congress (ANC) was founded, and was mainly managed by Xhosa.

The Xhosa formed the main driving force of the ANC from its founding in 1912. In 1910, the British allowed an elected government for a united South Africa, and slowly African rights enjoyed in the Cape began to erode with separatist, discriminatory policies. The ANC was an early response to this and an attempt to bring Africans into the political process. Subsequent governments passed more discriminatory legislation, where it was legal to live, the need to carry a pass, and the reduction of native agricultural lands and, in 1948, the Afrikaner National Party was able to gain control of the government and set the course of the next four decades of confrontation between African activists and the state. In 1960, the ANC and a number of other organizations were banned. The Xhosa and the other southern Nguni were assigned to the more barren parts of the Eastern Cape in the homelands of Ciskie and Transkei. Nelson Mandela, Thabo Mbeki, Desmond Tutu, Stephen Biko, Walter Sisulu, Oliver Tambo, and Mariam Makeba are notable Xhosa activists. Nelson Mandela became the first black president of South Africa in 1994.

Zulu

The Zulu state was formed by Shaka, who ruled as the king from 1816 to 1828. Shaka was the stuff of legends, and subsequent tales of his life include a prophecy that foretold of a child that would make the Zulu the most feared of nations. Shaka's success was due to the modifications he made to the traditional weapons (spear, club, and shield) as well as to new battle strategies. He took the traditional circumcision school-age sets and turned them into more effective military regiments or *impis*. Zulu regiments could cover up to 50 miles

Shaka Zulu: Founder of the Zulu Empire

Shaka was an exceptional leader who brought his relatively insignificant Zulu people to become the leaders of Natal's Nguni people. Shaka was born around 1787 and, from the time of his birth until the present, his life has been surrounded by myth and tales of magic. What is known is that Shaka was the eldest son of Zulu prince Senzangakhona and Nandi, daughter of Bhebhe, former chief of the Elangeni, an unimportant chieftancy in Natal. Senzangakhona and his family refused to acknowledge the child was his when Nandi sent word that she was pregnant. They told Nandi's messenger to say that she must have the stomach beetle or *ishaka* rather than be pregnant. When her son was born, she called him Shaka in order to drive home the point that Senzangakhona was the father.

Following custom, Senzangakhona had to recognize his son, and Nandi required no less than 50 head of cattle as *labola* or bride price. Nandi had problems with others in Senzangakhona's household, and eventually Senzangakhona expelled the mother and child. Shaka entered the service of Dingiswayo of the Mthethwa chieftancy, where he excelled as a warrior. Dingiswayo helped Shaka take the Zulu chieftancy when Sezangakkona died. When Dingiswayo was killed in battle, Shaka took over the Mthethewa as well. Shaka furthered Dingiswayo's military reforms and introduced a new, larger shield and the short, stabbing spear, which replaced the longer, throwing spear. He also modified battle tactics and introduced the "buffalo" format: two horns to encircle an enemy that forced them onto the front lines while the rear acted as reinforcements.

Shaka's half brothers Dingane and Mhlangana plotted to assassinate him. They were able to pull into their plot some of Shaka's closest advisers, importantly his chief aide Mbopa. With secure inside help, Shaka was assassinated in 1828.

(80 kilometers) a day and still be able to fight a battle at the end of the march, while European armies of the day could barely cover 20 miles (32 kilometers) in a day and rarely were able to engage an enemy at the end of a day's march.

Shaka was assassinated by his half brothers in 1828, and one of them, Dingane, became the king. He stopped the expansion of the empire, but was confronted by the arrival of Boers in 1837.

Dingane was deeply suspicious of the Boers and ordered the death of all that his regiments could find, resulting in the deaths of over 500 Boer men, women, and children. In 1838, the Boers were able to defeat a large force of Zulus at the Battle of Blood River and, in 1840, assisted Mpande, one of Dingane's many half brothers, in taking control of the Zulu state. Mpande and the Boers had Dingane assassinated.

Mpande ruled until 1872, though for the last year of his life, his son Cetshwayo was the real ruler. Cetshwayo eliminated any real rivalry by defeating several of his brothers while his father was still alive. In 1872, Cetshwayo was crowned king with the British representative in attendance. Cetshwayo reinstituted the military reforms of Shaka that had been allowed to slowly decline during Mpande's rule as well as introduced guns to his regiments. He expelled Christian missionaries, which the British deemed as an unfriendly act. The British sent him an ultimatum to disband his army, and to suspend traditional courts in favor of "modern, European" ones, which he refused to do. In reality, the ultimatum was worded deliberately to be rejected since Cetshwayo was an independent ruler, not a vassal of the British. The Zulu War began in 1879, and the British commanders at first greatly underestimated the Zulus. The Zulus inflicted one of the greatest defeats of a modern army by native forces at Isandhlwana, where the British lost over 1,300 men. The British recovered from their defeat and launched a new offensive, reaching the Royal Kraal at Ulundi in July, 1879. Cetshwayo was captured and exiled to London, where he lived until he was allowed to return in 1883.

Misrule of Zululand by a combination of inept local chiefs, British agents, and Christian missionaries forced the British to eventually bring Cetshwayo back, and they placed him on the throne once more. He died soon afterward and was succeeded by his son Dinizulu, who had the support of the Boers. Zululand lost its independence with the 1879 defeat and its land, and people were incorporated into Natal. Nonetheless, Zulu kings have continued to through the present day to be an important force in local politics, even if they have no real political power.

The Zulu were mainly a rural people. Despite the defeat of their king in 1879 and the subsequent misrule by the British and the disjointed nature of their homeland of KwaZulu, they have been able to maintain a fair degree of social cohesion to the present time. The current king, Goodwill Zwelithini kaBhekuzulu, commands great respect. In 1975, Chief Mangosuthu Buthelezi, a cousin of the king, formed the *Inkhatha YeSizwe* (Crown of the Nation) or Inkhatha Freedom Party, which the South African government recognized as the voice of the African people. Political violence between supporters of the ANC and Inkhatha lasted through much of the 1980s and ended only with the end of apartheid.

Swazi

The Swazi owe their independence to King Mbandzeni, who ruled from 1875 to 1889. He made agreements with a number of whites, both British and Boer, and though he allowed the sale of large parts of the kingdom to whites, he was able to preserve Swazi independence. Swazi kings maintained good relations with the British in particular, who declared Swaziland a protectorate in 1902, and like the kings of Lesotho, they were able to build a general national consensus of Swazi identity out of its different ethnicities, Nguni and others.

Swaziland's position as a British protectorate guaranteed its independence from South Africa, and in 1960, Great Britain granted its full independence.

Swaziland was ruled by King Sobhuza II (d. 1982), who had to straddle the divide between the traditional system of government and the attempt to implement parliamentary government. Swazi customs such as the yearly *Ncwala*, which renews the relationship between the king and his people, have come under pressure from modernists. At the *Ncwala*, the king has the traditional right to choose any young girl he sees and take her as his wife. More "modernist" Swazi women have refused to participate in the ceremony, and one even refused to be the current king's choice.

Ndebele

The Ndebele or Matabele originated with their first leader, Mzilikazi, who was chief of the Khumalo of the Ndwandwe, one of Shaka's main rivals. Mzilikazi joined Shaka, but in a quarrel over booty, Mzilikazi was forced to flee north. Mzilikazi at first established himself in the Transvaal, where he defeated local Sotho chiefs. The Boers defeated Mzilikazi in 1836, and by 1838, the Ndebele were forced to flee north of the Limpopo River, where they defeated the local **Shona** and set up a new kingdom in what the British called Matabeleland. They named their capital Bulawayo (meaning place of killing in isiZulu) after that of Shaka. Mzilikazi's son and heir Lobengula gave mining concessions to the British, which eventually led to two wars and the loss of independence in 1896. The Matabele were incorporated into the newly formed British colony of Rhodesia, where they, like most other Africans, became part of the workforce on the farms and mines of the whites.

The Matabele leader Joshua Nkomo founded the Zimbabwe African Peoples Union or ZAPU in 1961. ZAPU was one of two main groups, along with ZANU-PF, that formed the struggle against white minority rule in then Rhodesia. Nkomo's support came mainly from Matabeleland, while ZANU-PF had most of its support from the dominant Shona people. The two groups were able to work together until after the fall of white rule, and eventually ZANU-PF emerged as the single party in Zimbabwe. The union was not a happy one, and Robert Mugabe began a campaign to vilify Nkomo and the ZAPU leadership. In 2009, ZAPU declared that it would withdraw from its coalition with ZANU-PF.

Transvaal Ndebele

The Transvaal Ndebele claim to originate in the 17th century when their chief Muzi settled near where Pretoria is located today. The Ndebele split, with one division moving north as far as Botswana. In the 19th century, the Ndebele came into conflict with the Boers, who were not able to finally defeat the Ndebele until just before the Anglo-Boer War. Their chief Nyabela gave sanctuary to a rebel Sotho chief, which sparked war with the Boers. In 1882, the president of the Transvaal Republic, Paul Kruger, conquered the Ndebele and divided their lands among Afrikaner farmers, and the Ndebele became forced labor. In return for being able to continue living in their homeland, they were forced to provide Afrikaners with three months of labor a year. In 1955, as part of the apartheid laws, the Ndebele "homeland" was created in five tiny regions and families were required to leave their homesteads on white farms and move to one of the small areas in Transvaal called KwaNdebele. Despite the trauma suffered by them as a people, their cultural identity has been able to remain greatly intact. In recent years, South Africa's president Jacob Zuma has recognized the plight of the Ndebele and the heroic fight of Chief Nyabela.

John A. Shoup

Further Reading

Afolayan, Funso S. *Culture and Customs of South Africa*. Westport, CT: Greenwood Press, 2004.

Barthrop, Michael. *The Zulu War*. Durban: Bok Books International, 1980.

Bouttiaux, Anne-Marie. "Afrique Méridionale: Des perlespour le dire." In *Costumes et Textiles d'Afrique: Des Berbères aux Zulu*, by Anne-Marie Bouttiaux et al. Milan: 5 Continents Press, 2008.

Costello, Dawn. *Not Only for Its Beauty: Beadwork and Its Cultural Significance among the Xhosa-Speaking Peoples*. Pretoria: Unisa Press, 1990.

Courtney-Clarke, Margaret. *Ndebele: The Art of an African Tribe*. New York: Thames and Hudson, 2002

Crabtree, Caroline, and Pam Stallebrass. *Beadwork: A World Guide*. London: Thames and Hudson, 2002.

Hamilton, Carolyn. *Terrific Majesty: The Powers of Shaka Zulu and the Limits of Historical Invention*. Cambridge, MA: Harvard University Press, 1998.

Hammond-Tooke, W. D. *Bantu-Speaking Peoples of Southern Africa*. New York: Routledge, 1980.

Kuper, Hilda. *The Swazi: A South African Kingdom*. 2nd ed. Belmont, CA: Wadsworth/Thomson Learning, 2002.

Mofolo, Thomas. *Chaka*. Translated by Daniel Kunene. London: Heinemann, 1981.

Morris, Donald R. *The Washing of the Spears: The Rise and Fall of the Zulu Nation*. Cambridge, MA: Da Capo Press, 1998.

Mostert, Noel. *Frontiers: The Epic of South Africa's Creation and the Tragedy of the Xhosa People*. New York: Knopf, 1992.

Owomoyela, Oyekan. *Culture and Customs of Zimbabwe*. Westport, CT: Greenwood Press, 2002.

Peires, J. B. *The Dead Will Rise Again: Nongqawuse and the Great Xhosa Cattle-Killing Movement of 1856–7*. Bloomington: Indiana University Press, 1989.

Thompson, Leonard. *A History of South Africa*. New Haven, CT: Yale University Press, 1995.

Tyrrell, Barbara, and Peter Jurgens. *African Heritage*. Johannesburg: McMillan South Africa, 1983.

Nilotic

The Nilotes make up a large number of the population of southern Sudan, southwestern Ethiopia, Uganda, Kenya, and Tanzania. Today they number close to 10 million in total, though figures vary greatly from one group to another. In Sudan alone they represent one-third of the total population of the country, or close to 4 million people. The term *Nilote* comes from the language they speak, Nilote or Nilot, which belongs to the Nilo-Saharan language group. Nilotic peoples tend to be tribal in their traditional sociopolitical organization with an economy based mainly on cattle, though some Nilotes such as the Anuak in Sudan and the **Luo** in Kenya are primarily settled agriculturalists. The Shilluk of southern

Sudan developed into a state with a divine king called a *reth*, who embodies the Shilluk people and who is thought to possess the soul of their cultural hero and first *reth* Nyikang.

Nilotes, with a pastoral economic base, were only able to move south once the barrier of permanent river-flooding became seasonal in the second millennium and movement with their cattle was possible. These cattle people, called the Jii, also raised cereal crops and began to replace older populations called the Koman. Koman vocabulary was adopted particularly into Luo and aspects of Sudanic religion with the concept of a Divinity became part of Jii culture.

Nilotes are divided into three main groupings: the Southern Nilotes, who pushed into Kenya and Tanzania around 500 BCE; the Eastern Nilotes who also pushed south into Kenya around 500 to 1000 CE; and the Western Nilotes, most of whom live in southern Sudan. The Nilotes home region is in central (the Gazira) and southern Sudan, and they continued to occupy areas in the Gazira until into the 15th century, when the Dinka were eventually pushed south into their present area in southern Sudan. The Western Nilotes include the Luo, Shilluk, Anuak, **Acholi**, Jur, and the Dinka and Nuer, the most powerful groups in southern Sudan and among the largest. The Dinka are the single largest Nilotic population in Sudan and account for a full 10 percent of the country's population while the Nuer count for 5 percent. The Eastern Nilotes include the Maasai, Samburu, Karamajong, and Turkana. The Southern Nilotes include the Pokot, **Kalenjin**, and Kitoki. It is possible that the **Tutsi** of Rwanda and Burundi emerged from the combination of Hinda, Hima (southern Nilotic peoples) and ruling Bantu lineages, who imposed a system of vassalage on settled Bantu farmers who became the **Hutu**.

Nilotic peoples are characterized by being mainly cattle herders. Among many Nilotic peoples, such as the Nuer of Sudan, cattle play a vital role in the lives of the people, which the British anthropologist Evans-Pritchard notes, "Cattle are their dearest possession and they gladly risk their lives to defend their herds or to pillage those of their neighbors" (16). Deng notes the same sort of love for cattle by the Dinka: "[A] Dinka will kill and even risk his life for a single cow" (2). This strong attachment to their livestock, in particular to their cattle, has given rise to the concept of the "cattle complex" to describe the close relationship and social value placed on cattle by many Nilotic peoples. Cattle are adorned with large bells and woolen tassels attached to the ends of their horns; horns are weighted to be shaped for easier and quick identification, and bride wealth payments are calculated in numbers of cattle, as are payments such as in compensation for causing the death of another. Evans-Pritchard noted that the Nuer language has a large number of terms to describe the color or combination of colors and hide patterns for their cattle. Milk, rather than meat, is the main diet for many Nilotic peoples, and the Maasai, for example, mix milk with fresh blood drawn from

The Nuer and Evans-Pritchard

British anthropologist Edward Evan Evans-Pritchard arrived in Sudan in 1926, first working with the Zande, who inhabit southern Sudan. In 1904, the British had started a policy of separation between northern Sudan (seen as Arab and Islamic) and southern Sudan (African and non-Islamic) and by 1910, all Arab/ Muslim presence was cleared out from the south. However, both the tribal Dinka and Nuer were hard to understand or negotiate with, so much so that in 1930, the British authorities commissioned Evans-Pritchard to study the Nuer.

The result of his study is the theory (much debated now) of Segmentary Lineage Organization (SLO) and his book *The Nuer: A Description of the Modes of Livelihood and the Political Institutions of a Nilotic People* (1940). SLO helped give understanding to the individual independence found among groups like the Nuer as well as how they operated as a whole. He noted that kinship follows the breakdown from the largest recognized level where there are still responsibilities of kin which he called the "maximal level," to the "major level," to the "minor level" and finally to the household or "minimal level." He noted that leadership roles emerge along the kinship structure "when and where needed". Among the Nuer a special semireligious institution called the "leopard-skin" chiefs have any real political clout, but their political power and authority is weak. Being that they are the ones who can commune with the Sky-god and the spirits, their opinions are backed by their ability to read the signs left by the spirits. It was Evans-Pritchard's study that gave the British the ability to finally deal more effectively with the southern Sudanese pastoral peoples like the Nuer and the Dinka.

one of their cows for a high-protein drink that is the staple of their traditional diet. In the past, during the dry season when cows are not lactating, the Maasai drank fresh cow's blood from a wound on the neck which, and once a jug had been filled with the steaming, hot blood, it was closed with a plaster of mud and the cow was released.

Young boys among many Nilotic peoples are presented with their first ox as part of coming of age and, in many instances, even take on the names of their favorite ox. Deng relates the Dinka tale that explains their heavy reliance on cattle. In the past, while hunting, the ancestors of the Dinka killed the mother of both the buffalo and the cow. The buffalo became the enemy of man and will attack him whenever he approaches, while the cow took revenge in a different manner. The cow allowed herself to be domesticated and made man her slave to fight to possess her and to protect her. The Maasai justified cattle raiding in the past by saying that in the distant past, all cattle belonged to them, and cattle raids were a means to try to get them all back.

Many Nilotic peoples practice some form of scarification and/or circumcision of both boys and girls. Scarification is often part of initiation ceremonies, and for the Dinka, 7–10 incisions are made on the male initiate's forehead. Deng notes that the initiate tries to remain still and serene while chanting songs of bravery; however, the loss of blood can be great enough that they faint. The closely related Nuer also have long incisions made on the forehead of young men as a central part of the initiation ceremony. The Nuer usually cut three long incisions, and Evans-Pritchard noted that the cuts are deep enough to actually scar the skull. The incisions are rubbed with ash in order to stop the flow of blood and to cause the scars to form a raised ridge or lump. In Sudan, most Nilotes, with the notable exception of the Dinka, do not practice circumcision, perhaps as a means of separating themselves from their **Arab** Muslim neighbors. In Sudan, generally only those who have converted to Islam are circumcised. Elsewhere, such as in Kenya, Tanzania, and Uganda, Nilotic people mark coming of age with circumcision.

The Maasai practice both male and female circumcision. Once a young man reaches the age of between 15 and 18 and a young woman between the ages of 12 and 14, they are circumcised. The male is required to stay outside all night in the cold and is drenched in cold water (to help deaden the pain) before the operation. Taunted by his age mates (to mentally toughen him), he is circumcised in the early morning at the entrance to the family's cattle kraal. He is not to cry out or to give any indication that he has felt pain.

Maasai circumcision leaves a flap of skin under the head of the penis. The boy may bleed a great deal, and a calabash of fresh cow's blood is given to him to help replace the amount of his blood he might lose. Maasai girls are allowed to cry out from the pain of the operation. She is circumcised by woman who uses a special curved knife to cut away the clitoris and the labia minora. She is held by her female relatives who give her encouragement, laugh, and joke, while the girls frequently cry out and plead for the women to stop. All hope the operation is successful and the girl is inspected after her recovery. If not enough had been cut away due to the girl's struggling, she may be forced to endure the operation again.

Most Nilotic peoples have age set organization, and both boys and girls go through important steps in life, such as initiation, together in groups. Age sets help form other strong bonds between members of the group in addition to those of close kinship. Dinka of Sudan do practice circumcision, which they do when the child is around six years old. The operation is done by tying a string made of hair from a giraffe tail around the foreskin and then using a knife to cut it off. To help distinguish themselves from Arabs, they also remove the bottom six front teeth, using a fishing spear to pry loose each of the teeth and make sure the whole tooth, including the root, is forced out of the gums. Ritual scarification, removal of teeth, and lip plugs/dishes may have started as ways of making themselves less attractive to slavers.

Following their circumcision, Maasai boys become warriors or *moran*. This stage in their lives is marked by wearing their hair long, and their bodies are smeared with red ocher and animal fat as well as decorated with bead ornaments made by a warrior's numerous preteen sweethearts. Warriors are not allowed to marry, but may have as many sweethearts as they want from among the prepubescent girls of the camp. In order to lessen the problem of possible out-of-marriage pregnancies, no girl who has had a period is allowed to be a warrior's girlfriend. After seven years as warriors, the *moran* are ready for the next stage in their lives, to become elders or *ilterekeyani*. The time for the ceremony, called *eunoto*, is selected by a *laibon* or diviner-priest. The ceremony is marked with great emotion, as the warriors have their heads shaven by their mothers and all of the trappings of being a warrior are taken from them, and they are given instead those that mark them as elders, a cloak and walking stick, and they may then marry.

Closely related to the Maasai are the Samburu of northern Kenya. The term Samburu stems from the Maasai word *samburr* for the goatskin bag worn by most of the tribesmen and containing the essentials for travel. In the 19th century, the Samburu were frequently called the *Burkineji* or "people of the white goats." Their own name for themselves, *Lokop* or *Loikop*, and its meaning is an ongoing debate. It seems to mean something like "owners of the land." The people and their language are close to Maasai in that over 95 percent of the vocabulary is the same, and some have proposed that they descend from the Laikipiak Maasai, who were mainly destroyed in the 19th century.

Other sections of the Samburu may be of Turkana, Rendille, and other pastoralists who coalesced in the late 19th century.

The Samburu practice many of the same customs as the Maasai, including male and female circumcision. The Samburu are a pastoral people, and young men enter a long period of serving as warriors following their circumcision. The warriors, like their Maasai counterparts, dress up in beaded necklaces, bracelets, and earrings as well as wear beaded headbands. Their hair is elaborately coiffed with red clay. Most Samburu wore two pieces of cloth, one wrapped around the waist and a second around the shoulders. Until recently, colors and patterns of the cloth helped identify the age of the wearer. The Samburu have begun to wear nontraditional clothes such as trousers, shorts, and shirts since the 1990s.

Samburu camps remain generally small and may only consist of a single family. Each wife a man takes has her own hut and the housing is made of sticks, cattle dung, and grass. Nearby are the nightly cattle and sheep pens protected from wild animals and thieves made of thorn bush fences.

Among the greatest of changes that have been made on the Samburu in recent years is the change in their diet. More and more, they have become dependent on buying corn meal and other foods from local merchants with the monies they have made selling livestock. As a result, sugar is on the rise to sweeten porridge and tea. While the traditional milk-and-blood diet is still consumed, a few Samburu have turned to farming.

The Turkana are another greatly isolated Nilotic population living in the arid northwest of Kenya near the borders with Uganda and Ethiopia. The Turkana are also related to the Maasai, but claim their origin is from across the Red Sea in Arabia. They have taken on a number of aspects such as clothes that make them hard to distinguish from the Samburu, but in the past, they wore leather wraps and capes decorated with ostrich shell beads. An unusual aspect of traditional dress was the wrist knife. The wrist knife was shaped like a bracelet, and when swinging his arms, the wearer was able to slash his opponents. These are not worn today, but they are collectors' items in the African art market. Although isolated from much of Kenya, the Turkana have felt the impact of the modern state more keenly than the Samburu.

The majority of Nilotes still practice their traditional religions or have been converted mainly to Christianity. In Sudan, some have converted to Islam, such as one of the chiefly families of the Ngok Dinka. Figures for the numbers of Christian converts in Sudan are in doubt, as they are for all Nilotic peoples; for example, 25 percent of Maasai are estimated to be Christians, but this is questioned by some experts as being too high. Figures for the Turkana in Kenya, is between 5 and 10 percent Christian, which may be closer to the reality for most Nilotes. The remote region inhabited by the Samburu have both Protestant and Catholic missions established, and there has been some conversion, but these centers also offer education and health services that might be more attractive than the pull of conversion.

In Sudan, the British imposed a policy that isolated the south from the Arab, Muslim north of the country at the behest of the British Commissioner in Egypt, Evelyn Baring Lord Cromer, and British Governor-General of the Sudan, Sir Reginald Wingate. In an effort to keep East Africa British and Christian spheres of influence, the two men developed policies to lock out Arabs and Muslims from southern Sudan. The policy came into place in 1904 shortly after the reconquest of the Sudan and the fall of the Mahdist state in 1899. They opened up areas for Protestant and Catholic missionaries, and education was left in the hands of the missionaries. Sudanese independence in 1956 did not bring the north and south together in an easy bond. Shortly following independence, the northern-based government began to close missions and attempt to attract southerners to Islam. Today, it is estimated that only about 20 percent of southern Sudanese are Christians (including non-Nilotic peoples such as the **Zande**), and the majority follow traditional religions. Only a small minority of southern Sudanese converted to Islam, perhaps less than 10 percent. Among those who converted to Islam are some of the lineages of the Ngok Dinka.

Most Nilotes were brought under colonial authority only in the late 19th and early 20th centuries. It can be questioned whether or not the Nuer ever really recognized colonial authority. Sudan was incorporated into a larger Egyptian-Turkish state in 1821 when Ibrahim Pasha, son of the Egyptian ruler Muhammad 'Ali, began the conquest of Sudan. Ibrahim Pasha was able to extend Egyptian authority over much of Sudan and established what is called the *Turkiyah*, meaning the "Turkish State" (Egypt being nominally under the

Ottoman *Sultan*). Isma'il (1863–1879), one of Muhammad 'Ali's line to rule Egypt, was able to push ever further into Sudan and defeated the mixed Arab-**Nubian** Shayqiyah tribal forces, which he subsequently recruited as irregular cavalry. Khartoum was founded as the capital of the new province in 1825. Egypt's rulers wanted to be sure that Egypt, not the British or French colonial powers, would have control of the source of the Nile and encouraged the southern expansion by the Turko-Egyptian officers. They were successful in extending their control into southern Sudan, mainly along the course of the Nile, and established the province of Equatoria in the 1870s, though they exercised no real control over the Dinka and Nuer.

In 1881, Muhammad Ahmad ibn 'Abdallah rose to challenge the *Turkiyah*. The Turko-Egyptian government had generally been very abusive of Sudanese subjects, and Muhammad Ahmad opposed the legitimacy of the *Turkiyah* on religious grounds. He gathered a following whom he called the *Ansar* after those who gathered around the Prophet Muhammad in Madinah, and had significant victories over better-armed *Turkiyah* forces. He declared himself to be the *Mahdi* or "the Guided One" sent to renew Islam. By 1885, the Mahdi's forces had nearly all of Sudan under their control. That year, the Mahdi died and was succeeded by 'Abdallah ibn Muhammad as his *Khalifah* (a title first used by the successor of the Prophet Muhammad), who counted on his own Arab Baggarah tribe for support. The *Mahdiyah* state allowed enslaving of non-Muslims, and the Shilluk, Nuer, Dinka, and others were subject to raids.

Nonetheless, the Ngok Dinka forged ties with both the *Turkiyah* and with the *Mahdiyah* governments, resulting in a stronger, more centralized authority unlike the rest of the Dinka.

The British had little impact on most of the Nilotes in southern Sudan for the first several decades after the reconquest in 1899. The first two officers sent to deal with them were both killed in 1919 by the Dinka and 1927 by the Nuer, respectively. Incorporation of the south into the rest of Sudan did not really take place until 1956. Independence governments tended to marginalize the **Nuba**, Dinka, Nuer, **Fur**, and even the Arabic-speaking Baggarah in favor of the riverine Arabs such as the Shayaqiyah, Ja'aliyin, and Danqalah, the main sources for the Mahdis *Ansar* and the *Turkiyah*'s *Jihadiyah* troops. They are also called the *awlad al-bahr* or riverine Arabs who see themselves as being culturally superior to the *awal al-gharib* or Westerners, which include both Arabs, such as the Baggarah, and non-Arabs, such as the Fur, who are considered to be less "civilized." Conflict between the Arab, Muslim north and the non-Arab and non-Muslim south erupted as early as 1955 with a mutiny by southern soldiers. Problems escalated until 1958, when the Sudanese army took over the central government in a military coup. The long-running civil war in Sudan began. The rebel guerrilla army eventually took the name of *Anya-Nya* (the origin and meaning of the name is still obscure) which served as a refuge for the beleaguered civilian population of the south against the forced cultural unification policies of the central government.

Abyei

The Abyei region of Sudan was not included in the historic January 2011 referendum that formally separated the southern regions of Sudan from the north. Abyei will hold its own referendum later in 2011, and currently it is administered by the Abyei Area Administration headed by a Dinka, Deng Arop Kuol, from the Sudan People's Liberation Movement. Abyei is inhabited by both Arabic-speaking pastoral nomads, most of whom belong to the Masriyah (also spelled Messiria) division of the Baggarah tribe who inhabit a wide area in southern Dar Fur, Kordofan, and west into Chad. The Masriyah established themselves in the region by the 18th century and initially coexisted with nine separate Ngok Dinka groups who were also primarily pastoralists. The British in 1905 redrew the administrative districts and attached Abyei to Kordofan. The British also armed the Nuba with rifles to resist the expansion by Arabic-speaking pastoralists and serious conflict between the Arab and non-Arabs broke out in the post-independence period. In 1965, 72 Ngok men were killed in the trading town of Babanusa, within Masriyah territory. The Ngok Dinka became heavily involved in the civil war, and many fled further south to join the fight or north to Khartoum as a result. The government in Khartoum armed the Masriyah, and they developed into a highly effective mobile militia called the *murahilin*, who caused great damage in the south. By the end of the 1980s, the Ngok and other southerners had been generally displaced from Abyei and replaced by Masriyah. The conflict is greatly exacerbated by the fact that oil was discovered within the province, and by 2003, Abyei accounted for a full one-fourth of Sudan's oil exports. Issues remain such as the International Court in the Hague's ruling that gives Masriyah herders rights to access their common grazing lands as well as who will be able to vote in any referendum.

In 1972, the Addis Abba Agreement was signed in order to bring the 17-year war to an end. The attempt was to not include in any way things that would derail the negotiations, including any mention of the war's many atrocities against civilians. Not all southerners were willing to abide by the agreement, and those members of the *Anya-Nya* who refused to put down their weapons were referred to as *Anya-Nya II*.

The Southern Peoples Liberation Movement/Army (SPLM/A) was founded in 1983 by John Garang, a Dinka. The SPLA became so identified as a Dinka organization that anyone who was a Dinka was automatically seen to be a rebel and a member of the SPLA. Garang was a well-educated man with a BA in economics from Grinnell College in the United States and an MA in African agricultural economics from the University of Dar es-Salam in

Tanzania. As a student, he met Yoweri Museveni, later president of Uganda, and the two remained close allies. Garang joined *Anya-Nya* in 1971 and rose steadily through the ranks to become a colonel after completing the U.S. Army Infantry Officer's Advance Course at Fort Benning, Georgia, in 1974. He finished his PhD in economics at Iowa State University at Ames in 1980. In a period of reconciliation between the north and south, Garang was appointed to be the head of the Sudanese Staff College in Omdurman in 1982. Shortly afterward, he was sent south by the Sudanese government to deal with the Dinka, organized the SPLM/A, and the fighting erupted again. Garang defected to the rebels and quickly became their main voice. Garang died in 2005 after actively participating in the attempt for a comprehensive peace settlement signed in Kenya in January of the same year. Garang, unlike many other southern Sudanese, supported unification with the north in a type of federal system.

The Nilotes of Sudan voted during the week of January 9, 2011, in a referendum either for continued unity with the north or for total separation. Initially, the northern government of 'Umar Bashir declared that, though it would allow the referendum to take place, it would not agree to the south separating. The vote needed to have at least a 60 percent turnout of the southern electorate and in the weeks leading up to the referendum, it became clear that the south would vote to separate. Rhetoric from Khartoum began to change as did coverage on Sudanese satellite TV channels. President Bashir himself made a final visit to the south before the elections, during which he declared that Sudan would be happy to help with the emergence of its new neighboring state. After five decades of civil war, perhaps southern Sudan can now deal with the process of peace with the north and internal development.

Other Nilotes in Uganda, Kenya, and Tanzania tend to remain on the political fringes of the state. The Kalenjin produced one Kenyan president, Daniel Arap Moi, who served from 1978 to 2002, when the constitution did not allow him to run again. The Moi years saw the emergence of a single-party state in Kenya and the growth of human rights abuses. The Acholi in Uganda also produced one short-lived presidency in a military coup, but under Idi Amin, many Acholi military officers and soldiers were killed by government forces. In Tanzania and Kenya, Nilotic peoples tend to live in isolated areas and receive minimal education. Nonetheless, picturesque Samburu, Maasai, Turkana, and others serve as important draws for African safaris. Beadwork made by their women is an important source of local income for them.

John A. Shoup

Further Reading

Beckwith, Carol, and Angela Fisher. *African Ceremonies*. New York: Harry N. Abrams, Inc., 2002.

Collins, Robert. *A History of Modern Sudan*. Cambridge: Cambridge University Press, 2008.

Deng, Francis Mading. *The Dinka of the Sudan*. Long Grove, IL: Waveland Press, Inc., 1984.

Essien, Kwame, and Toyin Falola. *Culture and Customs of Sudan*. Westport, CT: Greenwood Press, 2008.

Evans-Pritchard, E. E. *The Nuer: A Description of the Modes of Livelihood and Political Institutions of a Nilotic People.* Oxford: Oxford University Press, 1956.

Fadlalla, Mohamed. *Customary Laws in Southern Sudan: Customary Laws of Dinka and Nuer.* Bloomington, IN: iUniverse, Inc., 2009.

Finke, Jens. *The Traditional Music and Cultures of Kenya.* http://www.bluegecko.org/kenya/ (accessed March 1, 2010).

Jenson-Elliot, Cynthia. *East Africa.* San Diego, CA: Lucent Books, Gale Group, 2002.

Jok, Jok Madut. *Sudan: Race, Religion, and Violence.* Oxford: Oneworld Publications, 2008.

Klein, Hanny Lightfoot, Ellen Cole, and Esther D. Rothblum. *Prisoners of Ritual: An Odyssey into Female Genital Circumcision in Africa.* New York: Routledge, 1989.

Lesch, Ann Mosley. *The Sudan: Contested National Identities.* Bloomington: Indiana University Press, 1998.

Otiso, Kefa M. *Culture and Customs of Uganda.* Westport, CT: Greenwood Press, 2006.

Sobania, N. W. *Culture and Customs of Kenya.* Westport, CT: Greenwood Press, 2003.

Non-Africans: Asians

Most of the Asian populations in Africa are from the Indian Subcontinent. Indian relations with East Africa stretch back at least to the early Islamic period, and Indians may even be among the peoples who helped form the **Swahili**. The Omani *Sultan* invited Indians to come to the East African cities to work in trade and finance following the establishment of the Omani east African empire in the 17th century.

Others came much later in the colonial period, in the late 1800s, when labor was needed for building mainly railroads. Others were brought by colonial authorities to work as farm laborers in sugar plantations in South Africa or coffee and tea plantations in Kenya and Uganda. In places such as Lesotho, Indians form an important merchant class beginning in the late 1800s. Indians are Muslim, Hindu, and other religions such as Christian, but the main religions are Islam and Hinduism. Today, Indians make up less than 1 percent of the total population of Africa, but in South Africa, they make up 2.5 percent. President Idi Amin of Uganda expelled 80,000 Asians in 1972, and since 1986, with the presidency of Yoweri Museveni, Asians have been coming back.

In much of French-speaking West Africa, **Arabs**, mainly from Lebanon, were encouraged to come by the French authorities. The Arabs were mainly from southern Lebanon's Shi'ite community and were seeking economic migration. Following the establishment of Israel in 1948, some Palestinians have also come. Most of the Arabs are Muslims, though some also belong to various Christian groups including the Eastern Orthodox or those connected to the Roman Catholic Church, such as the Maronites of Lebanon.

India became tied to the Indian Ocean trade with East Africa in the first millennium before the Christian era along with the Arabs. Indian products such as cotton cloth were traded for raw materials from Africa. In late antiquity, the city of Rhapta was established along the East African coast, from which commercial relations were extended inland. Other trading cities were built along the coast, and from these communities the Swahili culture emerged. Gold from the kingdoms in today's Zimbabwe came into the Indian Ocean trade by 1000 funneled through the city of Sofala on the Mozambique coast. The Portuguese took a number of these coastal cities in the late 15th and early 16th centuries and continued in trade for gold, ivory, and other African products, but in the 17th century, a revitalized Omani state pushed them out of most of East Africa. With reestablished Arab control over the cities along the coast, the *Sultan* encouraged Indians as well as Arabs to come and set up businesses.

Indians are mainly Muslim or Hindu, though there are others from Indian religions such as Sikhs and Jains. Islam is a religion shared with a good number of Africans, and where religion is shared, intermarriage with locals has occurred. Those Indians who came later, under British authority, did so mainly as work crews to build infrastructure such as railways. In 1860, Natal in South Africa brought 150 Indian men to work in sugar plantations as indentured labor. An appeal was made to allow small traders to come to South Africa and, by the start of World War I, Indians were in Natal and the Transvaal. By 1920, the number of Indians in Natal was larger than the white population, and legal restrictions were imposed to marginalize Indians economically and politically. The fight for Indian rights was led in part by the lawyer Mahatma Gandhi, and they were able to get the agreement that discriminatory laws would not be passed without consulting with Cabinet ministers. In 1914, Gandhi left South Africa for India, where he helped lead the movement for Indian independence.

In East Africa, large numbers of Indians were imported to build the Uganda-Kenya Railway, which was begun in 1896 and not completed until 1931. Around 32,000 Indians were contracted to build the railway, and by the end of World War II, the number of Indians in East Africa was 320,000. Most belonged to the small traders and artisans class called *dukawalla* in Hindi/Urdu. By the 1940s, Indians had gained control over 80 percent of the businesses and the majority of the cotton gins in both Kenya and Uganda.

Similar to the Indians, Arabs in the West African countries of Senegal, Côte d'Ivoire, Sierra Leone, Liberia, and Nigeria number fewer than 200,000.; but they fill important positions in the local economies as traders and deal in items such as cloth. They are considered by many locals as being highly exploitative of Africans and in the recent civil wars in Sierra Leone, Liberia, and Côte d'Ivoire, their shops were specifically targeted. In Senegal, where there have been historic tensions with the Arabs in Mauritania, Lebanese and Palestinians also have reputations for being exploitative.

Indians in South Africa felt the impact of apartheid and, like other nonwhite populations, were restricted by the government's laws. Faced with discriminatory access to funds for building schools, hospitals and the like, the Indian community raised the funds from within their own group and sent representatives to the United Nations and the newly independent government of India to complain about their treatment under apartheid. In 1984, in an attempt to break the Indians from the other nonwhite groups, a Tricameral Parliament system was put in place to give Indians a say in government. However, it was seen to be a political ploy and never gained much support among South Africa's Indians.

In 1972, Uganda expelled 75,000 Indians, who made up around 2 percent of the country's population. Most of Uganda's Indians had British passports, and 27,000 of them moved to Great Britain, 6,100 to Canada, and 1,100 to the United States. Since 1992, Ugandan president Yoweri Museveni has allowed them to return and regain their lost property.

John A. Shoup

Further Reading

Afolayan, Funso S. *Culture and Customs of South Africa*. Westport, CT: Greenwood Press, 2004.

Collins, Robert O. *Africa: A Short History*. Princeton, NJ: Markus Wiener Publishers, 2008.

Ehret, Christopher. *The Civilizations of Africa: A History to 1800*. Charlottesville: University Press of Virginia, 2002.

"Indians of East Africa." http://www.rudyfoto .com/IndiansofAfrica (accessed May 28, 2010).

Jenson-Elliot, Cynthia. *East Africa*. San Diego: Lucent Books, Inc., Gale Group, 2002.

Otiso, Kefa M. *Culture and Customs of Uganda*. Westport, CT: Greenwood Press, 2006.

Ross, Eric. *Culture and Customs of Senegal*. Westport, CT: Greenwood Press, 2008.

Sobanian, N. W. *Culture and Customs of Kenya*. Westport, CT: Greenwood Press, 2003.

"South African Indians: The Past, the Present, and the Future." http://www.ipoaa.com/south _african_indians (accessed May 28, 2010).

Non-Africans: Europeans

Europeans who are citizens of African countries make up a small number in the overall population statistics, but many hold significant positions in the economies of countries such as Namibia and South Africa. In Zambia and South Africa, they hold large commercial farms, and confiscations of white farmlands in Zimbabwe have left the economy in shambles. In 2003 alone, some 200 white commercial farmers relocated in Zambia from Zimbabwe. Generally speaking, Europeans make up only around 1 percent of the populations in most African countries, but in South Africa they number nearly 10 percent, and in Namibia, they represent 6–8 percent of the total.

The main European populations in Africa are Portuguese, French, Belgian, Dutch, and British, though in South Africa they also include Greeks and others who immigrated there after World War II. The earliest Europeans to establish a permanent post in Africa were the Portuguese, who began exploring the Atlantic coast in the early 1400s under the patronage of Prince Henry the Navigator. By 1460, they had reached as far south as Sierra Leone. In 1471, they reached the "Gold Coast" of Ghana and built their fort/trading station Elmina, from the Arabic word *al-Mina'* meaning a harbor. They also established another trading post in Benin and were greatly impressed by the highly centralized Benin state. In 1482, the Portuguese made it to the Kingdom of **Kongo**, where in 1505, the converted Catholic son of the king succeeded his father to the throne as King Alfonso. The Portuguese pushed south, and in 1487, they reached the Cape of Good Hope. Rounding the Cape, the Portuguese encountered **Arab**, **Persian**, Indian, and **Swahili** trading communities on the East African coast in 1498. The Portuguese were able to successfully compete with the Arab traders, and it was not until the rise of a renewed, strong Omani state in the 17th century that the Portuguese were pushed out of most of their East African holdings. .

The French, like the Portuguese, were interested in trade with West African states, and in 1659, the French established a trade station at Saint Louis at the mouth of the Senegal River. The island of Gorée, located just off the coast of Dakar, was originally a Portuguese trade station which was first occupied in 1444, but it became Dutch in 1588, and after a brief period of English control, it became French in 1677. The French were concentrated in West Africa and did not establish many trade posts further south along the Atlantic coast, nor did they have a strong presence along the East African coast.

The Dutch were among the more active commercial traders in the 16th and 17th centuries along the Atlantic coast, but were far more interested in developing strong trade relations with the East Indies (Indonesia) than in Africa. The Dutch decided their main interest in Africa was to have weigh stations for provisions for their fleets going on to and from the Indies, and in 1652, they founded the colony at Cape of Good Hope for this very purpose. The Cape Colony was allowed to expand when in 1657, the Dutch East Indies Company released farmers from their company contracts to develop farms outside of the lands owned by the company. The small group of Dutch settlers was further strengthened when, in 1685, French Protestants, the Huguenots, fleeing persecution in France were sent to the colony by the Dutch government. In 1658, slaves from Dahomey and Angola were brought into the colony, and slave labor on agricultural production became an important part of the colony's economy. While the company did allow for manumission of slaves, it was not that common, and the number of "free blacks" was never large. Nonetheless, they did become part of the growing Colored (**Creole**) community of mixed racial ancestry. Along with settled agricultural production, a pastoral group of Dutch emerged in the 18th century called the *trekboers*.

The British established a trading center at the mouth of the Gambia River in 1618, which confirmed a previous treaty between Portugal and England's Queen Elizabeth I that granted the English rights to trade in the Gambia and the Gold Coast, modern-day Ghana. The English, along with the other main European powers, were interested in developing the slave trade with African kingdoms and did little other than man coastal trading centers. Great Britain was the first European country to try to abolish slavery in 1807, and in 1811 slave trading was made a felony. In 1817, the European victors of the Napoleonic Wars all agreed to abolish slavery. In 1833, the British Parliament banned slavery in the British Empire, but it was not until 1845 that a fleet of British warships were assigned the duty of suppressing the slave trade, particularly the trans-Atlantic trade.

Strong British antislavery laws brought them into difficulties with the Dutch inhabitants of the Cape Colony, which became British during the Napoleonic Wars. In 1807, the British banned importation of new slaves into the colony, and in 1823, the British tried to impose a minimum standard of living for slaves similar to what had been imposed on Trinidad. Britain began sending British settlers to the Cape in 1815, and a much larger group that was to arrive in 1820. The increasing British presence in the Cape along with the antislavery attitude of the new immigrants provoked the Great Trek in 1830, with many of the Dutch leaving the colony to found new states in the interior.

It was not until much later in the 19th century that Europeans were able to venture into the African interior; first by explorers, then later by missionaries, and finally settlers. In 1882, a meeting was held in Berlin, and Africa was parceled out between the main powers, including Germany and Italy, who were recent entrants in the "Scramble for Africa." Germans did not send many colonists, but in 1884, they officially took control of Südwest Afrika (Namibia) and a number of German families moved to the colony. British colonists moved into the two Rhodesias in the1890s partially to counter moves by the Germans in Tanganyika and Südwest Afrika as well as renewed interest in the interior of Angola by the Portuguese. British interests in Kenya and Uganda were given a push by the Berlin Conference and French moves toward the sources of the Nile. In the early 20th century, British settlers were encouraged to develop commercial farms in both Kenya and Uganda. Following World War I, most of Germany's possessions in Africa became British, French, or Belgian.

Europeans brought with them western Christianity. **Copts** of Egypt and Ethiopia have long histories in the Nile Valley, and many of the peoples in Sudan converted to Islam in recent centuries. Many in West African countries such as Senegal converted to Islam following the defeat of traditional states by Europeans, Islam being a means of continued resistance to European political control. The western forms of Christianity introduced by Europeans were adopted and adapted by local peoples, and in many places syncretistic versions of Christianity emerged blending local belief systems with European. These syncretic churches, such as the Apostolic/Zionist forms in southern Africa and the Church of the Lord (Aladura), the Celestial Church of Christ, and the Cherebim and Seraphim Society in Nigeria, blend traditional beliefs in spirits with those of Christian salvation. Priesthoods in these churches follow the names and hierarchies of the Catholic or Anglican churches, and many use the Bible as a means of divination.

European colonial administration introduced the use of European languages that continue to be used today, since they allow communication across the numerous languages that may be found in one country. Following the independence of most African countries in the 1960s, the Organization of African Unity agreed to keep the colonial borders, and official colonial languages were easier to deal with than to reinstate all precolonial borders and languages. It has made education easier as well, using a single language, and the British, French, and Portuguese had set up postcolonial organizations that help deal with a wide range of issues using English, French, or Portuguese languages. Colonial languages are generally used for education in most of the former colonial territories, and English, French, and Portuguese in particular are languages of education.

European colonial powers invested in infrastructure to exploit the resources of the colonial possessions including roads and railways. Both the British and the French had plans to connect all of their colonial possessions by rail, though neither was brought to light. European settlers built European-styled homes and even cities, and some, such as the British, educated generations of young Africans. Among the Europeans who least prepared their former colonial possessions for independence were the Belgians and the Portuguese.

During the colonial period, Europeans had political power and gave their citizens the right to vote while indigenous peoples were, for the most part, denied. The exceptions to these policies were St. Louis and Gorée in Senegal and in the Cape Colony. In Portuguese Angola and Mozambique, the concept called Lusotropicalism emphasized the lack of racism among the Portuguese, but it has been noted that Luscotropicalism developed in Brazil, not in Africa, and should not be seen as a means of understanding Portuguese behavior in their African colonies. Portuguese in Angola and Mozambique did not encourage the type of mixing that occurred in

Brazil, and generally the numbers of *assimilados* in Africa were small. In Angola, the discrimination in jobs, etc., suffered by the *assimilados* helped encourage the growth of independence movements. In general, Europeans were reluctant to give up their special rights, and in places such as Kenya, local resistance erupted into violence. In 1961, Southern Rhodesia broke from the United Kingdom's negotiations for independence of Nyasaland and Northern and Southern Rhodesia, and declared itself to be Rhodesia ruled by a white (mainly British) minority. Eventually Rhodesia's minority government was forced to recognize its days were coming to an end, and in 1979, an interim government was elected. In 1980, white rule was over, and Rhodesia became Zimbabwe.

Namibia gained its independence from South African control in 1990. The South West African People's Organization was formed in 1960 and had a long struggle for independence and African representation. In 1994, Walvis Bay was reintegrated into Namibia after three years of negotiations with the South Africans. Generally, Namibia has been able to effectively integrate the Europeans into the nation's political fabric.

White rule in South Africa ended in 1990 when the government revoked a number of racial laws and the release of Nelson Mandela from jail. Elections were organized and, in 1994, Mandela was elected the first black president of South Africa, bringing an end to white minority rule. **Afrikaners** or Dutch speakers have opted to stay in the new multiracial South Africa, while a number of those of British origin have opted to leave, emigrating to Australia and other former British colonies.

John A. Shoup

Further Reading

Afolayan, Funso S. *Culture and Customs of South Africa.* Westport, CT: Greenwood Press, 2004.

"Background Note: The Gambia." http://www.state.gov/r/pa/ei/bgn/5459.htm (accessed May 28, 2010).

Bender, Gerald. *Angola under the Portuguese: The Myth and the Reality.* Trenton, NJ: Africa World Press, 2004.

Collins, Robert O. *Africa: A Short History.* Princeton, NJ: Markus Wiener Publishers, 2008.

Jegede, Dele. "Popular Culture in Urban Africa." In *Africa*, 3rd ed., edited by Phyllis M. Martin and Patrick O'Meara. Bloomington: Indiana University Press, 1995.

Murray, Jocelyn, ed. *Cultural Atlas of Africa.* New York: Facts on File, 1989.

Ndege, George. *Culture and Customs of Mozambique.* Westport, CT: Greenwood Press, 2006.

Owomoyela, Oyekan. *Culture and Customs of Zimbabwe.* Westport, CT: Greenwood Press, 2002.

Oyebade, Adebayo. *Culture and Customs of Angola.* Westport, CT: Greenwood Press, 2006.

Ross, Eric. *Culture and Customs of Senegal.* Westport, CT: Greenwood Press, 2008.

Sobania, N. W. *Culture and Customs of Kenya.* Westport, CT: Greenwood Press, 2003.

Thompson, Leonard. *A History of South Africa.* New Haven, CT: Yale University Press, 1995.

Wills, A. J. *An Introduction to the History of Central Africa: Zambia, Malawi, and Zimbabwe.* 4th ed. Oxford: Oxford University Press, 2002.

Nuba

Nuba, or Nubans (not associated with **Nubians**), is a general term given to people of non-**Arab** descent living in the Nuba Mountains of southern Kordofan, Sudan. There are more than 60 main groups with as many as 100 mutually unintelligible languages belonging to the Nilo-Saharan language phylum, and Arabic is the lingua franca. Most of the Nuba are subsistence farmers. Some groups are Muslim, some Christian, and many still practice a traditional religion. For centuries, they suffered slave raids, which devastated the population. Today, about 2 million live in the mountains.

The Nuba have occupied the mountains, long a place of escape for people fleeing surrounding areas, for 1,000 years. References to "Black Nubo" or "mountain people" appear as early as the 4th century, but there was no actual contact until the 16th century when an Arab holy man arrived and married the daughter of a chief, founding a kingdom and converting the inhabitants to Islam. Arab traders frequented the hills, which became a source of slaves. In the 18th century, the Baggara, nomadic Arabs to the north, began raiding lower regions, causing an increase in the numbers of refugees, pushing the Nuba higher into the mountains. The slave trade grew in intensity in the 19th century along with Arabization in the northern hills. Conversion to Islam was a means of protection against slave raids in that Islamic law forbids enslaving a free Muslim. The religion also encourages owners to a free slave who, as a slave, converts to Islam.

The Nuba live in permanent, clan-based settlements with farming dependent on rainfall. The leader of the community is the rainmaker, a hereditary position. Crops include sorghum, tobacco, cotton, and vegetables. Nuba also raise cattle, goats, and pigs. Women enjoy considerable freedom, choosing their husbands and participating in religious and cultural activities. Nuba are known for their intricate body art, including body painting and scarification. Wrestling is an important social activity practiced by both men and women.

Traditional religions are based on ancestor spirits contacted by means of an intermediary or *kujur* who can be male or female. The *kujur* is consulted in all aspects of life, including when to plant and harvest crops. Among Islamic groups, this role has been adopted by holy men. Ties to ancestors give Nuba an important connection to their homeland.

In the early 20th century, policies of the Anglo-Egyptian government were instrumental in minimizing Islamization and containing Arab herdsmen. Nuba was included in the southern area of British control that was closed to Arabs and Muslims. The policy was favored by Evelyn Baring Lord Cromer, the British commissioner in Cairo, and Sir Reginald Wingate, the Governor-General of the Sudan, following the defeat of the Mahdist state in 1899. As in the other parts of the south, the British encouraged English and Christianity instead of Arabic and Islam, and schools were in the hands of Christian missionaries. However, with independence in 1956 and an Arab central government,

Islamization in the region intensified and conflicts with Baggara herdsmen over grazing and water rights ensued. Independence also brought civil war to Sudan between the Arab north and the non-Arab south, catching the Nuba in between. Friction mounted in the 1970s and 1980s, leading some Nuba to join the rebel Sudan People's Liberation Army (SPLA). In retaliation, the government armed the Baggara, who killed thousands of Nuba. In 1992, the government forced Nuba into "Peace Villages," demanding conversion to Islam and enlistment in the army to fight against the southern rebels. At the same time, rebels were conscripting Nuba to fight the northern government forces. Years of civil war have brought the Nuba way of life to near extinction. A cease-fire negotiated in 2002 has brought some hope to the Nuba.

Geri Shaw

Further Reading

Insoll, Timothy. *The Archaeology of Islam in Sub-Saharan Africa.* Cambridge: Cambridge University Press, 2003.

Olson, James. *The Peoples of Africa: An Ethnohistorical Dictionary.* Westport, CT: Greenwood Press, 1996.

Ruhhal, Suleiman Musa. *The Right to Be Nuba.* Lawrenceville, NJ: Red Sea Press, Inc., 2001.

Seligman, C. G. and Brenda X. Seligman. *Pagan Tribes of the Nilotic Sudan.* London: Routledge & Kegan Paul Ltd., 1965.

Stokes, Jamie. "Nuba." In *Encyclopedia of the Peoples of Africa and the Middle East.* New York: Facts on File, 2009.

Taschen, Angelika, ed. *Africa: Leni Riefenstahl.* Cologne, Germany: Taschen, 2005.

Nubians

The Nubians are a non-**Arab** people who identify their ancestral homeland as a stretch of the Nile that runs hundreds of miles south from the First Cataract (large rapids in the course of the Nile River), near Aswan, to around the Fourth Cataract, in northern Sudan. Throughout its long history, Nubia had no clearly defined borders, but was a land where kingdoms rose to control the trade route between Central Africa and the Mediterranean, and territories from beyond the Sixth Cataract to, at one point, the Egyptian Delta were included in a Nubian kingdom.

Today, Egyptian Nubia and much of Sudanese Nubia are submerged under the waters of Lake Nasser. From 1963 to 1967, during the construction of the Aswan High Dam, approximately 47,000 Egyptian Nubians were resettled 30 miles north of Aswan on reclaimed land in Kom Ombo, and about 53,000 Sudanese Nubians to Khashm al-Girba, near the Ethiopian border. More recently, Sudan's construction of the Merowe Dam in 2009 and the Khartoum government's plans to build two more dams on the Nile could flood the last of traditional Nubia.

The name "Nubia" has been used only since medieval times. The ancient Egyptians and the Old Testament called the region "Kush." To the Greeks it was "Aithiopia," and in some Arabic sources, it was part of the great area stretching from the Atlantic to the Red Sea called *Bilad al-Sudan*, or "Land of the Blacks." Some scholars have suggested that "Nubia" is derived from either the ancient Egyptian word for "gold," a reference to the land's gold mines, or the Nubian word for "slave." Today "Nubia" is most accurately used as a linguistic term, applied to the area where Nubian-speaking people lived.

The Nubian languages are classified as an Eastern Sudanic Language, a branch of the Nilo-Saharan Group. Nubian-speaking peoples may have started to migrate from the Kordofan and Darfur regions of western Sudan to the Nile Valley about 2,000 years ago, settling in the Kush Empire. Over time, their numbers grew and their languages supplanted the Meroitic language. By the fall of the Kush Empire in the fourth century CE, Adams says, all of the peoples of southern Egypt and northern Sudan spoke Nubian languages and were called Nubian.

According to Marianne Bechhaus-Gerst, of the University of Cologne, two Nile Nubian languages survive today: Nobiin, previously known as Mahas, spoken in southernmost Egypt and north Sudan; and Kenzi-Dongolawi. Kenzi is spoken north of Mahas in Egypt, while Dongolawi is spoken in the south, around Dongola. Kenzi and Dongolawi are considered dialects of the same language. There are an estimated 605,000 Nobiin speakers and 1,045,000 Kenzi-Dongolawi speakers.

While there is evidence of human settlement in the Nile Valley that dates back more than 10,000 years, developing civilizations did not begin to emerge until the fourth millennium BCE. The first indigenous Nubian cultures are generally called the A- and C-Groups of Lower Nubia by archeologists (c. 3500–2800 BCE and c. 2200–1500 BCE). They were the first Nubians to develop agriculture and animal

Nubian sail ships, called *Fallukah* in Arabic, sail on the Nile in front of the Pharaonic ruins of Kom Ombo. The modern town of Kom Ombo is located beyond the range of the photo and is one of the resettlement communities for Nubians in Egypt displaced by the Aswan High Dam project. (John A. Shoup)

Nubians to develop agriculture and animal husbandry, and to the Kerma Culture of Upper Nubia.

Kerma, about 10 miles south of the Nile's Third Cataract, was settled as early the fourth millennium BCE and one of Africa's earliest urban centers. Kush—as Egypt began calling it in the second millennium—became wealthy through its control of southern trade routes. By 1650 BCE, the Nubian state was centralized state and stretched from the First to at least the Fourth Cataract, rivaling Ancient Egypt in size. Egypt absorbed Nubia into its empire in 1500 BCE, but the decline of Egyptian power over the centuries gave rise to a new Nubian

kingdom in Napata during the eighth century BCE that reclaimed traditional lands and even conquered Egypt.

Egypt's 25th Dynasty, also known as the Nubian Dynasty (760–656 BCE), ruled from the Egyptian Delta to the confluence of the Blue and White Nile until Assyrian pressures forced the Kushites back to their homeland. Kush never again extended its rule beyond the Second Cataract. But its civilization flourished in Meroe, between the Fourth and Fifth Cataracts, where contact with the classical world brought both wealth through trade and a cultural renaissance.

There is little recorded history of Nubia after Kush fell to the Kingdom of Axum (based in the Ethiopian highlands) in the fourth century CE. But in the sixth century, Monophysite Christian missionaries from Byzantium quickly converted the three Nubian kingdoms that had succeeded Kush: Nobadia, on the Egyptian borders; Makuria, in the Dongola region; and Aodia (Alwa), near modern Khartoum. Less than a century later, Nubia was resisting the Muslim Arab forces that had swept through Egypt. After two short invasions in 642 and 652, the Arabs signed a treaty with Nobadia and Makuria—the celebrated *baqt*, essentially a trade and nonaggression pact—that left Nubia in peace for centuries.

Nobadia and Makuria merged in the eighth century under a single king, and for the next several centuries, the united Christian kingdoms prospered from trade with Islamic Egypt. However, Nubia's Christian identity began to erode once **Arab** nomads and Arab traders began to settle in Nubia and tribal leaders married into leading Nubian families. Intermarriage led to the gradual conversion of the Nubian matrilineal kinship system to the Arab Muslim patrilineal system, shifting control of Nubian properties and princedoms to Muslims, and the adoption of Islamic religious practices by not only the ruling elite, but by the wider population as well.

After Arab tribes overran Alwa and most of Makuria in the 14th and 15th centuries, Arabic supplanted the Nubian languages in the south. The extreme desert environment spared Lower Nubia of the Arab invasions, but in the 17th and 18th centuries, as Islamic teachers settled among them, the Nubians in the north converted to Islam. Unlike their kin in the south, however, the Nubians of the north retained their language, which they continue to speak today.

Nubian villages were built as close to the Nile as possible, their economy based on subsistence farming, animal husbandry, and date production. For centuries, the scarcity of cultivable land, especially in Lower Nubia, encouraged the migration of male Nubians in search of work, leaving most of the agricultural work to women, children, and old men. *Eskalay* water wheels, an invention introduced during Roman times, were used in some areas for irrigation up until the 1960s.

Today, Egyptian Nubians use chemical fertilizers and modern irrigation systems, and cultivate sugar cane as a cash crop to be sold at government-controlled markets. Sudanese Nubians raise cotton, introduced by the British, as a cash crop. Dates, a staple in the Nubian diet and prized by villagers, grew poorly in the sandy soil at the resettlements in both Egypt and Sudan. Because the resettled Nubians' farmland is no longer just beyond their doorways, men are more involved in the agriculture work.

Nubian kinship is organized around the tribe. Cross-cousin marriage is preferred, but endogamous marriages occur with whichever relative is available. Intermarriage between the different Nubian groups was and is still rare. Nubians are Sunni Muslim, and adhere to the *Maliki* school.

After Great Britain assumed control of Egypt and Sudan between 1880 and 1900, the Nubians were generally left in peace and, for the first time, free of invading armies and slave raiders. But as Nile waters began to rise after the completion of the first Aswan dam in 1902, Nubia's destruction was sealed.

The first dam, and its subsequent elevation in 1912 and 1933, crippled Lower Nubia's agricultural system and had a profound social and cultural impact. While Nubian men had always left their villages in search of work, either as mercenaries or laborers, the increasing loss of Nubia's very limited agricultural land accelerated the labor migration. By the 1960s, 60 percent of Egyptian Nubia had been destroyed or rendered unfit for habitation, and 70,000 Egyptian Nubian men and women were living outside of Nubia. Those who had remained in the villages were overwhelmingly women, children, and the elderly.

Today, Sudan is embarking on a controversial series of dam construction on the Nile. About 70,000 indigenous people were forcibly resettled during construction of the Merowe dam, built near the Fourth Cataract and the largest hydro project in Africa. The government's plan to build dams at Kajbar, miles from ancient Kerma, and Dal, in northern Sudan, would likely require the displacement of tens of thousands more people. The government has either ignored or violently suppressed protests against the dams.

Scott Mattoon

Further Reading

Adams, William Y. *Nubia: Corridor to Africa.* Princeton, NJ: Princeton University Press, 1977.

Adams, William Y. "Nubia." *Encyclopedia of Africa South of the Sahara.* New York: Charles Scribner's Sons, 1997. Reproduced in History Resource Center. Farmington Hills, MI: Gale.

Adams, William Y. "Nubia." *Dictionary of the Middle Ages.* American Council of Learned Societies. New York: Charles Scribner's Sons, 1989. Reproduced in History Resource Center. Farmington Hills, MI: Gale.

Ammar, Nawal H. "Nubians." *Encyclopedia of World Cultures, Vol. 9: Africa and the Middle East.* Human Relations Area Files, 1995. Reproduced in History Resource Center. Farmington Hills, MI: Gale.

El Hakim, Omar. *Nubian Architecture.* Cairo: Palm Press, 1999.

Fernea, Robert A. *Nubians in Egypt: Peaceful People.* Austin: University of Texas Press, 1973.

Jennings, Anne M. *The Nubians of West Aswan: Village Women in the Midst of Change* Boulder, CO: Lynne Rienner Publishers, 1995.

Kennedy, John G., ed. *Nubian Ceremonial Life.* Cairo and New York: American University in Cairo Press, 2005.

Lewis, M. Paul, ed. *Ethnologue: Languages of the World*, 16th ed. Dallas, TX: SIL International, 2009. Online version: http://www.ethnologue.com/.

Taylor, John H. *Egypt and Nubia.* London: British Museum Press, 1991.

Nyamwezi

Nyamwezi or Wanyamwezi is a **Swahili** term meaning "People of the Moon" and refers to a large population of Bantu people in western Tanzania. Their homeland is called Unyamwezi, which are the provinces of Tabora and Shinyunga. The Nyamwezi are closely related Sukuma, and together they are the largest group in Tanzania, numbering over 5 million people; the Nyamwezi number about 2 million and the Sukuma 3 million, though the numbers are disputed. The Nyamwezi and Sukuma languages, Kinyamwezi and Kisukuma, are closely related, and there is some debate about whether one is a dialect of the other or if they should be considered separate languages.

The Nyamwezi began to settle in their present location in the 16th century. It has been noted that the region was not inviting for most Bantu farmers given the conditions of swamp, poor soils, drought, and sleeping sickness. The Nyamwezi, Kimbu, Sukuma, Turu, and Langi settled in widely dispersed settlements that made use of where soils were the most productive. This movement was among the last of Bantu displacements of earlier populations of **Khoisan**, though the **Hadza** and the Sandwe have survived up to the present day. The Bantu farmers generally absorbed others including many of the Southern Cushites.

As overland trade routes reached Lake Tanganyika by 1700, the Nyamwezi were in a position to take advantage. **Arab** and **Swahili** traders established two trade centers in Unyamwezi, Ujiji, and Tabora, that linked to other inland trade routes north to Buganda and west towards the kingdoms in Angola. Nyamwezi ivory traders were operating in Buganda by 1830. By the 19th century, the Nyamwezi were themselves recognized traders, often opening the way for later Arab and Swahili caravans. In the 1850s and 1860s, Arabs, Swahilis, and their Nyamwezi allies had tapped into the trade from the Kazembe kingdom in the Katanga in the Democratic Republic of Congo (former Zaire), where the Nyamwezi settled and took the name Yeke. The Yeke developed a conquest state that eventually brought down the Kazembe kingdom. Ivory and slaves were the main commerce and by the 1830s, slaves were needed in the clove plantations on Zanzibar and Pemba islands.

Islam was introduced in the 19th century, and some Nyamwezi adopted the religion, though generally the culture adopted much of the dress worn by Muslims even if they did not convert. Most Muslim Nyamwezi are Sunni of the *Shafi'i madhhab*.

The Nyamwezi developed a system of local leaders called *metimi* or *ntemi* or chiefs. Several of the chiefs were able to extend their rule over others, and in the 19th century, there was briefly a Nyamwezi Empire under Mirambo, who ruled from 1860 to 1884. The Germans extended their protectorate over the Nyamwezi in 1885 and imposed a hut tax in 1898. Great Britain took German East Africa following World War I as the colony of Tanganyika.

Most Nyamwezi have retained their original religion, and even those who have converted to Islam are not that strict in their belief. Nonetheless, Muslims celebrate the main *'Ids* or holidays; *'Id al-Fitr* at the end of the month of fasting, Ramadan, and *'Id al-Adha* or feast of the sacrifice that marks the end of the *Haj* period. In addition, the Prophet Muhammad's birthday or *al-Mawlid al-Nabawi* is celebrated.

Traditional Nyamwezi religion has several terms for the supreme being; *Likube* or High God, *Limatunda* (The Creator), *Limi* (The Sun), and *Liwelo* (The Universe). The creator god is rarely worshipped directly, and ancestors receive more of the peoples' reverence. The ancestors of chiefs are seen as even more important, and people give them, and their own ancestors, offerings such as grain or even a sheep or goat. Traditional religion believes in spirits and witches. Witchcraft or *bulongi* causes illness, and diviners called *mfumu* are needed to find out if a person has been bewitched.

The Nyamwezi were farmers as well as raised livestock. Farming included crops of millet, sorghum, and rice, and later, maize and cassava were introduced. Other crops include beans, mushrooms, onions, peanuts, bananas, and oranges. Cash crops were introduced in the 20th century, and the Nyamwezi today raise cotton, sunflowers, and tobacco as commercial crops. The Nyamwezi have long been involved in trade, and in the 19th century, between 1 million and 2 million men worked as porters between the inland and the Indian Ocean coast while others remained farmers.

As noted above, traditional Nyamwezi government involved local communities under a *ntemi*. They were very successful in absorbing others whose descendants consider themselves and are considered by others to be Nyamwezi. In 1961, Tanganyika became independent and, in 1964, Zanzibar joined Tanganyika to become Tanzania after a bloody revolt. The Nyamwezi traditionally lived in many somewhat isolated communities that came into trouble with official government policy called *ujamma* to collect isolated communities together. Tanzanian president Julius Nyerere wanted to implement a type of socialism, but to make it more familiar to Africans. He borrowed the idea of community/extended family from the Swahili *ujamma*, thinking that as an indigenous concept, it would be better accepted by all. The collectivization did not work, particularly with inland groups such as the Nyamwezi with long histories of private landownership. The *ujamma* farms failed and in the end, though amounting to over 90 percent of the farmlands, produced less than 5 percent of the agricultural output. Nyerere retired from office in 1985, and subsequent Tanzanian governments have abandoned the socialist policies. In more recent years, the Nyamwezi have suffered from drought and soil erosion, which has crippled their agricultural output.

John A. Shoup

Further Reading

Adekunle, Julius O. "East African States." In *Africa Volume 1: African History before 1885*, edited by Toyin Falola. Durham, NC: Carolina Academic Press, 2000.

Keller, Edmond J. "Decolonization, Independence, and Failure of Politics." In *Africa*, 3rd ed. Bloomington: Indiana University Press, 1995.

Mbajekwe, Patrick U. "East and Central Africa in the Nineteenth Century." In *Africa Volume 1: African History before 1885*, edited by Toyin Falola. Durham, NC: Carolina Academic Press, 2000.

"Nyamwezi." http://www.ethnologue.com/show_language.asp?code=nym (accessed June 10, 2010).

"Nyamwezi." http://www.everyculture.com/wc/Tajikistan-to-Zimbabwe/Nyamwezi (accessed June 10, 2010).

Oromo

The Oromo are a very large ethnic group occupying the south-central region of Ethiopia extending in the northern portion to the Sudanese border in what is now the state of Oromia. They also extend into northern Kenya. Previously the Oromo were referred to as "Galla," a term the Oromo find offensive. Though there is no consensus on where or how the term Galla arose, or what it means, the term Galla was used mainly by non-Oromo-speaking peoples and not by the Oromo themselves. The group consists of several main groups with as many as 200 subgroups who have a common culture and speak a common Cushitic language, Oromo. Traditionally, Oromo are pastoralists, though sedentary farming exists in northern areas. Oromo are both Muslim and Christian, with some still practicing their traditional religion. They number approximately 27 million to 30 million and comprise about a third of the Ethiopian population.

The Oromo probably originated in the far southern highlands of Ethiopia, where their Cushitic ancestors lived for thousands of years. They are related to the **Somali** with whom they have had a contentious relationship. In the 10th and 12th centuries, Somali expansion pushed the Oromo out of the eastern territories, driving the inhabitants south and west. During the Middle Ages, the region was central to power struggles between the highland Christians and the lowland Muslims. The Christian defeat of the **Arab** principality of Adal, near Harar, in the 16th century opened the door for the Oromo invasion of the Harar plateau, beginning the massive migration of the Oromo people that continued for several centuries.

In Harar, the Oromo became Islamized and acquired the use of horses, which enabled them to rapidly push westward. They were strong warriors who developed a full-length body shield, which further aided their conquests. The movement was driven by constant Somali pressure behind them. As the Oromo overran other ethnic groups, they assimilated the populations and adopted new influences. Their westward migration forced the **Amhara** into the higher regions of the mountains, prompting Christian chroniclers of the time to write about them as brutal and evil killers. The Oromo established several kingdoms in the southwest and west, some adopting Christianity, but employing Arab advisers, giving Islam a foothold in the region. Having successfully fought the Ethiopian imperial forces, they eventually came to terms with them, and in the 17th century, Oromo were influential in the imperial government.

The basis of Oromo culture is the age-grade system known as *Gadaa*. It is an egalitarian system through which all men pass. The system consists of 11 grade levels beginning with grades for small boys, moving up to warrior grades and later grades for advisers. At level 6, a man becomes part of the ruling class. Oromo leaders are elected by those who have attained a certain grade level. It takes 24 years to pass through the entire system of grades to retirement.

While most Oromo are Muslim or Christian, some still practice the traditional religion, which is based on a supreme celestial deity, *Wak*, whose eye is the sun. Minor deities or spirits live in trees, rivers, and mountains. Birth, circumcision, marriage, and death are celebrated with special rituals. The traditional religion mainly exists in the south of Ethiopia.

Traditionally, Oromo are cattle-herding nomads, and most are still rural. In the highlands of the north, they have settled and become farmers. Farmers adopted the plow when they came into contact with highland cultures. The main crops are cereals and coffee. In the southern lowlands, Oromo are pastoralists, raising cattle, sheep and goats, horses, and some pigs. Staples include milk, meat, and butter. Oromo women are known for their elaborate hairstyles.

In the 19th century, under Menelik II (1866–1913), the Ethiopian Empire extended control over Oromo territories, subjugating the people. Renewed Red Sea trade brought Arab slave traders, and during this time, thousands of slaves were taken to satisfy Arab demand; mostly Oromo were captured in Somali raids. The Ethiopian emperor Menelik II himself is said to have had 70,000 slaves.

In the 20th century, Haile Salassi pursued policies of modernization and government centralization. Amharic culture and language were forced on other ethnic groups. Land grants were given to Amhara settlers to settle in Oromo lands, bringing ethnic conflict. Encouraged by newly independent Somalia, Oromo joined Ethiopian Somalis in open rebellion for independence that erupted in 1963. Somalia later backed away and the rebellion failed.

During the 1960s and 1970s, Oromo suffered discrimination, which continued after the radical Derg government came to power in 1974. The Oromo Liberation Front (OLF) was one of several political parties that organized to fight government control. Oromo success, however, was marginal due to infighting and lack of cohesion, a direct result of the migration, which had a decentralizing effect. After the fall of the Derg in 1991, the ethnic state of Oromia was formed. Eventually the OLF was absorbed by the ruling Ethiopian People's Revolutionary Democratic Front, which was dominated by the more powerful **Tigray**. The Oromo, however, continued to agitate for independence, causing the region to come under military occupation.

Geri Shaw

Further Reading

Abdullahi, Mohamed Diriye. *Culture and Customs of Somalia*. Westport, CT: Greenwood Press, 2008.

Baxter, P. T. W. "Towards Identifying Some of the Moral Components of an Oromo National Identity." In *Ethnicity and the State in Eastern Africa*, edited by M. A. Mohamed Salih and John Markakis. Uppsala: Nordiska Africainstitutet, 1998.

Central Statistical Agency of Ethiopia (CSA). "Census 2007." http://www.csa.gov.et (accessed May 26, 2011).

Chanie, Paulos. "The Rise of Politicized Ethnicity among the Oromo in Ethiopia." In

Ethnicity and the State in Eastern Africa, edited by M. A. Mohamed Salih and John Markakis. Uppsala: Nordiska Africainstitutet, 1998.

Henze, Paul B. *Layers of Time*. New York: Palgrave 2000.

Lewis, I. M. *The Modern History of Somaliland*. New York: Frederick A. Praeger, Publishers, 1965.

Lewis, I. M. *Peoples of the Horn of Africa: Somali, Afar and Saho*. London: International African Institute, 1998.

Pankhurst, Richard. *The Ethiopians*. Oxford: Blackwell Publishers, 1998.

Ullendorff, Edward. *The Ethiopians*. London: Oxford University Press, 1965.

Ovambo

The Ovambo inhabit the far southwest of Angola and northern Namibia; they are among the smallest of Angolan populations, but represent a full 50 percent of the population of Namibia. In Angola, the Ovambo number only around 150,000, while in Namibia, they number close to 1 million. The Ovambo are a Bantu-speaking people, and their language is called Oshivambo. Collectively, they make up eight closely related groups who formed separate chiefdoms and whose economies were based on raising cattle, fishing, and farming. The Ovambo have a close historical tie with the **Herero**, who live further south in Namibia. The Herero and Ovambo claim they descend from brothers.

The Ovambo arrived in their current homeland sometime in the 16th century, being the spearhead of the great movement of Bantu peoples into areas where **Khoisan** peoples had lived for over 20,000 years. The Ovambo and the related Herero moved from the headwaters of the Zambezi, spreading the mixed economy of raising cattle and grain cultivation into the Cunene River valley. The Ovambo settled along the Cunene/Kunene River, which today forms part of the border between Angola and Namibia, entering the Atlantic at the small town of Foz do Cunene. The region the Europeans called Ovamboland stretched between the Cunene and the Kavango rivers.

The region where they settled has around 431 millimeters (17 inches) of rain each year, which floods the land, filling shallow pans called *oshana* that are exploited for fishing and for farming. The Ovambo kingdoms that emerged recognized Humbe overlordship: the Humbe being the ruling lineage of the Mataman kingdom that held sway over much of the area north of Ovamboland until the middle of the 17th century, when it fell to the **Ovimbundu**. The Ovambo lived far from European interests and escaped the worst of the Atlantic slave trade. They were not really in contact with Europeans until the Germans attempted to control Namibia, then called South West Africa, in 1884. The Germans had a difficult time trying to conquer the indigenous peoples and did not eventually bring an end to Ovambo resistance until 1917.

Diamonds were discovered in South West Africa in 1908, and German efforts concentrated on securing access to interior rivers. The Ovambo did not acquiesce to German control easily, but during World War I, the region was seized by South Africa and, in 1920, South African control was recognized by the League of Nations.

The Ovambo are matrilineal, and only the *akwanekamba* families produced the political leadership roles. Political leadership came through daughters and sons of political leaders, but they were treated no differently than any other male member of the group. Christian missions have made great strides in converting the Ovambo, and the Finnish Missionary Society has had a station in Ovamboland since 1870. Today, most Ovambo belong to the Lutheran Ovambokavango Church. Nonetheless, many still believe in their traditional religion, which centers on the creator god *Kalunga*.

Cultivation is mainly a woman's province, and they grow millet, maize, beans, sweet potatoes, peanuts, melons, and pumpkins. Millet is pounded and made into flour that is cooked as a dry porridge— much the way maize is prepared in South Africa, Botswana, or Lesotho—and maize is made into beer. Men tend livestock, but due to flooding, grazing is not as good as it is further south among the Herero. Ovambo who live in the western part of their homeland have developed skills such as copper and iron working. Since there are no deposits of either mineral in Ovamboland, it is assumed they knew the art of metalworking before they came to the area.

In the 1920s and 1930s, the Ovambo resisted the South Africans in a number of local uprisings. In 1948, South Africa introduced apartheid laws, which provoked a number of independence movements. In 1960, the South West People's Organization or SWAPO was formed, and from the beginning it was dominated by Ovambo. In 1973, an independent Ovamboland was

declared by South Africa. Similar to "independent" native homelands (usually called Bantustans by the international community) in South Africa, and, again similar to the others South Africa tried to set up at that time, Ovamboland was not internationally recognized. Ovamboland's government was cruel and harsh and existed only because it was backed by the South African government; again, not unlike the experience in South Africa. In 1990, SWAPO was able to gain Namibia's independence and, though heavily dominated by Ovambo, it has tried to be nonracial and not favor any one ethnicity. Unlike many other independent states on the African continent, the Namibian government remains open to full white participation in politics as well as in the economy. There is no talk of land confiscations or other forms of revenge or retaliations for what Ovambo and other Namibians suffered under the Germans or the South Africans.

John A. Shoup

Further Reading

Olson, James. *The Peoples of Africa: An Ethnohistorical Dictionary.* Westport, CT: Greenwood Press, 1996.

Stokes, Jamie. "Ovambo." In *Encyclopedia of the Peoples of Africa and the Middle East.* New York: Facts on File, 2009.

Ovimbundu

The Ovimbundu are one of the largest ethnic groups in Angola and number around 4 million, or approximately 37 percent of the total population. The Ovimbundu are a Bantu people whose language is called Umbundu. They are centered on the Bengula/Bié highlands, though today many live in Angola's main cities and, as migrant workers, others live in Zambia and South Africa.

The ancestors of the Ovimbundu arrived in Angola and settled along the main river courses in the Benguela/Bié Plateau sometime around 1000 CE. The Benguela/Bié Highlands allowed the Ovimbundu a wider range of crops to be grown, and in addition, they kept cattle. They were able to raise yams and oil palms as well as several varieties of millet and sorghum, embracing two distinct Bantu traditions. The Ovimbundu, like other Bantu who moved into Angola, encountered **Khoisan** peoples who were displaced and pushed to the south.

In the 16th century, the entire region of Angola was hit by long-term drought, and the *Jaga* or warrior class of the Ovimbundu was able to rise in importance. To the Portuguese on the Atlantic coast, *Jaga* came to mean outlaws and brigands as bands of highly disciplined warriors wrecked havoc on the coastal kingdoms such as the **Kongo**. A number of separate independent Ovimbundu kingdoms emerged in the course of the 16th and 17th centuries, and by the end of the 17th century, they numbered around 23 kingdoms or subgroups.

As the Portuguese built up the Atlantic trading post of Benguela in the 17th century, the Ovimbundu became major trading partners. The Portuguese did not venture far into the heartlands of Angola, but extended their influence through a trade network of local kingdoms. The Ovimbundu were well placed to extend Portuguese trade far into the interior and became important partners with the Portuguese traders in Benguela. The Ovimbundu quickly became major suppliers of slaves bound for Brazil and other parts of the Americas. They became adept traders with the interior kingdoms of the **Chokwe** and **Lunda**, trading for ivory, wood, wild rubber, and slaves. The height of this trade was between 1874 and 1900, by which time both slaves and Angolan rubber lost their economic importance. It is estimated that Angola supplied over 3 million slaves mainly to Brazil, most of whom were sold by the Ovimbundu.

In the early decades of the 20th century, the Ovimbundu economy was hard hit by the flood of rubber from Asia and Latin America. In addition, Ovimbundu trade caravans were replaced by the Benguela Railroad, which was begun in 1904 and completed in 1929.

The Ovimbundu have greatly been affected by the Portuguese, and their area was among those where European setters established farms in the 20th century. Scholar Gerald Bender has noted that many Ovimbundu left their rural homes for jobs in the city, and many lost both their traditional language and religion for that of the Portuguese colonial authorities. While Bender goes on to explain the large number of Ovimbundu who were thought to be adapting to Portuguese life, many colonial administrators looked to the Ovimbundu as models of assimilation. Today, more than three-fourths of all Ovimbundu are Catholics, and the rest adhere to their traditional religion, which centers on the chief who is responsible for fertility of the people under his control as well of plants and animals.

The traditional Ovimbundu lifestyle involved both patrilineal descent for access to lands and matrilineal descent in terms of rights to the mobile possessions of their mothers. The dual-lineage system allowed issues of land, associated with rights within village and kingdoms, to be separate from issues related to trade; patrilineal concerns kept to resident group concerns, and matrilineal concerns were more dispersed.

The year 1911 is called the "Year of Great Hunger" by the Ovimbundu and is the last year that trading caravans attempted to make commercial journeys to the interior—none of them returned. The Portuguese forces moved inland and, over the next several decades, reduced the kingdoms in interior Angola, awarded to the Portuguese by the Berlin Conference of 1884. Ovimbundu and others were forced into labor for European farmers, heavy taxation, and discriminatory practices by the Portuguese, and strong suppression of any political protest by Africans created strong feelings for independence. Portuguese from Europe and Cape Verdeans were encouraged to migrate to Angola, and soon made they made up 5 percent of the total population of the colony, most settled in Ovimbundu areas. The arrival of the new settlers and the alienation of Africans, along with the discrimination suffered by those who tried to assimilate to European culture, resulted in the growth of Angolan nationalism.

In 1961, the Angolan war for liberation began, and three groups emerged; the Popular Movement for the Liberation of Angola (*Movimento Popular de Libertacao de Angola*, or MPLA), the National Liberation Front of Angola (FNLA), and the National Union for the Total Independence of Angola (*Uniao Nacional para a Independecia Total de Angola*, or UNITA). From its inception, the Ovimbundu supported UNITA. The MPLA and UNITA were the two strongest parties, and by 1975, when Portugal withdrew from Angola, the two rebel groups were involved in a civil war that would drag on into the 21st century. UNITA was led by the charismatic Jonas Savimbi, an Ovimbundu, who used his media finesse to gain the backing of the United States (then serving President Ronald Reagan) and South Africa against the Marxist MPLA, which was backed by the Soviet Union and Cuba. In 1986, President Reagan invited Savimbi to the White House as a "Champion of Democracy."

The war devastated much of the Ovimbundu homeland; both the rural region and its cities such as Huambo were left with nearly not one building left standing. Kuito in Bié Province was bombed for nine months, leaving, again, nothing standing. A cease-fire was agreed upon in 1991, but following elections in 1992 that gave more support to the MPLA, Savimbi and UNITA once again began the war. Savimbi was able to finance the war by sales of diamonds through Zaire (now Democratic Republic of the Congo) when he lost the backing of both the United States and South Africa. The war was finally brought to an end in 2002 when Savimbi was killed by government forces in the remote area of Luva near the border with Zambia.

John A. Shoup

Further Reading

Bender, Gerald. *Angola under the Portuguese: The Myth and the Reality.* Trenton, NJ: Africa World Press, 2004.

Mbajekwe, Patrick U. "East and Central Africa in the Nineteenth Century." In *Africa Volume 1: African History before 1885*, edited by Toyin Falola. Durham, NC: Carolina Academic Press, 2000.

Meredith, Martin. *The Fate of Africa: A History of Fifty Years of Independence.* New York: Public Affairs, 2005.

Oyebade, Adebayo. *Culture and Customs of Angola.* Westport, CT: Greenwood Press, 2006.

Stokes, Jamie. "Ovimbundu." In *Encyclopedia of the Peoples of Africa and the Middle East.* New York: Facts on File, 2009.

P

Persians

The term Persian refers to a large ethnic and linguistic group of the Indo-Iranian branch of the Indo-European language family, to which belong also Slavic, Germanic, Romance, and Celtic peoples. Today, the terms Iranian and Persian are often used interchangeably, though Iranians themselves have historically self-identified as Iranians, since Persian refers historically to someone from the ancient province of Parsa, and its dialect Parsi, which was one of several Iranian languages, though it has become the dominant language of Iran today. The oldest-known Iranian languages were Old Persian, the distant ancestor of modern Persian, and Avestan, a close cousin of Sanskrit, which survives today as the liturgical Zoroastrian language. Other extinct members of the Iranian language family are Pahlavi (the court language of the Parthian and Sassanid empires) as well as the Bactrian, Khwarezmian, Old Ossetic (the ancestor of the modern Ossetian language of today), Saka (the language of the Scythians), and Sogdian. Modern Iranian languages include New Persian, also called Farsi, which is the official language of Iran and the native language of the majority of Iranians; also included are Dari, a dialect of Persian spoken in Tajikstan and Afghanistan, as well as **Baluchi, Kurdish, Luri**, and Pashto. The majority of Persians are Shi'ite Muslim, though a small minority are Zoroastrian, and also Baha'is, Christians, Jews, Mandeans, and Yezidis. Approximately 70 million Persians inhabit Iran, with minorities abroad in the Gulf countries, Europe, North America, and Turkey numbering between 2 million and 3 million.

Historically, early Iranians were a semi-nomadic people, similar in many ways to their other Indo-European cousins in that they were a patriarchal culture and relied heavily upon horses for raiding and warfare, and cattle for their sustenance. They developed chariot-based and cavalry-based warfare very early, and also possessed advanced skills in metalworking. Many early descriptions or depictions of such nomadic Persian tribes as the Parthians, Scythians, or Saka depict them with jewelry, weapons, and armor of their own making, and archeology has recovered material evidence supporting these descriptions. The early Persians were famed for their skill in archery, which served for both hunting and warfare; their bows were composite, allowing for attacks at great range. While some of the Persian tribes remained nomadic, many Persians eventually settled in the area that the Greeks later identified as Persia, and developed a sedentary and agricultural way of life.

In terms of religion, early Persians worshiped a similar group of divinities as those found in Hinduism; with the coming of Zoroaster (11th or 10th century BCE), a religious reform took place, not unlike

---

5er, 7er, or 12er Shi'ite

The Shi'ites developed following the first generation of supporters of the descendants of 'Ali ibn Abi Talib and Fatimah Zahrah. Their son Hussein died in battle at Karbala in 680 and the Shi'ites still mark the event with *'Ashurah*. Support for the descendants of 'Ali continued even with active persecution by the 'Umayyads (661–750) and the 'Abbasids (749–1258), but divisions arose between which of the descendants to follow. The first break took place during the period of the 4th *Imam*, 'Ali ibn Hussein Zayn al-'Abdin (658–715); his younger son Zaid led a rebellion against the Umayyads and therefore had more right to succession than the older brother Muhammad ibn 'Ali al-Baqir (676–743), who tried to stay out of politics. Those who remained loyal to Muhammad al-Baqir were faced with another split during the lifetime of the 6th Imam Ja'far ibn Muhammad al-Sadiq (703–765). His son Isma'il died before he did, but many had thought that Isma'il had embodied more of the spirituality of the *Imam* than his brothers. The Isma'ilis broke, and those who remained loyal to Musa ibn Ja'far al-Kadhim (745–799) and his sons became the core of the 12ers who claim the 12th *Imam* Hujjat ibn Hassan (b. 869) has gone into occultation (a suspended state of being) and will return as the *Mahdi* or guide before the last days. Shi'ism in the classical period was often the voice of rebellion and the oppressed, and at one point, the Isma'ilis produced the Fatamid dynasty (909–1171) to rival the 'Abbasids and the Umayyads in Spain (756–1031).

Buddha's reformation of Hinduism to Buddhism. This reformation maintained the tri-partite caste system, but moved toward a monotheistic theology with such concepts as the Day of Judgment, along with infernal and celestial abodes in the afterlife. Zoroastrianism became the dominant faith of Iran from the second millennia BCE until the coming of Islam.

In the first millennium BCE, Iran was a province of the Babylonian empire, until the Medes rose against Babylon and established Iran as an empire, which lasted until the coming of Islam in 651 CE. The three great dynasties that ruled Persia were the Achaemanids (from whom the emperors Darius, Xerxes, and Cyrus), the Parthians, and the Sassanids. Following the **Arab** conquest and the arrival of Islam, Persians became an integral part of the growing Islamic empire, and Persian language became the unofficial second language of Islam. Despite the presence of Arab (then **Turkish**) invaders, some degree of Persian self-rule continued, as demonstrated by the Tahirid, Saffarid, Samanids, Ghaznawid, Buyid, and Safawid/Safavid dynasties. Many Persians became leading scholars of early Islam, a practice continuing well into modern times. Likewise, Persians contributed to the growth of early Islamic thought through their contributions to Islamic arts, culture, literature, and court life. Prominent Persians of the classical and medieval period include such scholars as *Imam* al-Bukhar (810–870); Ibn Sina, known as Avicenna in the West (980–1037); and *Imam* al-Ghazali (1058–1111).

Persian culture is both rich and diverse, and each of the major cities of Iran is unique in terms of character and its contributions to the nation. Persia has always been synonymous with fine arts and craftsmanship. In terms of material culture, Persians have excelled in the production of rugs and carpets, for which they are rightly famed. Specifically, each region of Iran is known for its own designs and patterns, and so a skilled collector can determine the region of origin based on the patterns and colors employed in a carpet's design. Likewise, Persian miniature painting is famous throughout the artistic world. Many medieval Persian and Islamic manuscripts feature detailed, colorful illuminations, which not only serve to enhance the visual beauty of the text, but also deepen our understanding of the medieval Persian worldview. Perhaps most importantly among the Persian contributions to the arts is that of classical Persian literature, much of which is still extant. The rich body of literature from the classical period includes narrative, political science, scientific, and religious texts. This corpus also includes the poetry of Ferdowsi (940–1020), Nizami (1141–1203), Sa'adi (1184–1283?) , and Rumi (1207–1273)—all of which are widely available in translation and are numbered among the great poets of world literature. Medieval Persian poetry ranged from romantic epics, such as Nizami's *Qays and Leila*, to the mystical poetry of

Shahnameh illustration of the *Golden Age of Earthly Paradise*. The *Shahnameh* was written by the Persian poet Hakim Abu al-Qasem Ferdowsi. (Hulton Archive/Getty Images)

Rumi, which is easily available today in translation in English and other languages.

From ancient times, Persians have always been an athletic people, given to an appreciation of sports and competition. In ancient times, archery and equitation were important skills. One unique athletic institution that has survived from medieval times is the *Zur-Khaneh* or "House of Strength," a fraternal guild where men practice traditional Persian wrestling. Members of the *Zur-Khaneh* also practice traditional exercises using weighted clubs as a type of physical conditioning and strength development—and in recent

The *Shahnameh*

The *Shahnameh* (Persian "Book of Kings") is the famous epic poem of medieval Persia, which covers the deeds of Iranian kings and heroes from ancient times until the coming of Islam. Although composed in the 11th century by the celebrated poet Abu al-Qasem Ferdowsi, a Persian Muslim, the epic itself has roots in earlier oral legends dating back to the pre-Islamic period. The epic is a (lengthy) poem of nearly 100,000 lines; it begins with the creation of the world, then the epic narrates the history of Iran under the reigns of 50 *shah*s, ending with the Arab invasion of the seventh century. The hero Rostam features prominently, as does *Shah* Iskander (Alexander the Great), among a wide range of characters; and the villains of the epics include the traditional territorial rivals of Iran (the Turks, Arabs, and Mongols), and even supernatural enemies such as dragons and ogres. The *Shahnameh* poem remains popular today in Persian-speaking countries, and has even been adapted to a variety of popular contemporary media, including opera and comics.

decades, the Persians have done very well at the Olympics in strength-based competitions such as wrestling and weight lifting. Many contemporary Persians are great enthusiasts of soccer, which is perhaps the most popular sport in practice today.

Although a minority of Persians are non-Muslim (e.g. Zoroastrian, Christian, and **Jewish**), the vast majority are Shi'ite Muslim (from Arabic *shi'ah* "follower" or "partisan," i.e., follower of 'Ali ibn Abi Talib), or Muslims belonging to the Shi'ah creed. However, an important minority (approximately 22,000) belong to the Zoroastrian religion, which is generally considered the oldest monotheistic religion in the world. The Zoroastrian population in Iran today can be found primarily in the holy city of Yazd (holy to the Zoroastrians), but can also be found in such eastern regions as Kerman. Religion is an integral part of Persian society, especially since the

government is an Islamic republic, and the Supreme Leader is always a senior and ranking member of the Shi'ah cleric, known by the title *Ayatollah*. While admittedly much of the Middle East is Muslim, the Arab states and Turkey are mainly Sunni, which serves to differentiate Iran from its neighbors in modern times. Historically, Iran was a Sunni state until the early 16th century, when the Safavid (1501–1722) dynasty adopted Shi'ism as the creed of the official state. Shi'ites differ from the Sunni mainstream in that while they believe in the same pillars of Islam (the creed, prayer, fasting, tithing, and pilgrimage), they believe that the only legitimate spiritual successors ("*caliphs*" or "*imams*") of the Prophet Muhammad were those of his immediate family (through his daughter Fatima and her husband 'Ali), whereas Sunni Muslims believe that the first the caliphs were senior members of the

The Zur-Khaneh

The Zur-Khaneh (Persian "House of Strength") is a traditional Iranian guild dedicated to chivalry, fitness, and the art of wrestling. Dating back to pre-Islamic times, it was originally a place for the training of young warriors—yet the Zur-Khaneh still survives today in Iran and its neighboring countries as a sort of traditional gymnasium. Within its octagon pit, men develop their fitness and combat abilities through a series of complex exercises that focus on strength and endurance training through weight training, the wielding of heavy clubs in a series of practice patterns, and traditional wrestling. Yet the Zur-Khaneh is not only dedicated to physical fitness, but also spiritual fitness and Iranian culture. Students of the Zur-Khaneh are expected to be loyal to the guild and their teacher, and to develop the characteristics of chivalry (courage, honor, integrity); some guilds have even adopted an internal structure that is modeled on the hierarchy of Iranian Sufi orders. Many Zur-Khanehs also encourage the recitation of warrior epic *Shahnameh* in order to encourage the athletes in their training.

Prophet's close companions who were selected by vote by the companions. The subsequent quarrel over the successorship between Mu'awiyah and 'Ali, and the eventual emergence of the Umayyad dynasty (661–750) was the major break between the two communities, with the Sunni accepting the legitimacy of Mu'awiyah and the Shi'ites saying the successorship should have gone to one of the sons of 'Ali instead. Although similar in most areas of doctrine to their Sunni counterparts, Shi'ite Muslims also believe in the return of the *Mahdi* (from Arabic *mahdi* or "guided one"), equated by the Shi'ites with one of the early *imam*s, who is considered to be at present in occultation; various groups of Shi'ite dispute which historic *imam* will return as the *Mahdi*.

Despite the revolutionary rejection of the Shah and his excessive efforts to Westernize or Americanize Iran, many Persians today remain culturally secular and open to contact with the West. Indeed, despite its past of (and present political reliance upon) strong religious traditions, many of the youth are disaffected with religion, and in fact, secularism is common among university students and adults, though rarely admitted to openly. Iranian cinema is popular both at home and abroad, and Persian art and literature (especially poetry) maintains a strong presence in the global community. Western television, music, and media are very popular in Iran, and Internet culture is a growing and powerful phenomenon among Persian students. Although "dating" is forbidden by the religious authorities, many university students enjoy more Westernized forms of courtship, or even mixed-gender friendship, all of which is now made easier by the popularity of the Internet and electronic communications.

Medieval Persia was at the intersection of Ottoman Turkey, China, and the Arab states to its south. As a result, the culture and lifestyle of urban Persia was very cosmopolitan, and Persian court culture was very urbane and refined. Rural culture however, was considerably different, being primarily supported by farming, and lacked the vitality and advantages that cities offered to their inhabitants. In fact, the difficult conditions of rural life continue well into modern times in many parts of Iran. Between 1750 and 1921, Iran underwent several modern reforms, including the establishment of a parliament and the creation of several modern colleges. However, even greater efforts at change began in Iranian culture with the 1925 rise to power of the Pahlavi dynasty under Reza *Khan* (1925–1941) and his successor Muhammad Reza Pahlavi (1941–1979), who attempted to make Iran into a fully modern and Westernized state, economically and culturally. However, Reza *Khan* and his son Muhammad Reza Pahlavi's reforms were characterized by brutal oppression, most notably through the use of SAVAK (the American-supported Iranian intelligence service).

The increasingly Western lifestyle of 20th-century Persians changed again radically with the Islamic Revolution of 1979. While previous to the revolution, Muhammad Reza *Shah* was largely successful in modernizing and industrializing much of Iran, the *shah*'s policies became unpopular with the Iranian people by virtue of lavish spending on what many perceived to be affectations of decadence. With the support of the dissatisfied public, the powerful and popular cleric Ayatollah Ruhollah Khomeini (d. 1989) was able to force the *Shah* to abdicate in 1979, and thus Iran entered its current political state of being an Islamic republic.

During the reign of *Shah* Muhammad Reza, Iran enjoyed a close relationship with American administrations. However, as the *shah*'s policies of repression became more visible, the Iranian people began to associate the United States with the *shah*'s oppressive regime. To make matters worse, following the 1979 Islamic Revolution, during the same year, the American embassy was seized by Iranian students, and its members taken hostage. Although the hostages were eventually freed (some as late as 1981), relations between the United States and Iran have remained tense ever since. Iran later faced great hardship in the Iran-Iraq War of 1980–1988, in which Iraq suddenly invaded Iran without apparent provocation. The conflict lasted eight years, and is remembered today as having seen Iraq make use of such illegal means such as chemical weapons. Approximately 500,000 Iranian and Iraqi soldiers died in the war, and considerable damage was done to the social and economic infrastructure of Iran. Although initially unable to limit the conflict, the United Nations (UN) was eventually able to broker a cease-fire, though not without considerable difficulty.

Iran entered the 21st century under a new Supreme Leader, Ayatollah Khamenei, and since elections in 2005, the current president has been Mahmud Ahmadinejad, a staunch conservative and vocal critic of Israel and its perceived allies in the West. Ahmadinejad was reelected in 2009, but not without considerable media controversy about the legitimacy over the veracity of the official ballots. In 2008 and 2009, Iran has faced new challenges as it has attempted to develop its own nuclear generators for the production of electricity. Despite its claims that the nuclear power is for entirely peaceful purposes, the UN has expressed reservations about Iran's motives, and ongoing dialogue is still in progress to determine whether or not Iran will face sanctions if the UN is not satisfied that the project is not intended for military purposes. Still, many Persians and even members of the government have expressed cautious hope that under the new American administration of President Obama, a new era of more positive Iranian-Western relations may be possible.

Connell Monette

Further Reading

Amir-Moezzi, M. A. "Shi'ite Doctrine." In *Encyclopaedia Iranica Online*, 2006.

Boyce, M. *A History of Zoroastrianism*. 3 vols. Leiden: Brill, 1975.

Boyce, M. *Zoroastrianism: Their Beliefs and Practices*. Leiden: Brill, 1975.

Brosius, M. *The Persians: An Introduction*. New York: Routledge, 2006.

Chehabi, H. "*Zur-Kāna*." In *Encyclopaedia Iranica Online*, 2006.

Chelkowski, P. "Graphic Arts." In *Encyclopaedia Iranica Online*, 2008.

Curtis, V. *Birth of the Persian Empire*. Vol. 1 of *The Idea of Iran*. New York: I. B. Tauris, 2007.

Drews, R. *Early Riders: The Beginnings of Mounted Warfare in Asia and Europe*. New York: Routledge, 2004.

Gaffary, F. "Cinema." In *Encyclopaedia Iranica Online*, 1991.

Gieling, S. M. "Iran-Iraq War." In *Encyclopaedia Iranica Online*, edited by E. Yarshater. 2006.

Kent, R. *Old Persian: Grammar, Texts, Lexicon*. 2nd ed. New Haven, CT: Oriental Texts Society, 1953.

Lapidus, I. *A History of Islamic Societies*. Cambridge: Cambridge University Press, 1988.

Lindsay, A. *The Persian Empire*. Chicago: University of Chicago Press, 2005.

Morgan, D. *Medieval Persia: 1040–1797*. New York: Longman, 1988.

Sakhai, E., and I. Bennet. *Persian Rugs and Carpets: The Fabric of Life*. Woodbridge: Antique Collector's Club, 2008.

Thackston, W. *A Millenium of Classical Persian Poetry: A Guide to the Reading and Understanding of Persian Poetry from the Tenth to the Twentieth Century*. Bethesda, MD: Ibex Publishers, 1994.

Yarshater, E. "Iran: An Overview." In *Encyclopaedia Iranica Online*, 2005.

R

Rendille

The Rendille people of Kenya (also called Rendillé, Randille, Randile, Randali, Reendile, and Rendili) number between 32,000 and 34,000 people, and they inhabit the Kaisut Desert and Mount Marsabit (between Lake Turkana and Mount Marsabit) regions in the far north of the country. The Ituria and the Ariaal are subgroups of the Rendille. The Rendille language, also called Rendille, belongs to the Eastern branch of the Cushitic family of the Afro-Asian language phylum. The Rendille language is related to **Somali**, **Oromo**, and **Afar**, though not closely. The Rendille name in their language means "Holders of the Stick of God." The Rendille language is in danger of being replaced by **Nilotic** Samburu in recent years due to the close proximity of the Samburu and other Nilotic peoples such as the Turkana, and to the need to communicate with Kenyan officials. More and more young people no longer speak their own language to such a degree that in a broadcast over Kenya radio, the announcer stated that Rendille is extinct. While this statement is far from true, it does note the importance and degree of language loss among the younger generation of Rendille. Some Rendille have converted to Islam and Christianity, but belief in their traditional religion is strong.

Rendille history places their origins further north in Ethiopia, and they came to their present location in Kenya due to conflicts with the expanding Oromo and later Somalis. The Rendille are mainly pastoral nomads and keep herds of camels (in the northern part of their territory) or cattle (in the southern part of their territory). Rendille cosmology states that their god *Wakh* or *Ngai* prefers the desert, and the desert is the place *Wakh* created for them. *Wakh*, in their tales, does not like mountains or seas, and feels that the desert is the perfect place for Rendille because of their dependence on the camel.

Rendille society is divided into lineages, like other pastoral peoples, and it is forbidden to marry within the same, close families. Until today, couples prefer to have their marriages arranged between their parents to avoid too-close marriage partners. The social custom of exogamy (marrying outside the lineage) has encouraged many in the southern areas to marry Samburu or other pastoralist peoples of the region. Camping units or settlements vary greatly in size, from totals of 30 to 600 depending on the availability of grazing and water for their prized livestock. Anders Grum notes that Rendille groups may move to six times per year, depending on resources or for security reasons. A typical Rendille camp is surrounded with a bramble fence called a *tikhorat*, and in the center is a stone-walled enclosure called the *naabo*, where the main hearth burns and where the lineage elders meet. The camp's tents are built of wood and brush and near them are the brush pens or *sum-ki-gaal* for the livestock. When camps are large, they expand in semidetached semicircles for each of the lineages. The pattern is maintained when they move and set up a new settlement, and all persons know their place in society by their spatial placement in the camp. Camel herds are usually managed by unmarried males who now set up their own temporary camps closer to the grazing. These camps lack most of the structures other than brush enclosures for the young camels. Small stock are herded by girls and unmarried women in camps much closer to the main camps. Camels are the backbone of their society, and the people live on a diet of camel's milk sometimes mixed with blood in a drink called *banjo*.

The Rendille have age grades or *gadaa*, and they are 14 years apart in their system (though it is noted the space can be 7 to 14 years apart). There are six main grades, and circumcision of young men is an important part of moving from childhood to adulthood. Like many other East African peoples with age grades, the period of being a warrior lasts for 14 years, during which time they are not allowed to marry. The long period of being a warrior increased the military capabilities of any one group and may have developed first among Nilotic peoples. As warriors, the men are no longer only protectors of their precious herds of camels, but they become raiders against others as well. The warriors then move into the status of *ennui* around the age of 30 and mark this period by wearing a purple loincloth and a white feather in their hair. As adults they are allowed to own property, including land granted to them by the council of elders. The final

stage is that of elder; they then change to tartan cloth, and their headgear becomes far more important to them, no one being allowed to touch them. Though there are also age sets for women, they are not as well defined as they are for the men.

Traditional Rendille ceremonies are strictly gender divided. Most ceremonies are forbidden to women, and only men of certain age grades are allowed to attend. Rendille women are not allowed to touch objects or talk to men during the ceremonies. Only those around courtship are open to both men and women.

Rendille have been isolated from the national government during much of the colonial period; the British left them alone, and schools were opened in the 1960s following independence. In areas where Samburu are the majority, school and media (radio and later television) are in the Samburu language, making it easier to use Samburu rather than Rendille for the children. There are two towns where Rendille are the majority, Kargo and Korr, and in recent years, there have been attempts to revitalize the Rendille language; however, it is noted that attempts to do this in areas where Samburu is spoken have failed so far. Their region is still greatly isolated and became important to Kenya only with the raids by armed Somalis starting in the 1970s. The region is still prone to camel and cattle raids, and all sides are well armed.

John A. Shoup

Further Reading

Grum, Anders. "Rendille Habitation." In *African Nomadic Architecture: Space, Place, and Gender*, edited by Labelle Prussin.

Washington, DC: Smithsonian Institution Press and the National Museum of African Art, 1995.

"Rendille—Introduction." http://www.blue gecko.org/kenya/tribes/rendille/index.htm (accessed December 20, 2009).

"The Rendille Tribe." http://www.kenya -information-guide.com/rendille-tribe.html (accessed December 20, 2009).

"Rendille Tribe." http://www.softkenya.com/ tribe/rendille-tribe (accessed December 20, 2009).

S

Senufo

The Senufo or Senoufo number 3 million people and live in Mali, Burkina Faso, and Côte d'Ivoire. The Senufo do not speak one single language, but rather four, all of which belong to the Gur (formerly called the Voltaic) family of the Atlantic branch of the Niger-Congo phylum. The name Senufo was given to them by others from outside, and they do not have a single group name for themselves. Instead, the Senufo use different, specific names of the various subgroups that make up the larger group. The Senufo are composed of three main divisions: the northern group, called the Supide or the Kenedougou; the central group, which is composed of five different peoples each with its own name; and the southern group, which numbers over 2 million, again with their own self-designation. Nonetheless, they form a recognized cultural group and, as a single people, do have a broader identity that encompasses them all.

The Senufo emerged as a group of chiefdoms between the 15th and 16th centuries around their "capital" Korhogo, in northern Côte d'Ivoire. Senufo villages and towns were ruled by councils of elders based on matrilineal descent. Their location left them fairly free from outside control, and they did not fall under the control of the **Songhay** or **Hausa** states. In the 18th century **Mande**-speaking Dyula or Jula traders (Dyula being the Mande word for traders) were allowed to settle among them, and they introduced Islam.

Senufo society is class divided with three main divisions, similar to many other West African societies. These divisions or *katioula* are based on inherited crafts or the social level of each of these and between free and non-free classifications, with no or little intermarriage between social levels. These divisions are broken down into three main groups: "landowning" farmers; craftsmen such as blacksmiths, carvers, leather workers, and brass casters; and those who are slaves or descendants of slaves.

Senufo religion centers on both ancestral and natural spirits that are contacted through a number of secret societies. The Supreme Being is seen as a dualistic being both male and female; *Kolotyolo* or *Koulotiolo* (Creator God) and *Maleeo* or *Katieleo* (Ancient Mother) who regulate the world. The four masked secret societies are the *Poro*, *Sandogo*, *Wambele* (Sorcerers' society), and *Tykpa*. *Poro* is primarily for men, though some women join, and is responsible for regulating the world—the balance between the ancestors and the living. The spirit of *Nerejao*, an ancestress, is considered to be the head of the *Poro* society. Membership in the *Poro* society takes nearly 20 years of training before an initiate is able to perform the rituals that regulate life from agriculture to funerals.

The Senufo have a rich cultural life and were among the first African people

whose cultural artifacts European art dealers began to collect and sell. Most Senufo
pieces of art are part of ceremonial objects
used in masked societies, like many other
West African peoples. The Senufo art that
attracted art dealers and collectors the
most are the various masks used by the
Poro society. These are large, double-
faced helmet masks (often called Janus
masks) of buffalo. The masks are worn at
times of crisis and at funerals to help dis-
pel malevolent spirits. A similar type of
double-faced buffalo mask, but with antelope horns, is used at ceremonies marking
initiation into the *poro* society. Masks
used at planting and fertility ceremonies
are worn like a cap and are surmounted
by a figure of a woman. *Poro* society ceremonies also include large statues called
pombibele standing some 47 inches (120
centimeters) in height that are brought to
stand in the middle of the dance area
where they are then pounded into the
ground. The pounding provides rhythm
for the dancers and, as a result, they are
popularly referred to as "rhythm pound-
ers." Some, carried in pairs, represent
the first couple and the Senufo ideal of
the nuclear family. In addition, other large
statues called *kafigelejo*, including those
of birds, are brought to the *poro* ceremonies and represent various spirits who
have "judiciary or punitive powers"
(Bacquart, 73). Other objects of daily use
are also collected, including doors, boxes,
stools, and even beds. In recent decades,
Senufo art is being made for the tourist
trade some by carvers from other peoples
imitating Senufo work. Senufo mud cloth
depicting village scenes, masked dancers,
and animals called "Korhogo" for the

ancient Senufo capital city are also made
primarily today for the tourist market and
are sold throughout much of West Africa,
Europe, and North America. Korhogo
cloth is frequently called "mudcloth"
because the technique to make the designs
is similar to that of *bogolanfini* made by
Mande and **Dogon** craftsmen in Mali.
Similar to batik, the designs are stained
into the cloth with natural mineral and
plant pigments. While earlier versions of
Korhogo cloth seemed to have only geometric designs, newer ones on the market
have developed a set of symbols with animals and masked dancers to tell stories or
convey meaning.

Following World War II, the Senufo
have been less and less isolated from outside influences. Mali, Burkina Faso, and
Côte d'Ivoire became independent states
in the 1960s. All three have had periods
of intense nationalism, and all three have
had government policies trying to create
or promote single national identities. Conversion to Islam also increased, and today,
perhaps as many as one-half of Senufo, are
Muslim.

John A. Shoup

Further Reading

Bacquart, Jean-Baptiste. *The Tribal Arts
of Africa: Surveying Africa's Artistic Geography*. New York: Thames and Hudson,
2000.

Beckwith, Carol, and Angela Fisher. *African
Ceremonies*. New York: Harry N. Abrams,
Inc., 2002.

Fröster, Till. *Visions of Africa: Senufo*. Milan:
5 Continents Press, 2006.

Glaze, Anita. *Art and Death in a Senufo Village*. Bloomington: Indiana University
Press, 1982.

"Senufo Information." http://www.uiowa.edu/ -africart/toc/people/Senufo.html (accessed December 19, 2009).

Sereer/Serer

The Sereer or Serer are found almost exclusively in Senegal, where they number 1,154,760 speakers, or 15 percent of the total population of the country, making them the second-largest ethnic group in Senegal. Most Sereer still live in the area south of Dakar along the Atlantic coast from Rufisque, south of the mouth of the Saalum River. Small populations of Sereer live in Gambia and Guinea Bissau. The Sereer language is related to **Wolof** and Fulani (Pulaar, **Fulbe**) and belongs to the West Atlantic group of the Niger-Congo family.

The Sereer homeland forms large parts of the kingdoms of Siin (Sine) and Saalum (Saloum) that came into existence following the collapse of the Kingdom of Jolof in the 16th century. Portuguese traders established posts such as Rufisque along the Atlantic coast and introduced Christianity to the Sereer. Portuguese traders married local women and created the Luso-African population called *Luçado*, who facilitated trade with the kingdoms of Siin and Saalum. While many Sereer along the Petite Côte converted to Christianity, the majority remained faithful to their traditional religion based on shrines to ancestor spirits maintained by a priest class. Islam was introduced slowly and was greatly resisted by the Sereer until the late 19th century.

Sereer were historically divided into clearly defined social classes, similar to castes, of a ruling landed aristocracy (*Gelwaar*), a second class of free, landowning farmers, and a third occupational class made up of blacksmiths, weavers, potters, woodworkers, and historian-bards or *Griot*. The kings (*buur*) appointed nobles as lords/ governors (*laman*) over agricultural estates in a quasi-feudal organization. A special class of slave-warriors (*ceddo*) became more important following introduction of guns by Europeans and the expansion of the Atlantic slave trade.

Traditional Sereer religion recognized the existence of the supreme creator (*Roog*) as well as a number of natural forces. The natural forces needed to be placated by providing them with offerings such as libations. A few of these practices have continued such as the sacred lizards of Kaolack, who are fed by priestesses. The practice has now been reinterpreted in an Islamic context to fit the current cultural orientation. Most of the Sereer festivals relate to the pre-Islamic religious holidays; *gamo* was a divination ceremony, *korite* for boys' circumcision, and *weri kor* marked boys' initiation. While *tabaski* is the word used for the Islamic *'Id al-Adha* or feast of sacrifice, for the Sereer, the feast is similar to their pre-Islamic hunters' celebration. As noted, though the pre-Islamic festivals have all been given an Islamic meaning, the Sereer still associate them with their traditional animist religion as well.

Perhaps the older social organization of the Sereer was matrilineal, and as one moves from west to east in their area, and from Christian to Muslim in dominant religion, one also moves from matrilineal to patrilineal concepts of family. Islam

Traditional Wrestling

Traditional wrestling in Senegal is linked to the pre-Islamic past of the warrior or *ceddo* class. Wrestling fell into disfavor after the *ceddo* and the old ruling aristocracies were discredited after their defeat by the French and the subsequent rise of Islamic brotherhoods. Traditional wrestling depends on spirit forces that help the wrestler win, and that defeat the spirits evoked by the opponent. In the past, wrestling was done by young men who had been circumcised but who were not yet married. Today, professional wrestling was adopted by the youth *Bul Faale* (meaning "so what") movement in the 1990s and is popular especially with the Lebu and Sereer, who have only been recently Islamized.

Wrestling matches or *mbapat* are carefully organized, with each wrestler accompanied by an entourage of people who sing, dance, and parade with him. Wrestlers wear leather belts and neck, leg, and arm rings, all with protective charms sewn on to them. Matches last only a few seconds and end when one of the two touches the ground with any part of the calves, torso, back, or arms. Only the feet and hands may touch and not be considered a "throw." Wrestling matches are generally held in the afternoons and end in a festive mood of music and dance. Many of today's wrestlers have adopted professional names like "Tyson" and "Bombardier."

gained ground in Siin and Saalum following the incorporation of the two kingdoms by the French in late 19th century.

Contemporary history of the Sereer people begins in the middle of the 19th century and the *Jihad* of **Mande** leader Ma Ba Diakhou. Ma Ba overthrew the Kingdom of Saalum in 1862 and converted or destroyed the *ceddo*. The *ceddo* had maintained the strongest resistance to conversion to Islam, and part of their warrior prerogatives included public displays of drunkenness. In much of Senegambia, the *ceddo* were among the last to convert to Islam. In the same year, Ma Ba defeated the king of Siin as well. This brought the French colonial authorities from St. Louis into the picture who felt French interests were threatened by the growing power of a new Islamic state. The French were reluctant to lose French lives in the war with Diakhou and therefore rearmed the *gelwaar* and *ceddo*, ensuring an eventual victory of native troops over the Jihadist in 1867.

The two kingdoms of Siin and Saalum survived but, as a result of the initial victories of Ma Ba Diakhou, Saalum in particular greatly Islamized. Nonetheless, the war galvanized Sereer identity against that of Muslim Wolof; the victory being locally seen as the defeat of Muslim forces by the traditional spirit protectors of Siin. In addition, the king of Siin became a pliant ally of the French, which would work to the advantage of the colonial authorities in the slow conquest of the Wolof kingdoms.

The final defeat of the Wolof kingdoms and the introduction of the peanut economy in the 1890s impacted Siin, where assimilationist policies gave rise to a French educated class, especially among the Christians. Among the young men who went to France for university education in the 1930s and 1940s was Léopold Sédar Senghor, the first president of independent Senegal. Senghor developed a version of Black Pride called *Negritude*, which served as one of the main inspirations for African calls for independence from colonialism.

The Sereer have a strong sense of self-identity that has not been lost in the process of building a Senegalese national consensus following independence. Unlike their more pious and Muslim Wolof neighbors to the north, the Sereer have maintained customs such as traditional wrestling. Wrestling was associated with the warrior traditions of the *ceddo* that were outwardly un-Islamic. The warriors, and today's wrestlers, cover themselves with leather belts, armlets, leglets, and anklets with charms suspended from them. The charms are to ward off the spells and charms worn by their opponents and give the wrestler an advantage over the other. Wrestling and other *ceddo* practices were condemned and stopped in Wolof-speaking areas, but were maintained by the Sereer and the **Lebou**. While the aristocracy and warriors lost the confidence of the Wolof people, the impact of colonization in Sereer areas was not as dramatic, with the aristocracy being able to maintain themselves longer. In the Sereer areas, there was less tension between the old political elite and the

rising class of Islamic religious figures. In the 1990s, youth culture in Dakar adopted traditional wrestling as part of their "who cares" movement. There has been a revival of traditional wrestling since then, though not in the more conservative and Islamic Wolof heartland.

The Sereer language is now one of the official languages of Senegal along with Wolof. The high number of Sereer in professions and in Senegalese government is a direct result in the large numbers of Sereer who have sought high levels of education both under the French and after independence. Though the old kingdoms of Siin and Saalum did not outlast the French period, the descendants of the last king of Saalum still lives in the king's compound near the city of Kaolack.

John A. Shoup

Further Reading

Diouf, Mamadou, and Mara Leichtman. *New Perspectives on Islam in Senegal: Conversion, Migration, Wealth, Power, and Femininity.* New York: Palgrave MacMillan, 2009.

Galvin, Dennis. *The State Must Be Our Master of Fire: How Peasants Craft Culturally Sustainable Development in Senegal.* Berkeley: University of California Press, 2004.

Ross, Eric. *Culture and Customs of Senegal.* Westport, CT: Greenwood Press, 2008.

Schaffer, Matt, and Christine Cooper. *Mandinko: The Ethnography of a West African Holy Land.* Prospect Heights, IL: Waveland Press, Inc., 1987.

Searing, James. *God Alone is King: Islam and Emancipation in Senegal: The Wolof Kingdoms of Kajoor and Bawol, 1859–1914.* New York: Heinemann, 2001.

Searing, James. *West African Slavery and Atlantic Commerce: The Senegal River*

Valley, 1700–1860. Cambridge: Cambridge University Press, 2003.

Southerland-Addy, Esi, and Aminita Diaw. *Women Writing Africa: West Africa and the Sahel*. New York: Feminist Press at CUNY, 2005.

Shona

The Shona are a Bantu-speaking people who live mainly in the modern state of Zimbabwe, though some also live in Botswana, Zambia, and Mozambique. The Shona number between 4 million and 5 million in Zimbabwe with another 500,000 living in nearby countries. They represent the largest single ethnic group in Zimbabwe with 82 percent of the country's population. The Shona speak a number of dialects including Karanga, Zezuru, Korekore, Maniyka, Ndau, and Kalanga. Until the 19th century, their encounters with first the Ndebele (**Nguni**) and then British colonial authorities helped crystallize the Shona identity.

The Shona were among the Bantu peoples who spread south bringing with them iron technologies called the Lydenburg Tradition by archeologists. It is surmised that the iron-working tradition associated with Lydenburg culture subsequently spread both north again across the Limpopo River as well as further south into South Africa. North of the Limpopo, the Kutama tradition, associated with the site of Leopard's Kopje, is considered to be the origins of the Shona. The supposition is based on pottery and, though there is some controversy over the interpretation of styles and designs, nonetheless, the ancestors of the Shona seem to have been established between the Zambezi and the Limpopo rivers by the time gold mining became an important part of the economy around 900–1000 CE. **Arab** traders on the coast exchanged goods from the Middle East and India for gold and ivory, which developed into a thriving trade and helped give rise to states in the Zimbabwean highlands.

By 1100, central authority was extended over smaller chiefdoms, and the power of the king was such that wealth shifted from being measured in cattle to trade goods. Mapungubwe on the Limpopo River was the dominant power on the highlands and controlled the trade with **Swahili** and Arab merchants who came up the river or at their trade center Chibuene. Archeological excavations at Mapungubwe indicate that by 1075, there was strong social stratification, with elite living in large houses located toward the top of the hill, and cattle pens kept outside the city.

Mapungubwe declined in the 14th century and was quickly replaced by Great Zimbabwe. Archeology at Great Zimbabwe shows the site began in the 12th century, and trade objects such as glass beads and glazed pottery fragments have been found. The site is not close to where gold was mined, but is in a better strategic location to access trading centers on the coast. The rise of Great Zimbabwe may also be linked to changes in dominance of other Swahili cities on the Kenyan and Tanzanian coast and a shift north to Sofala. By the 14th century, Great Zimbabwe had a population of between 15,000 and 18,000 people and held dominion over a number of subordinate Shona-speaking states. There are a number of such large stone cities in Zimbabwe called

Great Zimbabwe

Great Zimbabwe was the capital city of the Kingdom of Zimbabwe that existed from 1100 to 1450. The term Zimbabwe comes from the Shona word *dzimbahwe* (plural *madzimbahwe*) meaning a site enclosed by a stone wall and a place of residence for a chief. Ruins of a number of smaller stone-walled cities exist, which most likely were regional centers dependent upon the main city of Great Zimbabwe politically, economically, and spiritually.

The site of Great Zimbabwe covers 1,784 acres and is estimated to have been able to house 18,000 people during its height. The city consisted of three parts; royal structures that skirt the exposed granite hill, the buildings around the Great Enclosure in the valley, and finally the area where the common people lived. The city became an important trading center with Muslim cities on the Indian Ocean coast such as Kilwa. Archeological excavations have found Arab coins, pottery from the Middle East and China, and glass beads. Arab and other Muslim merchants traded for gold that was supplied from mines scattered along the Zimbabwean plateau. It is argued that the regional *madzimbahwe* served as collection centers for the gold, which was then sent on to Great Zimbabwe to trade with the Muslims. Others argue that Muslim traders may have been in more direct contact with local chiefs. In either case, Great Zimbabwe served as the political and most likely the spiritual capital of the kingdom. Great Zimbabwe seems to have declined due to a shift in trade further north after the fall of its main partners on the coast to the Portuguese, or perhaps to the inability of the region to supply enough food to the city. Wealth was in cattle, and the large cattle herds of the king were moved in seasonal cycles, but farming may not have been able to produce enough food for the city to survive.

dzimbahwe in Shona and most likely are the seats of smaller states subordinate to the capital or were political and economic regional centers where governors acted for the king. The royal culture of Zimbabwe influenced others such as the **Venda**, who claim to have spent time with Karanga royalty and later Venda royalty claimed to be of Zimbabwean lineage.

Great Zimbabwe eventually collapsed and, though the reasons are not well understood, it is possible the environment around the capital simply could not support the numbers. The land could not support the agriculture needed to feed the population or the numbers of cattle. By 1450, the site was totally abandoned, and two other states grew to fill the political vacuum. These two, Torwa and Mutapa, are fairly well known from Portuguese texts. The Portuguese had been able to round the Cape of Good Hope in 1486, and by the end of the 16th century, the Portuguese had established their hegemony in the Indian Ocean. In 1505, they had taken the Arab trading center of Sofala and, in 1514, had successfully visited the capital of Mutapa. In 1556, the son of a Shona chief was baptized a Christian and, at his request, a mission was sent to convert the Shona in 1560.

The Mutapa state eventually collapsed partially due to Portuguese influence. The kings allowed Portuguese fort/trade stations to be built in their territory, diverting needed income from the state, and in 1663, the Portuguese deposed the ruler and put their own candidate on the throne. In 1693, the Mutapa king was able to force the Portuguese out of most of his kingdom, but in 1696, the Rozwi (or Rozvi) were able to overthrow the Mutapa dynasty and set up their own.

The Rozwi had controlled the Guruhuswa region on the southern part of the Zimbabwean highlands. The Rozwi state existed until the 19th century, when in 1834, Zwangendaba, at the head of the Ngoni (Nguni), fled the state building of Shaka **Zulu** and crossed the Limpopo River. His forces, using the military reforms introduced by Shaka, devastated the larger Shona army, and the last Rozwi king was killed. Zwangendaba did not stay in Shona lands, but continued his flight-turned-invasion north, spreading destruction until he finally stopped near Lake Victoria. In 1838, the Shona again were subjected to another group of Nguni speakers fleeing both Shaka and the **Afrikaner** Boers. Mzilikazi brought his Ndebele into Shona lands and established a state based at his new capital Bulawayo, in the Matopo Hills. Like the previous Ngoni invasion, the superior fighting skills, weapons, and

strategies first introduced by Shaka made the Ndebele of Mzilikazi unbeatable for the more traditional Shona armies. The Shona no longer had a central leader, and a number of small states emerged until the British forced their submission in the last decades of the 19th century.

The Shona have a long history of central state rule over large, settled agricultural communities. The region between the Zambezi and Limpopo rivers is composed of mainly fertile highlands, and Shona have traditionally raised millet and yams, and with the introduction of American crops, maize and pumpkins produce large yields. Cattle do well in the region as well, and originally the kings had control of one-half of all production including cattle. Some note the large numbers of cattle owned by the Shona kings of Great Zimbabwe perhaps led to land use pressure that resulted in the collapse of the state. Others note that, according to the written evidence by Arab and Swahili traders, the Shona kings moved their cattle around the country according to availability of seasonal pastures; thus, the numbers of cattle did not burden any one area too long. Since the 11th century, the Shona have been involved in international trade and, as noted above, trade replaced agricultural production as the mainstay of the economy and as a means of showing wealth. Copper, and later gold and ivory, formed the main base of their international trade for luxury goods such as glass beads and glazed pottery from Muslim merchants. The Portuguese also wanted gold and ivory, but also slaves to work their fort/trade posts called *prazo*. Unlike the local practice in which slaves eventually became part of their master's lineages, the Portuguese used slaves solely for their economic value.

Traditional Shona religion, like that of other Bantu in southern Africa, centers around the ancestral spirits called the *mhondoro*. Early Portuguese visitors to the Shona noted the fact that there were no idols and that the people believed in a single creator called *Molungo*—varying forms are *Murungu* or, more commonly today, *Mwari*. The Portuguese noted that witchcraft was strongly believed and that someone accused of witchcraft went through a trial of drinking a poisoned cup; if innocent, the poison would not hurt the accused. Shona have a long tradition of spirit mediums or *svikiro*, and special huts where mediums practice their art called *banya*. Such structures have been identified in ruins dating to the Great Zimbabwe period. Spirit mediums are called upon to settle disputes, ensure rain and good harvests, and to help enhance the authority of the nobility.

The *mbira* is one of the main musical instruments in Shona society. The *mbira* takes its name from the *bira* ceremony. A *bira* is called for by a traditional doctor or *n'anga* or a spirit medium (*svikiro*) should a person be ill or suffer from what seems to be the anger of his ancestors. The ceremony takes all night in a *banya*, some of which are large enough to hold 100 people. During the ceremony, the ancestors come and tell the medium the causes for their anger and what needs to be done to restore their goodwill. Groups of *mbira* players help the medium go into a trance in order for the ancestors to speak to him or her.

Traditional Shona doctor. Traditional doctors rarely wear this type of dress except at ceremonies or for tourist photos. Traditional doctors do play a major role in health care, being able to successfully treat a number of mental and physical illnesses. (John A. Shoup)

Christianity was brought to the Shona first by the Portuguese and later by the British. According to studies, 25 percent of Shona are Christians, and another 25 percent adhere to the traditional religion, while the majority belongs to the independent syncretic Afro-Christian churches that combine elements of traditional belief with Christianity.

The Shona were defeated and forced to accept British rule in 1896. Zimbabwe and Zambia were part of the colonial area called Rhodesia, named for British adventurer Cecil Rhodes who was granted the charter for the British South Africa Company in 1890. Attempts to develop gold and copper mines proved to be disappointments in Zimbabwe. Huge land grants of 3,000 acres or 1,214 hectares each were given out to early European settlers, and by 1923, 30 million acres or 12 million hectares were occupied by Europeans and only 10 million acres or 4 million hectares were allocated to the native peoples. Most Europeans established commercial farms worked by African labor.

Rhodesia was controlled by the British South Africa Company until 1923, when the British government took control and granted Rhodesia limited self-rule, but only whites could vote. Nearly half of the land and mineral rights were allocated to whites and the rest to the Tribal Trust Lands. British administration, trying to keep operation costs low, introduced forms of indirect rule, and traditional governments of chiefs were responsible to the colonial authorities. They were to collect taxes, ensure safety and security, deal out justice to "natives," and provide men for labor or the military.

A federation of Northern Rhodesia, Southern Rhodesia, and Nyasaland (Malawi) was formed in 1953, but it broke apart in 1963 as moves for independence grew in Northern Rhodesia and Nyasaland. Eventually, Northern Rhodesia became the independent states of Zambia and Nyasaland Malawi in 1964. White minority rule in Southern Rhodesia declared its independence in 1965. This began a 14-year struggle for majority rule in the country. Two main groups emerged to fight white rule, the Zimbabwean African National Union (ZANU) and the Zimbabwean African People's Union (ZAPU). ZANU was supported mainly by Shona speakers, and Robert Mugabe emerged as their political leader; while ZAPU was mainly supported by the Ndebele, and Joshua Nkome was its leader. White rule ended in 1979, and a transitional government was installed until elections in 1980 brought to power the now-united ZANU and ZAPU and ZANU-PF (Popular Front). Among the principles was the restoration of farmlands to Africans, and initially this was done through a policy called "willing buyer, willing seller," introduced in 1992. Not moving quickly enough, more pressure was put on white owners to transfer lands to black farmers, including forced eviction and killings starting in 1999.

Attempts to challenge Mugabe's control over the country have failed, and in 2002 he defeated his main rival, Morgan Tsvangirai, also a Shona. Subsequently, Zimbabwe has sunk into massive inflation, in 2007 calculated to be 26,000 percent and an unofficial rate of 100,000 percent. Average life expectancy has dropped from 60 years of age in the mid-1990s to 37 for men and 34 for women in 2006, the lowest in the world. More than 3 million Zimbabweans left for South Africa until a backlash against economic migrants hit South Africa in 2009.

John A. Shoup

Further Reading

Adekunle, Julius O. "East African States." In *Africa Volume 1: African History before 1885*, edited by Toyin Falola. Durham, NC: Carolina Academic Press, 2000.

Afolayan, Funso. "Bantu Expansion and Its Consequences." In *Africa Volume 1: African History before 1885*, edited by Toyin Falola. Durham, NC: Carolina Academic Press, 2000.

Berliner, Paul. *The Soul of Mbira: Music and Traditions of the Shona People of Zimbabwe*. Chicago: University of Chicago Press, 1981.

Fontein, Joost. *The Silence of Great Zimbabwe: Contested Landscapes and the Power of Heritage*. Oakland, CA: Left Coast Press, 2006.

Hall, Martin. *Farmers, Kings, and Traders: The People of Southern Africa 200–1860*. Chicago: University of Chicago Press, 1990.

Hall, Martin, and Rebecca Stefoff. *Great Zimbabwe*. Oxford: Oxford University Press, 2006.

Nyathi, Pathisa. *Zimbabwe's Cultural Heritage*. Bulawayo, Zimbabwe: amaBooks, 2005.

Olson, James. "Shona." In *Peoples of Africa: An Ethnohistorical Dictionary*. Westport, CT: Greenwood Press, 1996.

Owomoyela, Oyekan. *Culture and Customs of Zimbabwe*. Westport, CT: Greenwood Press, 2002.

Tyrrell, Barbara, and Peter Jurgens. *African Heritage*. Johannesburg: MacMillan South Africa, 1986.

Wills, A. J. *An Introduction to the History of Central Africa: Zambia, Malawi, and Zimbabwe*. Reprint of the 4th edition. Oxford: Oxford University Press, 2002.

Somalis/Issas

The Somali are a large homogeneous group occupying Somalia, southern Djibouti, southeastern Ethiopia, and northern Kenya. They are Muslim and speak Somali, a Cushitic language. There are approximate 12 million Somalis, mostly nomadic pastoralists. The Issa (Esa) are an important subgroup concentrated in the north, where they comprise 50 percent of the population of Djibouti.

Somali origins are uncertain, though contact with Arabia has existed from ancient times. **Arab** merchants introduced Islam in the seventh century, and Arab immigrants were founders of some Somali clans. Powerful principalities emerged in the 10th century, chiefly Adal and Mogadishu.

Somali expansion, fueled by Arab immigration, Islamic fervor, and need for grazing land, began in the 10th century. Tribal warriors in the north spread out west and south, pushing out local people and rival tribes. Movement west ended with the Christian defeat of Adal in the 16th century, but the expansion continued southward. By the 18th century, Somalis were established along the Shebelle and Juba rivers, and by the 19th century in northern Kenya, where they encountered other pastoral peoples such as the Cushitic Rendille. Conflict between the pastoral groups in northern Kenya continues to this day. Territorial borders set by European colonization finally contained Somali expansion.

Somali are divided into two classes. The "Somal" are the elite nomadic herdsmen who base wealth on livestock, primarily camels in the north and cattle in the south. Horses are the most prized possession of a Somal warrior and gave them superiority over many other groups they encountered. The largest Somal tribe is the Issa belonging to the Dir clan, considered to be the original Somal. The "Sab," viewed as inferior by the Somal, are sedentary farmers found between the Shebelle and Juba rivers, where they grow grains, fruit, and cotton. Outside of those who consider themselves to be Somali are classes of tradesmen such as blacksmiths, ironsmiths, and hunters, jobs detested by Somali. They live separately and cannot intermarry with Somali.

Tribal alliances are based on kinship traced through the male line to a common ancestor. Clans claim descent from the Prophet Muhammad, and Islam is the bond between clans. Somali follow Sufi orders with many saints, shrines, and holy men. Islamic holy men have played important roles in Somali history, and in the early 20th century, Sayyid Muhammad 'Abdille Hassan, who belonged to the Salihiyah Sufi order, was able to combine clan groups in organized resistance. He seemed to lack a larger set of political and religious ideology. Some of his supporters killed *Shaykh 'Uways*, leader of the Somali Qadiriyah Sufi order, and as a result, his conflict with the British lost needed Qadiri support. Eventually Sayyid Muhammad's followers were defeated by the British after his death.

In the late 19th century, colonial powers carved up Somali coastal areas into French, Italian, and British protectorates, with Ethiopia controlling Ogaden in the interior and Great Britain in Kenya. A struggle for unification began immediately. Angered by Christian domination, Muhammad 'Abdille Hassan, the "Mad Mullah," led a "Dervish" (from the fact he was a Sufi leader) revolt from 1899 to 1920 against the British and Ethiopians. As many as a third of the population of British Somaliland died as a result.

Unification of Italian and British Somaliland was achieved with independence of Somalia in 1960, but intense clan rivalries between the two areas followed. In efforts to unite all Somali people, Somalia waged several wars with Ethiopia over Ogaden and sought annexation of northern Kenya. These efforts all failed. The French territory of Afar and Issas gained separate independence as Djibouti in 1977, with the Somali Issas tribe dominating the government. In 1977, shortly after its independence, Djbouti joined the Arab League of States and Arabic, along with French, was declared an official language of the state. Admissions to the Arab League had much to do with the historical Arab sphere of influence along the Red Sea and East African coast, Somali belief in shared origins with **South Arabs**, and hopes for Arab money (from Saudi Arabia) to support the new state's economy.

In 1969, the socialist government of Said Barre came to power in Somalia, imposing policies that went against traditional and cultural life. Several clan-based rebel groups emerged. Fighting and famines caused widespread suffering. Since the collapse of the regime in 1991, there has been no functioning government in Somalia. Rebel factions continue to fight for dominance. In addition, since the emergence of groups such as Al Qaeda, the lack of a central government has allowed them to establish bases in Somalia. During the first decade of the 2000s, Somali pirate activities grew as lawlessness prevailed on land. Somali fishermen deprived of fishing due to pollution of their traditional waters used to clean out vessels such as oil tankers, helped to create the conditions for the pirates. Somali pirates began seizing ships and taking their crews hostage. Ransom demands grew, forcing Western governments to deploy naval detachments in the Indian Ocean to patrol for, intercept, and arrest pirates.

Geri Shaw

Further Reading

Abdullahi, Mohamed Diriye. *Culture and Customs of Somalia*. Westport, CT: Greenwood Press, 2001.

Central Statistical Agency of Ethiopia (CSA). "Census 2007." http://www.csa.gov.et (accessed May 26, 2011).

Lapidus, Ira M. *A History of Islamic Societies*. Cambridge: Cambridge University Press, 2002.

Lewis, I. M. *The Modern History of Somaliland*. New York: Frederick A. Praeger, Publishers, 1965.

Lewis, I. M. *Peoples of the Horn of Africa: Somali, Afar and Saho*. London: International African Institute, 1998.

Lewis, I. M. *Saints and Somalis: Popular Islam in a Clan-Based Society*. Lawrenceville, NJ: Red Sea Press, Inc., 1998.

Lewis, I. M. *Understanding Somalia and Somaliland: Culture, History, Society*. New York: Columbia University Press, 2008.

Murphy, Martin M. *Small Boats, Weak States, Dirty Money: Piracy and Maritime Terrorism in the Modern World*. New York: Columbia University Press, 2010.

U.S. Central Intelligence Agency. The World Factbook. https://www.cia.gov/library/publications/the-world-factbook/index.html (accessed May 26, 2011).

Songhay

The Songhay or Songhai peoples live along the Niger River in present-day Mali, Niger, Burkina Faso, and Benin, and they are one of the largest ethnic groups in Niger. In Niger, there are 2 million Songhay including the related Zerma (also called Djerma or Zaberma) and the Sorko. Songhay or Sonrai is also the name of their language, and it is thought to belong to the Western Sahelian family of the Nilo-Saharan phylum, though this is in doubt. Some linguists have proposed that the Songhay language is related to **Mande**, and more recently, some have proposed that it is a Tamsheq **Creole**—Tamsheq being the **Berber** language spoken by **Tuareg**.

It is generally assumed that the Songhay founded of the city of Gao, which the Arab geographers of the classical period called Kawkaw. It has been noted that the Arabic sources do not mention the Songhay by name, and that the Songhay people rarely use the term to refer to themselves, but there is no reason to believe that the Kingdom of Gao was not Songhay. Archeological evidence including grave markers in Arabic indicate that at least the ruling elite had converted to Islam sometime in the 10th century and the amount of Muslim material cultural items increases over the 11th and 12th centuries. The Arab geographer al-Muhallabi, writing before 985, stated that the king of Gao had converted to Islam as had many of his subjects. Gao was an important trading center that linked north to the Maghrib and east to Egypt. Gao exported large amounts of ivory and imported glazed pottery, glass, and items from the Indian Ocean such as cowrie shells. Goa was brought under the king of Mali in the 13th century and remained a province of Mali until the 15th century.

Songhay society has strong class divisions like most West African societies. There are three main levels: free (chiefs, farmers, and herders), servile (artists, musicians, and *griots* called *gesere*) and slave. Songhay rulers obliged the servile class to observe endogamy, similar to other social practices in West Africa, making it impossible to move class—and therefore, is similar to caste. Slaves, however, could be emancipated and over four generations could join the free class.

The highest social level in Songhay society is that of the sorcerer or *sohance*, who claim to descend from Sonni 'Ali Ber who ruled from 1464 to 1492. The American anthropologist Paul Stoller studied *sohance* arts, which he describes in his book *In Sorcery's Shadow*. His book gives insight into Songhay society and its strength in the face of globalization. The *Maamar haama* who descend from the next dynasty to rule Songhay, the Askiya (a military title) who overthrew the Sonni dynasty in 1493, are also among the highest ranking level of society. The *arma* are the descendants of the Moroccan troops who overthrew the Askiya dynasty in 1591, and the *sirayf* are the *shurufa'* or *sharif*s, descendants of the Prophet Muhammad. Songhay society has been able to balance strong Islamic identity with the pre-Islamic belief system in the epic of Askiya Muhammad I. His piety is balanced by stating that his father's people were a folk of good Muslims who lived under the water, or *holey*, spirits who look like men. His mother was a powerful sorceress, and her descendants are sorcerers in Niger today. Askiya Muhammad's descendants were protected by three *toorey* spirits when confronted by the Moroccan invaders, and thus the city of Gao did not fall to them.

Songhay was the last of the three great empires to rule the Sahel. The Songhay not only were able to break from Mali's control, but they defeated and took the Malian capital Timbuktu in 1468 under the able Songhay ruler Sonni 'Ali Ber. His harsh treatment of the Muslim scholars of Timbuktu offended one of his generals, Muhammad Ture, who seized power in a military coup against Sonni 'Ali's son, Abu Bakr, in 1493. Muhammad Ture's descendants ruled the Songhay Empire until 1591, when the Moroccan *Sultan* Ahmad al-Mansur sent an army equipped with guns across the Sahara and defeated the Songhay army. The Songhay kingdom was broken up, and Timbuktu was controlled by either the *arma* or the Tuareg until the French took it in 1893.

The Dendi kingdom emerged in the border region between Mali and Niger and tried to restore the glory of the earlier Songhay Empire. It was unable to dislodge the *arma* and eventually turned to lesser rivals. The kingdom was able to last until 1901, when the French conquered it as part of their conquest of the Niger River/ Sahara region.

Since independence from France in 1960, Niger has had a turbulent history with five republics interspersed with military rule. The Songhay-Zerma have dominated some of the governments that helped promote the north-south divide between settled farming south and pastoral—mainly Tuareg north.

John A. Shoup

Further Reading

Conrad, David. *Empires of Medieval West Africa: Ghana, Mali, and Songhay.* New York: Facts on File, 2005.

Hale, Thomas. "Can a Single Foot Follow Two Paths? Islamic and Songhay Belief Systems in the Timbuktu Chronicles and the Epic of Askia Mohammed." In *Faces of Islam in African Literature*, edited by Kenneth Harrow. Portsmouth, NH: Heinemann, 1991.

Hunwick, John O. "Songhay." In *Encyclopaedia of Islam*, 2nd ed., CD-ROM.

Hunwick, John O. *West Africa, Islam, and the Arab World.* Princeton, NJ: Markus Wiener Publishers, 2006.

Hunwick, John O., and Alida Jay Boye. *The Hidden Treasures of Timbuktu: Rediscovering Africa's Literary Heritage.* London: Thames and Hudson, 2008.

Insoll, Timothy. *The Archeology of Islam in Sub-Saharan Africa.* Cambridge: Cambridge University Press, 2003.

Lapidus, Ira. *A History of Islamic Societies.* Cambridge: Cambridge University Press, 1997.

Quigley, Mary. *Ancient West African Kingdoms: Ghana, Mali, and Songhay.* New York: Heinemann, 2002.

Stoller, Paul. *Fusion of the Worlds: An Ethnography of Possession among the Songhay of Niger.* Chicago: University of Chicago Press, 1997.

Stoller, Paul, and Cheryl Olkes. *In Sorcery's Shadow.* Chicago: University of Chicago Press, 1989.

Sotho/Tswana

The Sotho and closely related Tswana are Bantu peoples living in Lesotho, South Africa, and Botswana. They are divided into three main groups: Southern Sotho of Lesotho and the nearby regions in the Orange Free State; the Northern Sotho of the Transvaal; and the Western Sotho or Tswana, who live mainly in Botswana and the border region with South Africa. Together they number over 10 million people. *Mosotho* (*Basotho* plural) and *Motswana* (*Batswana* plural) is the usual way of referring to the people; *Sesotho* and *Setswana* are the adjectives used to refer to the languages; and *Lesotho* and *Botswana* are used to refer to the places where they live. The North Sotho dialect is called *Sesotho ea Leboa*, while South Sotho is simply called *Sesotho*. A more Lesotho specific term is *Seshoe* (pronounced *se-shway*), meaning the people of Moshoeshoe I who ruled from 1804 to 1870 (Moshoeshoe is pronounced *Mu-shway-shway*), the founder of the modern state of Lesotho.

The Northern Sotho are composed of peoples of Sotho origin such as the Pedi, while others have been absorbed into the Sotho such as the **Nguni** Transvaal Ndebele. The Pedi have lived around Phalaborwa since the fourth century CE. Other Northern Sotho includes the Lobedu, who are ruled by the Modjadji Rain Queens. The Ndebele are of Nguni origin and arrived in the Transvaal in the 16th century. As a result of their longtime residence among the Northern Sotho, the Ndebele have adopted a number of Sotho practices, including the language. However, they have also preserved some aspects of their Nguni origins in aspects of their language (words associated with the homestead and lineage) and customs. Ndebele women are famous for their beadwork, which is among the most elaborate in South Africa (see entry on **Nguni**).

Two forms of writing Sesotho developed in the 19th century. The Basotho of Lesotho were contacted by French Protestant Evangelical missionaries in 1833, who transcribed the language using French orthography. In South Africa, English missionaries transcribed both Tswana and Sotho languages using English orthography; for example, the word Sotho is spelled *Sutu* in South Africa. The difference in spelling the written languages has helped solidify separate identities among the Sotho/Sutu. In Lesotho, the mission station at Morija established a printing press in 1861, which initially was used for Christian texts, but with growing literacy among the Basotho in their own language, it began publishing other texts written in Sesotho by Basotho authors. Among the most famous examples of these is Thomas Mofolo's novel *Chaka*, which has been translated into English several times since it was first published in Sesotho in 1925. Sesotho and Setswana are among the widest spoken languages in South Africa and serve as part of the base for both *Tsotsitaal* and *Fanakolo*. Tsotsitaal, meaning gang/thug talk, is composed of all of the languages found in the townships, but is mainly Sotho, Tswana, and Zulu in origin, grammar, and vocabulary. Fanakolo is the work

Objects used by a traditional doctor in Lesotho who is also a devout Catholic. The materials include an array of beaded sashes—white beads mark him as a traditional healer, a police whistle to call the spirits of the ancestors, a beaded gourd or sehoana that is used to listen to the words of the ancestors or balimo, medicine horns filled with medicines, peacock feathers that are pleasing to the ancestors, and a list of prices for the various medicines and charms he can do under the portrait of the Virgin Mary and child. (John A. Shoup)

language that developed in the workers' dorms at the mines for work gang bosses to give orders more effectively.

The Sotho and Tswana received Christian missionaries from Protestant Evangelical churches in the 1830s. Sotho and Tswana leaders quickly recognized the value these missionaries had in subsequent dealings with the **Afrikaner** Boers and later with the British. In 1862, Catholic missionaries arrived in Lesotho, and today, the majority of the Basotho in Lesotho are Catholics. Christians total approximately 80 percent of Basotho and 71 percent of Batswana. In addition, a local version of Christianity emerged in South Africa that combined aspects of indigenous religion with Christianity, called the Zionist Apostolic Church. The Zionist Apostolic Church has wide appeal throughout southern Africa with adherents in Lesotho, South Africa, Botswana, and Zimbabwe. Nonetheless, there is still a minority of both Sotho (20 percent in Lesotho) and Tswana (6 percent in Botswana) who practice their traditional religion, which focuses on the relationship between the living and the ancestors called the *malimo/balimo* in Sesotho and the *medimo/bodimo* in Setswana. The ancestors contact the living through dreams, for example, and traditional doctors or *lingaka ea Sesotho* (pronounced *di-nyaka eya sesutu*—*lingaka* is the plural of *ngaka*, meaning a healer or doctor), a specialized class of traditional priest-healers, are able to interpret what the ancestors want. Traditional priest-healers use a range of tools to contact and understand the wishes of the ancestors, including throwing the bones and using drums. They provide medicines and cures for those who are ill, circumcise boys and make the medicines used after the circumcision operation, and provide charms against lightning, birds, and wild animals from destroying crops. They also provide charms against the actions of a *thokolosi* (an imp-like creature) and other familiars of witches.

In addition to the *lingaka*, traditional belief includes the *boloi* (*moloi* in singular) or witches. Unlike the *ngaka*, who uses his knowledge for the good of the people, witches are capable of evil. *Moloi* use covens to focus their power and are able to harm others simply by thinking it. In the past, *lingaka* were used by the ruling elite to "smell out" *boloi* in special ceremonies. Today in Lesotho, certain villages have reputations for witches such as Ha Toloane located within a few miles of Morija mission station.

The Sotho/Tswana arrived in southern Africa with other Bantu speakers sometime between the third and fourth centuries CE. The Bantu brought with them knowledge of iron working, and the iron mines around Phalaborwa in the Transvaal have been used since the third century and may be the original heartland for the Sotho/Tswana. The area is still inhabited mainly by the Sotho-speaking Pedi. The Sotho/Tswana moved out into the highveld and established large towns with stone-built homes. They engaged in intensive agriculture and raised large herds of cattle. Cattle came to play an important part of social values being held in high regard and a means of noting status. Raising and managing cattle became a male activity, with numerous taboos on women from even being able to touch a milking

Magic and Witchcraft

Magic plays an important role in many African societies, and those of southern Africa are no exception. Most Africans make a difference between witches and traditional doctors. Witches are born with the ability to make things happen, both good or bad, simply by thinking them, and many witches are not aware of their power. On the other hand, a traditional doctor must study as an apprentice for years to learn the use of medicinal herbs or minerals and making various charms.

Traditional doctors are not "witchdoctors," but they may learn aspects of sorcery depending on the skills of the person they study with. Most of their practice is dealing with a number of illnesses, including mental illnesses. They learn the use of various herbs, which they cultivate or collect and use in *muti* or medicines. In addition, they learn how to contact the ancestor spirits to help them deal with illnesses that someone else has "sent" to harm a person. They learn how to read and interpret divination tools like the bones; sets of bones, stones, and other objects that represent spirits. They learn how to make charms that protect a person or property, send illnesses to plague an enemy, capture lightning, direct lightning strikes either away from a crop or towards a person, among other useful skills. Traditional doctors help at circumcisions, performing the operation and making the medicines that heal the wound.

Baloi, or witches, are believed to be harmful and are greatly feared. *Baloi* focus their power on a tree or rock and can then travel immense distances. Witches have familiars they control and can send either as warnings or as agents of harm such as *thikoloshe*, believed to be a dwarflike creature with a strong sexual appetite. *Thikoloshe* occur naturally or can be made from corn meal porridge, but they have no independent will.

bowl. If a woman touches a milking bowl, it must be broken so that it can be never used again. A woman's touch will cause all of the milk to turn sour. Women are not allowed to cross a cattle path, or any cows that then use the path will stop giving milk. In rural Lesotho, such customs have been challenged not by the activities of feminists, but by the practicalities of large numbers of men needing to work in South Africa. Women may be all who are able to carry out caring for the livestock. Still, traditionalists try to keep women out of work with the livestock.

The different Sotho and Tswana peoples developed a complex kinship system based on the belief that they descended from different totems—that is, nonhuman ancestors—who gave their name to the different kin groups. For example, the Bakuena are the people of the crocodile and are the ruling clan in Lesotho. Politically, the Sotho/Tswana, as other Bantu in South Africa, had developed into chiefdoms and states ruled by elite families prior to the arrival of European settlers.

Modern history for both the Sotho and Tswana begins with the *Lifaqane* or Great Crushing caused by the expansion of the Zulu state under their great leader Shaka. In 1816, Shaka became the ruler of the Zulu, and by 1818, he had embarked on his policy of creating an empire. As the Zulus expanded, conquering and destroying those who opposed them, many of the peoples of Natal and nearby areas tried to flee, causing a ripple effect that reached as far north as the Lake District of Kenya and Tanzania. Modern Lesotho was born out of this time when the chief of the Bakuena, Moshoeshoe, was able to gather a number of Sotho under him. He relocated his capital to Thaba Bosiu, a large table-topped plateau a comfortable distance from Shaka in Natal, and not far from the modern capital of Maseru. Moshoeshoe was able to mollify Shaka by sending him gifts of cattle and young women and thus survived the period of expansion. Shaka was assassinated by his brothers in 1828, and Moshoeshoe was able to solidify his control over the different Sotho lineages by placing close relatives over them as principal chiefs.

The next major challenge came from the **Afrikaner** Boers who began to arrive in Sotho and Tswana territories in 1836. In a series of wars with the Griqua (Europeanized Khoikhoi [**Khoisan**]), the Boers, and the British, much of the better farmlands of the Basotho were taken. In 1868, Basotho independence from the Boer states was guaranteed by the British and Basutoland was declared a separate British colony. Administration of Basutoland was briefly turned over to the Cape in 1871; but, due to mismanagement, it returned to British control in 1884. In a similar process, the leaders of the various Batswana chiefdoms appealed to the British for help against the advance of Afrikaners and Nguni Ndebele, and in 1885, the British granted a protectorate over them called Bechuanaland. Political leadership in Lesotho developed into a centralized state with the paramount chief of the Bakuena being able to emerge as the king while Bechuanaland remained a collection of independent chiefdoms.

Both countries became independent states, the Kingdom of Lesotho and the Republic of Botswana, in 1966. Those Sotho and Tswana living in South Africa were grouped into two main native homelands, Basotho Qwa Qwa and Bophuthatswana. Lesotho and Botswana were brought into the antiapartheid struggle, and both served as bases for opposition operations inside South Africa. Both countries suffered from cross-border raids by South African military forces, and in 1986, South Africa blockaded Lesotho's borders, demanding that antiapartheid activists be expelled. The crisis caused a coup and the Lesotho military, with South African backing, took control of the government, although the king, Moshoeshoe II, was able to remain as the head of state.

Lesotho has become economically more tied to South Africa since 1986 and the beginning of the Lesotho Highlands Water Project was funded by South Africa. South Africa built much of the needed infrastructure—dams, roads, and hydroelectric generating plants—and pays the Lesotho government millions of dollars every year for both electricity and water. The project has electrified Lesotho and locals are able to make use of the improved roads, yet the cost is greater integration of Lesotho into South Africa.

Botswana has been able to capitalize on its own natural resources such as diamonds and from the fact that its population is small. Botswana has several major game reserves, the Okavango, Moremi, and Chobe, which bring in large numbers of tourists every year. Tourism is one of the main cornerstones of the national economy. Botswana has also encouraged local crafts for sale to tourists, and Botswana baskets have become internationally famous. Women compete for a yearly prize, and the baskets that are entered in the contest are auctioned off with international bidding. For many rural families, women's crafts are important sources of need cash. Women weave baskets and hats in Lesotho, where the traditional hat has become a symbol of the Basotho. The hat has a wide brim and comes up to a high point at the top. The top has usually four side loops, and tradition says the hat is the shape of a hill close to the site of Thaba Bosiu where Moshoeshoe established his capital. Basotho baskets and hats have not been well marketed outside of Lesotho and have not become established in the African arts market. Basotho are not well known for their beading, and most beading today is associated with traditional doctors and the costumes worn by both male and female initiates.

Both countries are greatly crippled with high rates of HIV, some of the highest infection rates in the world. In 2006, life expectancy in Botswana had dropped from 65 to 35 years of age due to the spread of HIV/AIDS. Life expectancy in Lesotho is similar, and there was no policy to combat HIV/AIDS until 2005. The Clinton Foundation assists the program in Lesotho and President Bill Clinton and Microsoft chairman Bill Gates visited the country in 2006 in an attempt to help push the fight against HIV/AIDS. Other international personalities such as Great Britain's Prince Harry have brought international awareness of the problems in Lesotho. However, as long as the pope refuses to sanction the use of condoms, Lesotho's Catholics will not use them.

John A. Shoup

Further Reading

Afolayan, Funso S. *Culture and Customs of South Africa.* Westport, CT: Greenwood Press, 2004.

Coates, Austin. *Basutoland.* London: Colonial Office, 1964.

Denbow, James, and Phenyo C. Thebe. *Culture and Customs of Botswana.* Westport, CT: Greenwood Press, 2006.

Good, Kenneth. *Diamonds, Dispossession, and Democracy in Botswana.* London; James Currey, 2008.

Letsema. http://www.letsema.org/html/clinton_foundation.php (accessed October 30, 2009).

"Missionary Settlement in Southern Africa 1800–1925." http://www.sahistory.org.za/pages/places/mission-stations/sources.htm (accessed October 30, 2009).

Mofolo, Thomas. *Chaka*. Translated by Daniel Kunene. London: Heinemann, 1981.

Murray, Colin. *Families Divided: Impact of Migrant Labor in Lesotho*. Cambridge: Cambridge University Press, 2009 (reissue).

Murray, Colin, and Peters Sanders. *Medicine Murder in Colonial Lesotho: The Anatomy of a Moral Crisis*. Edinburgh: Edinburgh University Press, 2005.

Sechefo, Justinus. *Customs and Superstitions in Basutoland*. Morija, Lesotho: Morija, n.d.

Thompson, Leonard. *A History of South Africa*. New Haven, CT: Yale University Press, 1995.

Tyrrell, Barbara, and Peter Jurgens. *African Heritage*. Johannesburg: MacMillan South Africa, Ltd., 1986.

South Arabian

South Arabian differs from the Arabic spoken by most **Arabs**. It descends directly from the Arabic of the ancient Yemeni kingdoms and is a major influence on the Semitic and Cushitic languages of the Horn of Africa. South Arabian speakers are limited to several small pockets in Dhufar, Socotra Island, and Musandam Peninsula in the modern states of Yemen, Oman, and the United Arab Emirates. There are five major groups left today: the Harasis, the Mahrah, the Qarah, the people of Socotra Island, and the Shihuh, totaling over 150,000. The majority speak a form of Mahri. The Harasis and Mahrah are primarily pastoralists; the Qarah are mainly settled agriculturalists, while the Shihuh of the Musandam live a transhumant life of mixed animal husbandry, subsistence farming, and fishing, moving up and down the mountains with the seasons, though many today work in jobs in the United Arab Emirates. The Shihuh migrated from Yemen in the second century CE and have subsequently mixed with **Baluch** from Iran/Pakistan. **Somalis** consider the Mahrah to be cousins (*ibn 'Amm*), and certain Somali tribes trace their descent back to Himyar, the semi-mythical founder of the Kingdom of Himyar, the most powerful of southern Arabian states in the sixth century CE.

The South Arabian kingdoms arose around 1000 BCE and lasted through the seventh century CE. In the eighth century BCE, the Kingdom of Saba dominated the region and influenced the development of the D'mt civilization of Ethiopia. By the fifth century BCE, Yemeni kingdoms had developed sophisticated stone architecture and complex social, political, and religious organizations. They exercised a good deal of political influence north into the peninsula and across the straights into the Ethiopian highlands. Archeological evidence in both Yemen and Ethiopia indicate strong connections between the two areas, including monumental stone architecture and temples to South Arabian gods similar to those of the Kingdom of Saba. The first major state in Ethiopia, Aksum, was founded by Yemenis around 100 CE, and in 525, the Ethiopians in turn conquered Yemen. In 570, the Ethiopians invaded the Hijaz from Yemen, but were turned back by perhaps an outbreak of plague; an incident mentioned in the Qur'an (*Surat al-Fil*; surah 105). In turn, the Sassanids of Persia forced the Ethiopians out of Yemen in 572, but by that time, the South Arabian economy was in decline and **Persian** rule was short-lived. Yemenis were among the first to convert to Islam and contributed to the success of the Arab-Muslim conquest of the Middle East and North Africa.

South Arabia developed its own alphabet, from which Ge'ez and other Ethiopian languages are derived. The South Arabian alphabet, though older, was replaced by the North Arabian alphabet with the spread of Islam, and is no longer used to write the language. Islam also brought the spread of Northern Arabic as the main medium of speech, and the number of South Arabian speakers declined to the situation of today.

The Mahrah and Qarah live close to each other in the Jabal Qarah region of Dhufar and across the Omani border with Yemen into the Hadramawt, where until the middle of the 20th century, they lived primarily from transhumant pastoralism. The two seem to share a common origin with the Mahrah stemming from the Qarah. The Mahrah established an independent *Sultanate* in Dhufar and the Hadramawt with its capital at al-Ghaydah. The *Sultans* of Mahrah gained control over Socotra Island in 1511, and it remained part of the *Sultanate* until 1967. The British established a protectorate over the *Sultanate* in 1886. The *Sultanate* of Mahrah was eventually abolished and incorporated into South Yemen in 1967.

The Harasis live mainly in the Jiddat al-Harasis, a large pebble plain between Dhufar and northern Oman. They are pastoral nomads famous for the quality of their camels. They joined a confederation of Bedouin tribes against their close relatives, the Mahrah, despite the fact that they speak a dialect of Mahri. The Harasis stayed out of the conflict between Oman and Dhufar rebels in the 1970s and allowed Mahri families to take refuge among them. Today, the Harasis are part of an integrated development program to preserve the wild oryx and provide grazing for their camels.

John A. Shoup

Further Reading

Carter, John R. L. *Tribes in Oman*. London: Peninsular Publishing, 1982.

Chatty, Dawn. *Mobile Pastoralists: Development Planning and Social Change in Oman*. New York: Columbia University Press, 1996.

De Maigret, Alessandro. *Arabia Felix: An Exploration of the Archeological History of Yemen*. London: Stacey International, 2002.

Heard-Bey, Frauke. *From Trucial States to United Arab Emirates*. Dubai: Motivate Press, 2004.

Insoll, Timothy. *The Archeology of Islam in Sub-Saharan Africa*. Cambridge: Cambridge University Press, 2003.

Lapidus, Ira. *A History of Islamic Societies*. Cambridge: Cambridge University Press, 1997.

Schippmann, Klaus. *Ancient South Arabia: From the Queen of Sheba to the Advent of Islam*. Princeton, NJ: Markus Wiener Publishers, 2002.

Shoup, John A. "Harasis." In *Saudi Arabia and the Gulf Arab States Today: An Encyclopedia of Life in the Arab States*, edited by Sebastian Maisel and John A. Shoup. Westport, CT: Greenwood Press, 2009.

Shoup, John A. "Mountains." In *Saudi Arabia and the Gulf Arab States Today: An Encyclopedia of Life in the Arab States*, edited by Sebastian Maisel and John A. Shoup. Westport, CT: Greenwood Press, 2009.

Shoup, John A. "Musandam." In *Saudi Arabia and the Gulf Arab States Today: An Encyclopedia of Life in the Arab States*, edited by

Sebastian Maisel and John A. Shoup. Westport, CT: Greenwood Press, 2009.

Thesiger, Wilfred. *Arabian Sands*. London: Readers Union, Longmans, Green, and Co., 1960.

Surma

Surma is the general term used for a number of tribal peoples who live in the southwest of Ethiopia along the Omo River. The Ethiopian census of 2007 notes that there are around 186,875 people belonging to one of the three main groups: the Suri, the Mursi, and the Me'en. Others who live in the same area and speak related languages include the Bodi, Chai, and Tirma. They all speak Nilo-Saharan language referred to as Surmic, which seems to be closely related to **Nilotic**, though is distinct from it being part of the Eastern Sudanic language family. The small but separate group called the Kwegu (which numbers only around 500 in total) also seems to belong to the general language group, but have been dominated by the Mursi, Bodi, and others for several centuries. The Kwegu are bilingual, speaking their own language as well as those of the larger groups who dominate them in a patron-client relationship. The Kwegu depend on having a Musri or Bodi patron to protect them from other Mursi and Bodi and provide various services such as navigation on the dangerous Omo River.

The Surma and related peoples live in one of the most remote areas of the world and appear to have done so for millennia. They developed an economic system that utilizes the various environmental conditions of the region. The Omo River runs through an arid area subject to drought; thus they practice agriculture growing crops of millet or *dura*, sorghum, maize, peppers, cabbage, beans and sweet potatoes along with raising herds of cattle. Their diet consists of cereals such as millet and sorghum with milk and blood from their livestock. British anthropologist David Turton notes that the Kwegu work for the Mursi and Bodi, clearing needed agricultural fields while the Muris and others take their cattle away from the river during the wet season. The Surma and related peoples supplement their diet with some hunting and gathering, though again, Turton notes that hunting and gathering is also expected of their Kwegu clients. Kwegu not only help clear fields for cultivation once the seasonal floods recede, but also provide their patrons with honey, which is traded with Ethiopians in the highland towns for bullets, a practice that continues today. Among themselves, cattle, goats, and bullets function as currencies. Since the Italian invasion of Ethiopia in the 1930s, Italian guns have been available to the Surma, but they are dependent on highland Ethiopians for bullets.

The Surma place high value on their cattle and once had large herds that ranged into Sudan for pasture. Like the Nilotic peoples, cattle play a significant role in Surma society. Part of their domination over the Kwegu was the change in Kwegu marriage patterns; today, they are forced to use cattle and other livestock in bride wealth payments, which, according to David Turton, they have a remembered past, before being dominated, where livestock played no role in marriage.

The Surma are well known for their body paint. Children learn to paint their bodies with chalk and earth by imitating their elders, and close friends frequently paint identical designs. For adult Surma men, body painting is part of the "dress" for stick fighting and to attract women. Surma women extend their ear lobes and their lower lip by inserting clay disks. Extending the lower lip may have begun to discourage slavers, but, for the Surma, they are seen as enhancing a woman's beauty, and the size of the lip insert increases the number of cattle a potential husband will have to pay as bride wealth.

The Surma and related peoples celebrate harvest time, when there is enough food in November with *Donga* tournaments. *Donga* tournaments are stick fights, considered one of the most vicious of all African sports. The *donga* are held twice a year, in November and in February, and the fights are a means to relieve tension and to settle disputes. It has been noted that the competition is also part of courtship practices, as the winner of the tournament becomes the first choice of the most desirable girls. Each man carries a 6-foot (1.82 meters) wooden pole tipped to look like a phallus. The object is to knock down the opponent, and tournaments will draw men from up to 50 villages. The winner is the one man left still standing at the end. While the men wear little other than elaborate body paint, unmarried girls wear a *cache sexe* made of heavy iron beads that can weigh up to 10 pounds (4.5 kilograms).

In the 19th century, the Surma were subjected to slave raids from **Arabs** and Highland Ethiopians. Following the Italian occupation of Ethiopia and after World War II, slavery came to an end, but due to subsequent long droughts and epidemics of livestock diseases, the Surma have lost a good number of their cattle. Since the beginnings of the Sudanese Civil War in the 1950s, the Surma have been subjected to violence that spilled over across the border, causing the Surma to migrate north, which put them into armed conflict with other pastoral peoples over water and grazing lands. In the 1980s, the Sudanese Peoples Liberation Army moved its operational headquarters into Surma land; and many of the local people were able to purchase automatic guns, which have generally replaced older makes from the Italian occupation. The wide availability of automatic weapons, and the cultural ideals of manliness and revenge, in conjunction with greater restrictions on water and grazing lands for their precious herds of cattle, have started rounds of localized warfare among the Surma.

More recently, the Omo has been targeted for a national park, the Omo National Park, which threatens the grazing lands of seven Surma and related peoples, the Mursi, Suri, Dizi, Me'en, Nyangatom, Kwegu and Bodi. The park was "established" in 1966, but the boundaries were designated only in 2005, and local people were forced to sign away their lands, with no compensation. Many were unable to read the documents they were forced to sign. David Turton warns what the consequences of such forced removal would be in terms of violent conflict with the national government as well as the environmental consequences to lands humans have used for millennia.

John A. Shoup

Further Reading

Beckwith, Carol, and Angela Fisher. *African Ceremonies*. New York: Harry N. Abrams, Inc., 2002.

"*The Kwegu*." http://www.therai.org.uk/film/volume-ii-contents/the-kwegu (accessed April 1, 2010).

Native Solutions to Conservation Refugees. http://www.conservationrefugees.org/ (accessed April 1, 2010).

Silvester, Hans. *Ethiopia: Peoples of the Omo Valley*. New York: Harry N. Abrams, Inc., 2007.

Swahili

Swahili is both a culture and a language that emerged on the east coast of Africa and combines elements of **Arab**, **Persian**, and African cultures. The term Swahili comes from the Arabic word *sahili* or coastal; *sawahili* is the plural. The Swahili language or Kiswahili belongs to the Bantu family of the Niger-Congo phylum, but has a significant number of loanwords from Arabic, enough for some to think of it as an Arabic pidgin. Kiswahili has also borrowed words from Persian, Urdu, and Gujarati as well from English and Portuguese. Nonetheless, Kiswahili is a Bantu language, with its closest cognates being the Mijikenda and Pokomo languages of the coastal area near the Tana River.

Kiswahili is widely spoken in East Africa and served as a trading lingua franca well into the 20th century. German and British colonial authorities adopted Kiswahili as their administrative language in much of East Africa as far inland as Rwanda and Burundi. Kiswahili was originally *written* in Arabic script, and the Swahili people have a long history of literacy in Arabic, Persian, and Kiswahili; and partially for this reason, the Germans chose it for their administrative language in their colony of Tanganyika. Rather than use Arabic script, Europeans introduced writing Swahili in Latin script, and today, Swahili speakers use both scripts to write the language. The fact that it was an official administrative language helped its spread among non-Swahili peoples of the interior. Today, some 30 million people speak the language, of whom around 1 million speak it as the first language of the home. Most Swahili speakers live in Kenya and Tanzania, but the language has spread into Uganda, Somalia, Djibouti, Mozambique, and the Comoros Islands as well as into the Lakes Region of Central Africa. Due to the recent historical connections with Oman, there are still bilingual Arabic and Kiswahili communities in Oman as well.

The origins of the Swahili community may stretch back into antiquity. The anonymous Greek text called *Periplus of the Erythrean Sea*, a guide to trade in the Indian Ocean, notes two main trading centers on East African coast, Rhapta and Qanbalu. While there was contact with the coastal Bantu peoples in antiquity, following the rise of the Umayyad dynasty in the seventh century, Arab contacts with the coast increased and permanent settlements were built. As with the language, there is debate about whether the Swahili people are Arabized Africans or Africanized Arabs. The Swahili are a mix of Arab, Persian, and African origins; Arabs and

Persians married into African families and perpetuated Islam as well as contributed to the wealth of vocabulary to the emerging Swahili language.

Arab and Persian merchants set up a number of trading centers from Somalia to the Mozambique coasts, and it seems a number of the early Arab Muslims were *Zaidi* Shi'ites (called "5ers" in they follow the line of *Imam*s from 'Ali ibn Abi Talib five generations to Zaid) from Yemen. By the year 1000, a number of stone buildings replaced earlier wattle-and-daub structures. The Swahili people are Muslims, and archeological evidence in Islamic burials, monumental inscriptions in Arabic, and mosques supports the fact that local Muslim families were in evidence by the end of the 10th century.

In the 14th century, Muslim influence expanded in East Africa, perhaps as a response to the growing influence of Islam in India and Indonesia. More immigrants from especially Yemen and Oman came bringing with them both Sunni *Shafi'i* and *Kharaji Ibadi* Islam; though the presence of *Ibadi*s may stretch back into the eighth century. When the Moroccan traveler ibn Battuta (1304–1369) visited the East African coast around 1332, he noted not only large mosques, but also *madrasah*s (Islamic schools) and communities of *shurufa'* (descendants of the Prophet Muhammad). Since the 14th century, the majority of Swahili have been Sunni of the *Shafi'i madhhab*.

Swahili society and culture flourished until the arrival of the Portuguese explorer Vasco de Gama in 1498. In 1505, the Portuguese took the great trading city of Kilwa and sacked Mombassa. By 1530,

the Portuguese were in control of the East African coast, and in 1542, they helped the Ethiopians defeat Ottoman expansion. However, the Portuguese were eventually defeated and forced to retreat from their conquests in Oman, Pakistan, and East Africa by the newly established Al BuSa'idi dynasty in Oman. They lost their forts along the Omani coast in 1630, Zanzibar and Pemba in 1652, and finally Mombassa in 1696. East Africa's Swahili communities generally regained their independence, with only Zanzibar remaining under the *Sultan*s of Oman until *Sultan* Sayyid Sa'id bin Sultan (1804–1856) expanded his authority over them between 1822 and 1837. In 1832, he moved the capital of the *Sultanate* from Musqat in Oman to Zanzibar.

Swahili society is divided into a number of groups, if not distinct social classes. The non-Arab farmers and fisherman of Pemba and Zanzibar Islands are called the *WaHamidu* (from the Arabic word *khadimin* meaning servants) and *WaTumbatu* (the people of the island of Tumbatu) or more generally *WaPemba* (the people of the island of Pemba). The *WaShirazi* (people of Shiraz) claim to descend from Persian immigrants who, in 1200, established seven coastal cities with Kilwa as their center. Kilwa controlled the region from Mogadishu to the Comoros, and the *WaShirazi* are credited with the conversion of much of the local population to Islam.

Arabs from the Hadramawt in Yemen established themselves early in the region, but in the 12th and 13th centuries, larger numbers came to the East African coast and are often referred to as the "Old Arabs." Among them are the *MaSharifu*, the Swahili form of *Shurufa'* who gained control over religious matters and provide *barakah* or blessings to the community of Muslims. Later Arab immigrants from Oman established themselves in the late 17th century, when Oman became a major sea power and are locally called *Manga*. While they have become part of the Swahili, they have kept their Arab identities through family genealogies. The *WaShihiri* are the immigrants who came mainly from the Hadramawt in the 19th and 20th centuries. Their name comes from the port city of al-Shihr, from where most of them sailed when they left Yemen. Oman came to dominate the region starting in the 17th century, following their defeat of the Portuguese. The *Sultanate* of Oman briefly moved the capital from Oman to Zanzibar in 1832, and a number of Omani families moved not only to Zanzibar, but to Mombassa and other cities along the coast. Family names such as Mazru'i, such as the famous historian 'Ali Mazru'i, are Omani in origin. Following the overthrow of the *Sultan* of Zanzibar in 1964, many Omani families returned to Oman.

Indians make up the final element in Swahili society. Indian merchants from mainly Gujarat were involved with trade with Arabs from the Arabian/Persian Gulf as well as with the Swahili from East Africa. Indians were Muslims and married into the Muslim Swahili families and brought with them *Isma'ili* Shi'ism (or 7ers in that they follow the line of *Imams* from 'Ali ibn Abi Talib to Isma'il), architectural elements, clothes, and cuisine that have become part of Swahili culture.

Swahili society is also class divided between gentry and commoners. Called the *WaUngwana*, the urban gentry hold the highest position in Swahili society. The term is best translated as gentlemen and gentlewomen, as it comes from the root *uungwana* meaning courteous behavior. Most of these families claim to originate in Yemen or Oman. Below them are the *Madada* (female domestic slaves), *WaZalia* (locally born slaves), *WaTumwa* (plantation slaves), and *WaShenzi* (all other Africans). Slavery was part of the Swahili economy as well as social organization until the Germans banned it in Tanganyika and Zanzibar in 1897 and the British banned it in Kenya in 1907. Slaves were first obtained in Ethiopia, but eventually slavery concentrated on the interior around Lakes Nyasa and Tanagnyika. Slave traders such as the 19th century Hamid bin Muhammad bin Juma' al-Marjabi, known and feared as Tippu Tip (from the sound his men's muskets made when being cocked), established trading centers at Ujiji and Kasongo (founded by Tippu Tip) deep into the interior and helped spread Kiswahili.

Swahili has a long history of literacy in Arabic and Kiswahili. As in Arabic, poetry has an important place in Swahili society. Swahili poetry includes religious themes as well as erotic love poems. There are accounts of Swahili history or the Swahili chronicles that tell their history from their point of view. The *Kilwa Chronicle* or *History of Kilwa* tells of how the city was founded by a prince from Shiraz, his marriage to the daughter of a local king, the defeat of traditional spirit based religions by the Islam of the Persian prince, and the establishment of trade with interior peoples. Other stories chronicle the life of the cultural hero Fumo Liongo, a prince poet and the model of a sophisticated urban Swahili. Swahili society produced more secular poetry historically than any other type, much of which is oral in nature, while more religious themes are part of the written heritage. One of the oldest poetic patterns is called *utenzi*, which uses the least number of lines and makes use of the fact that Kiswahili has a large corpus of rhyming words.

The Swahili under the Omani *Sultan*s thrived with trade in spices, mainly cloves, and in slaves. Swahili and Omani merchants moved from the coast inland, setting up new trade centers and influencing African states around them. The Swahili merchant 'Abdallah ibn Salim established an independent state at Nkhota Kota, and his descendants instituted both Arabic and Islam as the official language and religion. In turn, the chief of the nearby **Yao** converted to Islam in 1870, and in 1885, Muslim missionaries persuaded the Yao that Arabic and Islam were vehicles of modernization as well as resistance to European expansion. Swahili settlers at Tabora and Ujiji introduced Islam and Kiswahili to the Buganda (**Ganda**) of Uganda as well as into Congo, Burundi, and Rwanda. The Ganda *Kabaka* Mutesa encouraged Islam and Arabic literacy in what were called "Readers" who served as pages in his court. Arab and Swahili merchants traded arms for slaves; and those who converted to Islam had privileged trade positions as well as being exempted from being raided for slaves themselves. In the 1860s, 20,000 to 25,000 slaves passed through the markets of Zanzibar.

In 1856, *Sultan* Sayyid Sa'id died and divided the state between two of his sons, one ruling the Omani mainland and possessions along the Arab/Persian Gulf and the second ruling Zanzibar and the East African coast. Sayyid Majid ibn Sa'id (1856–1870) and his brother Sayyid Bargash ibn Sa'id (1870–1888) saw the height of the Omani Zanzibar and the spread of Islam and Swahili language and culture into the interior. Their ability to keep European powers at bay served as an example to other African rulers. During this period, many of the Swahili urban elite took on as much Arab identity as possible, including Arab genealogies, in order to compete with the newly arrived Omani Arabs who were seen as taking over much of the economy of Pemba and Zanzibar.

In the later part of the 19th century, Britain, Germany, France, and the United States made political moves to gain control of the Zanzibar *Sultanate*. Trade from the interior in ivory, whale oil from the Indian Ocean, and cloves made it a valuable prize. In the end, Great Britain and Germany divided the *Sultanate* between them as a protectorate with Germany taking much of the mainland possessions in 1888 and Great Britain the island of Zanzibar in 1890. In 1918, as a result of Germany losing World War I, Great Britain took Germany's mainland possessions and renamed it Tanganyika.

Between 1961 and 1963, Kenya, Tanganyika, and Zanzibar all became independent, but in 1964, a bloody revolution overthrew the last *Sultan* of Zanzibar and many of the Omani/Arab families returned to Oman. Zanzibar was united with Tanganyika as Tanzania. With incorporation into Tanzania, the Swahili lost a good deal of economic and political power. Nonetheless, centers of Swahili culture such as Pemba, Zanzibar, Dar al-Salam, and Mombassa remain vibrant producers of the culture.

John A. Shoup

Further Reading

Horton, Mark, and John Middleton. *Peoples of Africa: The Swahili*. Oxford: Blackwell Publishers, 2000.

Insoll, Timothy. *The Archaeology of Islam in Sub-Saharan Africa*. Cambridge: Cambridge University Press, 2003.

Jenson-Elliot, Cynthia. *Indigenous Peoples of Africa: East Africa*. San Diego, CA: Gale Group, Lucent Books, Inc., 2002.

Lapidus, Ira. *A History of Islamic Societies*. Cambridge: Cambridge University Press, 1997.

Lewis, David. *The Race to Fashoda: European Colonialism and African Resistance in the Scramble for Africa*. London: Bloomsbury, 1988.

Mazrui, 'Ali. *The Africans: A Triple Heritage*. New York: Little Brown and Co., 1987.

Middleton, John. *African Merchants of the Indian Ocean: Swahili of the East African Coast*. Long Grove, IL. Waveland Press, Inc., 2004.

Noor Sharif, Ibrahim. "Islam and Secularity in Swahili Literature: A Overview." In *Faces of Islam in African Literature*, edited by Kenneth Harrow. Portsmouth, NH: Heinemann, 1991.

Robinson, David. *Muslim Societies in African History*. Cambridge: Cambridge University Press, 2004.

T

Talysh

The Talysh, Talish, or Tolish people live along the far western shore of the Caspian Sea and into Azerbaijan; the Iranian provinces of Gilan and Ardabil, and in Azerbaijan northern Talysh is the historic region of Talish-i Gushtasbi. The Talysh language, like **Gilaki** and **Mazandarani**, belongs to the Northwestern Iranian language group and seems to be related to that of the ancient Medes. It is estimated that there are between 500,000 and 1 million speakers of Talysh. Most Talysh also speak Azeri **Turkish**, Gilaki, and **Persian**.

The Talysh are noted in ancient texts; the oldest mention of them as a people comes in an **Armenian** translation of the Epic of Alexander, which dates to around 278. Early **Arabic** sources called them the al-Taylasan and they were under the administrative district of Gurgan. Between 1747 and 1813, a descendant to the Safavids (1501–1722) established an independent *Khanate* called the Talysh Khanate that served as a buffer between Iran and Russia until the defeat of the Persian army in 1813. The Treaty of Gulistan in 1813 ended the hostilities, and Iran lost a number of other Khanates to Russia as a result. A small part of the Talysh region remained under Persian rule. Those in Azerbaijan were able to continue to utilize the Mukan steppes for pastoral nomadism. Talysh are both Sunni and Shi'ites; the percentages are in dispute. Shi'ism was imposed by the Safavid *Shah* Abbas I (r. 1587–1629), himself a native of Azerbaijan, was able to bring the region under Safavid control.

In June 1993, seven districts around the town of Lankaran declared the Talysh-Mughan Autonomous Republic under Colonel Surat Huseynov and his close companion Alikram Hummatov, with Russian support, independent of the Republic of Azerbaijan. Both men were Talysh nationalists, and Hummatov was made president of the new republic. However, there was little public support, and in August of the same year, the republic was crushed. Hummatov fled but was eventually caught, tried, and condemned to death. His sentence was commuted in 2004, and he was released from prison on the condition that he not be active in politics. The Talysh people today are split between the Republic of Azerbaijan and Iran and have no separate political organizations.

John A. Shoup

Further Reading

"Afghanistan Most Significant Riser in Global *Peoples under Threat* 2011 Survey." www.minorityrights.org/?id=1927&tmpl=print page (accessed February 14, 2010).

Bosworth, C. E. and E. Yarshater. "Talish." In *Encyclopaedia of Islam*, 2nd ed., CD-ROM.

Daniel, Elton L., and 'Ali Akbar Mahdi. *Culture and Customs of Iran*. Westport, CT: Greenwood Press, 2006.

Roudik, Peter L. *Culture and Customs of the Caucasus*. Westport, CT: Greenwood Press, 2008.

Smith, Dan. *The State of the Middle East: An Atlas of Conflict and Resolution.* Berkeley: University of California Press, 2006.

Stokes, Jamie. "Talysh." In *Encyclopedia of the Peoples of Africa and the Middle East.* New York: Facts on File, 2009.

Téda/Tubu

The Téda, also known as Tubu or Toubou (also spelled Tibu or Tebu) are found in northern Chad, southern Libya, and eastern Niger. Their name, in **Kanuri**, "means inhabitants of Tu," "Tu" meaning "rocks" and "Bu" meaning "a person" or "people of the Rocks." The word "Tu" is also used to mean the Tibesti Mountains; thus their name means "people of the Tibesti," a remote, inaccessible area that remains today a major Tubu stronghold. They are predominantly pastoralists, raising camels and other livestock, and cultivating date palms and small gardens where water supplies permit. Some scholars have proposed that the Tubu are among the most ancient of the Sahara's inhabitants.

The Tubu is divided into two major branches, the Téda and Daza. The Téda are the core of the Tubu of today, centered on the Tibesti and adjoining areas north and east and are primarily camel nomads and cultivating dates in the oases. The southern Daza are cattle herders, given that their area is Sahel rather than Saharan in climate. The Daza are generally considered a separate group, are clustered toward the southwest, but they speak a dialect of (not a separate language from) that of the Téda. Some have said the Téda are the Tubu of the desert and the Daza are the Tubu of the steppe. Both the Téda and Daza are further subdivided into a number of clans, the more effective unit of identity; in the 1990s, the total population was estimated at 250,000, with about a half in Chad, a third in Libya, and the remainder in Niger. The area where the Tubu live is not good for settled agriculture, and all Tubu, whether belonging to the Téda, Daza, or the Bediyat (a division of the **Zaghawa**) "are either camel or cattle pastoralists" (Prussin, 108). The area they inhabit is immense, covering much of the south central Sahara and the northern parts of Kanem and Borku in Chad, where they have intermarried with the Kanuri. The two speak closely related dialects; the Téda call their dialect Tedaga, and the Daza call theirs Dazaga. Both languages belong to the Western branch of the Nilo-Saharan phylum, making claims of Berber origins doubtful.

Some scholars still hold that the Tubu may be of at least partial Berber origin (though now dark-skinned, reflecting centuries of intermixture with other groups), perhaps having migrated from the Nile Valley in the late first millennium CE. Tubu pushed both north into Fezzan in Libya and south toward Kanem after 1000. Although linked to the founding of the kingdom of Kanem, they were being pushed back toward the north by the early 13th century. Their northern limits were set by their need for Savannah pastures, reinforced by Ottoman (after the 16th century) pressures from Libya.

The Tubu have been Muslim for centuries, although still retaining certain pre-Islamic spirit beliefs and practices. As warrior nomads, they were able to exact protection rents both from caravans and from sedentary settlements in the vicinity of their territories. Subservient to the Daza are a craft-making people called the Azza. The Azza work wood, metal, and leather and provide the tent poles for the Tubu. The Azza are, or were, hunters who sold to the Tubu a number of items from their hunting, including finely tanned leather bags as well as fresh and dried meat. The Azza hunting abilities are held in a degree of awe, and the skins of animals they provide are used for a number of magical items by the Tubu. The most important are the charms suspended at the head of the bed and on camel palanquins called *kubu*, *odri*, or *dela*. The charms are made from finely tanned leather decorated with designs in cowrie shells and are similar to the same type charms among the **Beja**. The Azza hunters, unlike the Tubu who have taboos against wearing leather clothes, are clad in leather when hunting and which they wear at celebrations. The Azza also provide music and entertainment for the "more noble" Tubu. Prussin notes, that like many other African societies, as blacksmiths, the Azza occupy an "outsiders" place among the Tubu, which is referred to as *mellen* or vassals (110).

The Azza make the tent poles used by the Tubu out of acacia trees and acacia roots. The poles are carved and shaped, and holes are drilled where they come together to allow ties to bind the structure together. Tubu women also make some of the poles; especially the ridge poles made from bent acacia roots. The acacia roots are pulled out while alive and are bent into the needed shape and allowed to dry. Tubu tents are covered with mats made from

doum palm, and generally Tubu women make them. Tubu women have a reputation for being "free" and are known to embarrass their husbands by stripping in public. Azza women make a number of items used by the pastoralist, including woven baskets, leather containers, and items made from calabash (dried gourds).

Despite the existence of a titular traditional head among the Téda, called the *Derdei*, the Tubu have remained highly decentralized. By the 19th century, however, they had established a *Sultanate* at Kaouar (in present-day Niger), replacing the Kanem-Bornu Kingdom as overlords of the oases and salt pans around Bilma. At the same time, they themselves became subject to the even more powerful **Tuareg**.

At the onset of colonial penetration, the Tubu allied themselves with the *Sanusiyah*, a reformist Sufi Muslim order, based in Libya, strongly opposed to foreign rule. The Téda, particularly, played a leading role in ongoing anti-French resistance in both Niger and Chad, with the Tibesti regaining an effective independence between 1914 and 1930.

Only lightly controlled, at best, during the colonial period, the Tubu have been involved in a series of rebellions against the various governments of Chad that followed independence in 1960. The Tubu were also impacted in the 1980s by conflicts between Libya and Chad, focused on control of the "Aozou Strip" along Chad's northern border and more recently the conflict in Sudan's Dar Fur. The Tubu have produced a number of important political figures in Chad, such as Goukouni Oueddai, son the Téda *derdei* who was Chad's chief of state from 1979 to

1982; and Hissène Habré, who ruled Chad from 1982 to 1990. Habré was overthrown by Idriss Deby, with Libyan help, who belongs to the Bediyat of the Zaghawa. In Niger, the Tubu, like the Tuareg, have been involved in various armed resistance movements since the early 1990s.

K. P. Moseley

Further Reading

Decalo, Samuel. *Historical Dictionary of Niger.* Lanham, MD: Scarecrow Press, 1997.

Novaresio, Paolo. *The Sahara Desert: From the Pyramids of Egypt to the Mountains of Morocco.* Cairo: American University in Cairo Press, 2003.

Prussin, Labelle. "The Tubu: Nomads in the Eastern Sahara." In *African Nomadic Architecture: Space, Place, and Gender,* edited by Labelle Prussin. Washington, DC: Smithsonian Institution Press and the National Museum of African Art, 1995.

Le Quellec, Jean-Loïc. *Maisons du Sahara: Habiter le désert.* Paris: Editions Hazan, 2006.

Temne

The Temne are also called the Time and the Timmanee, and their language belongs to the Mel group of the Niger-Kordofanian family. The Temne are one of the largest ethnic groups in Sierra Leone, numbering between 1 million and 1.5 million, making them the second-largest group in Sierra Leone (after the **Mende**). They make up approximately one-third of the country's population.

The Temne seem to have originated in the Futa Jalon region of Guinea and moved south to occupy the region north of the Sow River in the early 15th century. They were occupying the Freetown Peninsula before the arrival of the Portuguese in the late 15th century.

In the 17th century, Islam arrived among the peoples of Sierra Leone, brought by Mende Muslim traders or **Diola** from the interior. Many Temne converted to Islam, though others have kept their original religion, referred to as *Poro*, from one of the main masked secret societies. The *Poro* society centers on males and circumcision ceremonies for boys while the *Bondo* is the masked society for women, connected to fertility. Other Temne converted to Christianity, but nearly half of all Temne are Muslims today and are generally hostile to those who have kept their traditional religion.

The Temne were the most hostile of Sierra Leone's peoples to the British and their **Creole** colony at Freetown. The Temne were grouped into 44 chiefdoms, which made organized resistance to the British difficult. The Temne invaded the British colony and nearly destroyed it at one point, but the British and the Creole were able to push inland and settled Creole on lands taken from the Temne. When the British imposed the hut tax in 1896, the Temne resisted, and the Temne chief Bai Bureh was able to defy the British until he was defeated in 1898. The British brought all 44 chiefdoms under their control, and today they form the Northern Province of Sierra Leone.

The Temne continued resistance to the British by conversion to Islam, and by the early 20th century, the majority was Muslim. The Temne became politically active following independence in 1961, forming the major supporters for the Sierra Leone's People's Party and the All Peoples Conference. The leaders of the now-discredited Revolutionary United Front (RUF) including Fody Sankoh, its ideological and political leader, were mainly Temne. The RUF originally sought to free the country from the political and economic control of the Creole elite and foreign companies. The RUF was responsible for launching the vicious civil war that lasted from 1991 to 2002. The civil war was ended by British military intervention, and the RUF's attempt to change to a civilian political party ended in defeat in the 2002 elections.

John A. Shoup

Further Reading

Bacquart, Jean-Baptiste. *The Tribal Arts of Africa: Surveying Africa's Artistic Geography.* 1st paperback ed. New York: Thames and Hudson, 2002.

Ferme, Mariane. *The Underneath of Things: Violence, History, and the Everyday in Sierra Leone.* Berkeley: University of California Press, 2001.

Olson, James. "Temne." In *The Peoples of Africa: An Ethnohistorical Dictionary.* Westport, CT: Greenwood Press, 1996.

Surhone, Lambert M,. Miriam T. Timpledon, and Susan F. Marseken. *Sierra Leone Civil War: Revolutionary United Front, Foday Sankoh, Joseph Momoh, Recreational Drugs, Child Soldiers.* Beau Bassin, Mauritius: Betascript Publishing, 2010.

Tigray/Tigrinya

The Tigray-Tigrinya people occupy the highlands of northeastern Ethiopia and western Eritrea. In Ethiopia, they are called Tigray, and in Eritrea, Tigrinya. The common language is Tigrinya, a Semitic language. The people are sedentary farmers, Christian, and conservative. Throughout history, they have had an important political role. About 5 million Tigray live in Ethiopia and 2.5 million Tigrinya in Eritrea, making up 50 percent of the population. The Tigray people, in their Ethiopian region, are sometimes called "Tigre"; however, the **Tigre** people of Eritrea form a separate group.

The Tigray highlands have been inhabited from ancient times. Tigray was the center of the Kingdom of Axum, first through ninth centuries, which had strong trade ties with southern Arabia. Slaves, skins, and ivory were major exports. Orthodox Christianity was adopted in the fourth century. Ge'ez, the language of Axum and basis of the Tigrinya language, remains the language of the church. As Axum declined in the ninth century, power shifted southward to the **Amhara**. **Arab** merchants penetrated inland along trade routes, bringing Islam to low-lying areas, while the highlands remained Christian. Cut off from other Christian societies, the Ethiopian church developed independently. Connection with Axum is the core of Tigray-Tigrinya culture and language, which has resisted change.

The Tigray remained important over the centuries, controlling vital trade routes. It was the center of the salt trade, which was used as currency in the empire, and later the trade of firearms. The most important ruler from Tigray was Emperor Yohannes IV (r. 1872–1889) in the 19th century, whose reign was marked by invasions from Egypt, Sudan, and Italy. The

Italians seized Eritrea, dividing the Tigray and Tigrinya people, but were defeated in Tigray province in 1896.

Most Tigray-Tigrinya people are rural, living in villages surrounded by cultivated fields. Many also raise cattle. Fields are plowed using draft animals, also used in threshing grain during harvest. A major crop is *tef*, a small indigenous grain, from which *injera*, traditional flat bread, is made.

The church is the religious and social center of village life. During religious celebrations, *tabots*, representing the Ark of the Covenant, are brought from the church in processions accompanied by music and dancing. One of the important religious festivals is *Timkat* (Epiphany), commemorating the baptism of Christ.

The wars of the 19th century devastated Tigray, which became neglected and poverty stricken in the 20th century. After World War II, Eritrea was briefly rejoined with Ethiopia, but Amhara dominance and forced Amharization brought ethnic revolts and the Eritrean struggle for independence. Fighting intensified during the brutal Derg regime (1975–1991) which overthrew the imperial government in 1975. The Eritrean People's Liberation Front (EPLF), led by Isaias Afewerke, a Tigrinyan, took the brunt of most battles in Eritrea. In Tigray, the Tigrayan Peoples Liberation Front (TPLF) led the fight for ethnic autonomy. After the collapse of the Derg in 1991, Tigray became an autonomous region in Ethiopia, dominating the current ruling political party. Eritrea gained independence with Isaias Afewerke as president. In recent years, there has been rising opposition to the Afewerke government and the domination of the Tigrinya.

Geri Shaw

Further Reading

Adhana, Adhana H., "Tigray—the Birth of a Nation within the Ethiopian Polity." In *Ethnicity and the State in Eastern Africa*, edited by M. A. Mohamed Salih and John Markakis. Uppsala: Nordiska Africainstitutet, 1998.

Central Statistical Agency of Ethiopia (CSA). "Census 2007." http://www.csa.gov.et (accessed May 26, 2011).

Henze, Paul B. *Layers of Time*. New York: Palgrave, 2000.

Insoll, Timothy. *The Archaeology of Islam in Sub-Saharan Africa*. Cambridge: Cambridge University Press, 2003.

Pankhurst, Richard. *The Ethiopians*. Oxford: Blackwell Publishers, 1998.

Ullendorff, Edward. *The Ethiopians*. London: Oxford University Press, 1965.

U.S. Central Intelligence Agency. The World Factbook. https://www.cia.gov/library/publications/the-world-factbook/geos/er.html (accessed May 26, 2011).

Tigre

The Tigre are a group of heterogeneous tribes living in the northern lowlands of Eritrea and the Dahlak Islands in the Red Sea. The people are nomadic pastoralists, Muslim, and speak Tigre, a Semitic language. They number about 1.5 million, 30 percent of the population and the majority of Muslims in Eritrea. The Eritrean Tigre should not be confused with the **Tigray** of Ethiopia, who can also be referred to as "Tigre" (see entry **Tigray**).

The Tigre are Cushitic people, once part of the first-century Kingdom of Axum whose close ties to Arabia introduced **Arab** influence to the lowlands. The Tigre language is rooted in Ge'ez, the language of Axum, and is closely related to Tigrinya, the language of the highlands.

The Tigre of the Dahlak Islands were the first converts to Islam in the 7th century. Ottoman Turks controlled Tigre coastal areas in the 16th century. Revival of Arab trade in the 19th century brought widespread Islamization inland. The century also brought Italian colonization to Eritrea. The opening of the Suez Canal in 1869 brought greater European interest in the Red Sea, since ships needed secure stops to take on coal for the steamships. Great Britain already claimed the Red Sea port of Suakin in Sudan, which had become Anglo-Egyptian in 1881. The Mahdi Revolt in Sudan threatened Suakin, but never took it. Other European countries decided they also needed access to fuel stops—not under British control— and Italy began to expand in Eritrea and Somalia. In 1890, Italy formally annexed Eritrea as a colony and in 1893, Italian attempts to conquer Ethiopia were dashed at the Battle of Adawa. Italians started occupying other coastal towns in Somalia in 1895.

The Tigre are divided into two social classes: the ruling elite, and Tigre vassals. The rulers of the northwestern plains are the Beni Amer, the southern branch of the **Beja** of Sudan. The Beni Amer are the single largest Tigre-speaking tribe. In the eastern plains, the ruling class is the Bet Asgede, originally Tigrinya-speaking Christians from the highlands who eventually converted to Islam and adopted the language of their Tigre serfs.

Most Tigre are nomadic herdsmen, moving seasonally with herds of camel, goats, and sheep between seasonal grazing areas. During the rainy season, the Beni Amer camp on the Barka River is where it is possible for sedentary farming to exist. In the coastal plains of Massawa, the Tigre move seasonally with their herds between the arid plains and low hills near Ginda again following rains that bring fresh grazing. The Dahlak Islanders are mainly fishermen.

At the end of World War II, Ethiopia took control of Eritrea and pursued a policy of Amharization, greatly resented by many ethnic groups. The Marxist regime that overthrew Ethiopian emperor Haile Sellase in 1971 persecuted Muslims and attempted to force the Tigre and other nomads into permanent settlements. The Eritrean Liberation Front (ELF), a mostly Muslim political party, organized in opposition to state control. It joined the Eritrean People's Liberation Front (EPLF), led by Tigrinyans, in seeking Eritrean independence. Tigre regions suffered severe fighting during the struggle and many escaped to Sudan. At independence in 1991, the EPLF took control of the government. Muslims, however, have been dissatisfied in recent years with Tigrinyan dominance and an undemocratic government.

Geri Shaw

Further Reading

Lapidus, Ira M. *A History of Islamic Societies.* Cambridge: Cambridge University Press, 2002.

Lipsky, George A. *Ethiopia*. New Haven, CT: HRAF Press, 1967.

Pankhurst, Richard. *The Ethiopians; A History*. Oxford: Blackwell Publishing, 2001.

Ullendorff, Edward. *The Ethiopians*. London: Oxford University Press, 1965.

Visscher, Jochen, and Stefan Boness. *Asmara: The Frozen City*. Berlin: Jovis Verlag, 2007.

U.S. Central Intelligence Agency. The World Factbook. https://www.cia.gov/library/publications/the-world-factbook/geos/er.html (accessed May 26, 2011).

Tiv

The Tiv people are one of the many minority ethnic groups in Nigeria. They are sandwiched between their larger Muslim **Hausa** and Fulani (**Fulbe**) neighbors to the north, and the **Igbo** and **Yoruba** to the south. While it is very difficult to establish their actual population, current estimates put the Tiv people as 2.2 million. Mostly Catholic Christians, the Tiv are linguistically classified as belonging to the Bantu language group. They can be found beyond the boundary of modern Nigeria, especially in the neighboring country of Cameroon, where many historians believed they originally came from. Located in the middle belt or north central Nigeria, the Tiv are primarily farmers producing subsistence food crops. They are found mainly in provinces of Benue, Nassarawwa, Plateau, and Taraba, all of which are newly created states during military rule in Nigeria.

The most common myth of origin of the group had it that God (*Aondo*), who created the earth (*tar*), originally inhabited the land where the Tiv people live today, and created the Tiv people as his children. One day, the legend goes, *Aondo* or God was accidentally hit with a paddle by a woman pounding yam. Annoyed of this act, *Aondo* packed his bags and fled to heaven from where he continues to protect his children (*Tiv*) until today. No matter how farfetched this story of origin may sound, many Tiv believed in this myth of creation, and it is taught to their children in schools today. However, official history points to southern Africa, where the group are believed to be a breakaway band of the Bantu ethnic group that migrated northward to their present location, where they are known as Tiv. A more believable fashion of the historical origin of the Tiv is one that claims that the group migrated from the Swem Mountain in the Cameroon in search of fertile land and ended up settling in this section of modern Nigeria. This makes sense because there are other ethnic groups in the Cameroon that share the same Bantu language of the Benue-Congo group with the Tiv. The Benue-Congo language group was officially classified by the British as a subdivision of the Niger-Congo language phylum.

The Tiv are a patrilocal group composed of closely related patrifamilies. Kinship ties are established through marriage (affinity) and through blood relatives (consanguinity). Several extended families live together inside big compounds in which members are allocated their own huts (*ate*). In the main, the Tiv practice polygamy like their neighbors to the southeast and southwest. One unusual marriage system was *Yamshe* (exchange marriage), in which sisters are exchanged in marriage

(*Ya Ngyor*), but this was abolished by the British administrators in 1927. Under the traditional *Yamshe* marriage system, older male children were allowed to take over their deceased father's (also brothers) wives as a form of social security for Tiv women. With the advent of British rule, traditional *Yamshe* marriage has since been replaced by "bride-price marriage," whereby the family of the groom is required to pay the bride's family an exorbitant amount of money. In some cases, the family may also request articles of clothing, yams, goats, and drinks. Also replaced by the British was the practice of endogamous marriage (in-group marriage) except in remote areas of Tivland. Finally, polyandry was also a common practice amongst the Tiv whereby a woman can marry more than one husband. This often takes the form of a sexual arrangement that involves a woman moving from one village to the other to provide sexual favor for a lover or a faraway husband without the condemnation of the clan members. In the past, the Tiv practiced their traditional religion, which in some places are called *Akombo*, *Azov*, and, *Tsav*. They are basically a form of ancestor worship. One of the legendary figures in Tiv's oral tradition was Takuruku, whom they believed led the migration to their current place from the top of the mountain in Cameroon. He is accorded the status of god or a creator in Tiv the belief system and oral traditions.

Before the advent of British administration, the Tiv were governed by their king called the *Tor-Tiv* and assisted by lower-level chiefs. Today, they are part and parcel of modern-day Nigeria, and they are ruled by a civilian administration at the head of which is the state governor. However, most Tiv still perceive their king as their natural ruler to whom they pledge allegiance more often than to the appointed civil administration.

Pade Badru

Further Reading

Bohannan, P. "The Migration and the Expansion of the Tiv," *Africa*, vol. 24.

Bohannan, P. *The Tiv of Central Nigeria*. London: Oxford University Press, 1952

Logams, Chunun. "The Middle Belt Movement in Nigerian Political Development: A Study of Political Identity, 1949–1967." PhD diss., University of Keele, England, 1985.

Makar, T. *The History of Political Change among the Tiv in the 19th and 20th Centuries*. Enugu: Fourth Dimension Publishers, 1994.

Meek, C. K. *The Northern Tribes of Nigeria: An Ethnological Account of the Northern Provinces of Nigeria Together with a Report on the 1921 Decennial Census*. New York: Negro Universities Press, 1969.

Torkuka, Alfred, A. "A Survey of Marriage and Burial Institutions Amongst the Tiv." PhD diss., St. Clements University, British West Indies, 2004. http://www.stclements.edu/librphil.htm#top (accessed February 21, 2010).

Tseayo, J. I. *Conflict and Incorporation in Nigeria: the Integration of the Tiv*. Zaria: Gaskiya Corporation Ltd., 1975.

Tonga

The Tonga or Batonga represent one of the main ethnicities in Zambia and stretch across the Zambezi River into northern

Zimbabwe as well as into Malawi. In Zambia, the Tonga represent about 12 percent of the total population and number over 1 million people. They speak a Bantu language called Citonga, which is shared with a number of other closely related peoples in the Zambezi River area, including the Ila, Toka, and Leya.

The Tonga descend from peoples who have inhabited the Zambezi River valley since around 1000 CE, referred to as the Botatwe and the closely related Sabi. In both societies, importance of females was consolidated in matrilineal descent patterns and in the development of religion. Between 300 and 1400, Botatwe culture developed, incorporating concepts from Sudanic cattle-raising peoples who were already settled in the Zambezi River area before they arrival of the Bantu. The Botatwe brought with them yam-based agriculture, iron working, and matriclan political organization of small chiefdoms. Sudanic concepts of patrilineages were developed along the lines of male-based organizations for the ownership and protection of livestock. Male circumcision was most likely already in place among the Sudanic inhabitants of the area, but female initiation ceremonies grew in number and in importance. The Tonga were generally safe from the rise and fall of trade-related states, being too remote for this to have much of an effect on them. However, developments of **Shona** states of the 16th to the 19th centuries did bring some Tonga under their control.

The first European to write much about the Tonga was the British explorer and traveler David Livingstone, who traveled into their area in 1855. The Tonga were described as friendly, but European travelers noted that their cattle herds were the subject of a large number of raids by others, such as the **Lozi** and Ndebele that they were no longer wealthy by the late 19th century. Tonga farmlands were located in areas that were rich in production, and early on, European settlers preferred to take lands from them, and many Tonga found themselves displaced.

The Tonga were mainly farmers and stock raisers and produced crops of millet, sorghum, vegetables, and, after the introduction of cash crops in the late 19th and early 20th centuries, cotton. Since the imposition of British rule and the relocation of many Tonga to reserves in the early 20th century, many have left to work in the growing cities of Zambia (then Northern Rhodesia) or in the various mining camps.

Traditional Tonga religion was based on the idea of a nurturing god figure that emerged in the early Botatwe period. In addition, like many other Bantu religions, ancestral spirits or *mizimo* play a central role in peoples' lives. *Mizimo* occupy a similar space as their descendants and interfere in their daily lives. The wishes of the *mizimo* are understood by mediums or *nganga*. People are also subject to the actions of malicious spirits called *masabe*, who cause illness or even death. The same mediums deal with the *masabe* through use of what is described as magic. The spirit mediums interpret dreams, throw the bones, or use other means to contact and understand the wishes of the spirits. They can also "write" prescriptions of what a person afflicted has to do to put him or herself right with spirits.

Most Tonga are Christians today, though most belong to indigenous churches that combine both Christianity and local religion. Christianity was spread by missionaries and even more by mission schools, where most people were educated. The mission-educated elite became the leaders of the independence movements that grew up in Northern Rhodesia in the 20th century.

The Tonga did not form a centralized state the way many other Bantu peoples did, but remained broken into a number of small matrilineal-based chiefdoms. Although the clans were matrilineal, the heads of families and of political institutions were men. The lack of a strong political structure meant that the Tonga were not able to effectively resist European settlers, and in a deal between the British and the Lozi king Lewanika, Tonga were placed in three reserve areas, the Plateau Tonga, the Kalomo Tonga, and the Gwembe Tonga. Their lands were divided up among white settlers who established commercial farms with Tonga labor.

In 1924, the British South African Company turned over the rule of Northern Rhodesia (Zambia) to the British Colonial Office, and from 1953 to 1963, Northern Rhodesia, Nyasaland (Malawi), and Southern Rhodesia (Zimbabwe) became a federation. The Kariba Dam project on the Zambezi River was initially to help reduce the costs of the copper production, but it meant that the Gwembe Tonga had to be relocated. Around 50,000 Gwembe Tonga were relocated, some forcibly. The result is that many moved to large cities to find work, since where they were relocated had poor, rocky soil.

Zambia became independent in 1964, and the idea of native reserves was done away with. The Tonga, like other Africans, were once again able to move freely, though interethnic problems emerged in the early 1970s. President Kenneth Kaunda used the growing ethnic support for specific political parties to declare Zambia a one-party state and outlawed other political parties in 1972. War in Southern Rhodesia against white minority rule ended in 1980 and Tonga in the newly created Zimbabwe were also freed from colonial reserves.

John A. Shoup

Further Reading

Ndege, George. *Culture and Customs of Mozambique*. Westport, CT: Greenwood Press, 2006.

Owomoyela, Oyekan. *Culture and Customs of Zimbabwe*. Westport, CT: Greenwood Press, 2002.

Stokes, Jamie. "Tonga." In *Encyclopedia of the Peoples of Africa and the Middle East*. New York: Facts on File, 2009.

Taylor, Scott D. *Culture and Customs of Zambia*. Westport, CT: Greenwood Press, 2006.

Wills, A. J. *An Introduction to the History of Central Africa: Zambia, Malawi, and Zimbabwe*. 4th ed. Oxford: Oxford University Press, 2002.

Tsonga

The Tsonga or Shangaan live mainly in southern Mozambique and Swaziland. They also live in the Transvaal in South Africa with small numbers scattered into Zimbabwe and Malawi. Approximately 3,265,000 people speak *xiTsonga*, which is a Bantu language. It is one of the official languages of the Republic of

South Africa. Tsonga-speakers make up about 25 percent of Mozambique's population, less than 2 percent of Swaziland's population, and 2 percent of South Africa's population.

The Tsonga originated with the Bantu populations who migrated along the coast of the Indian Ocean, arriving in Mozambique sometime in the fifth or sixth century CE, and seem to be related to the **Shona**. Their economy was based on fishing, shellfish, and cultivation, and they lived in small, scattered settlements. Unlike the Bantu on the highveld of South Africa or in Natal, the Bantu who settled in Mozambique did not rely on livestock, particularly cattle, due to the presence of the tsetse fly and other sources of diseases that affect livestock. The lack of cattle impacted their agricultural practices, since animals are a major source of energy used in intensive agricultural practices (such as pulling plows). When the Portuguese established a trading post on Delagoa Bay in the early 16th century, the Tsonga reacted by moving closer to the trade center while others moved inland, establishing their own trade networks with other Bantu peoples of the interior. The Portuguese took the **Arab**-African trading center at Sofala and systematically tried to destroy Arab shipping in the Indian Ocean during the 16th century as well as attempted to move up the Zambezi River to gain better access to the gold trade from the kingdoms in Zimbabwe.

The Tsonga do not have their own name for themselves and both Tsonga and Shangaan are relatively new names others have given them. Shangaan comes from the name of Soshangane, a Zulu (**Nguni**) chief who was able to establish

his own state in the early 19th century that lasted until the Portuguese conquered it in 1895. The term Shangaan comes from the word *amaShangana*, meaning the People of Soshangane, and was shortened to Shangaan. Soshangane brought Zulu culture and language to the Tsonga, including the value of cattle in both culture and economy. Before unification under Soshangane, the Tsonga lived in a number of small, independent chiefdoms clustered around Portuguese trading centers or as itinerant traders among other Bantu peoples of the interior. Other Tsonga established themselves as farmers in southern Malawi. After the fall of the Tsonga/Shangaan state, many fled to the Transvaal.

The Tsonga developed a reputation for magic and as herbalists among the other Bantu in South Africa. "Around Richmond (and in other parts of the Republic) the Shangana/Tsonga diviners are surrounded by a dark aura of power and awesomeness. Any farmer in Natal wishing to protect a crop against pilfering does well to employ the services of such a fearful personage" (Tyrell and Jurgens, 101).

The Tsonga are mainly Christian; those in Mozambique were exposed to Catholic missionaries, those in South Africa to Protestant missionaries. The indigenous Apostolic Zionist Church and traditional religions are also strong.

The political identity of the Tsonga begins with the founding of the Gaza Empire by the Zulu chief Soshangane in the early part of the 19th century. Following the example of Shaka Zulu, other chiefs escaping the state building of Shaka, Soshangane established his state among the Tsonga, which was called the Gaza Empire in 1824. Soshangane and his Nguni warriors became the elite, but the Tsonga were incorporated and served in the army and were required to learn to speak the Zulu language of the military elite. Soshangane named the kingdom "Gaza" after the name of his grandfather. In the 1860s, the Gaza Empire was at its height of power and controlled a large area along the Sabi River in modern-day Zimbabwe. Subsequent droughts and the expansion of Portuguese control weakened the state. The Gaza Empire fell in 1895, one of the last independent kingdoms to fall to the Europeans. The last king, Gungunyana, strongly resisted the Portuguese and, when finally defeated, was exiled to the Azores, where he died in 1906.

Under apartheid in South Africa, the Tsonga/Shangaan were placed on the "homeland" called Gazankulu in eastern Transvaal. In a number of acts passed starting in 1951, eventually 10 homelands were set up for the different African populations of South Africa, and Gazankulu was declared "self-governing" in 1971. Like all other "Bantustans," Gazankulu was reintegrated into South Africa in 1994. In Mozambique, the war of liberation against Portugal began in 1962 and lasted until 1975, and the subsequent civil war, which lasted until 1992, caused many of Mozambique's people to flee to South Africa where the men were able to find work in the mines. Recently, those who fled from Mozambique have returned as a result of South Africa's recent turn on migrant laborers.

John A. Shoup

Further Reading

Afolayan, Funso S. *Culture and Customs of South Africa*. Westport, CT: Greenwood Press, 2004.

Ndege, George. *Culture and Customs of Mozambique*. Westport, CT: Greenwood Press, 2006.

Newman, James. *The Peopling of Africa: A Geographic Interpretation*. New Haven, CT: Yale University Press, 1995.

Owomoyela, Oyekan. *Culture and Customs of Zimbabwe*. Westport, CT: Greenwood Press, 2002.

Thompson, Leonard. *A History of South Africa*. New Haven, CT: Yale University Press, 1995.

Tyrrell, Barbara, and Peter Jurgens. *African Heritage*. Johannesburg: McMillan South Africa, 1983.

Tuareg/Tuwariq

The Tuareg are a **Berber**-speaking people who live in southern Algeria, Mali, Niger, Burkina Faso, and the far southwest of Libya. The name Tuareg, or more correctly *Tuwariq*, is an Arabic plural (singular *Tariqi*) and is the name others call them. The Tuareg call themselves *Kel Tamasheq*, meaning speakers of *Tamasheq* or *Kel Tagulmust* or veiled people, for the large turban or *talgumust* worn by the men. Tamasheq is one of the dialects of Berber, which belongs to the Afro-Asiatic group of languages. Berber seems to have split from the main family some 9,000 years ago when the Berbers migrated west into North Africa from the Nile Valley.

The Tuareg are estimated to number between 1.5 million and 2 million according to government agencies, though Tuareg themselves give numbers closer to 3 million. Major civil strife between the governments of Mali and Niger with Tuareg starting in 1990 (a low-grade civil war began in Niger in 1963) caused a diaspora with Tuareg seeking refuge in Mauritania, Algeria, Libya, and Burkina Faso, making accurate population statistics difficult. In Algeria and Libya, state Arabization programs in place since independence have also eroded the number of *Tamasheq* speakers. Wherever they live today, Tuareg are minorities. Relations with the new national governments have been strained from the beginning of independence in the 1960s, whether the governments are Arab-Mediterranean or African-Sahelian. Historical relations between the Tuareg and the dominant ethnicities were not always good and are reflected in national attitudes towards Tuareg as rebels, bandits, or racist slavers.

The Tuareg may be the descendants of the Garamantes mentioned by classical sources such as Strabo. They are mentioned by the early Arab geographers such as ibn Hawkal (10th century) and al-Bakri (11th century), who provided detailed descriptions of the "people of veil." The Tuareg converted to Sunni Islam, and like the rest of North and West Africa, adhere to the *Maliki* school of law.

Tuareg are divided into nine confederations or *ettabel* "drum groups" (from the Arabic word *al-tabal* or drum based on the idea of a war drum that would bring all of the clans of a single confederation together in times of war), each with an elected leader called an *amenokal* or *amghar*. Traditional Tuareg society is divided into four major classes: the nobles or *imajeghen/ihaggaren*, religious lineages called *inesleman*, free commoners or *imghad/imrad*, and a final group of specialized craftsmen and laborers, many of whom descend from former slaves called *ilkan/Bella*. The craftsmen or *inadan* and bound agriculturalists of non-Tuareg origin, the *izeggaren*, are part of the *ilkan* group that forms the bottom of Tuareg society.

Islam is still taught to Tuareg youth by a special social class of religious scholars, the *ineslemen*, who historically acted also as counselors to tribal leaders and as mediators to settle intertribal disputes. In addition to the *ineslemen*, other Islamic religious figures (usually called *marabout* in French) have influenced the spread of Qadiri Sufism from centers such as in the Azwad region of western Mali. Among the most influential was the Arab Sufi *shaykh* Sidi al-Mukhtar al-Kabir (1729–1811) of the Kuntah tribe. Qadiri Sufism and Islamic law as also taught by the Tuareg Kel es Suq lineage. The Kel es Suq established several places of religious learning, some of which were later taken over by the Kuntah. These religious centers today have large collections of valuable manuscripts bought by private owners/teachers in the past. These libraries were declared a UNESCO World Heritage site (including those in Mauritania). Many of the manuscripts are private libraries belonging to their descendants, some of which are hidden in large wooden coffers and buried literally under the sands. Attempts are now being made to preserve them by digitizing them and restoring the fragile pages. While many Sahel and Saharan communities have

A Tuareg brush "tent" is typical of the Sahel regions (here in Mali) where there are more materials to construct this type of structure. The haze is dust due to wind. (John A. Shoup)

literate pasts in Arabic, the introduction of French during the colonial period has had a negative impact on the Arabic libraries.

The Tuareg are mainly pastoral nomads keeping large herds of camels. In the past, the Tuareg were able to use pasture lands south of the Niger River in Mali, and even today, some Tuareg are permanently located in northern Burkina Faso, such as the Oudlen. In Mali, the traditional grazing lands of the Gourma are located south of the river, but much of these were taken by the government during the struggle with the Tuareg in the 1990s. Further east and south, the Kel Geres compete with the **Hausa** in Niger and northern Nigeria for grazing lands. As pastoral nomads, the Tuareg traditionally live in tents, but unlike the goat-hair tents of the Arab Bedouin, the Tuareg tent is made of leather or of dum palm mats. Tuareg material culture was, and is, mainly the realm of the specialized craftsmen or *inadan* (*enad* in singular). Like many artisans in the Sahel and Sahara, the *inadan* remain "outsiders" yet provide most of the metalwork (including fine silver jewelry), woodwork, leather work (done by the *inadan* women) and other crafts. The *inadan* claim the Prophet and Old Testament king, David, taught them their craft, and some scholars believe that Jews from the Saharan oases may have been the first of the specialized craftsmen. They make all of the required equipment for the camels (saddles, bridles, cinches, buckles, etc.), swords, jewelry, bags of various types, bowls (for eating, milking, etc.), and nearly everything except the tent.

The Tuareg word for tent, *ehen*, is also their word for marriage, and the expression "to make a tent" also means "to get married." Tents belong to the woman who made it, and for a man to express the idea that he is getting married, he says that he is "entering a woman's tent." The ownership of the tent is such that in Tamasheq, a collective (and polite) way of referring to women is to say "those of the tents" (Prussin, 92). Women make most of the parts of the tent (frame and mat siding) but the highly decorative ridgepole and ridgepole pieces are made by *inadan*.

Conflict with national governments caused large numbers of Tuareg to seek protection in refugee camps in Mauritania, Algeria, and Libya where the youth were educated mainly in Arabic. Youth groups organized and developed a resistance music called *ishumar*, from the Tamasheq word *shimar* meaning rebellion. In Algeria, where the government was reluctant to recognize the growing number of refugees, the term *ishumar* was associated with the French term *chomeur*, meaning unemployed. The association with the French term was far less politically charged. The *ishumar* bands were greatly inspired by those of the Mauritanian and Western Saharan Hassani Arabs broadcasted from the POLISARIO headquarters in Tindouf. The POLISARIO struggle with Morocco was seen in the same light as the Tuareg struggle with Mali and Niger, and the music first spoke to the issues of being refugees, the beauty of their original homes in the Sahara, and fights against government troops. Once the peace settlement with Mali and Niger was signed, the *ishumar* groups performed at weddings and other Tuareg cultural events. One group, Tinariwen (meaning

desert in Tamasheq), has become successful in Europe and North America, releasing three albums through 2009 with good sales despite the fact that the words are all in Tamasheq.

The Tuareg proved difficult to defeat as the French expanded their control over Algeria, Mali, and Niger. The French military were only able to finally defeat them in 1917 and bring resistance to French control of the Sahara to an end, though the Tuareg in Niger were not defeated until 1920. French officers liked the image of the Tuareg warriors and likened them to medieval knights of Europe. A degree of romanticism grew around the Tuareg even as the French tried to impose their rule. The first Frenchman to travel through part of the Tuareg territory was the explorer Henri Duveyrier (1840–1892), who was completely enamored of them and described them as "veiled, turbaned Carolingian paladins" (Novaresio, 45). The French explorer and Catholic priest Charles de Foucauld, who settled in the Hoggar Mountains in 1905 and was killed by Tuareg in 1916, remained a Tuareg romantic until his death. His death at the hands of the Tuareg helped cause the final French push to bring them under French control. French, Italian, and British claims to colonial territories in the Sahara required that all plant their flags and delineate colonial borders, which were completed in the 1930s.

In 1931, the French brought Tuareg to France, as they did a number of peoples from their colonial empire. The exhibit was to highlight the different cultures of the French colonial empire and convince the French public that colonialism spread civilization. The Tuareg, in their flowing garments, helped set the romanticization of them among the general public. The romantic view of the veiled "Blue Men of the Sahara" was adopted by Hollywood as well in such films as *Beau Geste* (released in 1939).

The Tuareg have had a difficult time with the national governments of Mali and Niger since independence of these states in 1960. National governments have been dominated by other peoples and, as noted above, the Tuareg are minorities in all of the countries where they live. Relations between them and the majority governments are clouded by past history of Tuareg military domination and enslavement of non-Tuareg peoples. In Mali, the first government after independence was run by Modibo Keita (president from 1960 to 1968), a **Mande**, who tried to socialize the nation. He pushed for collectivizing agricultural production, including pastoralism, and tried to force settlements on the Tuareg and other pastoral peoples. He was overthrown in a military coup, but the harsh policies on the Tuareg and other pastoralists continued. Tuareg were barred from bringing their animals into areas south of the Niger River, and other, settled agricultural peoples were brought in to settle. Conflicts over grazing lands and water rights were further complicated by the great drought in the Sahel region from 1975 to 1980. The drought brought famine to many Tuareg, as large portions of their livestock died. In Niger, the independence government became a single-party state in 1961 and remained so until it was overthrown in 1991. Niger, one of the world's poorest nations, has had five

republics since independence, but all of them have been dominated by peoples from the Niger River rather than from the Sahara. The Tuareg in Niger were identified by the state as "racist-slavers," and armed conflict began as early as 1963. Conflict in Niger included the **Tubu** who, as pastoralists, were targeted by the government.

In 1990, armed conflict flared into open war in Niger spilling across into Mali. In 1995, hostilities came to an end with an elaborate ceremony held in the town of Timbuktu in Mali. A stockpile of weapons was destroyed, and Tuareg fighters were incorporated into the national army. In Niger, the Tuareg and Tubu were also supposed to be incorporated into the army. Tuareg refugees in Algeria, Libya, and Mauritania were allowed to return to both Mali and Niger, but in 2007, hostilities flared up again in Niger and threaten to spill across into Mali. In addition, both Mali and Niger have become involved in the global fight against terror. Both countries have been accused of harboring cells of Al Qaeda in the desert regions. Foreign tourists have been kidnapped from hotels in desert towns and cities such as Timbuktu, and in 2010, several were killed. Until the situation is better understood, it is difficult to see how much the Tuareg are involved in these cases.

John A. Shoup

Further Reading

Claudot-Hawad, Hélène. "A Nomadic Fight against Immobility: The Tuareg in the Modern State." In *Nomadic Societies in the Middle East and North Africa: Entering the 21st Century*, edited by Dawn Chatty. Leiden: Brill, 2006.

Hachid, Malika. *Les Premiers Berbères: Ente Méditerranée Tassili et Nil*. Paris: Edisud, 2001.

Hunwick, John O. *West Africa, Islam and the Arab World*. Princeton, NJ: Markus Wiener Publishers, 2006.

Hunwick, John O., and Alida Jay Boye. *The Hidden Treasures of Timbuktu: Rediscovering Africa's Literary Culture*. London: Thames and Hudson, 2008.

Novaresio, Paolo. *The Sahara Desert: From the Pyramids of Egypt to the Mountains of Morocco*. Cairo: American University in Cairo Press, 2003.

Prasse, K.-G. "Tawarik." In *Encyclopaedia of Islam*, 2nd ed., CD-ROM.

Prussin, Labelle. "The Tuareg: Kel Ahaggar and Kel Ferwan." In *African Nomadic Architecture: Space, Place, and Gender*, edited by Labelle Prussin. Washington, DC: Smithsonian Institution Press and the National Museum of African Arts, 1995.

Quellec, Jean-Loïc. *Maisons du Sahara: Habiter le désert*. Paris: Editions Hazan, 2006.

Seligman, Thomas. "An Introduction to the Tuareg." In *The Art of Being Tuareg: Saharan Nomads in a Modern World*, edited by Thomas Seligman and Kristyne Loughran. Los Angeles: UCLA Fowler Museum, 2006.

Shoup, John A. "Saharan Blues: Contemporary Music in Mauritania, Mali, and Senegal." In *La Culture populaire et les defiles de la mondialisation*. Fez: 2008.

Turks

The term Turks refers to the diverse ethnic and linguistic group of the Turkic language family, to which belong such Eurasian peoples as Azeri, Kazakhs, Kirgiz, Tatar, Turkmen, Turkish, Uighur, and Uzbek; smaller groups include such peoples as the Bashkirs, Chuvashes, Gagauz, Karakalpaks, Karachays, and Krymchaks. While originating from Mongolia, the Turkic people today inhabit several countries ranging from Eastern Europe to as far east as Siberia, with the majority of them settled in such Western and Central Asian nations as Azerbaijan, Kazakhstan, Kyrgyzstan, Turkey, Turkmenistan, and Uzbekistan; a sizable minority inhabit North America and Western Europe. The early Turks of Central Asia were pastoral nomads and militarily organized into *khanate*s (confederated tribal societies) under a *khan* (prince or ruler); the individual *khanate*s vied for control of the steppe. However, several of the more ambitious *khan* were able to expand their territory into Western Asia and Eastern Europe, namely the powerful Oghuz and the Seljuk tribes. While some Turkic rulers in the early medieval period entered into diplomatic relations with the Iranian and Byzantine empires, both empires were later conquered by Turkic tribes, paving the way for the rise of the mighty Ottoman Empire (1281–1924), one of the longest-lived dynasties in global history. Today, the Turkic peoples of the world number approximately 190 million. Turkey, the largest of the Turkic countries, occupies a strategic position as both part of Europe and part of Asia, and is considered a political power in the Middle East and the Mediterranean region. The vast majority of Turks today are Sunni Muslim, though a small minority of Turks is Shi'ite.

Historically, early Turks were a Central Asian people inhabiting Mongolia and Siberia, known for their hardiness and militant lifestyle; as early as the third millennia BCE, they had begun to domesticate the horse. Though the early Turks were organized by tribes and clans related by blood or descended from a common heroic figure, the development of the *khanate* allowed for multiple tribes to unite under a single charismatic leader or prince (*khan*), who would rule with the aid of lesser lords (*tegin*). As such, the Turkic tribes were able to dominate a large part of Mongolia, though not without considerable conflict with other Mongolian (and later Chinese) rulers. In the ninth century, the 'Abbasid (750–1258) caliphate took many Turkic slaves (called *Mamluk*s) into military service territory, beginning large-scale Turkic conversion to Islam; a century later, those Turkic slaves revolted and took a sizeable part of the **Persian** Empire for their own. By the 11th century CE, the Oghuz and Pecheneg were at war with the Byzantine Empire, and with the victory at the Battle of Manzikert in 1071, the new Seljuk *Sultanate* of Rum (1077–1302 CE) took possession of the eastern part of Byzantium. Founded by a lesser Turkish *beg* or *bey* (lord), Osman ('Uthman) of Bithynia, the Ottoman Empire, which followed in the wake of the disintegration of the Seljuk state in 1299 CE, rose to prominence. At the height of its power, Ottoman territories included large parts of North Africa, Western Asia, and Eastern Europe, and it endured for six centuries, ending only in 1924. With the conquest of Constantinople in 1453, the Turks (who had previously disdained cities) became leaders in urban engineering and development. The Ottoman Empire secured for itself the power both of the *Sultan* and *khilafah* (caliphate or successor to the Prophet Muhammad's temporal powers), and is credited with contributing greatly to development of Islamic architecture, science, and mysticism as well as Islam's continued presence as a military power in the medieval and early modern periods.

Given the ethnic and cultural diversity of Turkic people, it is not surprising that Turkish culture demonstrates influences from both Europe (especially Greece and the Balkans) and the Middle East (**Armenia**, **Persia**, and the Levant); Turkish culture has likewise left its mark in these regions. The great city of Istanbul boasts great architectural sites as the Hagia Sophia church/mosque, now a museum, though it was originally a Byzantine site (originally built between 532 and 537); and the *Sultan* Ahmad (r. 1603–1617) or "The Blue Mosque," named for both its builder and the for the extensive use of blue tiles in the interior decoration (built between 1609 and 1616). Turkish, especially Ottoman, cuisine has been very influential in the Mediterranean region, particularly in the Levant and Egypt. The rise of the coffee industry and the development of the coffeehouse, the ancestor of the modern coffee franchise, occurred first within the Ottoman Empire, from whence it spread to Europe via Italy. Turkey has long held a reputation for the production of poetry; the early Turkic tribes upheld the institution of the bard, or professional poet. One of the many surviving bardic poems, famous today, is the Oghuz epic of *Dede Korkut*, a poem about the conflict between the Oghuz and Pecheneg tribes. With the

Karagöz: Turkish Shadow Play

Turkish shadow theater has a long history reaching back perhaps to the 13th century; however, it is not clear as to when, where, how, or why it was introduced. There are numerous stories, both popular and scholarly, but there is no consensus on the matter. Turkish shadow plays developed during the early Ottoman period, and two main characters, Karagöz and Hacivat (Hajivat), were perhaps based on real people. The two characters have a number of tales around whom they were and when they lived. The most widespread tale of their origin states that during the time of *Sultan* Orhan (1326–1359), the two were employed in building a mosque in the then Ottoman capital of Bursa; Hacivat being a mason and Karagöz being a blacksmith. Their conversations were full of wit, so much so that the other workers forgot their tasks to listen to the two exchange quips. One day, Orhan visited the construction site to find no one working, but instead listening to the two men. In his anger, Orhan ordered their execution, but later regretted his action and sent a messenger with the order to stay the execution. The messenger arrived too late, and Karagöz and Hacivat had already been hanged. The *Sultan* greatly regretted ordering their execution, and *Sheyh (Shaykh)* Küshetri tried to comfort him by recreating some of the witty exchanges. He used two leather slippers behind a cloth screen which cast shadow on the cloth and became the founder of the Turkish shadow theater. *Sheyh* Küshteri is buried in Bursa in the cemetery behind where the city honors Hacivet and Karagöz with a monument. So popular did the two become, that generally shadow theater is called Karakgöz in much of the former Ottoman Empire after the name of one of the characters.

coming of Islam and exposure to Persian court culture, Turkic poetry developed new meters and styles, which showed influence from **Arabic** and Persian styles.

Likewise, Turkish music showed significant development during the Ottoman period, using such musical instruments as the *dutar* (lute) and the *tunbur* (a stringer instrument akin to the *satar*); while much of this traditional music was repressed under the Soviets, it has experienced a revival since the 1990s. Turkish literature has a very rich tradition, both in terms of script and text. Early Turkic texts were written in various scripts adapted from neighboring cultures such as Aramaic, Armenian, Greek, and Sogdian; following conversion to Islam, the Arabic alphabet (or its Persian variant) was widely adapted for use, and a rich corpus of Turkish manuscripts written in the Arabic script is extant today.

The 20th century has seen considerable development in Turkish arts and culture, and an expansion beyond traditional Islamic norms with the secularization of

Sinan: Master Architect of the Ottomans

Sinan or Khujah Mi'mar Sinan Agha (Hoca Mimar Sinan Aga in modern Turkish) was a master architect who set the stamp on what is called the Ottoman style. He was born around 1490 and was recruited in 1512 through the *devsrime* into service for the state. The *devsrime* (devshirme) was the Ottoman practice of recruiting young boys from the Christian provinces of the empire into government service. The boys were taught to read and write, given military training, converted to Islam, and eventually emerged to man the government posts throughout the expanding empire.

Because he was 22 when recruited, Sinan was not admitted to the top Endreun School in the imperial palace. He learned quickly and served *Sultan* Sulayman the Magnificent in several campaigns in the Balkans. Sinan's performance attracted the attention of the *Sultan*, and he was promoted to captain commanding a troop of infantry. Sinan participated in further military campaigns against the Persians, Austrians, and Greeks. His engineering skills were noted, and by 1535, he was promoted to the level of *Agha* of the Janissaries.

In 1539, the *Vazir* Chelebi Lütfi Pasha appointed Sinan Architect of the Abode of Felicity. He became not only the chief architect of the capital city, but also chief engineer, maintaining public facilities such as water drains and firefighting equipment. Later, he was appointed Architect of the Empire and served three *Sultan*s; Sulayman (r. 1520–1566), Salim II (r. 1566–1574), and finally, Murad III (r. 1574–1595). Throughout his long career, Sinan built or supervised the building of 476 projects, including bridges, mosques, schools, hospitals, soup kitchens, aqueducts, caravanserai, Sufi lodges, tombs, baths, and houses, of which 196 still survive. His work has been compared to Italian masters such as Michelangelo.

Turkey and other Turkic states. The Cyrillic and Latin scripts became widely used by many of the Turkic states in Central Asia and Azerbaijan; in 1928, Turkey itself officially adopted the Latin script over Arabic. Contemporary Turkish literature has done very well in the 21st century, as evidenced most recently by awarding of the 2006 Nobel Prize to novelist Orhan Pamuk. Likewise, Turkish cinema has done very well in the last 50 years, especially at the international level in the prestigious Cannes Film Festival. In terms of sports, while from ancient times Turks have favored their own traditional style of wrestling (and also related strength training), the 20th and 21st centuries have seen soccer take the limelight as the favorite sport of Turkey and the other Turkic nations today. However, wrestling (both Turkish and Olympic) remains popular in contemporary culture.

The Whirling Dervish Festival held each December in Konya, Turkey honors Mawlana Jalal al-Din Rumi, the 13th-century mystic and poet who founded the Mevlevi Order of Whirling Dervishes. (Corel)

The vast majority of Turks are Sunni Muslim of the *Hannafi* school of jurisprudence, although a significant minority are Shi'ite of the Alevi movement, and a minority of Turkey's population practice Judaism and Christianity (mainly Armenian and Greek Orthodox). The ancient Turks of Central Asia historically practiced a shamanic tradition known as Tanrism; however, due to their nomadic nature, the Turks encountered different religions, and a certain amount of syncretism and conversion took place. Islam, itself a missionary faith, made repeated attempts to proselytize the Turkish tribes—for example, ibn Fadlan's mission (a Hollywood adaptation of this was *The Thirteenth Warrior* with Antonio Banderas as ibn Fadlan, released in 2000); but the greatest rate of conversion came in the 9th and 10th centuries CE, when large numbers of Turkish children were raised as Mamluks. As Constantinople (indeed Anatolia) was itself a major Christian center, Turkey maintains many important sites of Christian heritage. Islam in Turkey has been marked by strong influence of Sufism and specifically the "Dervish" tradition of the great mystic and poet *Mawlana* Jalal al-Din Rumi (1207–1273), who was himself widely known for his appreciation of the Christian mystic tradition, and a proponent of religious tolerance.

One of the Turkish contributions to Islam was the creation of an elite military unit known as the Janissaries (from the Turkish *Yenicheri* or new warriors): these were slave-soldiers who were from non-Muslim origins, taken as children and raised to be Muslim elite troops in service to the Ottoman *Sultan*. The Janissaries provided the Ottoman *Sultans* with a powerful weapon with which to better maintain the empire. Although an Islamic state for centuries, in the early 20th century, Turkey became a secular republic; and it has been widely considered as a model of moderate religion by both Muslim and non-Muslim states. Though it is a secular state, the *Diyanet* ("Presidency of Religious Affairs") is still a part of the Turkish government, and many of the country's *Imam*s (lead prayer at mosques) are salaried as civil servants.

The 20th century brought great change to Turkey and the other Turkic states.

Perhaps the most significant political change came with World War I: the Ottoman Empire sided with the Central Powers in the war, and during this period, the empire attempted a genocidal purge of foreign elements in Turkey, most notably of Armenians, and to a lesser extent of Assyrians and Greeks. Following Turkey's defeat and the subsequent disintegration of the Ottoman Empire in 1922 (the last *Sultan* was deposed in 1924), the Republic of Turkey was born in 1923 under Mustafa Kemal Atatürk. A military officer, Atatürk began an overhaul of the political and administrative system of Turkey. This is not to say that the Ottoman Empire left no mark on Turkey or the surrounding nations—quite the reverse. Atatürk's major policies focused on secularization and modernization of Turkey, in hopes of bringing economic and social economic development that would place Turkey on equal footing with the European powers; this process was largely successful, but not without its challenges, especially in terms of the struggles between Islamists and secular political tensions. Though traditionally considered part of the Middle East–North Africa region, modern Turkey sees itself as European, and in 2010, Istanbul was elected the European cultural capital.

Turkey and the other Turkic states today have undergone significant modernization (or Westernization), such that life in major urban centers such as Istanbul or Ankara is not significantly different from life in other European cities. Turkey is very much aware of globalization, and the Internet and communications media are widely used. Given the secularization of Turkey, there is less taboo surrounding the consumption of alcohol or entertainment establishments, which might otherwise be prohibited in other predominantly Muslim countries. Likewise, dating and mixed-gender friendship or socializing is not considered abnormal. In recent years, Turkish television and cinema have developed a popular international following; Turkish soap operas are especially popular in Arab countries, as they do not require the usual censorship that North American–produced or European-produced programming frequently require.

As a Mediterranean state that lies across two continents (Europe and Asia), Turkey has always enjoyed a privileged position for trade and diplomacy; as such, Turkey was a founding member of the United Nations in 1945 and later NATO in 1952; however, despite its associate member standing with the European Union, it has yet to attain full member status as a European nation. As a traditionally Muslim nation, Turkey enjoys generally good relations with its neighboring Arab states; further, it was the first Muslim state to recognize Israel in 1949, and consequently, they have enjoyed very strong relations. As a member of NATO and a democratic state, Turkey also has strong ties with the United States, which is considered its primary ally. However, Turkey has had poor relations with Greece over the dispute of Cyprus, and likewise very strained relations with Armenia over the Turkish refusal to accept the genocide as a historical fact. However, in 2009, the Turkish government made several diplomatic overtures to Armenia, which have been generally well received as beginning steps toward a better relationship. Overall, in the first decade of the 21st century, Turkey has generally been considered to be one of the most successful nations of the Middle East–North Africa region, not just economically, but also in terms of its relations with neighboring states.

Connell Monette

Further Reading

Ambros, Edith G. et al. "Turks." In *Encyclopaedia of Islam Online*, 2nd ed., 2009.

And, Metin. *Karagöz: Turkish Shadow Theater*. Istanbul: Dost Publications, 2005.

And, Metin. *Turkish Miniature Painting: The Ottoman Period*. Istanbul: Dost Publications, 1987.

Atasoy, Nurhan. *Iznik: The Pottery of Ottoman Turkey*. London: Laurence King Publishers, 2008.

Bali Aykan, M. "The Palestinian Question in Turkish Foreign Policy from the 1950s to the 1990s." *International Journal of Middle Eastern Studies* 25, no. 1 (1993): 91–110.

Bealer, B., and B. Weinberg. *The World of Caffeine: The Science and Culture of the World's Most Popular Drug*. New York: Routledge, 2001.

Broome, B. "Reaching across the Dividing Line: Building a Collective Vision for Peace in Cyprus." In *Journal of Peace Research* 41, no. 2 (2004): 191–209.

Brown, D. *A New Introduction to Islam*. Chichester: Wiley-Blackwell, 2004.

Büchner, V. F., and G. Doerfer. "Tañri (t.)." In *Encyclopaedia of Islam Online*. 2009.

Goodwin, Godfrey. *A History of Ottoman Architecture*. London: Thames and Hudson, 1987.

Goodwin, Jason. *Lords of the Horizons: A History of the Ottoman Empire*. New York: Hold and Company, 1998.

Heper, M. "Islam and Democracy in Turkey: Toward a Reconciliation?" *Middle East Journal* 51, no. 1 (1997): 32–45.

Hovannisian, R. G. *The Armenian Genocide: History, Politics, Ethics*. New York: St. Martin's Press, 1992.

Keyman, E. F., and B. Koyuncu. "Globalization, Alternative Modernities and the Political Economy of Turkey." *Review of International Political Economy* 12, no. 1, *Aspects of Globalization* (2005): 105–28.

Lewis, Geoffrey, ed. *The Book of Dede Korkut*. Harmondsworth: Penguin, 1974.

Loewenthal, R. *The Turkic Languages and Literatures of Central Asia*. Central Asiatic Studies, I. The Hague: Mouton, 1957.

Montgomery, J. ed. "Ibn Fadlan and the Rūsiyyah." *Journal of Arabic and Islamic Studies* 3 (2000):1–25.

Quataert, D. *The Ottoman Empire 1700–1922*. Cambridge: Cambridge University Press, 2000.

Republic of Turkey. *Presidency of Religious Affairs*. December 2009. http://www.diyanet.gov.tr/english/default.asp (accessed May 27, 2011).

Rogers, J. M. *Sinan*. London: I. B. Tauris, 2006.

Rouleau, E. "The Challenges to Turkey." *Foreign Affairs* 72, no. 5 (1993): 110–26.

Royal Academy of the Arts. *Turks: A Journey of a Thousand Years, 600–1600*. http://www.turks.org.uk (accessed May 27, 2011).

Saktanber, Ayse. *Living Islam: Women, Religion, and the Politicization of Culture in Turkey*. London: I. B. Taurus, 2002.

U.S. Central Intelligence Agency. The World Factbook. https://www.cia.gov/library/publications/the-world-factbook/ (accessed May 27, 2011).

Walliman, I., and M. Dobkowski. *Genocide and the Modern Age: Etiology and Case Studies of Mass Death*. Westport, CT: Greenwood Press, 1987.

Webster, D. *The Turkey of Atatürk: Social Process in the Turkish Reformation*. New York: AMS Press, 1973.

Yesilada, B. "Turkey's Candidacy for EU Membership." *Middle East Journal* 56, no. 1 (2002): 94–111.

Zachariadou, E. "The Oğuz Tribes; the Silence of the Byzantine Sources." In *Itinéraires d'Orient: Hommages à Claude Cohen*, edited by Y. Monsef et al. Leuven: Peeters Press, 1994.

Tutsi

The Tutsi are called by a number of similar names, including Tusi, Watutsi, or Watusi, and number around 2.5 million in the central African states of Rwanda and Burundi. They comprise around 14 percent of the total population of Rwanda and Burundi combined. A small number of Tutsis, usually called Banyarwanda—indicating that they are originally from Rwanda—are found in the Democratic Republic of Congo (formerly Zaire). In order to distinguish those who have been in the Lake Kivu region since the 17th century, the term Banyamulenge has been used since the 1970s. The Tutsis speak Kinyarwanda or Kirundi, the same Bantu language spoken by their **Hutu** neighbors. It is more likely the division between Hutu and Tutsi is one of economics than one based on different ethnicities. The cattle-owning Tutsi patrons made clients of the farming Hutu and movement between the categories was based on owning cattle. Much later, these categories became more rigid, and strong social stratification between the two groups emerged. It has been noted that until the advent of European colonial rule, it was possible for Hutu to become Tutsi, and a Tutsi who lost his land and cattle would become a Hutu.

The term "Tutsi," meaning cattle herders, seems to have originated in the southern part of the region and was first recorded by European explorers in the 19th century. In the north, the term "Hima," also meaning "cattle herder," was used well into the 20th century, and in the 1924 dictionary compiled by colonial authorities, Hima" is noted to mean "an inferior race of Tutsi." The term "Tutsi" was adopted by the ruling Nyiginya dynasty and by the end of the 19th century, and "Tutsi" was generalized to mean cattle herders and "Hima" came to mean seminomadic herders and was a term of scorn.

James Newman notes that the Tutsi most likely arose from the mix of Hinda and Hima cattle herders with local Bantu royalty. The Hinda and Hima moved into Rwanda in the 15th century from the north (the Hima people of Uganda are **Nilotic** though their connection with the Hima in Rwanda is controversial, and others have speculated Ethiopian or Horn of Africa origins). The first king of the Nyiginya, Ruganzu Ndori, is said to have been a Hima who came from the north. The Hima were, until recently, thought of as exclusively Tutsi lineages.

Ndori introduced a form of unequal contract/agreement between himself and his clients called *ubuhake*, whereby the royal herds of cattle are distributed to clients for use, but the ownership remains with the king. The relationship was hereditary, and only the patron could dissolve the contract. When the contract was dissolved, the client was not only to turn over the cattle that belonged to the patron, but also all of those that belong to the client as well. The competition for lands between herders and farmers was acute in the densely populated Lakes Region, and cattle needed large areas to graze, more than could be provided by stubble fields. The two main forms of economic production, intensive farming and cattle herding, were closely interlocked, and cattle ownership became an important social indicator of wealth and privilege. Kings used cattle as a means of bestowing honor on an individual as well as for establishing control through *ubuhake* relationships. *Ubuhake* divided cattle herds into smaller units of around 30 to 50 head of cattle, making it easier to find grazing for the animals. The division of labor between Hutu farmers and Tutsi herders solidified, and it has been noted that the concept of class grew into "distinctions of caste."

Ndori was able to gain alliances with other small kingdoms, but his own region of his direct rule is estimated to be only around 10 percent of modern Rwanda. The *umwami* or king was considered to be semidivine. It became a belief by the end of the 19th century that any attempt to overthrow the *unwami* would bring ruin and severe punishment of *Imana* or God. Among the titles of the Tutsi king was *Nyagasani* meaning "Lord," and the Christian missionaries chose this term to translate their concept of God into Kinyarwanda.

The history of the precolonial period comes mainly from a corpus of oral literature; epic poems of kings, battles, and cattle raids. The list of kings suggests that Ndori founded his kingdom around 1650. Political and social institutions grew as the Kingdom of Nyiginya was able to expand, especially in the 19th and 20th centuries, creating what have come to be seen as natural and ancient in origin.

The basic social unit was the *unzu* (household) that was a local, exogamous, patrilineal group. It was the smallest social unit required to respond to needs of war or vengeance, and the whole group bore the burden of vendetta or the culpability for revenge. When the *unzu* grew in size, it would break into new *unzu*, but still belonged to the same general lineage or *umuryango*. Over time in central Rwanda, alliances of several *imiryango* (plural of *umuryango*) emerged who did not share a common ancestor. The *imiryango* were never composed of a single economic category; they were to behave as kinsfolk when they met and were ritually assisted by an *umuse* or godfather.

Women had the right to own cattle and were able to exercise a good deal of freedom of action once they became mothers. Their status was attached to that of the men of their family—fathers, husbands, and sons. Queen mothers ruled along with their sons, but their status was due to their sons being the monarch. Women played an important role in the mystical religion *Ryangombe*, which was spread and maintained by women within the household. Women were also seen as those responsible for all household work and the education of children. Most slaves in the precolonial time were women who assisted the women in the great households.

Cattle play an important part in Tutsi culture and serve as the basis of Tutsi identity. A particular breed of long-horned cattle called *Inyambo* and called internationally as the Watutsi breed was developed. The massive and magnificent horns of the cattle were a living embodiment of the *umwami*'s power. They were given out to special herders to take care of and to train for parades before the king and his retainers. Cattle were the base for Tutsi domination of Hutu and the *shebuja* or patron established the relationship with a *garagu* or client by giving him a cow. Cattle were the subject of a special form of praise poetry called *amazina y'inka* or names of cows. Using similar praise as for warriors, the cattle would be described for their beauty and bravery. Cattle are still culturally important today among the Tutsi, but many have given up raising cattle and have turned to farming or work in the cities.

Germany declared that Rwanda and Burundi fell under their colonial authority, and in 1894, Count von Götzen met the Tutsi *umwami* Rwabugiri. Rwabugiri died in 1895 and was succeeded by Rutarindwa, who ruled for one year before he was replaced by Musinga in 1897. Jan Vansina's study of the Nyiginya Kingdom shows that far from being the strong state many have proposed, Rwanda was, at the time of German incorporation of the social and political systems, at a critical point, and perhaps ready for major changes that help shape modern historical events. In 1911, German authorities helped the Tutsi king put down a Hutu rebellion. The Germans also began opening both Burundi and Rwanda to Christian missions.

Germany lost control of its African colonies during World War I, and both Burundi and Rwanda were given to the Belgians in 1916. Their control was recognized by the League of Nations in 1923. Europeans introduced the idea that the Hutu and Tutsi can be distinguished by physical differences, the Tutsi being taller, nobler, and more "advanced" than the shorter, darker Hutu. It was popularly believed that the Tutsi were Hamites from the Horn of Africa rather than Bantu. Colonial stereotyping was partially adopted by the Hutu and Tutsi in the post-independence era and served to separate peoples in the subsequent conflict, often wrongly assuming, for example, that a taller or lighter-skinned person must be a Tutsi. Hutu politicians kept up a state of fear of the Tutsi enemy returning and imposing their rule. Stereotyping of Tutsis by Hutu were used in the 1994 genocide in Rwanda where the Hutu radio station Radio-Télévision Libre des Mille Collines broadcast, "Defend your rights and rise up against those who want to oppress you. The Tutsis are ferocious beasts, the most vicious hyenas, more cunning than a rhino; The Tutsi cockroaches are bloodthirsty murderers. They dissect their victims, extracting vital organs, the heart, liver, and stomach [used in traditional magic for power] " (Berkeley, 2).

Colonial authorities maintained the indigenous kingdoms and further solidified social distance between Hutu and Tutsi. The Belgians seemed to favor the Tutsi and used them to expand colonial production of coffee and tea plantations using Hutu labor. Christian missions opened schools and both Tutsi and Hutu children were educated, and in the 1950s, Hutu desire for democratic representation was presented in the Bahutu Manifesto of 1957. The Tutsi responded, saying that the traditional institutions of patron and client were to remain. The two sides began to harden against each other, and the Belgians began to shift their support from the Tutsi to the Hutu, resulting in the 1959 Rwandan Revolution. Many Tutsis were killed including the last king, Kigeri V, while 200,000 fled to neighboring countries. The Hutus and the Belgians agreed to the official end of the Tutsi kingdom in 1961 and the full independence of Rwanda in 1962.

Burundi's colonial history was similar to that of Rwanda, except that the Tutsi were able to keep control. In 1961, Burundi separated from Rwanda (colonial Ruanda-Urundi) and became the independent Kingdom of Burundi. In 1962, it was internationally recognized as the Kingdom of Burundi and its Tutsi king, Mwambatsu IV, announced that it would be a constitutional monarchy and allow political participation of the Hutu. In 1965, the king refused to officially appoint the elected Hutu prime minister, which led to a rebellion by the Hutu-dominated police. The rebels were crushed by the Tutsi-dominated army. The army then staged a coup and established a republic. Hutu and Tutsi conflict has erupted several times since then, resulting in large numbers of mainly Hutu deaths. Recently, Burundi has attempted to form governments with quota representation of ethnic groups and have elected two Hutu presidents since 2003.

Rwanda's independence history has been equally bloody. Tutsis driven out in 1959 made incursions into Rwanda and, in 1963, launched major attacks from bases in Burundi. The result was a backlash on Tutsi civilians, leaving more than 10,000 Tutsis dead at the hands of the Hutu. The Hutu-led government imposed a 9 percent quota on Tutsis in schools, universities, government service, and every

sector of employment. President Kayibanda was overthrown in a military coup led by hard-line Hutu Power leader Juvénal Habyarimana in 1973. General Roméo Dallaire notes that the policies of Rwandan president Juvénal Habyarimana to expel the Tutsis resulted in a diaspora population that could not be ignored. The diaspora coalesced into the Rwandese Patriotic Front (RPF) in 1987 that proved it was more than a match for the French-backed Rwandese Government Forces. Habyarimana was forced to open negotiations with the RPF and, in 1994, a peace agreement was finally struck between the parties. However, Habyarimana's airplane was shot down while landing at Kigali airport, which unleashed the 1994 genocide of Tutsis and moderate Hutus in Rwanda. It is still a matter of debate as to who shot down the plane, but it is generally believed it was the Rwandan army.

The best account of the subsequent events is, perhaps, the account given by the head of the United Nations peacekeeping mission UNAMIR, General Roméo Dallaire, in his book *Shake Hands with the Devil*, first published in 2003. The Hutu militia, called the *Interahamwe*, with support from the Rwandan regular army, killed between 500,000 and 800,000 Tutsis and moderate Hutus before the RPF was able to take nearly the whole country. Ironically, the mother of the president of the *Interahamwe*, Robert Kojuga, had been a Tutsi. The *Interahamwe* targeted Tutsi women and characterized them as seductress-spies out to bring down Hutu men. Tutsi women were thought to be witches, and the *Interahamwe* leader Georges Rutagunda encourages his men to capture and rape Tutsi women thinking them to be so. The *Interahamwe* had training from the Rwandan army and had made lists of Tutsi for their eventual extermination; 1,000 were killed in the first 20 minutes of the organized slaughter. With RPF victory, 2 million Hutu fled Rwanda for Congo (Zaire), Tanzania, and other neighboring countries; approximately 1.7 million in Congo (Zaire) alone. In the 100 days of the genocide, between 500,000 and 800,000 people were killed— three-fourths of the Tutsi population of Rwanda.

The RPF was led by Paul Kagame, whose family fled the killings in 1959 when he was two years old. Kagame has tried to bring about a sense of reconciliation and the first post-genocide president of the new regime was a moderate Hutu and a member of the RPF, Pasteur Bizimungu.

Around 130,000 Hutu are awaiting trial in Arusha, Tanzania, on murder charges.

John A. Shoup

Further Reading

Adekunle, Julius O. *Culture and Customs of Rwanda*. Westport, CT: Greenwood Press, 2007.

Berkeley, Bill. *The Graves are Not Yet Full: Race, Tribe, and Power in the Heart of Africa*. New York: Basic Books, 2001.

Dallaire, Roméo. *Shake Hands with the Devil: The Failure of Humanity in Rwanda*. Cambridge, MA: Da Capo Press, 2005

Meredith, Martin. *The Fate of Africa: A History of Fifty Years of Independence*. New York: Public Affairs, 2005.

Twagilimana, Aimable. *Hutu and Tutsi*. New York: Rosen Publishing Group, Inc., 1998.

Vansina, Jan. *Antecedents to Modern Rwanda: The Nyiginya Kingdom*. Madison: University of Wisconsin Press, 2004.

U

Ubykh

The Ubykh are originally from the Caucasus region near Sochi. The Ubykh language, now extinct, was a member of the Northwestern Caucasian group and was related to the other languages spoken by the Circassians and Chechens, such as Abkhaz and Adyghe. However, some linguists propose that it may also be related to Hattic, one of the ancient languages spoken in Anatolia. The last fluent speaker of the language died in 1992, but there is interest in reviving the language by members of the Ubykh community who are mainly in Turkey. There are no specific numbers for the Ubykh as a separate community in Turkey, but Turkey's Circassians number around 3 million, most of whom belong to or identify with the Adyghe language group. As noted above, the last native speaker of Ubykh, Tevfik Esenç, died in 1992.

The Ubykh originated in the Abkhazia region of the Caucasus and may be the Brouchoi mentioned by Procopius. Their closest neighbors were Abkhazians and Circassians, and the Circassians had the greatest influence on them. Little is known of them though from the 13th to the 15th century, but at least part of the Caucasus was under the Golden Horde. In the 14th century, Egypt's Mamluks began buying Circassians instead of Kipchak **Turks** for their slave military, and from 1382 until the Ottoman conquest in 1517, Circassian Mamluk *Sultans* ruled from Cairo.

In the 17th century, a coalition of Circassian tribes under the leadership of the Kabard tribe defeated an invasion by the Turkic Kalmiks, and from that time until the Russian defeat of the Circassians in the mid-19th century, the Circassians were the most important power in the Caucasus. The Circassians resisted Russian attempts at controlling the Caucasus, and Circassians fought alongside the Crimean Tartars and later the Ottomans against Russian expansion. The first part of Circassian territory lost to the Russians was in 1774 as a result of the Treaty of Küchük Kaynard, and Russia annexed the lands north of the Kuban River in 1783. Russia continued to try to advance into the region and took the Ottoman fort at Anapa in 1791. In the Treaty of Adrianople in 1828, the Ottomans were forced to give up their authority over the Circassians and allow Russia to advance into the area. Circassian resistance was fierce, and it took the Russians 50 years to defeat them. In 1864, the Russian czar Alexander II expelled large numbers of Circassians and Chechens, while others decided to leave and seek the protection of the Ottoman *Sultan* rather than live under Russian military rule. The Ubykh were the last to surrender and were removed en masse in April 1864, at the end of what was called by the Russians "a war of extermination."

The Ubykh population was greatly reduced by the war to only 25,000. Most settled in Turkey, but others moved on to Jordan where, starting in 1878, Circassians, Chechens, and others from the Caucasus were encouraged to settle by the Ottomans.

The Circassians, including the Ubykh, were converted to Sunni Islam of the *Hanafi madhhab* by the Nogai and Crimean Tartars starting in the 16th century. Before that time, the various Circassian peoples were Christian or continued to worship their ancestral gods; however, little is known of their ancestral religion.

The Ubykh, like all Circassians and like their Turkish neighbors today, are patrilineal. In the past, they were seminomadic horse pastoralists until forced to leave their homeland in 1864. Once the Ubykh settled in Turkey and Jordan, they became settled farmers. Their elders encouraged living together in settled communities in order to protect themselves from assimilation into their Turkish and **Arab** neighbors. In the early 20th century, Ubykh villages were found near Izmit, Bandirma, Marash, and Samsun.

During the Greco-Turkish War of 1919–1920, Ubykh villages suffered destruction at the hands of the Greeks, and the remaining population was dispersed among other Circassian communities throughout Turkey. Today, the Ubykh have greatly assimilated into the general Circassian communities in Turkey and identify themselves as Circassians (though as Ubykh-Circassians). Following the rise of Republican Turkey and the assimilation policies of Atatürk, the Turkish language began to replace Ubykh among the young. With less strict official policies in place in Turkey today, there has been an increase in Ubykh identity and a desire to revive their language.

John A. Shoup

Further Reading

Abazov, Rafis. *Culture and Customs of Turkey.* Westport, CT: Greenwood Press, 2009.

Lewis, Norman. *Nomads and Settlers in Syria and Jordan, 1800–1980.* Cambridge: Cambridge University Press, 1987.

Quelquejay, Ch., D. Ayalon, and H. Inalcik. "Cerkes." In *Encyclopaedia of Islam*, 2nd ed., CD-ROM.

Raymond, André. *Cairo: History of a City* (English edition). Cairo: American University in Cairo Press, 2000.

Roudik, Peter L. *Culture and Customs of the Caucasus.* Westport, CT: Greenwood Press, 2008.

Smeets, H. J. A. "Ubykh." In *Encyclopaedia of Islam*, 2nd ed., CD-ROM.

Venda

Venda or Vahvenda, meaning the people of Venda, are a Bantu-speaking people who live in the northern Transvaal in South Africa and in southern Zimbabwe in the region also known as Venda, though the majority of them live in South Africa. The Venda language is called *Tshivenda* or *Luvenda*, and it is estimated that there are over 550,000 speakers. *Thsivenda* seems to be transitional between **Shona** (one of the main languages in Zimbabwe) and **Sotho**, and the Venda represent only about 2 percent of Bantu speakers in South Africa. Others note the Venda may have Nilotic ancestry rather than Bantu and have adopted Bantu language over their original Nilo-Saharan language.

The Venda migrated from the central African Lakes Region to their current homeland near the Limpopo River in a series of waves starting around 1100. They crossed the Limpopo perhaps around 1600 and were able to dominate the Ngona peoples who already lived there. The Venda arrived in two main waves; the first of the Venda to arrive were the Vhatavhatinde, followed by the MaKhwinde. The MaKhwinde came to dominate, and their leader Dimbanyika placed his sons as local chiefs over the various districts. Around 1720, Dimbanyika died, and his son Phophi took his place as the paramount chief and changed his name to Thoho-ya-Ndou, meaning Head of the Elephant. Thoho-ya-Ndou moved the capital to Dzata, which "is regarded as the ancestral home of the BaVenda" (Fokwang, 23). Rivalry between the descendants of Thoho-ya-Ndou broke the Venda into a number of chiefdoms. The mountainous nature of their land helped them repel an invasion by the Swazi (**Nguni**) and later by the **Afrikaners**.

The Venda are mainly Christians or belong to the Apostolic Zionist Church, though there are still a small minority who hold to their traditional religion, which is based on the wishes of the ancestors or *midzimo*. There is a strong belief in magic among the Venda, and they have a reputation for powerful magic by other groups in South Africa. Many Venda believe in the existence and power of witches, and their priest-diviners use the bones to help them in divination.

The Venda have maintained the puberty celebration for girls called the *vhusha*, which lasts six days. They attend the initiation school called the *domba*, which used to be for both boys and girls, but today the boys no longer attend. The school can last up to three months in which the girls are instructed on their future duties as women. The girls dance the python dance, which is unique to the Venda. They form a line, each girl body tight to the girl in front of her, and the entire line moves to the rhythms of massive drums played by men.

The Venda was able to maintain their independence from white domination, and various chiefdoms were recognized and made agreements with the whites. Finally, in 1896–1897, the Boer Republic of Transvaal was eventually able to defeat the various chiefdoms. In 1910, the Union of South Africa was formed, and the Venda, like all other African peoples, were more and more subject to a series of racist laws. The Venda's relative poverty and isolation meant that they were generally ignored, especially after the 1948 election of the National Party government.

In 1913, the Venda were forced onto a much reduced native reserve and, in 1979, the "independent" Venda homeland was created around the families of the ruling chiefs and the first president was the Venda paramount chief Patrick Mphephu, who was a direct descendant of Thoho-ya-Ndou. The economy was primarily based on traditional agriculture and lacked any real investment other than a gambling casino that opened in the early 1980s. South Africa under apartheid did not allow gambling casinos to operate and many of the "Bantustans," technically no longer under South African law, did allow organized gambling, which frequently became an important source of revenue. Patrick Mphephu was followed by Frank Ravele as president in 1988, but in 1990, a military coup toppled the government. Venda was reabsorbed into South Africa in 1994. In that same year, the new province of the Northern Province was established, which changed its name to Province of Limpopo in 2003. Tourism was developed and is now the third pillar of the province's finances. The natural beauty of the Venda homeland has helped the development of ecotourism, and the growth in cultural tourism brings in needed foreign capital. Some 5 percent of all foreign visitors to South Africa spend time in the province.

John A. Shoup

Further Reading

Fokwang, Jude. *Mediating Legitimacy: Chieftaincy and Democratisation in Two African Chiefdoms*. Bamenda, Cameroon: Langaa Research and Publishing CIG, 2009.

Thompson, Leonard. *A History of South Africa*. New Haven, CT: Yale University Press, 1995.

Tyrrell, Barbara, and Peter Jurgens. *African Heritage*. Johannesburg: Macmillan South Africa, 1986.

Vili

The Vili or Bavili people established the Kingdom of Loango before the arrival of the Portuguese in 1485. The Bavili are also called Tsivili, Civilii, Ivili, Fiote, and Fiot and number around 11,200 people in Gabon, Congo, and the Cabinda enclave of Angola. Their language, Vili, is closely related to **Kongo** and belongs to the Bantu language group.

The Loango kingdom was established long before the arrival of the first Europeans and was located at the mouth of the Congo River in the 13th or 14th century. The kingdom included in what are today parts of Gabon, Congo (Brazzaville), and the Democratic Republic of Congo (formerly Zaire) and included not only Vili, but also Kongo people. When the Portuguese first encountered them, they had one of the most powerful states along the Atlantic coast of central Africa. The Vili were fishermen, hunters, and farmers, but their main strength was in trade. The Vili made salt from seawater and also made raffia cloth that they traded inland along with metal tools for items such as ivory and iron ore.

Europeans had initially little impact on the Vili and the Loango kingdom until the demands for slaves increased in the 17th century. The Vili opened new trade routes in the interior to the Imbangala kingdom, which were linked to the Vili capital city of Loango. The Vili sought slaves for the European market up the Congo River and into Angola, but later, as the Portuguese and the Luso-African (**Creole**) *pombeiros* came to dominate the slave trade further south in Angola, and the Vili lost control. Nonetheless, they maintained their link to the slave trade well into the 18th century.

The Vili are well known for their naturalistic art. They make a number of objects similar to those of the Kongo, such as nail fetishes and figurines of animals. One of the most important pieces are double-faced (Janus) masks called *ndungu* worn by a diviner during the coronation of the king, when invoking the gods, or pronouncing a divine judgment. The *ndungu* masks are characterized by a slightly open mouth and are painted black, red, and white and topped by a crown of feathers.Other masks are used in various masquerades to celebrate or mark events such as funerals. Masks used in the boys' circumcision school are painted in symmetrical white and black designs.

The Vili practiced a slash-and-burn form of agriculture to free lands for farming and the burned trees and bushes helped fertilize the light tropical soil. They still practice this form of agriculture and raise corps of manioc, custard greens, and peanuts. While women garden, men engage in fishing using a wide variety of nets to catch fish, shrimp, and crabs. In addition, men still hunt game in the surrounding forests with traditional weapons (such as bow and arrow) and shotguns.

In the late 19th century, the Vili were brought under French control. Using their knowledge of local trade and routes, the French engaged the Vili as both agents for French firms and as porters. Vili settled in the new European colonial towns where they have been influential, though small in total numbers. Vili were particularly important in places such as Libreville and Port-Gentil.

In 2002, then President Omar Bongo of Gabon established 13 national parks covering a full 10 percent of Gabon. This has affected the local populations, many of whom are Vili. The Loango National Park does have a few villages within its borders, but they are located along the Ngove Lagoon on the opposite shore from where most of the park is located. The villagers are allowed to maintain farming, fishing, and hunting as their staple economy, and so far they have not been brought that much into the operation of the park.

John A. Shoup

Further Reading

Collins, Robert O. *Africa: A Short History.* Princeton, NJ: Markus Wiener Publishers, 2008.

"History of Cabinda." http://www.cabinda .tripod.com/HISTORY_OF_CABINDA.html (accessed June 1, 2010).

Stokes, Jamie. "Vili." In *Encyclopedia of the Peoples of Africa and the Middle East.* New York: Facts on File, 2009.

"Tribal African Art: Vili (Bavili, Ivili)." http://www.zyama.com/vili/pics..htm (accessed June 1, 2010).

Vansina, Jan. *Paths in the Rainforests: Toward a History of Political Tradition in Equatorial Africa.* Madison: University of Wisconsin Press, 1990.

"Vili (Tsivili, Civili, Ivili, Fiote, Fiot, Bavili)." http://www.christusrex.org/www1/pater/JPN-vili.html (accessed June 1, 2010).

Wolof

Wolof (also called Ouolof, Olof, Wollof, and Woloff) belongs to the Atlantic family of the Niger-Congo language phylum and is closely related to **Sereer** and **Lebou**. Wolof speakers form the largest single ethnic group in Senegal and are among the largest groups in Gambia. In Senegal, over 3.5 million people speak Wolof as their first language (around 50 percent of Senegalese) and another 20–30 percent of Senegalese speak it as their second language. Wolof make up around 17 percent of Gambia's population, making them the second largest group after the Mandinka (**Mande**). Wolof is also spoken by about 7 percent of Mauritania's people; there are minorities of Wolof speakers in Guinea, Guinea Bissau, and Mali; and among the Senegalese diaspora in Europe and North America, there are around 7 million people. Wolof is written in Latin script as well as in Arabic called *'ajami*. Wolof texts in Arabic script are called *Wolofal*.

The Wolof trace their origins to the Senegal River before the rise of the first historic state, Takrur, in the 12th century. The Kingdom of Jolof challenged Takrur's control and Jolof's founder, Ndiandiane Ndiaye, established independence in the 13th century. Wolof sense of identity begins with Jolof, and the kingdom expanded its control over the region between the Senegal River south to the Gambia and held a number of other Wolof and Serer kingdoms as tributaries.

The famous and legendary founder of the Kingdom of Mali, Sundiata Keita, conquered and subjugated those around him in the mid-13th century, and both Jolof and Takrur were made tributary, though able to keep their own kings. Mali began to weaken in the 15th century, and local authorities reestablished their independence. The Mandinka in the Casamance and Gambia established the Kingdom of Gabu, Mandinka warrior aristocrats consolidated their control over the Serer in Sine, and Jolof reasserted its independence and extended its control over much of the rest of the Atlantic seaboard north of the Gambia. This coincided with the arrival in 1444 of Portuguese traders who sought to gain access to West African gold fields. The period also saw the conquest of Takrur by the HaaPulaarin (**Fulbe**), who established a new kingdom under the Denyanke dynasty. Jolof was unable to defeat revolts by several of its tributary states and, in 1549, Amari Ngoone Sobel Fall of Kayor defeated the king of Jolof, declaring Kayor's independence. He also established himself as the king of Baol. Following the loss of Kayor and Baol, Walo, Sine, and Salum also gained their independence. Nonetheless, Jolof was able to survive until 1890, when the French imposed their rule.

The presence of European traders along the coast and their need for slaves for the newly established colonies in the Americas caused an intense local competition for European goods such as weapons. The intensive warfare for the purpose of obtaining slaves caused the rise of the *ceddo* or royal slave warriors of the Wolof kings at the expense of the landed aristocrats. Continued warfare was cause for concern for the growing Islamic clerical class. In Islamic law, it is unlawful to enslave free Muslims; only non-Muslims are legally allowed to be captured as slaves. The enslavement of Muslims was not only condemned, but gave rise to Islamic reform movements or *jihads* in the Senegambia. The first such *jihad* had its origins in the fight between **Berbers** and newly arrived Awlad Hassan **Arabs** in today's western Mauritania, but it spread to Futa Toro (former Takrur), Jolof, and Kayor in 1673. In 1693, an Islamic state was founded in Bundu called an *Imamate*.

The end of slavery in the French Empire in 1848 ended much of the trans-Atlantic slave trade, though the Portuguese illegally dealt in slaves for several more decades. The mixed French-African Métis (**Creole**) families from St. Louis looked to the trade in gum Arabic as the main substitute for slaves as the backbone of the colony's economy. In 1840, the French began to encourage the production of peanuts—the oil was used to lubricate machines of the Industrial Revolution, and Kayor, being close to St. Louis, became the focus of French interests. Kayor was also used for grazing by camel pastoral nomads from Mauritania who provided transportation of the peanuts to St. Louis before the French built a railway. Peanut production was adopted by the

Arab Sufi leader, Bu Kunta, who had established a semi-independent Islamic community in Kayor as a means to give his community of followers a sense of self and strengthen their Muslim identity. His numerous followers/students, called *taalibe*, provided the labor.

Kayor and Baol were linked kingdoms and had been united by the Geej dynasty in the 18th century. Wolof society in the 19th century was divided between the traditionalists and newly emerging power of Muslims under the leadership of Muslim scholars. The French wanted to build a railway to link St. Louis with Dakar, which became a focal point of the battle between the main divisions in Wolof society. The king of Kayor, Lat Dior Diop, was cool to the idea of the railway, which he saw as merely an extension of French control, while the Islamic leader Bu Kunta saw it as a means to bring greater wealth to his community. The railway was finished in 1885. Lat Dior converted to Islam in 1861, and by the 1880s, most Wolof had also converted. Islam was seen as a means of passive resistance against the Europeans; a cultural resistance rather than an armed resistance. Eventually, felt pushed to no other recourse, Lat Dior rose against the French and was killed at the Battle of Dekhlé in 1886, which brought an end to the old regimes of Senegal. By 1891, all of the old kingdoms had been taken over by the French, even those that had developed friendly relations. The older social-political order did not end, but was quickly surpassed by that of the Muslim scholar supported by his students. Conversion to Islam by even the most anti-Islamic elements of society, the *ceddo*, created a new social order that exists up to today. Lat Dior has become a Senegalese national hero, and his interaction with the Sufi *shaykh* Ahamdu Bamba's life intertwines Islam with nationalism.

Wolof society had been based on a system often called a caste system due to the fact that it was hard, if not impossible, to change one's social class. The main division was between those who could own and inherit property and those who could not. The *baadoolo* were the free, landholding peasants and form the major base of Wolof society until today. Above them are the *jaambuur*, who were free commoners but described as having respect, and the *liman*, the titled landowners who, in the past, were given *lew* or land grants by the kings. Above them were the aristocrats, called *geer* or those who have honor. The *garmi/lingeer* were the special lineages of kings. The *neeno* or inherited occupation groups were made up of iron workers, weavers, leather workers, and the *géwél* or *griots* brads. Even today, few who are not of *géwél* origin have been able to break into the music profession. Youssou N'Dour, perhaps Senegal's most famous performer, has had to emphasize the fact that his mother is connected to traditional *géwél* families as well as his devotion to his Murid *shaykh*, Abd al-Ahad Mbaké, to be able to make it as a singer-musician. The *neeno* were below the *baadoolo* and though necessary, were clients of others and therefore had no personal honor. The bottom of the social organization was the *thiam* or slaves. Slaves were differentiated by those owned by men and those owned by women, and between those who were royal slaves and those owned by ordinary people. Among the royal slaves were the *ceddo*, who served as a standing army. The *ceddo* were allowed a good deal of public bad behavior such as public drunkenness and with the rise of the Atlantic slave trade, *ceddo* gained a good deal of political power.

The *serin* (for males) and *sokhna* (for females) are the Islamic scholars whom the French styled *marabout* from the Arabic word *murabit*. The French conquest of the traditional kingdoms helped with the spread of Islam as people turned to the *serin* for protection. By the end of the 19th century, several scholars were able to establish not only their moral authority, but a working relationship with the French authorities. David Robinson's book *Paths of Accommodation* details how each one was able to do this. For the Wolof, the most important was *Shaykh* Ahamdu Bamba (1853–1927), who founded the Muridiyah Sufi order. Chiekh Anta Babou's book *Fighting the Greater Jihad* details the life of Ahamdu Bamba.

The vast majority of Wolof are Muslims, following the Sunni Maliki *madhhab*, but women hold a much stronger position in Senegal than they do in Morocco or Algeria. Wolof extended family groups/households or *ker* form much of the basis for Wolof society and are patrilineal and patriarchal, but the female line is counted as equally important. A person's status is determined by noting both sides of descent and, historically, Wolof society has given important position to women. The Métis *signares* of St. Louis have often run the businesses of their European "husbands" since the 17th century. Today, the female line of descent is

Wall art in the town of Diourbel tells that the owner of this bakery is not only a member of the Murid Sufi order, but also a Baye Fall. The man in white is the founder of the order, Ahamdu Bamba M'beki, and kneeling before him is his disciple Ibra Fall in typical Baye Fall patchwork robes. (John A. Shoup)

important for the leaders of the Sufi orders. Among the Murids, *Sokhna* Seyata Aidara and *Sokhna* Bintou Massmba Mbaké contest the leadership of one of the branches of the Baye Fall subgroup of the Murid order.

Senegal became independent in 1960, and its first president was the well-known Serer intellectual Léopold Senghor. Since 1981, the subsequent presidents of the country have been Wolof, Abdou Diouf (1981–2000) and the current president Abdoulaye Wade (2000–). Wolof have produced several major intellectuals such as Cheikh Anta Diop, who challenged the Eurocentric view of world history. The Muridiya Sufi Order is one of the most powerful forces in Wolof and Senegalese

life today. It permeates everyday life and its symbols are a dominant part of the Senegalese scene, from popular music and street art to personal adornment. Allen and Mary Roberts's study on the iconography of Ahamdu Bamba was the subject of a display at the Fowler Museum of Cultural History in 2003, and a publication *A Saint in the City* further explores the pervasive Murid presence in contemporary Wolof and Senegalese life.

John A. Shoup

Further Reading

Babou, Cheikh Anta. *Fighting the Greater Jihad: Ahmadu Bamba and the Founding of the Muridiyya of Senegal, 1853–1913.* Athens: Ohio University Press, 2007.

Cham, Mbeye. "Islam in Senegalese Literature and Film." In *Faces of Islam in African Literature*, edited by Kenneth Harrow. Portsmouth, NH: Heinemann, 1991.

Ewens, Graeme. *Africa O-Ye! A Celebration of African Music*. London: Guinness Publishing Ltd., 1991.

Newman, James. *The Peopling of Africa: A Geographic Interpretation*. New Haven, CT: Yale University Press, 1995.

Roberts, Allen, and Mary Nooter Roberts. *A Saint in the City: Sufi Arts of Urban Senegal*. Los Angeles: UCLA Fowler Museum of Cultural History, 2003.

Robinson, David. *Paths of Accommodation: Muslim Societies and French Colonial Authorities in Senegal and Mauritania, 1880–1920*. Athens: Ohio University Press, 2000.

Ross, Eric. *Culture and Customs of Senegal*. Westport, CT: Greenwood Press, 2008.

Searing, James. *God Alone Is King: Islam and Emancipation in Senegal: The Wolof Kingdoms of Kajoor and Bawol, 1859–1914*. Portsmouth, NH: Heinemann, 2002.

"Wolof (Wollof)." http://www.omniglot.com/writing/wolof.htm (accessed December 31, 2009).

Yao

The Yao or waYoa (also called the Wahyoa, Vciao, Achawa, and Adjoa) are a Bantu people numbering over 2 million in East Africa, mainly in Mozambique, Tanzania, and Malawi. It is noted that the Makua-Lomwe, who also live in Mozambique and Tanzania, are closely related to the Yao and are frequently grouped with them as are the **Makonde** (also called Chimakonde, Konde, Maconde, or Matambwe) of Tanzania. In total, the entire group of Yao, Makonde, and Makua-Lomwe number over 8 million people. The Yao language is called Chiyao, but many speak **Swahili**, Portuguese, English, and Chichewa as well. The Yao claim their home region is in Niassa Province in northern Mozambique, centered on the village Chiconono between the Rovuma and Lugenda rivers and seem to have lived there since the early first or second century CE. Today, more Yao live in Malawi (over 1 million) than in Mozambique (around a half million, and another half million live in Tanzania) due in part to their movements in the 19th century.

Yao were in early contact with **Arabs** along the Indian Ocean coasts and developed trading partnerships with them. The Yao traded slaves, beeswax, and ivory to the Arabs in exchange for cloth and glass beads, and later guns, gunpowder, and tobacco that could be traded with inland peoples. The Yao were heavily impacted by their close contact with Arabs and other Muslim traders from the coast, and today most Yao are Sunni Muslims of the *Shafi'i* school, though they maintain a good number of their own, pre-Islamic beliefs even today. They became powerful and wealthy, and by the 15th century, they had established several kingdoms in northern Mozambique.

In the late 15th and early 16th centuries, the Portuguese took the Arab/Muslim coastal trading cities, which impacted the Yao. The Portuguese pressed inland in Mozambique setting up commercial farming plantations based on African labor. The Yao were pressed into work, but resented being forced to work for Christians. As a result, Yao Muslim identity was greatly reinforced, and they were able to maintain their traditional social organization as well as subsistence agriculture as part of group resistance to the Christian Portuguese. They began to move inland themselves, away from Portuguese control. Nonetheless, some did attend Christian schools and learn Portuguese, though few were attracted to Christianity as a religion.

Portuguese domination came to an end along much of the East African coast with the expansion of the Omani empire in the 18th and 19th centuries. While Mozambique remained Portuguese, regions of what would become Tanzania and Malawi remained outside of European control. Yao established their own states in these areas and reopened links with the Omani and Swahili traders on the coasts of Kenya and Tanzania. Yao leaders called themselves *Sultans*, following the Arab examples they knew. The Yao once again had markets for the slaves they took or bought from inland peoples. During the 19th century, Yao borrowed a good deal from the Arabs, including forms of dress and architecture, particularly for mosques. The Arabs also continued to provide them with guns that gave the Yao a decided advantage over the **Chewa** and other nearby peoples. The Chewa were, in particular, frequently the victims of Yao slave raids because of their lack of centralized leadership. Yao established several states in Malawi between 1850 and 1870 with strong cultural ties with the Arab and Swahili coastal communities. Yao states remained important links for trade from the interior with the Indian Ocean coast until the Germans established the German East Africa Colony.

Yao rulers were able to deal on near equal terms with the colonial government once Tanganyika was declared "German territory" in 1885. In 1888, the *Sultan* of Zanzibar had his coastal territories on the mainland stripped from him and given to Germany with British help. The Yao had not politically recognized the *Sultan*'s authority over them; nonetheless, their main trading ties were to the *Sultan*'s Arab and Swahili subjects, who were no longer allowed to deal in slaves. The German encroachment on the *Sultan* was a direct threat to Yao independence, and in 1890, the Yao leader Machemba told the Germans he was willing to open up trade with them, but that was all. He would not submit to European authority. The Germans pushed into Yao territory, and eventually the Yao were defeated.

The Germans in 1905 faced the Maji Maji Rebellion that brought numerous different African peoples together to rid themselves of the European colonials. The term Maji Maji comes from the Swahili word for water, as the "priests" of the movement blessed their men with water that was to turn away the Europeans' bullets. The Maji Maji Rebellion was the last of a series of rebellions by local people against German rule and eventually, by 1907, the last of the rebels was defeated and German rule in the colony was not challenged again. In 1918, the former German East Africa Colony was divided up, with a small part being added to the north of Portuguese Mozambique, Rwanda and Burundi were given to Belgium, and the major share taken by Great Britain, which renamed the colony "Tanganyika" after the lake.

Yao, with the end of the African slave trade and the disappearance of the legal ivory trade, maintained their subsistence agriculture, raising crops of millet and sorghum. Though they were able to maintain a bit of political independence under the British, economic needs forced many to move to the growing cities to seek jobs. Even today, the same pattern continues, with it being noted that a full one-third of the adult male population is away working in Tanzania's and Malawi's cities during most of the year and returning home to help with harvests and for holidays.

The British tried to unify Kenya and Tanganyika in a number of different ways, but the two countries were bound to remain separated. In 1958 and 1959, Tanganyika held its first local elections, and in 1961, the country became independent. It did not go through the struggle with the British as Kenya did. The Yao in Tanganyika were not impacted too much by the bloody revolt on Zanzibar and the eventual unification of Zanzibar with Tanganyika in 1964 as the new country Tanzania. However, they were impacted by the new socialist policies of President Julius Nyerere. His policy of *ujamaa*, a Swahili word meaning "togetherness" or "familyhood," was not liked by the highly independent Yao. The policy failed not only because of Yao passive resistance, but other peoples in Tanzania did not like the collectivization of their lands. Before the policy was officially abandoned in 1979, 90 percent of Tanzania's lands were enrolled in the *ujamaa* system, but they produced only 5 percent of the agricultural output of the country.

In Malawi, the Yao have faired fairly well, and from 1994 to 2004, one of theirs, Elson Bakili Muluzi, served as president of the republic. When he tried to run in the presidential race for 2009, he was arrested and charged with allegedly plotting a coup and later charged with corruption. In 2009, Muluzi made a public statement over state-controlled media that he retired from politics, but he is still facing 86 charges of corruption in Malawi courts. In his statement, he told the people that the charges have no basis and are only a ploy of the government to keep him out of office.

John A. Shoup

Further Reading

Lewis, David Levering. *The Race to Fashoda: European Colonialism and Africa Resistance in the Scramble for Africa*. London: Bloomsbury, 1988.

Mbajekwe, Patrick U. "East and Central Africa in the Nineteenth Century." In *Africa Volume 1: African History before 1885*, edited by Toyin Falola. Durham, NC: Carolina Academic Press, 2000.

Mitchell, J. Clyde. *The Yao Village: A Study in the Social Structure of a Malawian Tribe*. 3rd ed. Manchester: Manchester University Press, 1971.

Yoruba

The Yorubas, also known as the Yariba and Yarba, are found in the southwestern corner of modern-day Nigeria, where they constitute the second-largest ethnic group. While census data is not very reliable in this most populous country in sub-Saharan Africa, estimates put the population of the Yoruba people is between 30 million and 36 million of the country's 140 million people. Their neighbors are **Igbos**, Ibiobio, and Shekiris to the east, and the **Hausa-Fulani** to the north. The Yorubas are spread across West Africa especially in Benin Republic and Togo (formerly part of the Dahomey Empire), and Ghana, where they are known as the **Ewe**. A significant portion of the Gan ethnic group of Ghana can also trace their ancestry to Yorubaland. Beyond Nigeria, the descendants of Yorubas can also be found in the African diaspora, especially Trinidad and Brazil, most of whom were transplanted as slaves by the British and the Portuguese between the 15th and 17th centuries. Linguistically, the Yorubas are classified by the Europeans as belonging to the Negroid linguistic group (of the Benue-Kwa group) despite their close historical relationship to the Hausa of northern Nigeria, who are linguistically classified as a Chadic language of Afro-Asiatic phylum.

In the oral tradition of the Yoruba, Ile-Ife, the center of Yoruba life and culture, was said to be the cradle of human civilization where all human forms (human beings) first emerged, and it is the ancestral home of all members of the black race. Much of the early history of the Yoruba people is shrouded in mythology as opposed to historical facts. While there are many and diverse mythical accounts of the origin of the Yoruba in oral history, there are very scanty evidence to back up these accounts. The most common account of the origin of the Yoruba is one that states that God or *Olodumare* sent his messenger, Obalufon (also referred to as Obatala in other accounts) from heaven to create the earth out of the vast expanse of water that was below. Accompanied by a priest, Ojumu, Obalufon, or Obatala descended from heaven with a dove with a bag of sand attached to its toes , which Obalfon or Obatala scattered over the water below in a place called *More* (or *Moore*), in Ile-Ife. According to this account, the first habitable land emerged from the bosom of the seawater. This spot is known today as Ile-Ife. The second task given to Obatala, by *Olodumare*, was to populate the earth with humans, and with the help of the priest named Owu, human forms were made from mud dug from the earth until he (Owu) became drunk and fell asleep.

The more accurate historical version of the origin of the Yoruba pointed to Makkah, one of the oldest cities in the pre-Islamic Arabian Peninsula. Makkah, according to this account, was ruled by King Lamurudi, an idol worshiper who was exiled to Egypt with his children, one of whom was Oduduwa, who was credited for founding Ile-Ife as a dynasty, while his two other brothers went from Mecca to Egypt before finally founding the old kingdoms of Gobiri and Kukana in present-day Hausaland in modern Nigeria. On arrival at Ile-Ife, Oduduwa was warmly welcome by the king, Ooni Oba Oluwaiye Orunumila, who gave his only daughter, Okanbito Oduduwa, in marriage. Between them they produced seven children, the oldest of which was Olowu. All the children left Ile-Ife to found their own dynasties. Oluwu married a priest in Owu, and their only son became the first king, Olowu of Owu. The other children of Oduduwa were Alaketu of Ketu, *Oba* of Benin, and Orangun, the founder and first king of Ila. The others were Onisabe of Sabe; King Olupopo of Popo; and Oranmiyan, the youngest of the children, who founded Oyo. Oranmiyan later abandoned his throne in Oyo to revenge the death of his grandfather, Lamurudu, who was dethroned as a paganic king of Makkah. The seven kingdoms or principalities, founded by the seven offspring of Oduduwa, constitute the core of the Yoruba nation today.

The Yoruba are organized into patrilineal groups in which kinship is established through marriage. As a patriarchal group, the eldest male in the family unit (*Agba ile*) exercises absolute power within the unit, and in some instances, through his male children. Property is passed down through the male side of the family, and only male children can inherit from their father. However, there are pockets of matrilineal groupings where the female head of household exercised power; and through her, properties are passed down to the first female child, who in turn may pass the properties to her brothers after she is married. Polygamy is practiced widely among the Yoruba. The man must take a wife outside of his clan (exogamous marriage) and the wife is expected to bear him children—but more importantly, male children. The choice of a wife is often arranged between two families and the aunt or the best friend of the mother of the prospective groom is expected to initiate the marriage process once a mate has been identified. On the other hand, daughters of the king usually identify a male for themselves, and that mate could be a male from any strata of the society. There are instances of princesses marrying amongst their father's court servants like in the case of Olowu, the founder of the Owu dynasty, who married her father's priest.

The Yorubas have a rich culture which is expressed through their elaborate dress forms, dance, ceremonies, and numerous festivals like the *egunguns*. They are often dressed in colorful flowing garments, *sokoto* and *agbaada* for men, and *iro* and *buba* with flowing *gele* for women, which are often worn during important ceremonies like funerals and a naming ritual for a newborn baby. Of the many festive ceremonies celebrated by the Yoruba, the *egunguns* festival is one of the most important. The *egunguns* are masquerades dressed in colorful mystic garb, and they are supposed to be the impersonation of the ancestors that have passed to the next level of existence. The *egunguns* festival is performed every year at the end of the

farming season, and the symbolism is that those alive, through the *egunguns*, give thanks to the ancestors for the abundance of food, especially yams, for that planting season.

The main religion of the early Yoruba was the worship of *Orisa*, some of which was transported to the New World like *Lucume* in Cuba, *Santeria* in the Caribbean Island, and *Yemoja* in other parts of the African diaspora. Although the Europeans classified the Yoruba as animists, in actual fact, their traditional religion of ancestor worship is, in general, centered on a powerful creator god and predates Christianity. They believe in the existence of a universal God called *Olodumare* or *Olorun*, the creator of the universe, and through him, life is made possible. In addition to the *Olodumare*, there are other lesser gods known as *Orisa* (365 of them) and through these lesser gods, the Yoruba send their wishes and prayers to the Supreme God, *Olodumare* or *Olorun*, the owner of heaven. Today, half of the Yoruba population still practices their traditional religion, while the remaining half either practices Christianity or Islam.

The Yoruba are governed by their kings through an autonomous system of democratic governance embodied in the *Agbo-Ile* system. Within each *Agbo-Ile* system (comprising of related clan members) monthly assemblies are held to discuss issues relating to the welfare of its members and to resolve conflicts. There are two parallel assemblies; one for women chaired by the eldest female (usually called *Iyalode*), and the other by the eldest male of the clan (called *Baale ile*). Through the two assemblies, order and peace are maintained within the clan and at the village level, which is often geographically contiguous with the *Agbo-Ile*. At the town level, governance is carried out by the king, who is assisted by selected elders (usually *Baale* and *Iyalode* of different compounds). He also appoints a *Bashorun* (secretary of state) and a war commander, *Balogun* or *Seriki* (also known in some parts of Yorubaland as *Ajagun* or *Aare Ona Kakanfo*), and *Giwa* (chief of staff), to assist him in the maintenance of peace and order throughout the areas of his jurisdiction.

One of the historical figures in Yoruba history was a female heroin called Moremi. Moremi was the wife of the then-king of Ile-Ife, Obalara, who volunteered to be captured by enemy forces so that she could reveal the secrets of the Igbo invaders who camouflaged as masqueraders. Legend had it that, the Igbo, the Yoruba's neighbors, routinely raided Ile-Ife in desperation for food and women. The king, being helpless to stop these raids, was maligned by his subjects. This led Moremi to volunteer to be captured by the marauding Igbos and very soon, she became the favorite wife of the Igbo's king. In the heat of passion, the Igbo king revealed the secrets of his attacks on Ile-Ife to Moremi, after which she escaped and went back to Obalara, her husband, who then organized his men to ward off the annual Igbo attacks. Before Moremi left, she had promised the gods a sacrifice upon her successful return to Ile-Ife, but, unfortunately, the gods demanded her only child, her daughter named Oluorogbo as a sacrifice. She complied and threw her daughter into the Oshun River where she

became the goddess *Yemoja*. In Yoruba religion, *Yemoja* is one of the goddesses worshiped today in Yorubaland, and in Trinidad and Brazil.

Today, Nigeria is a democracy with a presidential-type system of political governance based on the American model, with a chief executive, two chambers, and a Supreme Court. One of the Yoruba who led the independence movement against the British was Chief Obafemi Awolowo, who, together with other nationalist leaders like Dr. Nnamidi Azikiwe and Chief Anthony Enahoro, fought the British for early independence, and later became the first governor of Western Nigeria. He was probably the most respected leader of the Yoruba in living memory, and most certainly, the most controversial.

Pade Badru

Further Reading

Ajayi, Omofolabo, S. *Yoruba Dance: The Semiotics of Movement and Body Attitude in a Nigerian Culture.* Trenton, NJ: Africa World Press, 1998.

Akinjogbin, E. A. *Dahomey and Its Neighbors.* Cambridge: Cambridge University Press, 1967.

Asiwaju, A. I. *Western Yorubaland Under European Rule, 1889-1945: A Comparative Analysis of French and British Colonialism.* London: Longman, 1976.

Atanda, J. A. *The New Oyo Empire.* London: Longman, 1973.

Biobaku, S. O., ed. *Sources of Yoruba History.* Oxford: Clarendon Press, 1973.

Clapperton, H. *Journal of a Second Expedition into the Interior of Africa from the Bight of Benin to Soccatoo.* Philadelphia: Carey, Lea and Carey, 1829.

Clapperton, H. *Into the Interior of Africa: Record of the Second Expedition 1925–1927*, edited by Jamie Bruce Lockhart and Paul Lovejoy. Leiden: Koninklyjke Brill N.V., 2005.

Clapperton, H. *Record of Expedition to the Interior of Africa*. London: Murray, 1829.

Clapperton, H. "Travels and Discourses in Northern Nigeria and Central Africa." In *Journal of a Second Expedition into the Interior of Africa from the Bight of Benin to Soccatoo*. Philadelphia: Carey, Lea and Carey, 1829.

Ford, D. *The Yoruba-Speaking Peoples of South-Western Nigeria*. London: International African Institute, 1951.

Gleason, Judith. *Oya: In Praise of the Goddess*. Boston: Shambhala Publications, 1987.

Idowu, E. B. *Olodumare: God in Yoruba Belief*. London: Longmans, 1962.

Johnson, Samuel. *The History of the Yorubas*. Lagos: CSS (CMS) Press, 1921.

Ojo, G. J. A. *Yoruba Culture: A Geographical Analysis*. London: University of London Press, 1966.

Olupona, J. K. *Kingship, Religion and Rituals in a Nigerian Community*. Stockholm: Almqvist & Wiksel International Press, 1991.

Parrinder, E. G. "The Yoruba-Speaking Peoples of Dahomey." *Africa* 17 (1956): 122–48.

Peel, J. D. *Ijesha and Nigerians: The Incorporation of a Yoruba Kingdom, 1890s–1970s*. Cambridge: Cambridge University Press, 1983.

Verger, P. "Yoruba Influences in Brazil." *Odu*, 1, 3. Ife, Nigeria: University of Ife, 1976.

Z

Zaghawa

The Zaghawa is one of the major divisions of the Beri peoples who live in western Sudan and eastern Chad, and their language, also called Zaghawa, belongs to the Saharan branch of the Nilo-Saharan language group. The Zaghawa make up more than 90 percent of the Beri numbering over 300,000 and are related to the **Tubu**. H. T. Norris notes that it is believed that the Zaghawa once included the Tubu (the Téda and Daza) and the Bediyat, the Zaghawa element keeping their original name. The Zaghawa are predominantly nomadic pastoralists, highly decentralized, with clans and sub-clans as effective units of identity and organization.

According to a number of the classical Arabic sources, the Zaghawa were associated with **Berber**-speaking Sadrata and were semi-sedentary under a monarch with divine powers living in a capital city located in the Burku region of northern Chad (located just south of the Tibesti Mountains). Most of the classical Arabic sources refer to the Kingdom of Kanem (located near Lake Chad) as the Kingdom of Zaghawa (rather than as Kanem) until the geographer al-Ya'qubi (d. 897) joined them and provided detail on the Zaghawa people in the Kingdom of Kanem.

The Zaghawa were involved in the trans-Saharan trade both toward the Nile Valley and Egypt and west to the Algerian city of Wargla. Islam spread from the Nile westward, and it is noted that the Zaghawa kings in the 11th century were at least nominally Muslims. Only gradually and partially Islamized until the mid-20th century, the Zaghawa are Sunni Muslim, but still practice a number of traditional rites. For example, they sacrifice animals, a practice they call *karama* "to ward off evil or bring rain and a good harvest" (Olson, 608).

Zaghawa society was tribal, and in the past, political power was exercised by *'umdahs*, a term borrowed from the Nile region where it refers to a village headman or a tribal elder. During the colonial period, after the collapse of Dar Fur as an independent *Sultanate*, the region was more or less left to itself with minor interference from the few British officers stationed in al-Fasher or other towns. The Zaghawa were mainly camel nomads and moved between the far west of Dar Fur and the eastern areas of northern Chad. Those who did settle, lived in small villages of 100 or fewer people and farmed millet, sorghum, peanuts, okra, sesame, and pumpkins as well as kept livestock, sheep, goats, and cattle. Once the borders between French-controlled Chad, Italian-controlled Libya, and British-controlled Sudan (and Egypt) were demarcated in the 1930s, Zaghawa found themselves split between French and British areas. The British divided Dar Fur into 30 regions governed by a local headman. Since independence, Sudanese state officials have generally replaced more traditional political positions, though day-to-day affairs remained in the hands of the local headmen until the droughts of the 1980s and nomadic herdsmen, including the Zaghawa, lost their grazing lands to desert. The Zaghawa became embroiled in the 1980s in a series of wars in Chad that also involved the Libyan leader Mu'ammar al-Qadhafi. Qadhafi wanted to expand Libyan control over the northern Aozou Strip (and even briefly tried to annex it), and came into conflict with the Tubu. Libya became less interested in Aozou and concentrated its efforts on limiting the influence of **Arab** *mujahidin* recently returning from fighting the Russians in Afghanistan on their own people. The Zaghawa leader, Idriss Déby, was willing to take money and arms from Libya and, in 1990, successfully launched an invasion of Chad from Dar Fur, which resulted in the fall of the Tubu president of the country, Hissène Habré. Déby and Qadhafi came to an agreement over the Aozou Strip in 1994 leaving it in Chadian hands. Although the Zaghawa make up only small minorities in either Chad or Sudan, their involvement in key conflicts and military prowess have lent them considerable political importance.

In Dar Fur, the Zaghawa had been experiencing increasing competition with Arab pastoralists for land and water; by 2001, many Zaghawa joined the **Fur** in the Sudan Liberation Army (SLA), engaging in a broader war against both Arab militias and the government of Sudan. Khalil Ibrahim, with a base in the eastern Zaghawa subgroup, the Kobe, created a separate Islamist rebel group in 2003, the Justice and Equality Movement (JEM). Lack of cooperation between the different organizations in Dar Fur have led some to make agreements with the national government in Khartoum while others continue to try to fight.

Since 1994, Chad and Libya have been able to keep fairly good relations. In 2007, four Chadian rebel groups signed deals with the Chadian government overseen by Libya. Libya and Chad have worked together on issues related to trying to halt shrinkage of Lake Chad and how the African Union can be more effective in negotiating peace between African states.

K. P. Moseley

Further Reading

Collins, Robert O. *A History of Modern Sudan.* Cambridge: Cambridge University Press, 2008.

Flint, Julie, and Alex de Waal. *Darfur: A New History of a Long War.* London: Zed Books, 2008.

Insoll, Timothy. *The Archaeology of Islam in Sub-Saharan Africa.* Cambridge: Cambridge University Press, 2003.

Jok, Jok Madut. *Sudan: Race, Religion, and Violence.* Oxford: Oneworld Press, 2007.

Lesch, Ann Mosely. *The Sudan: Contested National Identities.* Bloomington: Indiana University Press, 1998.

Norris, H. T. "Zaghawa." In *Encyclopedia of Islam*, 2nd ed., CD-ROM.

Olson, James S. "Zaghawa." In *The Peoples of Africa: An Ethnohistorical Dictionary.* Westport, CT: Greenwood Press, 1996.

Zande

The Zande or Azande are also called the Niam Niam and number between 1 million and 4 million people living mainly in the Central African Republic, but they are also found in Sudan and the Democratic Republic of Congo. Their language, called Pazande, belongs to the Adamawa family of the Niger-Congo language phylum.

The origins of the Zande are vague, and they do not appear until in the 18th century, when the Vungara or Avongara ruling elite of the Ambomou from the region east of the Mbomou-Uele confluence began a series of wars of conquest. The Vungara pushed their frontiers up the Mbomou River toward the Middle Nile Basin as well as southwest up the Uele River. The Zande conquered the peoples already living along these two rivers and quickly absorbed them by marrying their women and forcing the men into the military. A series of subject chiefdoms emerged within the new identity; that of Zande emerging from the mixing of conquered peoples with the original Ambomou clans. By the 19th century, the Zande had reached the Bahr al-Ghazal region in southern Sudan, and they came into contact with **Arab** and **Fur** slavers as well as clashed with the Dinka (**Nilotic**) over land.

By the time of the first European contacts, the Zande had become a formidable kingdom, and their fighting force was equipped with a deadly three-bladed throwing knife called a *shongo*. In the late 19th and early 20th centuries, the Zande were divided between the British in southern Sudan, the French in the Middle Congo, and Belgians in the Congo Free State. In 1899, the borders between French and British zones were agreed upon, the Nile and its tributaries going to Great Britain, and Congo and its tributaries to the French and Belgians. The French established the colony of the Middle Congo (today's Central African Republic) in 1885, while the Belgians, also in 1885, established the Congo Free State, today's Democratic Republic of the Congo.

The Zande are farmers and have traditionally raised crops of maize, rice, peanuts, sesame, cassava, and sweet potatoes. The Zande live in an area where various fruit can also be raised, such bananas and mangos. Livestock did not play an important role in their economic system until during the 20th century other than chickens, with meat being supplied by hunting. In the 1920s, cotton was introduced by the Anglo-Egyptian authorities as means for Zande to access the international market and improve their economy, but the introduction of cotton required reorganization of Zande farmlands, which brought about the loss of number of cultural features.

Zande recognize a king, and there are 180 nonroyal lineages (each with a genealogy that links them to a common male ancestor). The lineage system is patrilineal. Each of the Zande kingdoms were divided into provinces governed by "princes" of the royal Vungara line or by a commoner appointed by the king. Scholar E. E. Evans-Pritchard noted that the princes were more or less autonomous, but still had to obey summons for war and pay tribute to the king. Traditional Zande culture centered on the family compounds, which were self-sufficient and generally located along the riverbanks. The cotton scheme in the Sudan required that families move away from the riverbanks and in the process, most households lost their self-sufficiency.

The Zande believe in a single creator god called *Mboli* in addition to the ancestor spirits; however, runs of bad luck are attributed to witches. The Zande were the subject of British anthropologist and colonial agent Edward Evans-Pritchard's study of witchcraft and magic first published in 1937. Evans-Pritchard's study helped understand the principles of witchcraft as distinct from magic. As he points out that, for the Zande and other African peoples, being a witch is an inherited quality, and witchcraft is a "psychic art" (1). Zande believe in the ability of a witch to think something and it befall the person he/she is thinking about. Any misfortune is reasoned to be the work of a witch. He notes that generally, those accused of being a witch are close neighbors, and those who live at some distance are not seen as causing harm. Commoners may accuse other commoners, but not members of the ruling Vungara clan, who cannot be witches—witchcraft being an inherited trait through the father's line. Concerns about witchcraft are taken to traditional doctors who practice magic or to the oracles who use *benge*, a poison, that is given to a chicken and the response of the chicken to the poison in relation to the questions being asked tell the oracle the answer.

Zande art has become collectors' items, and they are skilled in not only weapons of exceptional beauty, but also wood carvings, storage bowls, and *sanza* or thumb pianos made in human shape, and even items that were once given by royalty as marks of honor. *Yande* figures are used in one of the men's associations. Evans-Pritchard notes that all such associations are recent introductions to Zande society after European conquest and the decay of Zande social order.

Zande society was greatly affected by European contact. Although the British in particular tried to use indirect rule among the Zande in Sudan and limited influence from the Arabic-speaking Muslim Sudanese, nonetheless, economic schemes, such as the cotton project introduced in the 1920s, had profound effects on the people. The Sudanese Zande have been affected as well by the Sudanese civil wars and participated in the first war between 1955 and 1972. Subsequent civil strife in Sudan has caused food shortages, which caused some Zande to move to the Central African Republic and the Democratic Republic of Congo, though the Zande were not active participants in the conflict.

John A. Shoup

Further Reading

Bacquart, Jean-Baptiste. *The Tribal Arts of Africa: Surveying Africa's Artistic Geography.* London: Thames and Hudson, 2002.

Evans-Pritchard, E. E. *Witchcraft, Oracles, and Magic among the Azande.* Abridged and Introduction by Eva Gillies of original 1937 edition. Oxford: Clarendon Press, 1976.

Stokes, Jamie. "Azande." In *Encyclopedia of the Peoples of Africa and the Middle East.* New York: Facts on File, 2009.

Tishken, Joel E. "Indigenous Religions." in *Africa Volume 2: African Cultures and Societies before 1885*, edited by Toyin Falola. Durham, NC: Carolina Academic Press, 2000.

Zaza/Dimli

The Zaza home area is in eastern Turkey concentrated between the three cities of

Siverek, Erzincan, and Varto. The Zaza are also called Dimli, which supposedly comes from the ancient name Daylam or Dailam for the region to the south of the Caspian Sea. The term "Zaza "comes from the pejorative label meaning incomprehensible speech, and as noted in the *Encyclopaedia of Islam*, it is similar to the English "blah-blah." The Zaza call their language Dimli while others call it Zazaki. Like many ethnicities in Turkey, there are only estimates to their size, since the state does not recognize minorities. It is estimated that there are between 1 million and 4 million speakers, though it seems that the estimate of between 1.5 million and 2 million is perhaps closer. There is a good deal of debate if Zazaki is a dialect of **Kurdish** or not, but it is an Indo-European language and seems to have closer relation with languages such as **Gilaki** than with other main dialects of Kurdish.

As noted above, Zazaki seems to have been derived from ancient languages spoken around the southern end of the Caspian Sea before the arrival of Islam. Scholars on Iran such as Minorsky noted that early **Persian** and **Arab** geographers included the Zaza among the different peoples called Kurds. This is further confused due to the fact that many also speak Turkish and Persian, and therefore are able to switch identities easily. They converted to Islam some time in the eighth century and welcomed 'Alids seeking refuge from 'Abbasid persecution. The Shi'ite Buwayhid (Buyid) dynasty was Daylamite in origin and in 932 seized Baghdad. The 'Abbasid *Khalifah* was under their control for 109 years before the Saljuq **Turks**, recently converted Sunni Muslims from Central Asia, took Baghdad and defeated the Buwayhids. The Zaza seem to have originated with soldiers of the Buwayhid armies and were settled in the upper regions of the Tigris River in the region of Diyarbakr.

The Zaza are split between those who are Sunni and adhere to the *Shafi'i madhhab*, similar to Sunni Kurds living to the south of them, while the rest belong to the Shi'ite splinter group called the *Alevi* or *'Alawi*. The Anatolian Alevi are less "extreme" than the *Nusayri 'Alawi* of Syria, but are different enough from the mainline Shi'ites to be considered as *ghulat* or going beyond the doctrine of the 12er Imams. Most Anatolian Alevi only share the *shahadah* or declaration of faith with other Muslims, but do not pray five times a day, fast the month of Ramadan, pay *zakat*, or make the pilgrimage to Makkah. There are a number of other, non-Muslim aspects to their belief system coming from Yazidism, Mithraism, and even Christianity. It is argued by some that the Christian elements are due to intermarriage with **Armenians**.

Zazaki seems not to have been a written language until the later part of the 19th century, when Ehmedê Xasi and 'Usman Efendiyo Babic published religious texts using the Arabic script in Damascus in 1933, and since the 1980s, more has been written about and in the Zazaki language. The language is now written using the Latin script, and the revival of interest in language began in the 1980s first among Western scholars. Zazi living in Europe have begun to learn the language and to question whether or not they are Kurds.

John A. Shoup

Further Reading

Abazov, Rafis. *Culture and Customs of Turkey*. Westport, CT: Greenwood Press, 2009.

Daniel, Elton L., and 'Ali Akbar Mahdi. *Culture and Customs of Iran*. Westport, CT: Greenwood Press, 2006.

"Ethnic Differentiation among the Kurds: Kurmancî, Kizilbash, and Zaza." http://members.tripod.com/zaza_kirmanc/research/paul.htm (accessed May 1, 2010).

Izady, Mehrdad. *The Kurds: A Concise History and Fact Book*. London: Taylor & Francis, 1992.

Kurdish Academy of Language. http://www.kurdishacademy.org/?=node/47 (accessed May 1, 2010).

Paul, L. "Zaza." In *Encyclopaedia of Islam*, 2nd ed., CD-ROM.

List of Contributors

Pade Badru
University of Maryland, Baltimore County (UMBC)

Tierno S. Bah
Smithsonian Institution

Houssam Jedda,
Student assistant, Al Akhawayn University, Ifrane, Morocco

Jack Vahram Kalpakian
Al Akhawayn University, Ifrane, Morocco

Scott Mattoon
Independent researcher and writer

Karen E. Milbourne
National Museum of African Art, Smithsonian Institution (NMAfA)

Connell Monette
Al Akhawayn University, Ifrane, Morocco

K. P. Moseley
Independent scholar

Geri Shaw
Southwestern College

Geographical Index

Index

Note: Page numbers followed by i indicate illustration.

Apartheid: doctrine, 5, 78; fighting against, 6; laws, South Africans' introduction of, 236; in South Africa, the Tsonga under, 295

Apostolic Zionist Church, Venda and, 315

'Arab al-'Arabah/Arabian Arabs, 17

Arabic language: Acholi and, 1; al-Taylasan and sources in, 283; Armenians and, 26; Assyrians use of, 30; Baluch and, 39; Beja and, 50; Berbers and, 54, 57, 58; Copts and, 75; Dogamba and, 85; Fur and, 100, 101; *Fusha* and Modern Standard Arabic, 17; Greek philosophers' translations into, 21; Haratin and, 115; Hassaniyah, 35; Jews and, 138; reign of 'Abd al-Malik and, 19; South Arabian, 273; as West Semitic language, 16, 133

Arab League, 16, 264

Arab Rizayqat, 102

Arabs, 1, **16–26**, 156; Assyrians and, 30; Bakhtiyari and, 36; Beja and, 50; Bemba and, 52; Berbers and, 54, 55; Chewa and, 70; circumcision and, 213; conquest of Southern Spain, 97; Copts and, 75; decline of Axum and influence of, 13; descendants of, 17; in the fifth century, 18; Fur and, 101; Gilaki and Mazandarani regions and, 109; Herero's escape from enslavement by, 120; holy war against Christians, 13; intermarriages with Kurds, 159; Islam and, 16, 18, 38; Israel and, 25; Kamba and, 144; Lele and, 165; Libya and, 334; Lunda Empire and, 172; Lurs and, 177; Malayo-Indonesian, 180; modern history of, 23–25; Mutesa I and, 106; Nubia and, 229; origin of, 17–18; Persians after the conquest of, 242; Portuguese traders and, 222; rise of Zimbabwean highlands and, 258; Sunni or Shi'ite, 17; Surma and slave raids from, 276; Swahili and, 277; trade centers, 231; during Umayyad period, 19; use of weapons, 189; in West Africa, 219; Yao contact with, 325, 326; Zande and, 335; Zaza/Dimi and, 337. *See also* Arabic language

Arameans. *See* Assyrians

Architecture: Andalusian, 57; Arab, 19, 22–23, 22i; Berbers, 57; Dogon, 88

Ark of the Covenant, 13, 14, 288

Armenagan (Armenian National Democratic) Party, 29

Armenia, 26, 28, 29, 30, 159

Armenian movements, 29

Armenian National Democratic Party (Armenagan), 29

Armenian nationalism, 29

Armenians, **26–30**, 28i, 337

Armenian Soviet Socialist Republic (1936–1991), 29

Art; Mask(s): Arab, 22; Armenian, 27–28; Bamileke, 41; Baule, 38; Benin, 64; Berbers, 57–58; Bini/Edo, 64; Chokwe, 73, 74; Dan, 82; Fon, 94, Fulbe, 97, 98, Kuba, 157, Lozi, 168, Makonde, 179; Mangbetu, 189; Mossi, 199; Persian, 243, 245; Rock of San peoples, in South Africa, 148; Senufo, 254; Songhay, 266; Tribal, 60; Turkish, 302–3; Vili, 317; Wolof, 321, 321i; Zande, 336. *See also* Body painting

Asaimara (nobles), in Afar, 2

Asamankese. *See Asantehene*

Asantehene, 8, 10

Asante kingdom (Ashanti kingdom), 8, 10, 47

Asante Manso. *See* Asante kingdom (Ashanti kingdom)

Asante region, 7

Asante society, 8, 9

Ashantis (Asantes), 7, 7i, 10

'Ashurah, 242

Asian population, in Africa, 219

Asiwa (or betrothal), 10

Askiya dynasty, 266

Askiya Muhammad I (epic), 266

Association des Bakongo (Belgian Congo), 155

Assyrian Democratic Movement, 32

Assyrians, **30–33**, 33i, 134

Atatürk, Mustapha Kemal, 161, 305

Ateker speakers, 1

Atlantic slave trade, 255; *ceddo* and, 321; the Fon involvement in, 93; French Empire and, 320; in the 19th century, 15; Ovambo and, 235

Auma, Alice. *See* Lakwena, Alice

Aussa, *Sultanate* of, 2, 3

Austronesian language phylum, Malagasy language, 180

Autonomous Afar Region, 3

Avicenna in the West. *See* Ibn Sina (980–1037)

Awash River, 2

Awash valley, 3

Awemba. *See* Bemba

Awolowo, Obafemi, 330

Awura Poku, 477

About the Author

John A. Shoup is a Professor of Anthropology who has his BA and MA in Middle Eastern Studies/Arabic from the University of Utah and his PhD in Cultural Anthropology from Washington University in St. Louis. He has conducted field work in Lesotho, Jordan, Syria, Egypt, Tunisia, Morocco, and most recently in Mauritania on topics related to pastoralism, impact of tourism on local communities, traditional land use systems, trans-Saharan trade, and popular culture. He has authored and coauthored several articles and book chapters, and has published *Culture and Customs of Jordan* (2007) and *Culture and Customs of Syria* (2008), and coauthored *Saudi Arabia and Gulf Arab States Today: An Encyclopedia of Life the Arab States* (2009), all three with Greenwood Press. He was part of the research team for the Baseline Survey conducted in the Middle Atlas region of Ifrane (2000) and on the impact of tourism in Atlantic port city of Essaouira (2001–2002), published as *Assessing Tourism in Essaouira* by Al Akhawayn University (2002). Professor Shoup taught at the American University in Cairo from 1990 to 1996 and at Al Akhawayn University in Ifrane, Morocco, from 1996 to the present.